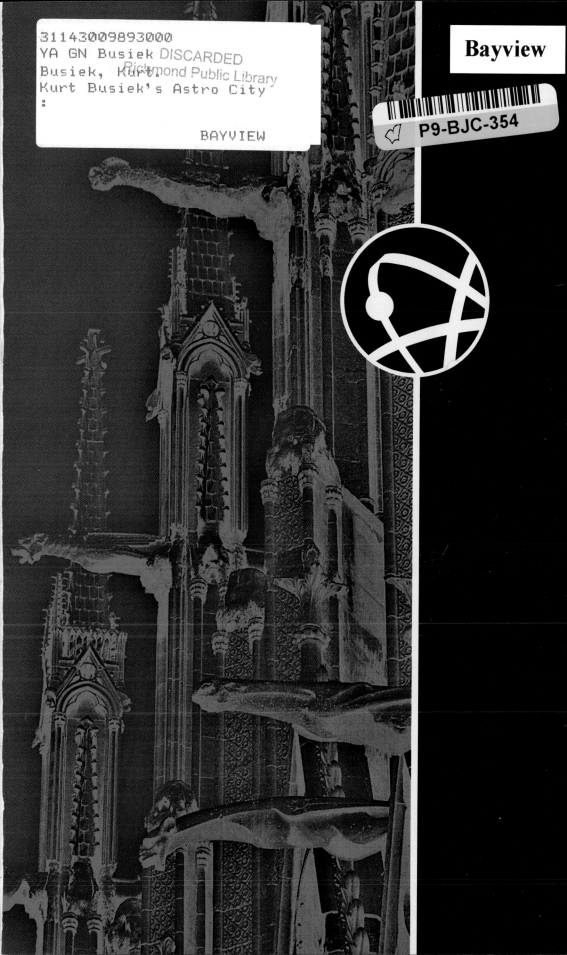

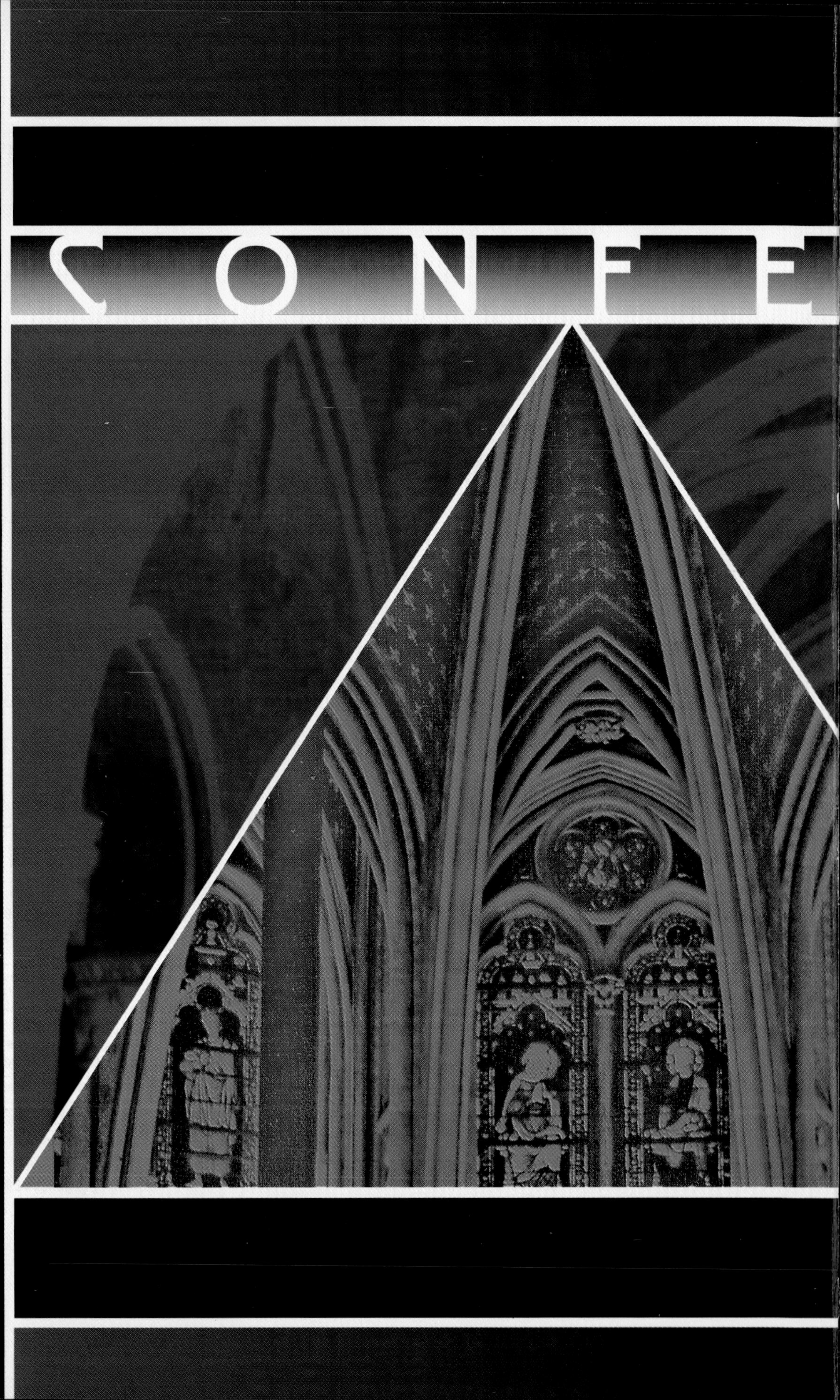
CONFE

ASTRO CITY
CONFESSION

KURT BUSIEK
WRITER

BRENT ERIC ANDERSON
PENCILER

WILL BLYBERG
INKER

COMICRAFT'S JOHN ROSHELL
LETTERING & DESIGN

ALEX SINCLAIR
COLORS

ALEX ROSS
COVERS

BUSIEK, ANDERSON & ROSS
CITY FATHERS

Juke Box

PRODUCTIONS

ANN HUNTINGTON BUSIEK
MANAGING EDITOR

PURVEYORS OF UNIQUE DESIGN & FINE LETTERING

RICHARD STARKINGS
PRESIDENT & FIRST TIGER

BY THE SAME CREATORS

ASTRO CITY:
LIFE IN THE BIG CITY

ASTRO CITY:
FAMILY ALBUM

ASTRO CITY: THE
TARNISHED ANGEL

ASTRO CITY:
LOCAL HEROES

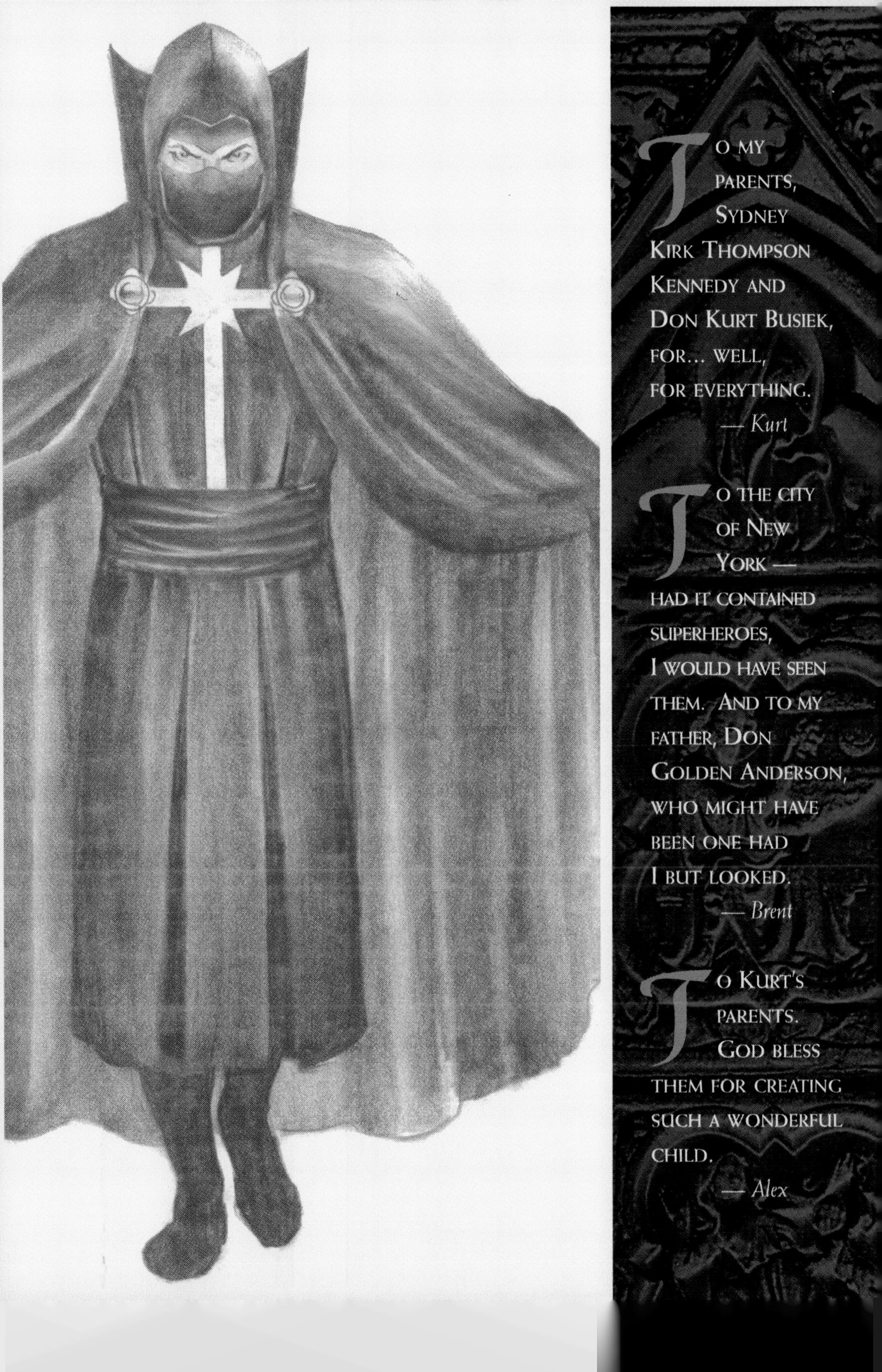

To my parents, Sydney Kirk Thompson Kennedy and Don Kurt Busiek, for... well, for everything.

— *Kurt*

To the city of New York — had it contained superheroes, I would have seen them. And to my father, Don Golden Anderson, who might have been one had I but looked.

— *Brent*

To Kurt's parents. God bless them for creating such a wonderful child.

— *Alex*

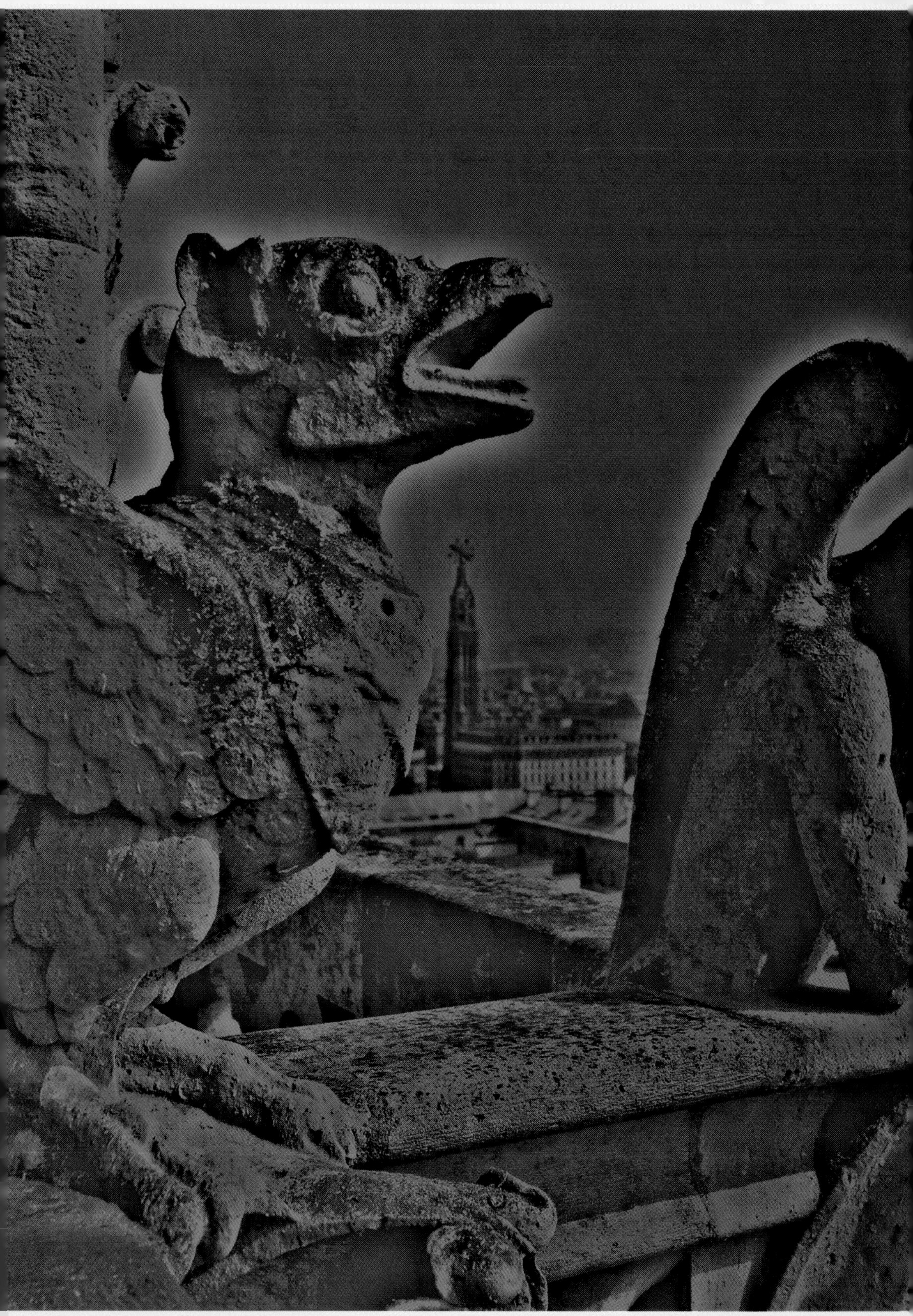

CONTENTS

Page 8 • INTRODUCTION

Page 13 ① NEW KID IN TOWN

Page 39 ② LEARNING THE GAME

Page 65 ③ THE GATHERING DARK

Page 91 ④ EYE OF THE STORM

Page 117 ⑤ PATTERNS

Page 143 ⑥ MY FATHER'S SON

Page 169 • THE NEARNESS OF YOU

Page 187 • DRAMATIS PERSONAE

Page 193 • COVER GALLERY

Page 208 • ACKNOWLEDGMENTS

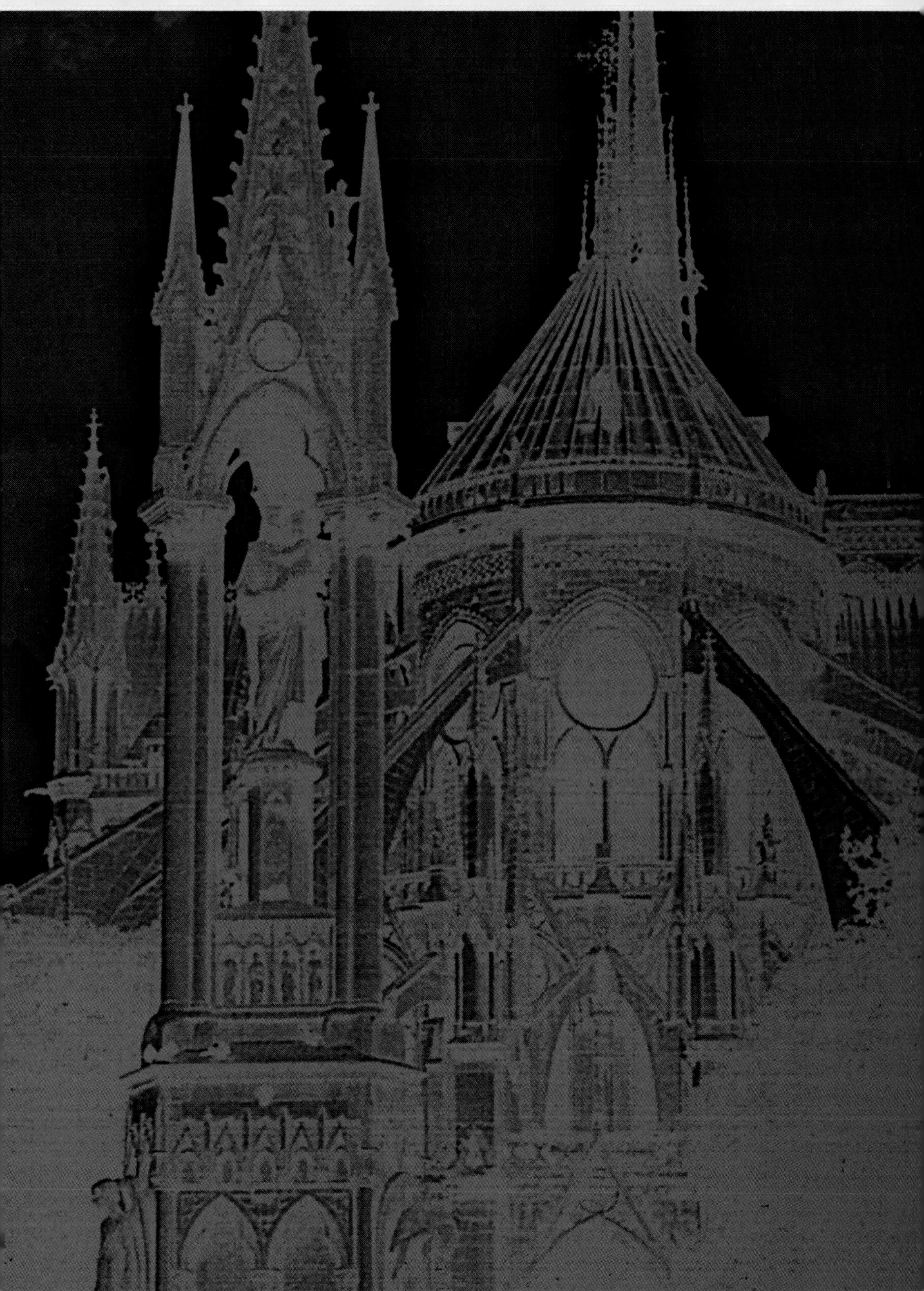

INTRODUCTION

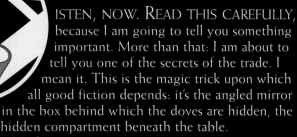

ISTEN, NOW. READ THIS CAREFULLY, because I am going to tell you something important. More than that: I am about to tell you one of the secrets of the trade. I mean it. This is the magic trick upon which all good fiction depends: it's the angled mirror in the box behind which the doves are hidden, the hidden compartment beneath the table.

It's this:

> *There is room for things to mean*
> *more than they literally mean.*

That was it.

Doesn't seem that important to you? Not impressed? Convinced you could get deeper, sager advice about writing from a fortune cookie? Trust me. I just told you something important. We'll come back to it.

THERE ARE, IN MY OPINION, TWO MAJOR WAYS in which superheroes are used in popular fiction. In the first way superheroes mean, purely and simply, what they mean on the surface. In the second kind of fiction, they mean what they mean on the surface, true, but they also mean more than that — they mean pop culture on the one hand, and hopes and dreams, or the converse of hopes and dreams, a falling away of innocence, on the other.

The lineage of superheroes goes way back: it starts, obviously, in the 1930s, and then goes back into the depths of the newspaper strip, and then into literature, co-opting Sherlock Holmes, Beowulf and various heroes and gods along the way.

Robert Mayer's novel *Superfolks* used superheroes as a metaphor for all that America had become in the 1970s: the loss of the American dream meant the loss of American dreams, and vice versa.

Joseph Torchia took the iconography of Superman and wrote *The Kryptonite Kid*, a powerful

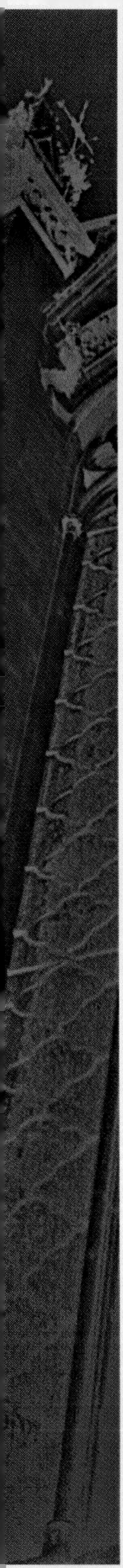

and beautiful epistolary novel about a kid who believes, literally, in Superman, and who, in a book constructed as a series of letters to Superman, has to come to terms with his life and his heart.

IN THE 1980S, FOR THE FIRST TIME, WRITERS BEGAN WRITING comics superheroes in which the characters were as much commentary upon superheroes as they were superheroes: Alan Moore led the way in this, as did Frank Miller.

One of the elements that fused back into comics at that time was the treatment of some comics themes in prose fiction: *Superfolks* and *The Kryptonite Kid*, short stories such as Norman Spinrad's "It's a Bird, It's a Plane...," essays like Larry Niven's (literally) seminal "Man of Steel, Woman of Kleenex."

The resurgence that hit comics at this time also surfaced in prose fiction — the early volumes of the George R.R. Martin-edited *Wild Cards* anthologies did a fine job of reinvoking the joy of superheroes in a prose context.

The problem with the mid-80s revival of interesting superheroes was that the wrong riffs were the easiest to steal. *Watchmen* and *The Dark Knight Returns* spawned too many bad comics: humourless, grey, violent and dull. When the *Wild Cards* anthologies were turned into comics everything that made them interesting as commentaries upon comics evaporated, too.

So after the first Moore, Miller and Martin-led flush of superheroes (they weren't deconstructed. Just, briefly, respected), things returned, more or less, to the status quo, and a pendulum swing gave us, in the early 90s, superhero comics which were practically contentless: poorly written, and utterly literal. There was even one publisher who trumpeted four issues of good writers as the ultimate marketing gimmick — every bit as good as foil-embossed covers.

There is room to move beyond the literal. Things can mean more than they mean. It's why *Catch-22* isn't just about fighter pilots in the second world war. It's why "I Have No Mouth, And I Must Scream" is about more than a bunch of people trapped inside a supercomputer. It's why *Moby Dick* is about (believe fifty thousand despairing college professors or not, but it's still true) a lot more than whaling.

And I'm not talking about allegory, here, or metaphor, or even The Message. I'm talking about what the story is about, and then I'm talking about what it's *about*.

Things can mean more than they literally mean. And that's the dividing line between art and everything that isn't art. Or one of the lines, anyway.

Currently, superhero fictions seem to break into two kinds: there are the workaday, more or less pulp fictions which are turned out by the yard by people who are trying their hardest, or not. And then there are the other kind, and there are

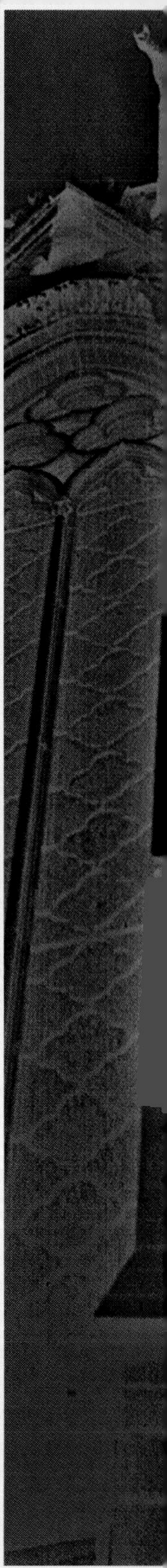

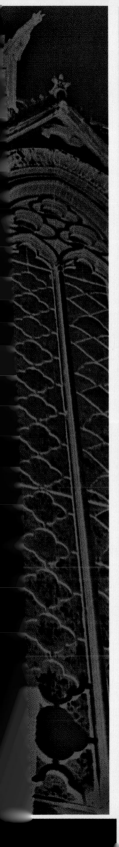

precious few of them.

There are two obvious current exceptions — Alan Moore's *Supreme*, an exercise in rewriting fifty years of Superman into something that means something.

And then — and some of you might have thought that I might have forgotten it, given how far we've got into this introduction without it being mentioned, there is *Astro City*. Which traces its lineage back in two directions — into the world of classic super-hero archetypes, but equally into the world of *The Kryptonite Kid*, a world in which all this stuff, this dumb wonderful four-colour stuff has real emotional weight and depth, and it means more than it literally means.

And that is the genius and the joy of *Astro City*.

ME? I'M JADED, WHERE SUPERHEROES ARE CONCERNED. Jaded and tired and fairly burnt out, if truth be told. Not utterly burned out, though. I thought I was, until, a couple of years ago, I found myself in a car with Kurt Busiek, and his delightful wife Ann. (We were driving to see Scott McCloud and his wife Ivy, and their little girl Sky, and it was a very memorable and eventful evening, ending as it did in the unexpected birth of Scott and Ivy's daughter Winter.) And in the car, on the way, we started talking about Batman.

Pretty soon Kurt and I were co-plotting a complete Batman story; and not just a Batman story, but the coolest, strangest Batman story you can imagine, in which every relationship in the world of Batman was turned inside out and upside down, and, in the finest comic book tradition, everything you thought you knew turned out to be a lie.

We were doing this for fun. I doubt that either of us will ever do anything with the story. We were just enjoying ourselves.

But, for several hours, I found myself caring utterly and deeply about Batman. Which is, I suspect, part of Kurt Busiek's special talent. If I were writing a different kind of introduction, I might call it a super power.

Astro City is what would have happened if those old comics, with their fine simplicities and their primal, four-colour charac-ters, had been about something. Or rather, it assumes they *were* about something, and tells you the tales that, on the whole, slipped through the cracks.

It's a place inspired by the worlds and worldviews of Stan Lee and Jack Kirby, of Gardner Fox and John Broome, of Jerry Seigel and Bob Finger and the rest of them; a city where anything can happen: in the story that follows we have (and I'm trying hard not to give too much away) a crimefighter bar, serial killing, an alien invasion, a crackdown on costumed heroes, a hero's mysterious secret... all of them the happy pulp elements of a thousand comics-by-the-yard.

Except that, here, as in the rest of *Astro City*, Kurt Busiek man-ages to take all of these elements and let them mean more than they literally mean.

(Again, I am not talking about allegory here. I'm talking story, and what makes some stories magic while others just sit there, lifeless and dull.)

Astro City: Confession is a coming of age story, in which a young man learns a lesson. (Robert A. Heinlein claimed in an essay in the 1940s, published in Lloyd Esbach's collection of SF writer essays *Of Worlds Beyond*, that there are only three stories, which we tell over and over again. He said he had thought there were only two, "Boy Meets Girl" and "The Little Tailor," until L. Ron Hubbard pointed out to him that there was also "A Man Learns A Lesson." And, Heinlein maintained, if you add in their opposites — someone fails to learn a lesson, two people don't fall in love, and so on — you may have all the stories there are. But then, we can move beyond the literal.) It's a growing up story, set in the city in Kurt's mind.

One of the things I like about *Astro City* is that Kurt Busiek lists all of his collaborators on the front cover. He knows how important each of them is to the final outcome: each element does what it is meant to, and each of them gives their best and a little more: Alex Ross's covers ground each issue in a photoreal sort of hyper-reality; Brent Anderson's pencils and Will Blyberg's inks are perfectly crafted, always wisely at the service of the story, never obtrusive, always convincing. The colouring by Alex Sinclair, and the Comicraft lettering by John Roshell are both slick, and, in the best sense of the word, inconspicuous.

Astro City, in the hands of Kurt Busiek and his collaborators, is art, and it is good art. It recognizes the strengths of the four-colour heroes, and it creates something — a place, perhaps, or a medium, or just a tone of voice — in which good stories are told. There is room for things to mean more than they literally mean, and this is certainly true in Astro City.

I look forward to being able to visit it for a very long time to come.

Neil Gaiman
26 October 1997
ROME.

Neil Gaiman used to have more Eisner Awards than anyone else, but he suspects that Alan Moore, Kurt Busiek or James Robinson must have caught up by now. His most recent works are *Stardust*, a four-part short novel illustrated by Charles Vess, *Neverwhere*, a longer novel illustrated only by the power of the imagination, and *Beowulf*, a re-telling of the original saga which he wrote with film-maker Roger Avary, and which goes into production in 1998. Unless it doesn't, this being Hollywood, after all.

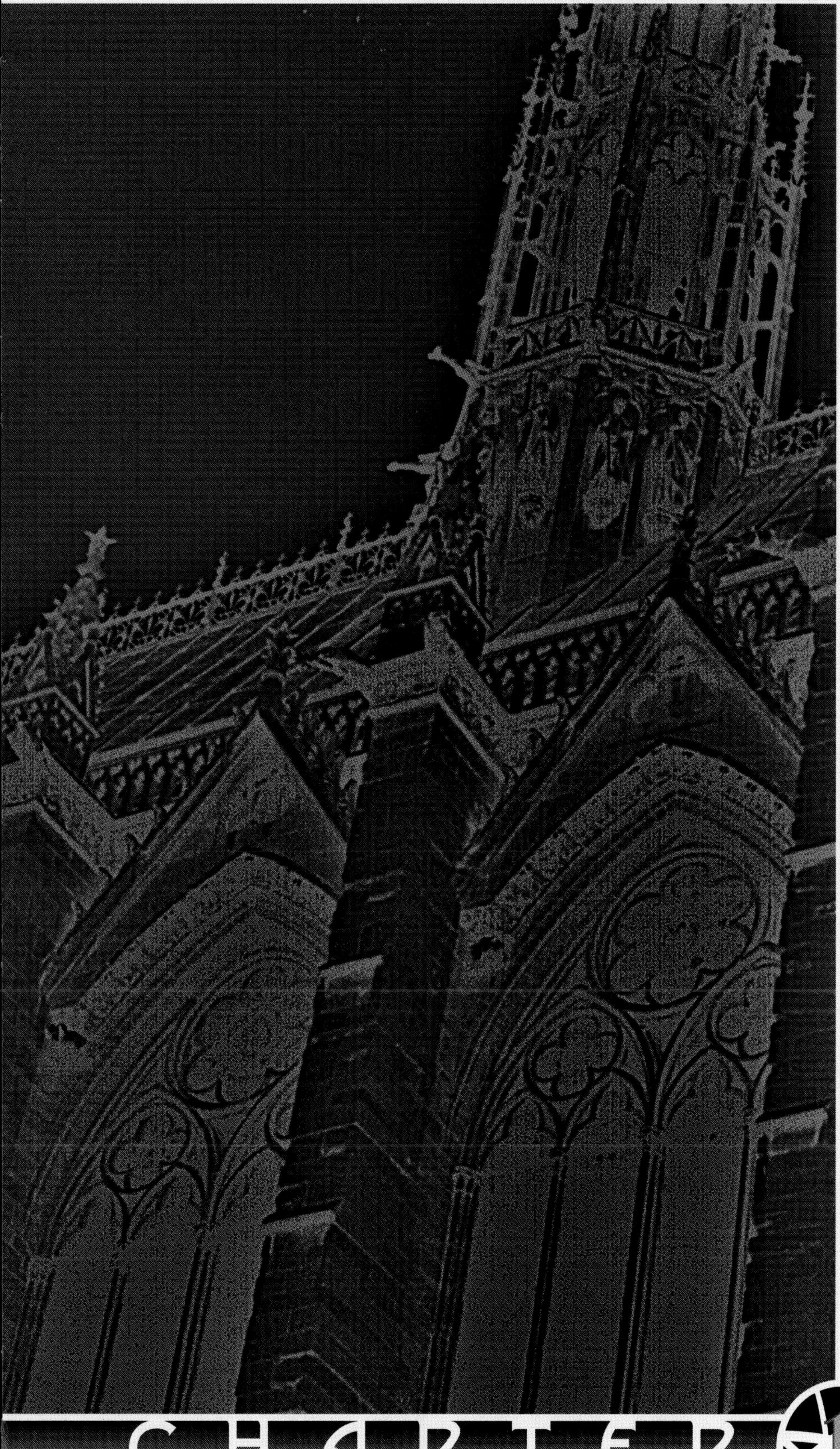

CHAPTER 1

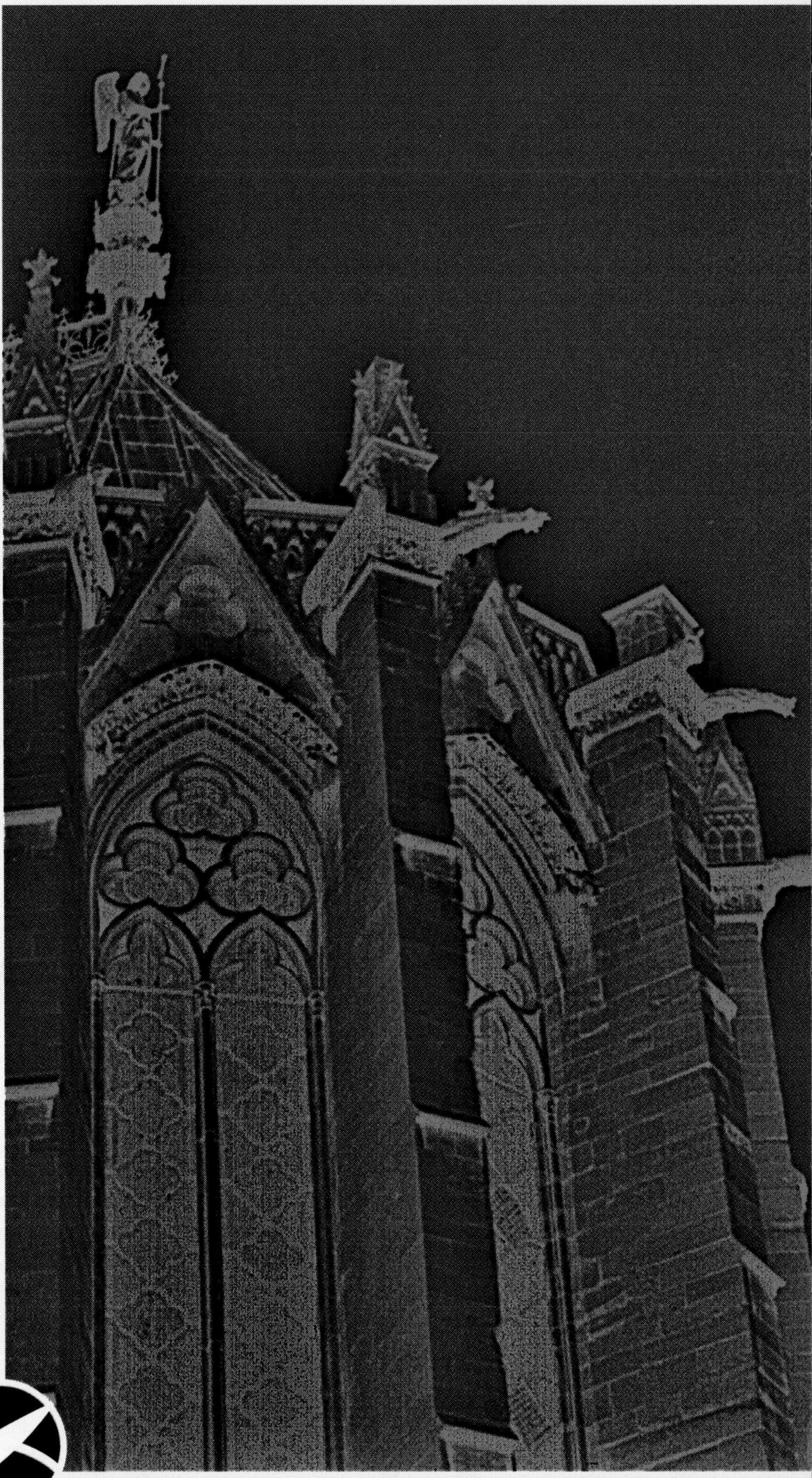

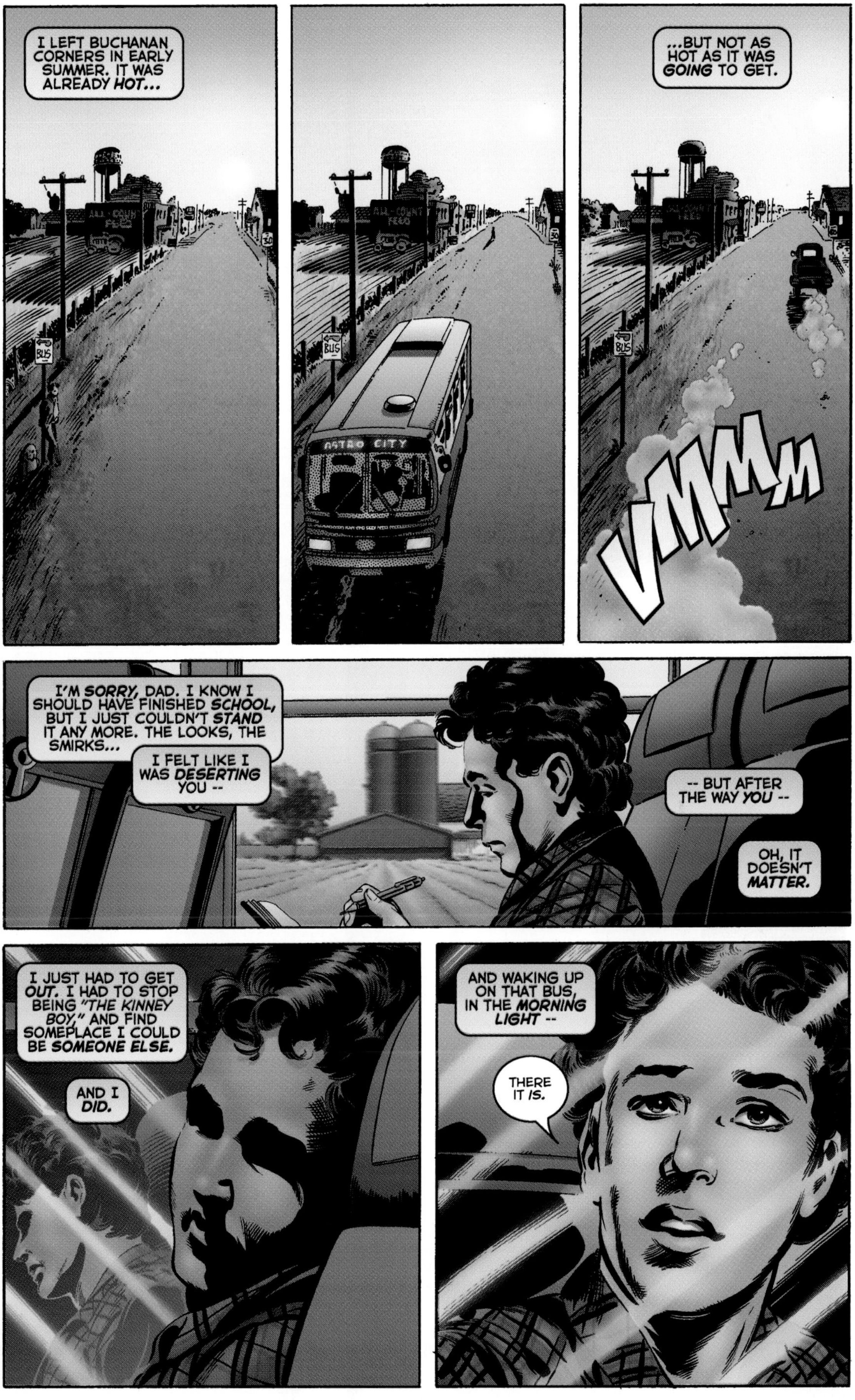

I LEFT BUCHANAN CORNERS IN EARLY SUMMER. IT WAS ALREADY *HOT...*
...BUT NOT AS HOT AS IT WAS *GOING* TO GET.
ALL-COUNTY FEED
BUS
ASTRO CITY
VMMMM
I'M *SORRY,* DAD. I KNOW I SHOULD HAVE FINISHED *SCHOOL,* BUT I JUST COULDN'T *STAND* IT ANY MORE. THE LOOKS, THE SMIRKS...
I FELT LIKE I WAS *DESERTING* YOU --
-- BUT AFTER THE WAY *YOU* --
OH, IT DOESN'T *MATTER.*
I JUST HAD TO GET *OUT.* I HAD TO STOP BEING *"THE KINNEY BOY,"* AND FIND SOMEPLACE I COULD BE *SOMEONE ELSE.*
AND I *DID.*
AND WAKING UP ON THAT BUS, IN THE *MORNING LIGHT* --
THERE IT *IS.*

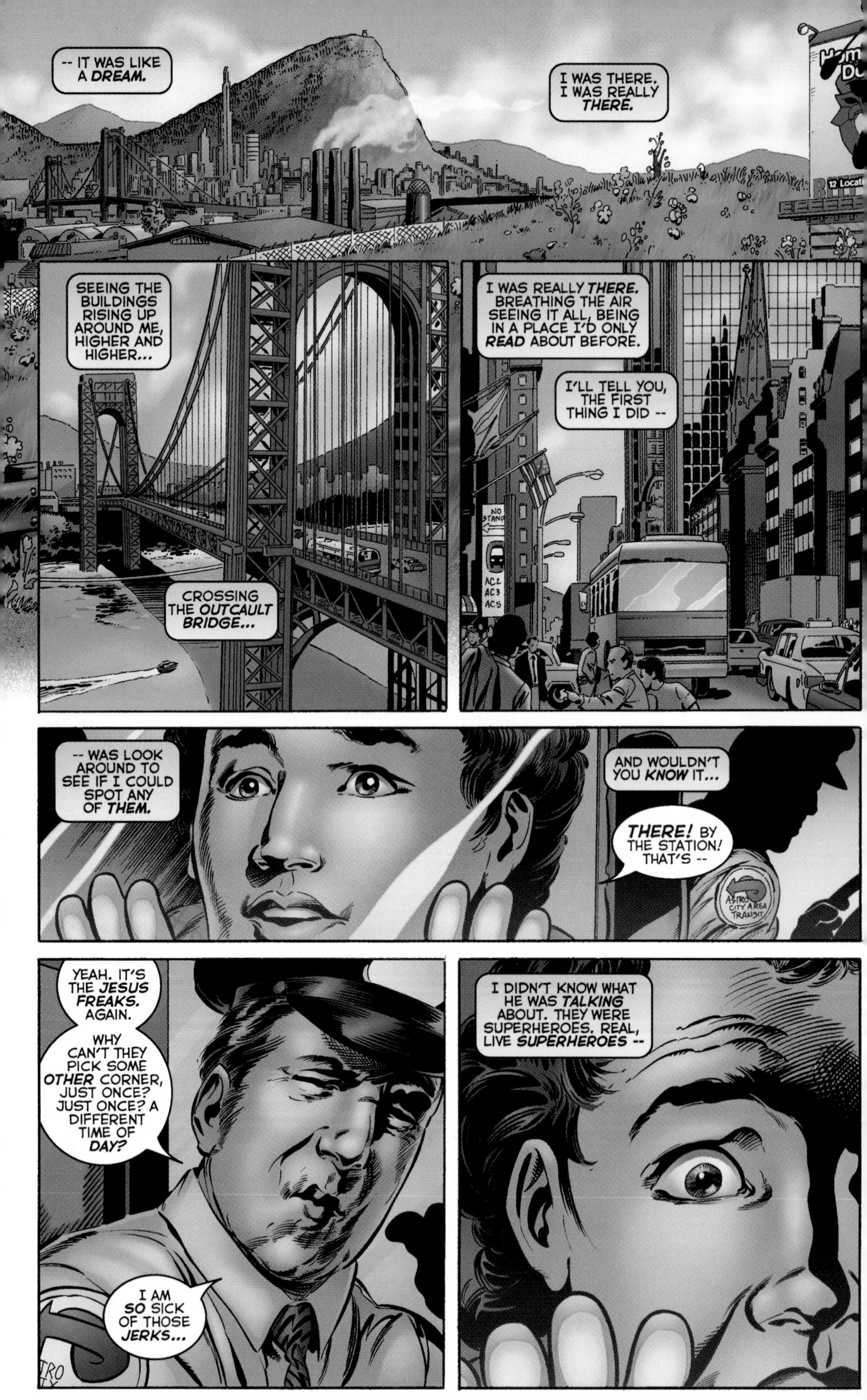
-- IT WAS LIKE A DREAM.
I WAS THERE. I WAS REALLY THERE.
SEEING THE BUILDINGS RISING UP AROUND ME, HIGHER AND HIGHER...
CROSSING THE OUTCAULT BRIDGE...
I WAS REALLY THERE. BREATHING THE AIR SEEING IT ALL, BEING IN A PLACE I'D ONLY READ ABOUT BEFORE.
I'LL TELL YOU, THE FIRST THING I DID --
NO STAND
AC2 AC3 AC5
-- WAS LOOK AROUND TO SEE IF I COULD SPOT ANY OF THEM.
AND WOULDN'T YOU KNOW IT...
THERE! BY THE STATION! THAT'S --
ASTRO CITY AREA TRANSIT
YEAH. IT'S THE JESUS FREAKS. AGAIN.
WHY CAN'T THEY PICK SOME OTHER CORNER, JUST ONCE? JUST ONCE? A DIFFERENT TIME OF DAY?
I AM SO SICK OF THOSE JERKS...
I DIDN'T KNOW WHAT HE WAS TALKING ABOUT. THEY WERE SUPERHEROES. REAL, LIVE SUPERHEROES --

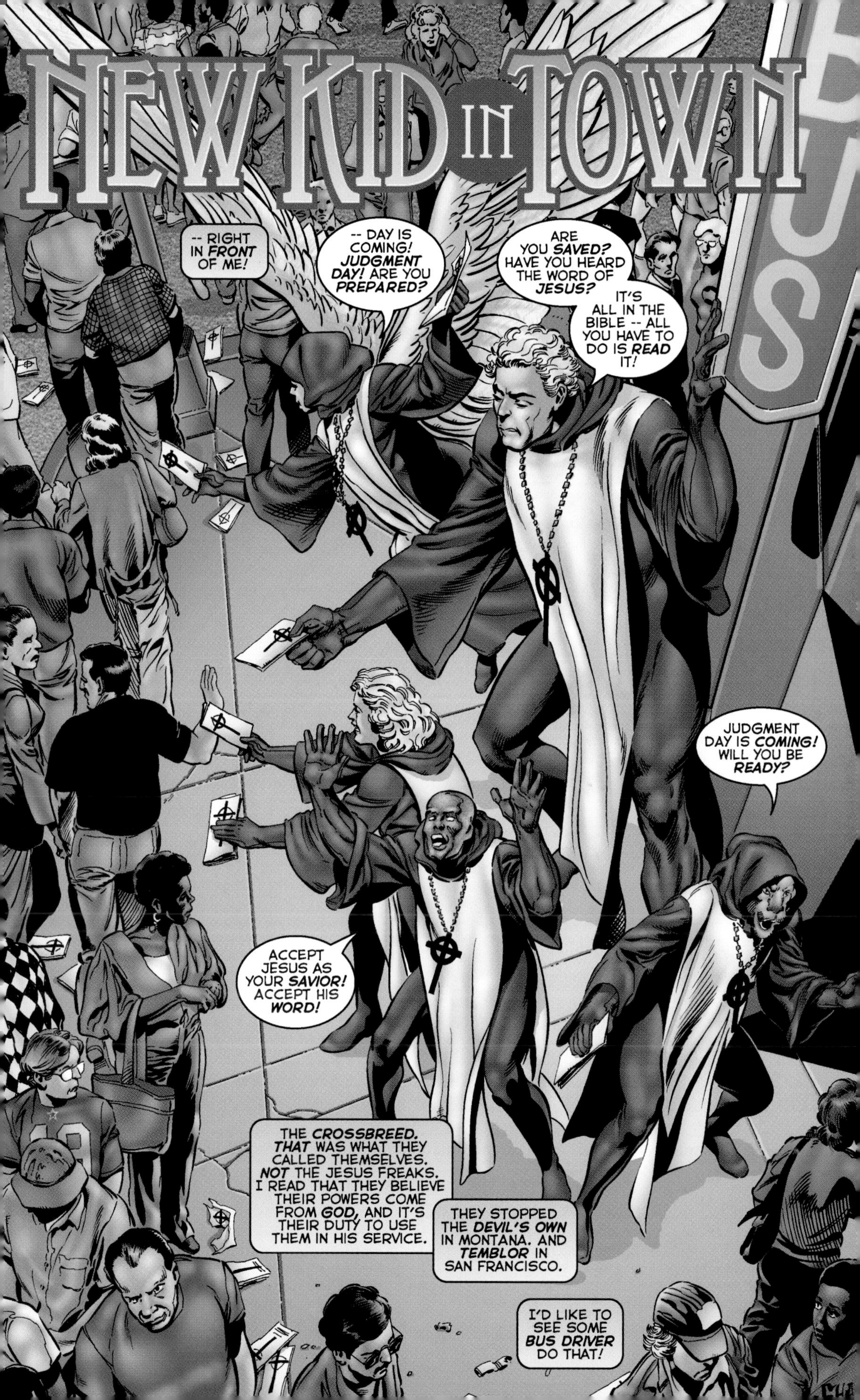
NEW KID IN TOWN
-- RIGHT IN FRONT OF ME!
-- DAY IS COMING! JUDGMENT DAY! ARE YOU PREPARED?
ARE YOU SAVED? HAVE YOU HEARD THE WORD OF JESUS?
IT'S ALL IN THE BIBLE -- ALL YOU HAVE TO DO IS READ IT!
JUDGMENT DAY IS COMING! WILL YOU BE READY?
ACCEPT JESUS AS YOUR SAVIOR! ACCEPT HIS WORD!
THE CROSSBREED. THAT WAS WHAT THEY CALLED THEMSELVES. NOT THE JESUS FREAKS. I READ THAT THEY BELIEVE THEIR POWERS COME FROM GOD, AND IT'S THEIR DUTY TO USE THEM IN HIS SERVICE.
THEY STOPPED THE DEVIL'S OWN IN MONTANA. AND TEMBLOR IN SAN FRANCISCO.
I'D LIKE TO SEE SOME BUS DRIVER DO THAT!

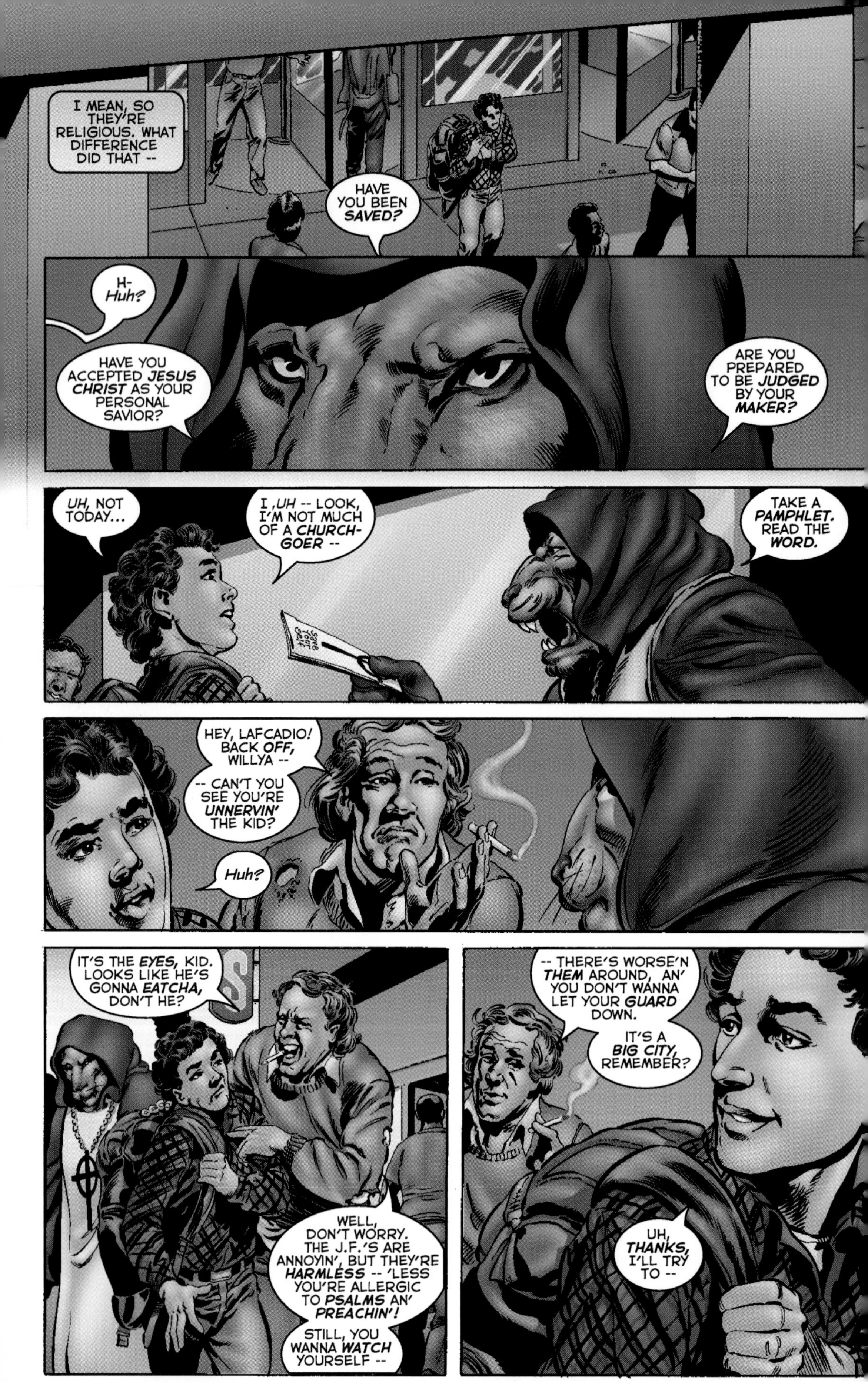

I MEAN, SO THEY'RE RELIGIOUS. WHAT DIFFERENCE DID THAT --
HAVE YOU BEEN SAVED?
H- Huh?
HAVE YOU ACCEPTED JESUS CHRIST AS YOUR PERSONAL SAVIOR?
ARE YOU PREPARED TO BE JUDGED BY YOUR MAKER?
UH, NOT TODAY...
I ,UH -- LOOK, I'M NOT MUCH OF A CHURCH-GOER --
TAKE A PAMPHLET. READ THE WORD.
HEY, LAFCADIO! BACK OFF, WILLYA --
-- CAN'T YOU SEE YOU'RE UNNERVIN' THE KID?
Huh?
IT'S THE EYES, KID. LOOKS LIKE HE'S GONNA EATCHA, DON'T HE?
WELL, DON'T WORRY. THE J.F.'S ARE ANNOYIN', BUT THEY'RE HARMLESS -- 'LESS YOU'RE ALLERGIC TO PSALMS AN' PREACHIN'!
STILL, YOU WANNA WATCH YOURSELF --
-- THERE'S WORSE'N THEM AROUND, AN' YOU DON'T WANNA LET YOUR GUARD DOWN.
IT'S A BIG CITY, REMEMBER?
UH, THANKS, I'LL TRY TO --

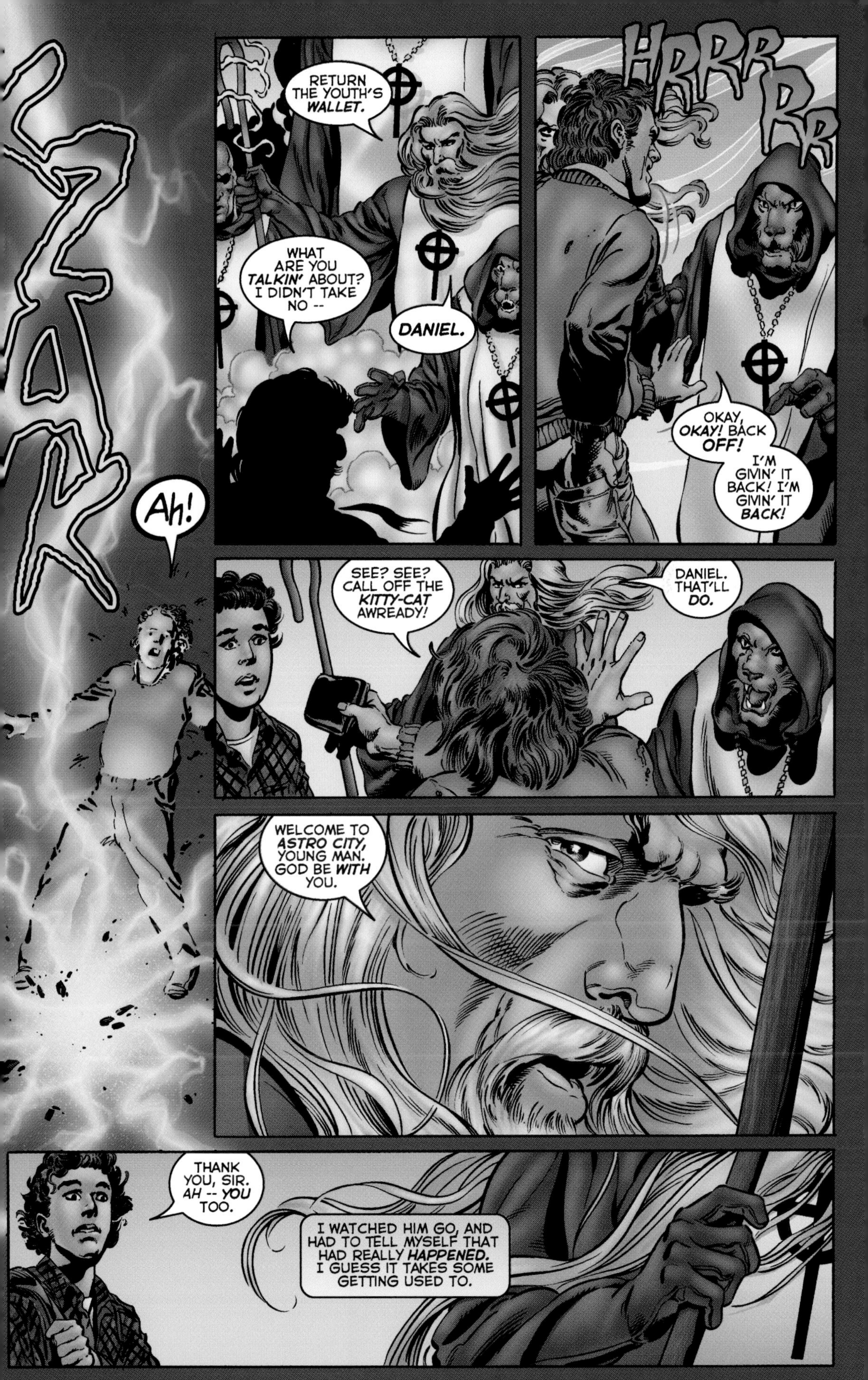
RETURN THE YOUTH'S *WALLET.*
WHAT ARE YOU *TALKIN'* ABOUT? I DIDN'T TAKE NO --
DANIEL.
HRRRRR
OKAY, *OKAY!* BACK *OFF!*
I'M GIVIN' IT BACK! I'M GIVIN' IT *BACK!*
Ah!
SEE? SEE? CALL OFF THE *KITTY-CAT* AWREADY!
DANIEL. THAT'LL *DO.*
WELCOME TO *ASTRO CITY,* YOUNG MAN. GOD BE *WITH* YOU.
THANK YOU, SIR. *AH -- YOU* TOO.
I WATCHED HIM GO, AND HAD TO TELL MYSELF THAT HAD REALLY *HAPPENED.* I GUESS IT TAKES SOME GETTING USED TO.

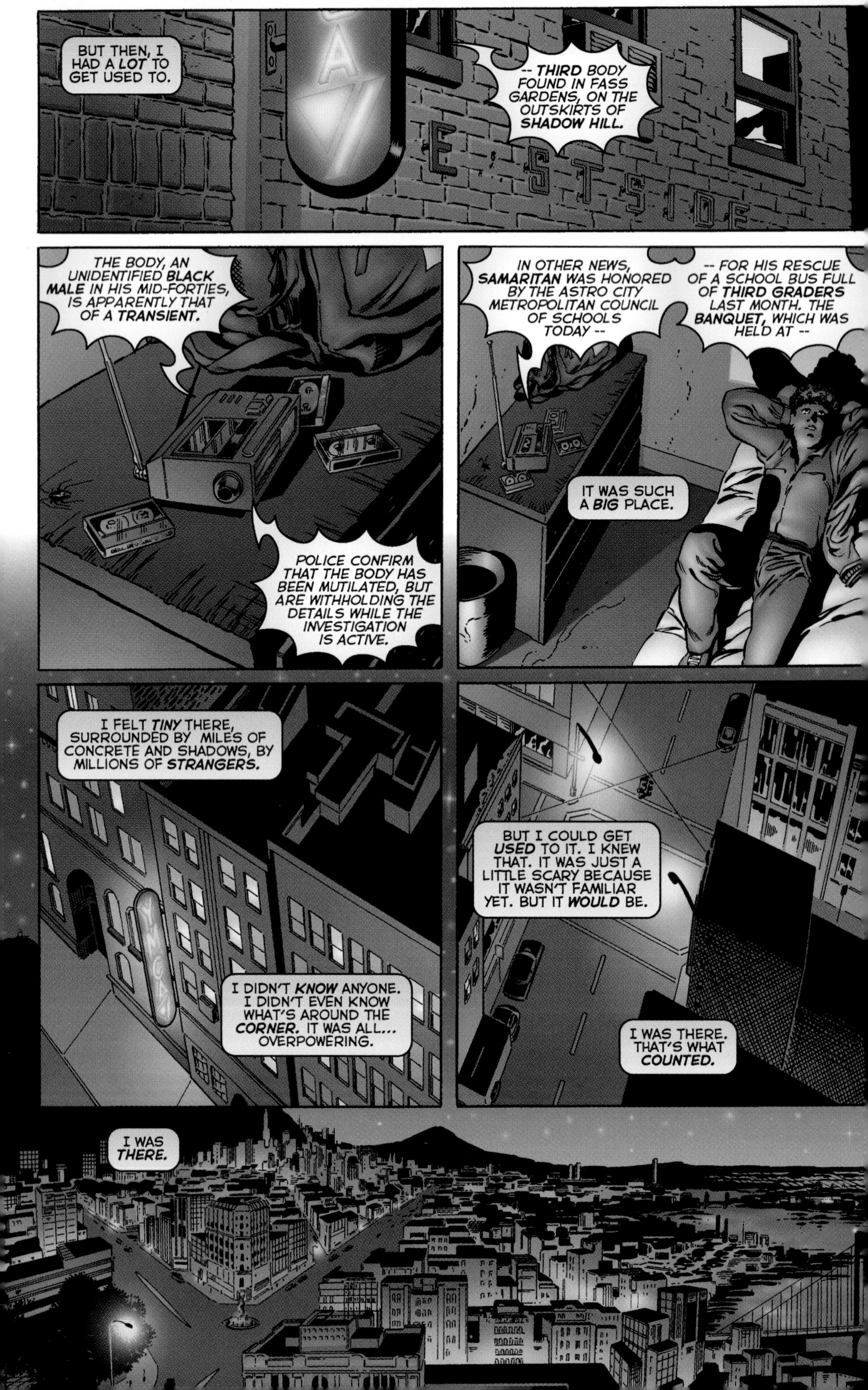

BUT THEN, I HAD A *LOT* TO GET USED TO.
-- *THIRD* BODY FOUND IN FASS GARDENS, ON THE OUTSKIRTS OF *SHADOW HILL.*
THE BODY, AN UNIDENTIFIED *BLACK MALE* IN HIS MID-FORTIES, IS APPARENTLY THAT OF A *TRANSIENT.*
POLICE CONFIRM THAT THE BODY HAS BEEN MUTILATED, BUT ARE WITHHOLDING THE DETAILS WHILE THE INVESTIGATION IS ACTIVE.
IN OTHER NEWS, *SAMARITAN* WAS HONORED BY THE ASTRO CITY METROPOLITAN COUNCIL OF SCHOOLS TODAY --
-- FOR HIS RESCUE OF A SCHOOL BUS FULL OF *THIRD GRADERS* LAST MONTH. THE *BANQUET,* WHICH WAS HELD AT --
IT WAS SUCH A *BIG* PLACE.
I FELT *TINY* THERE, SURROUNDED BY MILES OF CONCRETE AND SHADOWS, BY MILLIONS OF *STRANGERS.*
I DIDN'T *KNOW* ANYONE. I DIDN'T EVEN KNOW WHAT'S AROUND THE *CORNER.* IT WAS ALL... OVERPOWERING.
BUT I COULD GET *USED* TO IT. I KNEW THAT. IT WAS JUST A LITTLE SCARY BECAUSE IT WASN'T FAMILIAR YET. BUT IT *WOULD* BE.
I WAS THERE. THAT'S WHAT *COUNTED.*
I WAS *THERE.*

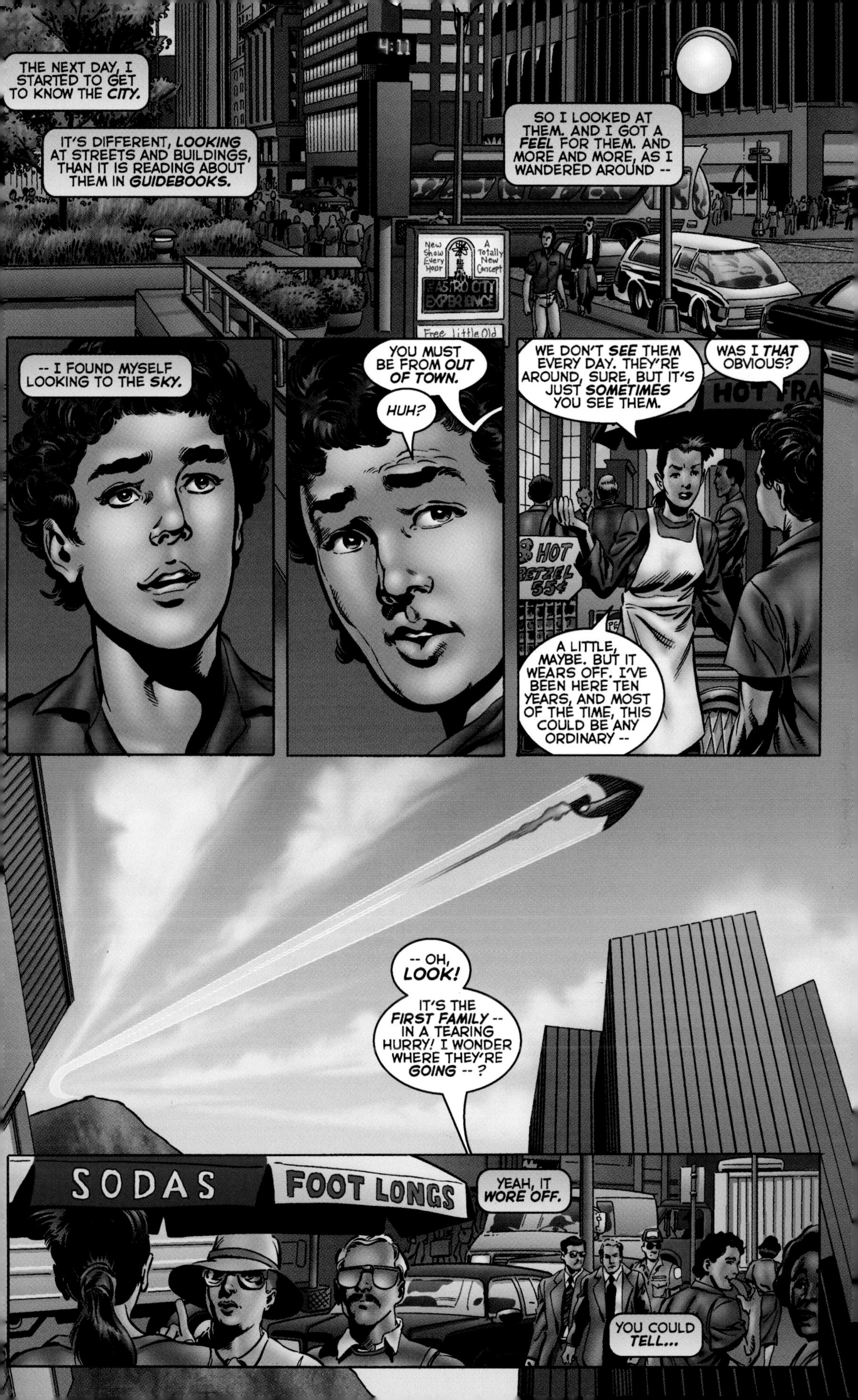

THE NEXT DAY, I STARTED TO GET TO KNOW THE CITY.
IT'S DIFFERENT, LOOKING AT STREETS AND BUILDINGS, THAN IT IS READING ABOUT THEM IN GUIDEBOOKS.
SO I LOOKED AT THEM. AND I GOT A FEEL FOR THEM. AND MORE AND MORE, AS I WANDERED AROUND --
4:11
New Show Every Hour
A Totally New Concept
ASTRO CITY EXPERIENCE
-- I FOUND MYSELF LOOKING TO THE SKY.
YOU MUST BE FROM OUT OF TOWN.
HUH?
WE DON'T SEE THEM EVERY DAY. THEY'RE AROUND, SURE, BUT IT'S JUST SOMETIMES YOU SEE THEM.
WAS I THAT OBVIOUS?
HOT PRETZEL 55¢
A LITTLE, MAYBE. BUT IT WEARS OFF. I'VE BEEN HERE TEN YEARS, AND MOST OF THE TIME, THIS COULD BE ANY ORDINARY --
-- OH, LOOK!
IT'S THE FIRST FAMILY -- IN A TEARING HURRY! I WONDER WHERE THEY'RE GOING -- ?
SODAS
FOOT LONGS
YEAH, IT WORE OFF.
YOU COULD TELL...

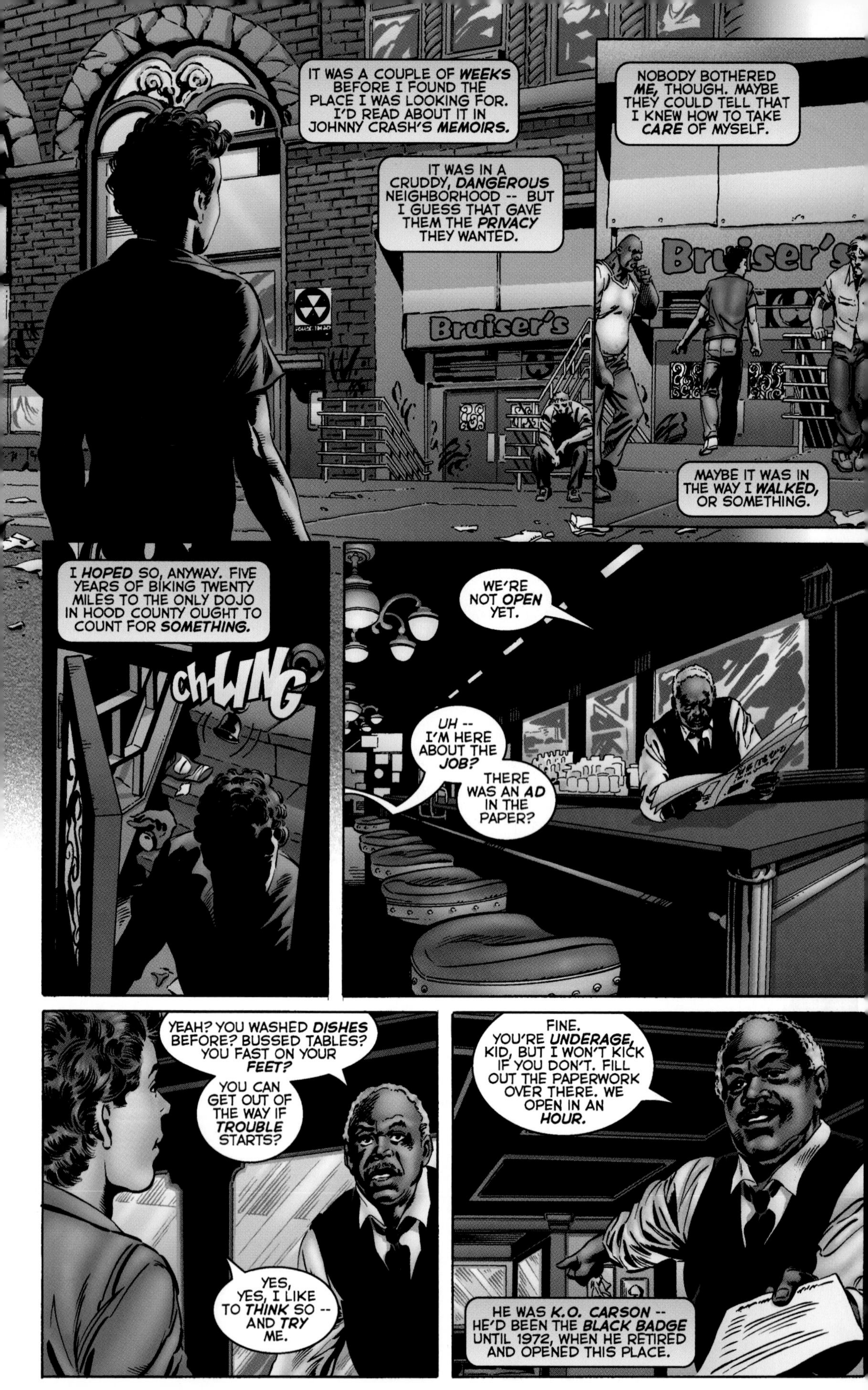

IT WAS A COUPLE OF WEEKS BEFORE I FOUND THE PLACE I WAS LOOKING FOR. I'D READ ABOUT IT IN JOHNNY CRASH'S MEMOIRS.
IT WAS IN A CRUDDY, DANGEROUS NEIGHBORHOOD -- BUT I GUESS THAT GAVE THEM THE PRIVACY THEY WANTED.
Bruiser's
NOBODY BOTHERED ME, THOUGH. MAYBE THEY COULD TELL THAT I KNEW HOW TO TAKE CARE OF MYSELF.
Bruiser's
MAYBE IT WAS IN THE WAY I WALKED, OR SOMETHING.
I HOPED SO, ANYWAY. FIVE YEARS OF BIKING TWENTY MILES TO THE ONLY DOJO IN HOOD COUNTY OUGHT TO COUNT FOR SOMETHING.
CH-LING
WE'RE NOT OPEN YET.
UH -- I'M HERE ABOUT THE JOB?
THERE WAS AN AD IN THE PAPER?
YEAH? YOU WASHED DISHES BEFORE? BUSSED TABLES? YOU FAST ON YOUR FEET?
YOU CAN GET OUT OF THE WAY IF TROUBLE STARTS?
YES, YES, I LIKE TO THINK SO -- AND TRY ME.
FINE. YOU'RE UNDERAGE, KID, BUT I WON'T KICK IF YOU DON'T. FILL OUT THE PAPERWORK OVER THERE. WE OPEN IN AN HOUR.
HE WAS K.O. CARSON -- HE'D BEEN THE BLACK BADGE UNTIL 1972, WHEN HE RETIRED AND OPENED THIS PLACE.

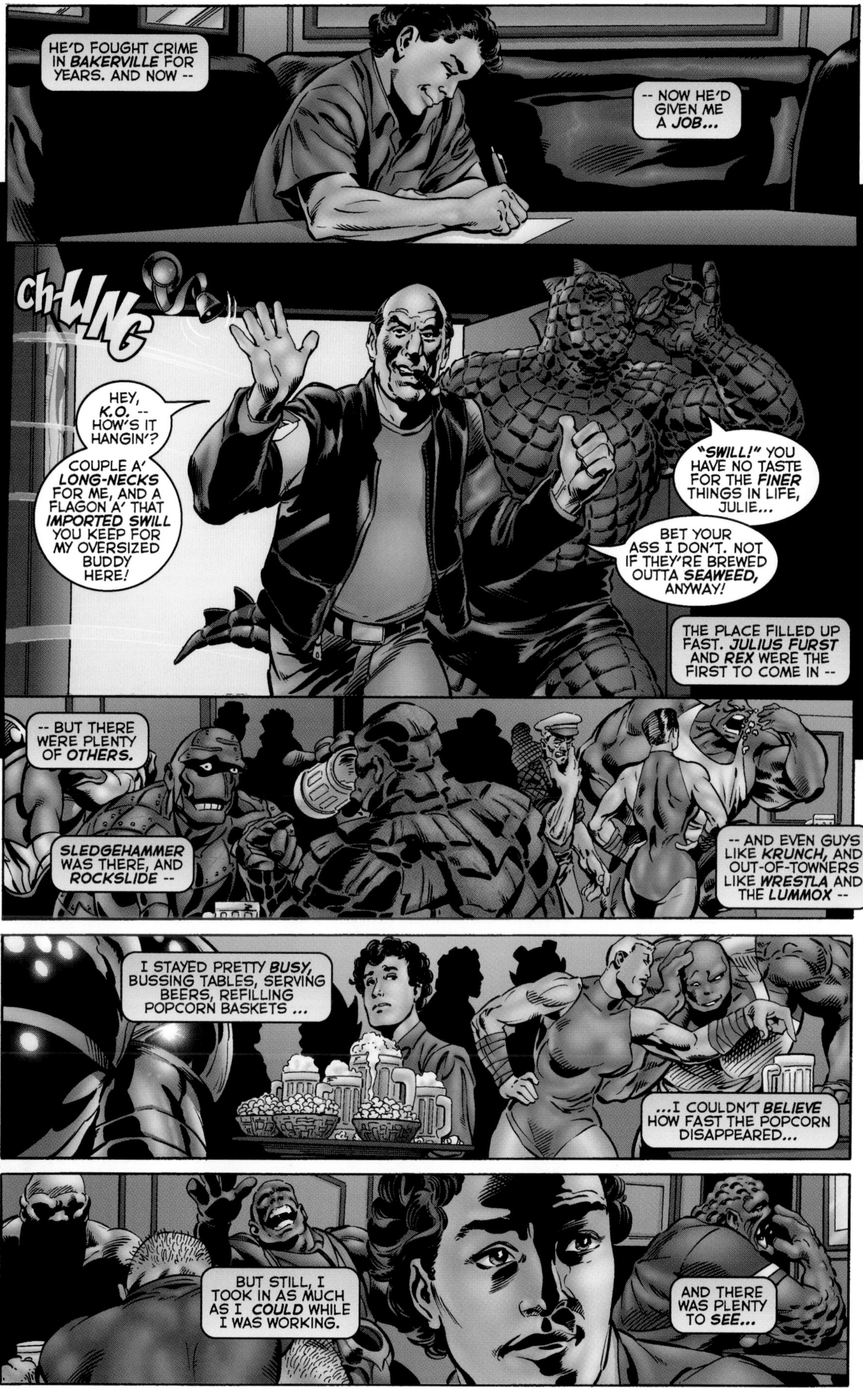
HE'D FOUGHT CRIME IN BAKERVILLE FOR YEARS. AND NOW --
-- NOW HE'D GIVEN ME A JOB...
CH-LING
HEY, K.O. -- HOW'S IT HANGIN'?
COUPLE A' LONG-NECKS FOR ME, AND A FLAGON A' THAT IMPORTED SWILL YOU KEEP FOR MY OVERSIZED BUDDY HERE!
"SWILL!" YOU HAVE NO TASTE FOR THE FINER THINGS IN LIFE, JULIE...
BET YOUR ASS I DON'T. NOT IF THEY'RE BREWED OUTTA SEAWEED, ANYWAY!
THE PLACE FILLED UP FAST. JULIUS FURST AND REX WERE THE FIRST TO COME IN --
-- BUT THERE WERE PLENTY OF OTHERS.
SLEDGEHAMMER WAS THERE, AND ROCKSLIDE --
-- AND EVEN GUYS LIKE KRUNCH, AND OUT-OF-TOWNERS LIKE WRESTLA AND THE LUMMOX --
I STAYED PRETTY BUSY, BUSSING TABLES, SERVING BEERS, REFILLING POPCORN BASKETS ...
...I COULDN'T BELIEVE HOW FAST THE POPCORN DISAPPEARED...
BUT STILL, I TOOK IN AS MUCH AS I COULD WHILE I WAS WORKING.
AND THERE WAS PLENTY TO SEE...

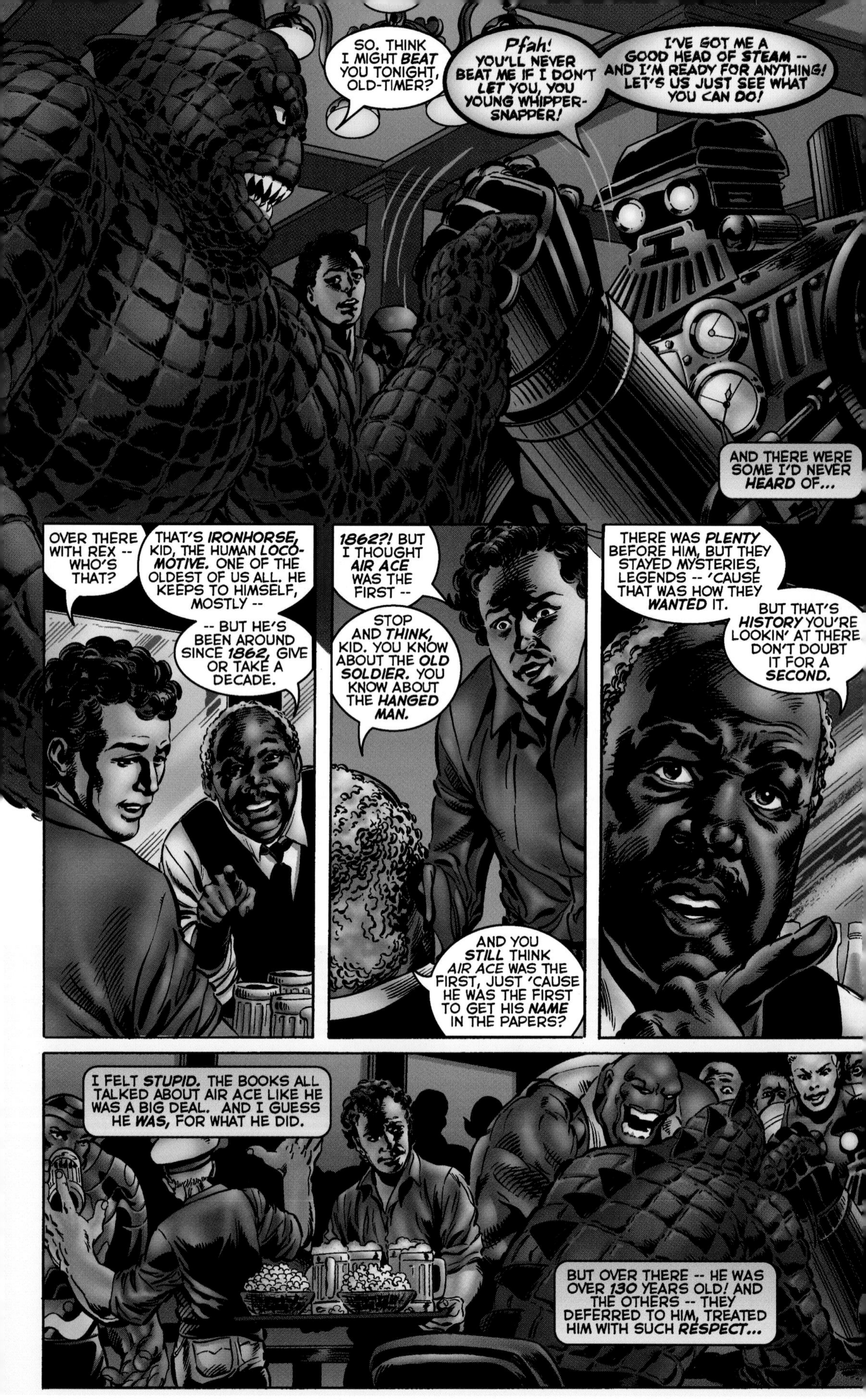
SO. THINK I MIGHT BEAT YOU TONIGHT, OLD-TIMER?
Pfah! YOU'LL NEVER BEAT ME IF I DON'T LET YOU, YOU YOUNG WHIPPER-SNAPPER!
I'VE GOT ME A GOOD HEAD OF STEAM -- AND I'M READY FOR ANYTHING! LET'S US JUST SEE WHAT YOU CAN DO!
AND THERE WERE SOME I'D NEVER HEARD OF...
OVER THERE WITH REX -- WHO'S THAT?
THAT'S IRONHORSE, KID, THE HUMAN LOCOMOTIVE. ONE OF THE OLDEST OF US ALL. HE KEEPS TO HIMSELF, MOSTLY --
-- BUT HE'S BEEN AROUND SINCE 1862, GIVE OR TAKE A DECADE.
1862?! BUT I THOUGHT AIR ACE WAS THE FIRST --
STOP AND THINK, KID. YOU KNOW ABOUT THE OLD SOLDIER. YOU KNOW ABOUT THE HANGED MAN.
AND YOU STILL THINK AIR ACE WAS THE FIRST, JUST 'CAUSE HE WAS THE FIRST TO GET HIS NAME IN THE PAPERS?
THERE WAS PLENTY BEFORE HIM, BUT THEY STAYED MYSTERIES, LEGENDS -- 'CAUSE THAT WAS HOW THEY WANTED IT.
BUT THAT'S HISTORY YOU'RE LOOKIN' AT THERE DON'T DOUBT IT FOR A SECOND.
I FELT STUPID. THE BOOKS ALL TALKED ABOUT AIR ACE LIKE HE WAS A BIG DEAL. AND I GUESS HE WAS, FOR WHAT HE DID.
BUT OVER THERE -- HE WAS OVER 130 YEARS OLD! AND THE OTHERS -- THEY DEFERRED TO HIM, TREATED HIM WITH SUCH RESPECT...

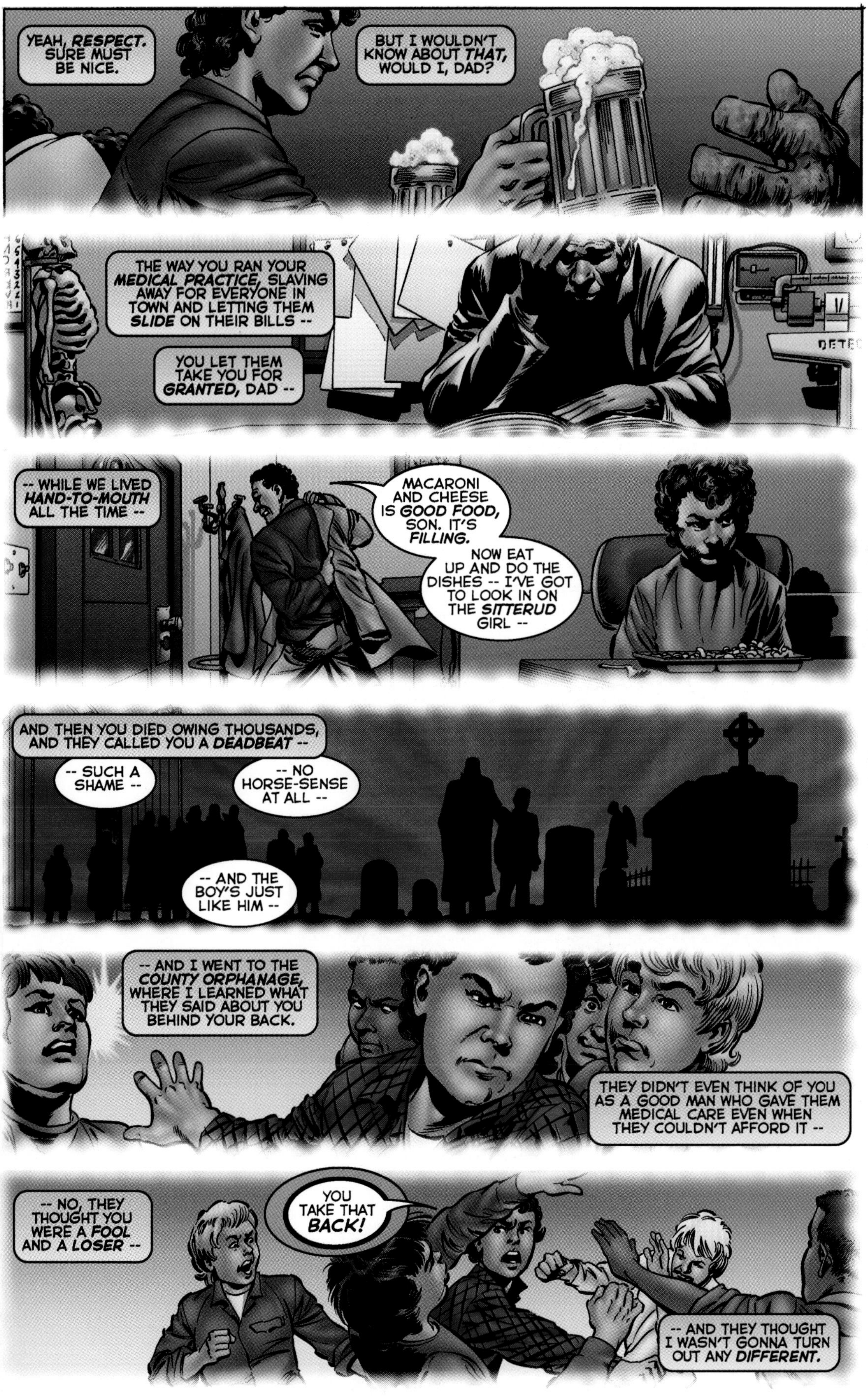

YEAH, RESPECT. SURE MUST BE NICE.
BUT I WOULDN'T KNOW ABOUT THAT, WOULD I, DAD?
THE WAY YOU RAN YOUR MEDICAL PRACTICE, SLAVING AWAY FOR EVERYONE IN TOWN AND LETTING THEM SLIDE ON THEIR BILLS --
YOU LET THEM TAKE YOU FOR GRANTED, DAD --
-- WHILE WE LIVED HAND-TO-MOUTH ALL THE TIME --
MACARONI AND CHEESE IS GOOD FOOD, SON. IT'S FILLING.
NOW EAT UP AND DO THE DISHES -- I'VE GOT TO LOOK IN ON THE SITTERUD GIRL --
AND THEN YOU DIED OWING THOUSANDS, AND THEY CALLED YOU A DEADBEAT --
-- SUCH A SHAME --
-- NO HORSE-SENSE AT ALL --
-- AND THE BOY'S JUST LIKE HIM --
-- AND I WENT TO THE COUNTY ORPHANAGE, WHERE I LEARNED WHAT THEY SAID ABOUT YOU BEHIND YOUR BACK.
THEY DIDN'T EVEN THINK OF YOU AS A GOOD MAN WHO GAVE THEM MEDICAL CARE EVEN WHEN THEY COULDN'T AFFORD IT --
-- NO, THEY THOUGHT YOU WERE A FOOL AND A LOSER --
YOU TAKE THAT BACK!
-- AND THEY THOUGHT I WASN'T GONNA TURN OUT ANY DIFFERENT.

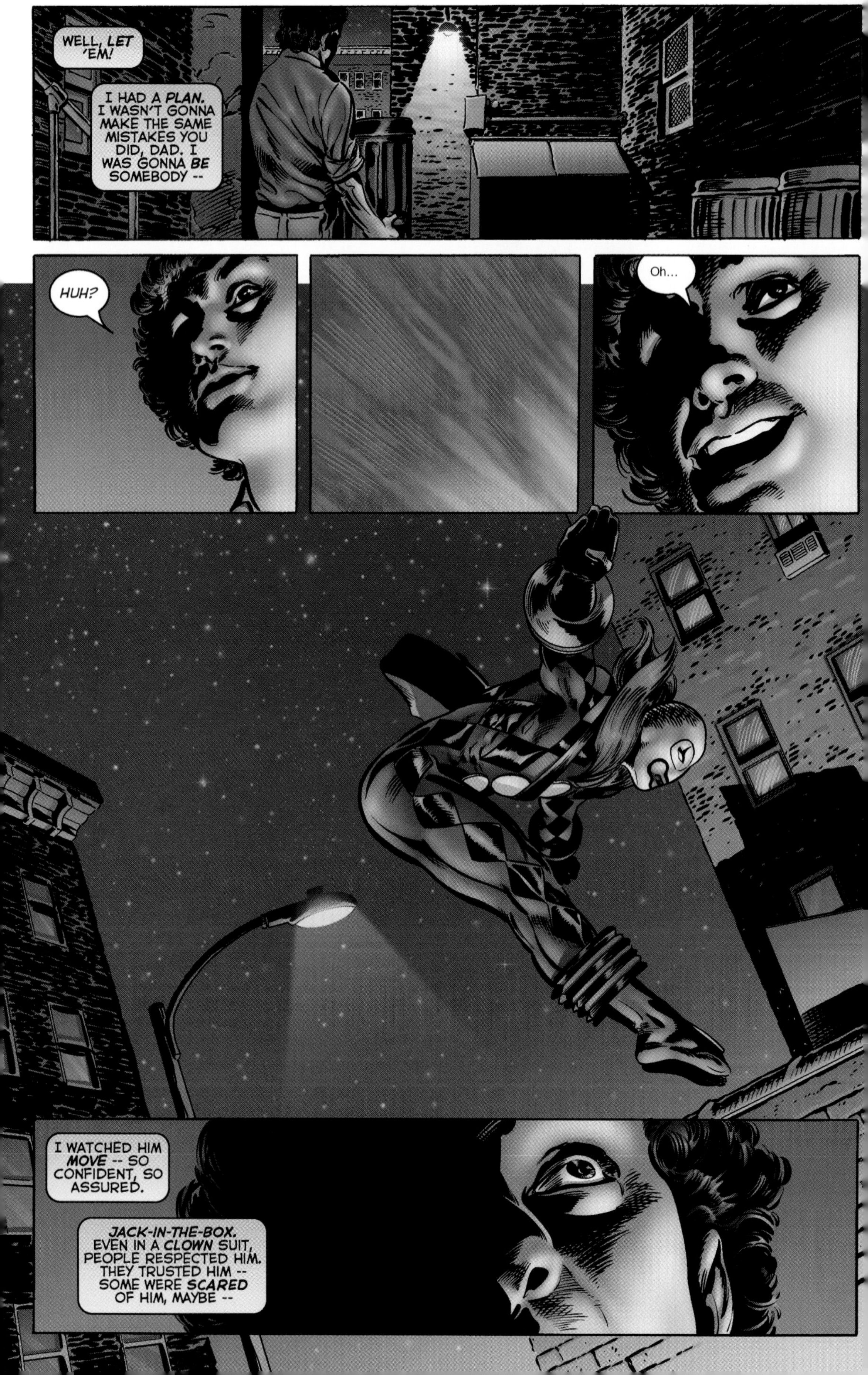
WELL, LET 'EM!
I HAD A PLAN. I WASN'T GONNA MAKE THE SAME MISTAKES YOU DID, DAD. I WAS GONNA BE SOMEBODY --
HUH?
Oh...
I WATCHED HIM MOVE -- SO CONFIDENT, SO ASSURED.
JACK-IN-THE-BOX. EVEN IN A CLOWN SUIT, PEOPLE RESPECTED HIM. THEY TRUSTED HIM -- SOME WERE SCARED OF HIM, MAYBE --

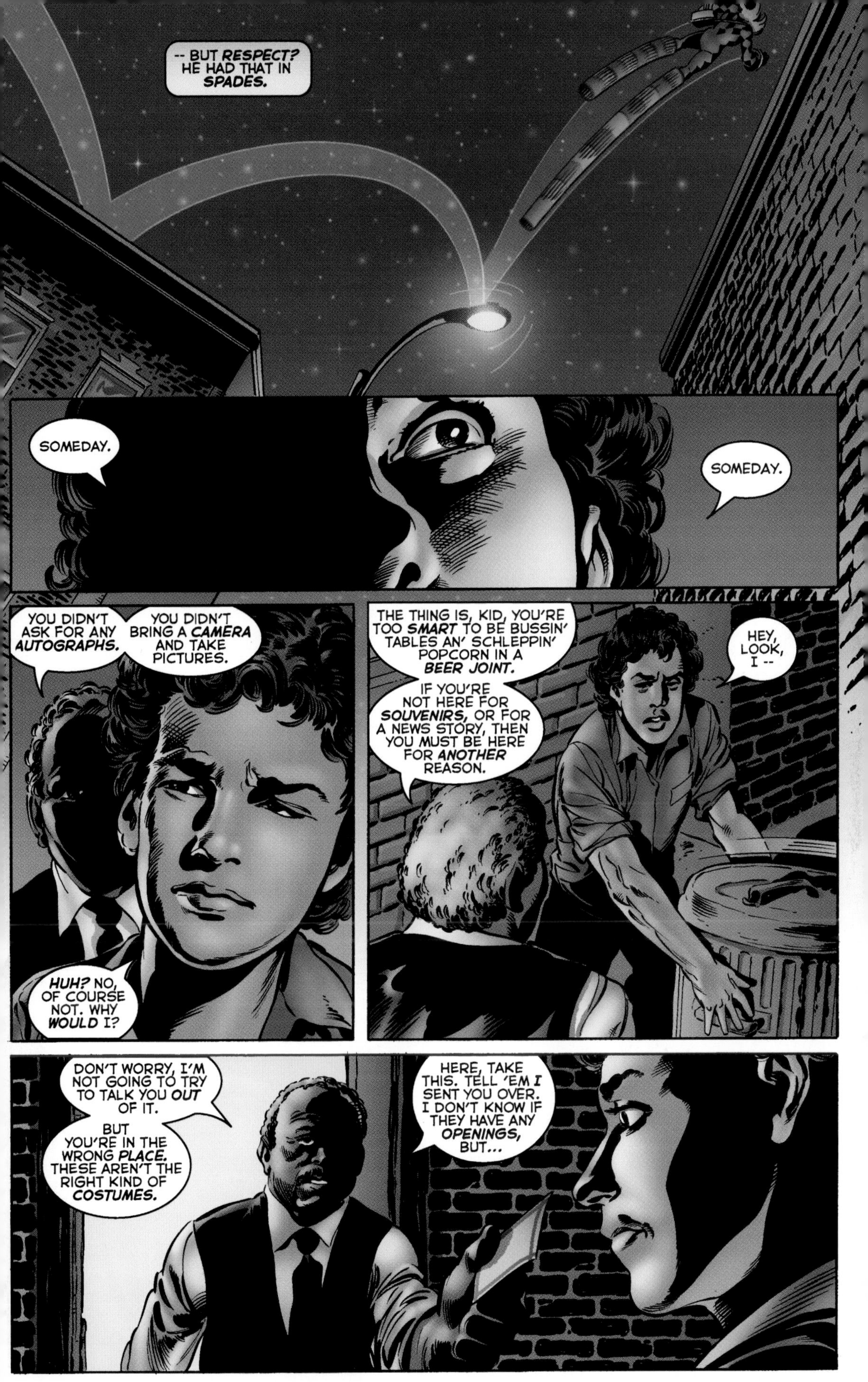
-- BUT RESPECT? HE HAD THAT IN SPADES.
SOMEDAY.
SOMEDAY.
YOU DIDN'T ASK FOR ANY AUTOGRAPHS.
YOU DIDN'T BRING A CAMERA AND TAKE PICTURES.
HUH? NO, OF COURSE NOT. WHY WOULD I?
THE THING IS, KID, YOU'RE TOO SMART TO BE BUSSIN' TABLES AN' SCHLEPPIN' POPCORN IN A BEER JOINT.
IF YOU'RE NOT HERE FOR SOUVENIRS, OR FOR A NEWS STORY, THEN YOU MUST BE HERE FOR ANOTHER REASON.
HEY, LOOK, I --
DON'T WORRY, I'M NOT GOING TO TRY TO TALK YOU OUT OF IT.
BUT YOU'RE IN THE WRONG PLACE. THESE AREN'T THE RIGHT KIND OF COSTUMES.
HERE, TAKE THIS. TELL 'EM I SENT YOU OVER. I DON'T KNOW IF THEY HAVE ANY OPENINGS, BUT...

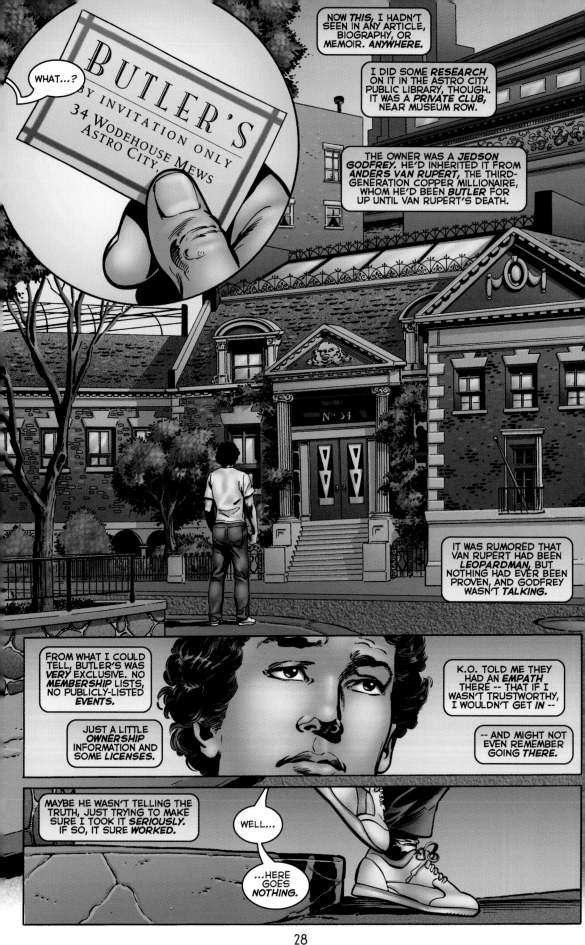

WHAT...?

BUTLER'S
BY INVITATION ONLY
34 Wodehouse Mews
Astro City,

NOW *THIS*, I HADN'T SEEN IN ANY ARTICLE, BIOGRAPHY, OR MEMOIR. *ANYWHERE.*

I DID SOME *RESEARCH* ON IT IN THE ASTRO CITY PUBLIC LIBRARY, THOUGH. IT WAS A *PRIVATE* CLUB, NEAR MUSEUM ROW.

THE OWNER WAS A *JEDSON GODFREY.* HE'D INHERITED IT FROM *ANDERS VAN RUPERT*, THE THIRD-GENERATION COPPER MILLIONAIRE, WHOM HE'D BEEN *BUTLER* FOR UP UNTIL VAN RUPERT'S DEATH.

IT WAS RUMORED THAT VAN RUPERT HAD BEEN *LEOPARDMAN*, BUT NOTHING HAD EVER BEEN PROVEN, AND GODFREY WASN'T *TALKING.*

FROM WHAT I COULD TELL, BUTLER'S WAS *VERY* EXCLUSIVE. NO *MEMBERSHIP* LISTS, NO PUBLICLY-LISTED *EVENTS.*

JUST A LITTLE *OWNERSHIP* INFORMATION AND SOME *LICENSES.*

K.O. TOLD ME THEY HAD AN *EMPATH* THERE -- THAT IF I WASN'T TRUSTWORTHY, I WOULDN'T GET *IN* --

-- AND MIGHT NOT EVEN REMEMBER GOING *THERE.*

MAYBE HE WASN'T TELLING THE TRUTH, JUST TRYING TO MAKE SURE I TOOK IT *SERIOUSLY.* IF SO, IT SURE *WORKED.*

WELL...

...HERE GOES *NOTHING.*

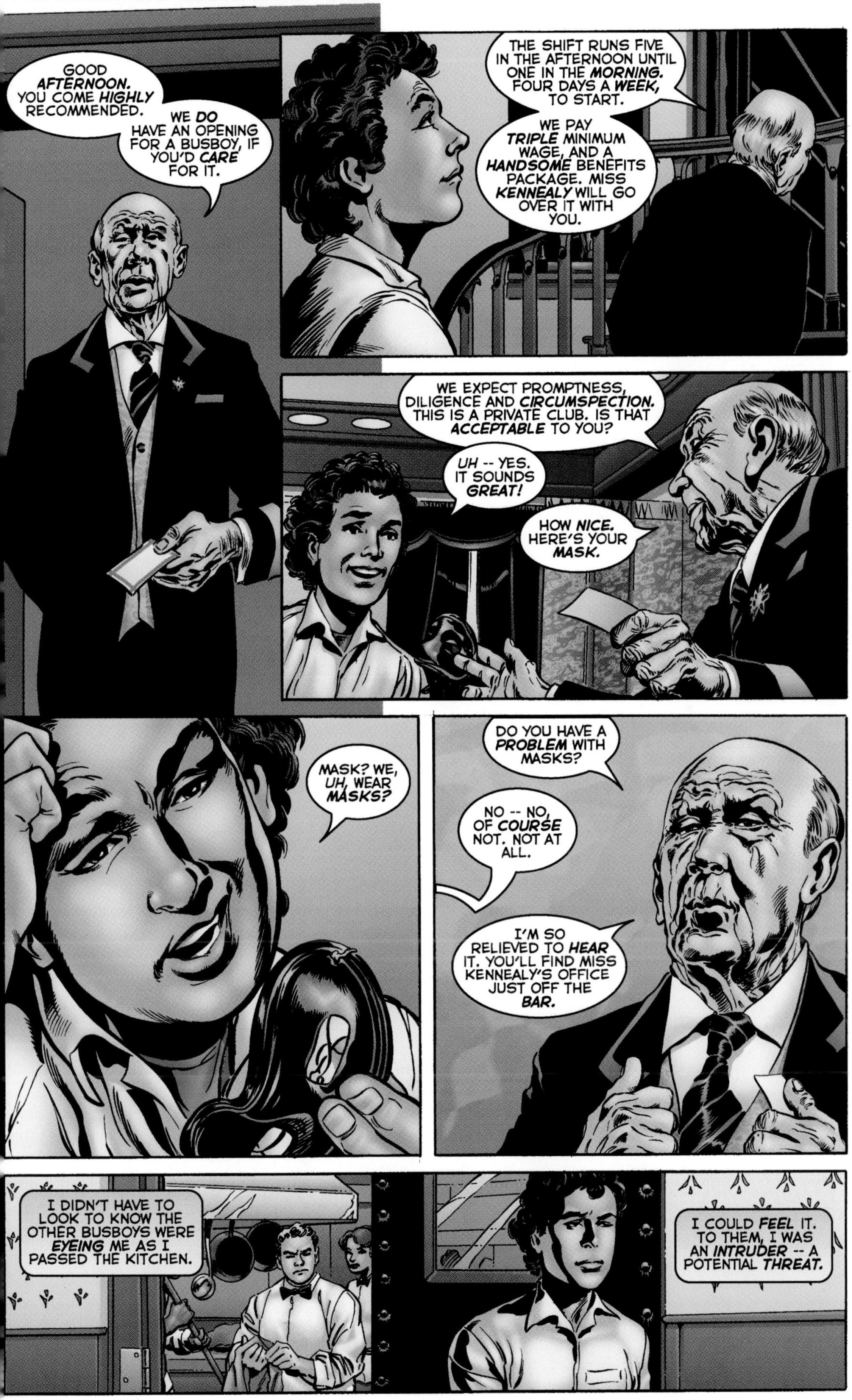
GOOD AFTERNOON. YOU COME HIGHLY RECOMMENDED.
WE DO HAVE AN OPENING FOR A BUSBOY, IF YOU'D CARE FOR IT.
THE SHIFT RUNS FIVE IN THE AFTERNOON UNTIL ONE IN THE MORNING. FOUR DAYS A WEEK, TO START.
WE PAY TRIPLE MINIMUM WAGE, AND A HANDSOME BENEFITS PACKAGE. MISS KENNEALY WILL GO OVER IT WITH YOU.
WE EXPECT PROMPTNESS, DILIGENCE AND CIRCUMSPECTION. THIS IS A PRIVATE CLUB. IS THAT ACCEPTABLE TO YOU?
UH -- YES. IT SOUNDS GREAT!
HOW NICE. HERE'S YOUR MASK.
MASK? WE, UH, WEAR MASKS?
DO YOU HAVE A PROBLEM WITH MASKS?
NO -- NO, OF COURSE NOT. NOT AT ALL.
I'M SO RELIEVED TO HEAR IT. YOU'LL FIND MISS KENNEALY'S OFFICE JUST OFF THE BAR.
I DIDN'T HAVE TO LOOK TO KNOW THE OTHER BUSBOYS WERE EYEING ME AS I PASSED THE KITCHEN.
I COULD FEEL IT. TO THEM, I WAS AN INTRUDER -- A POTENTIAL THREAT.

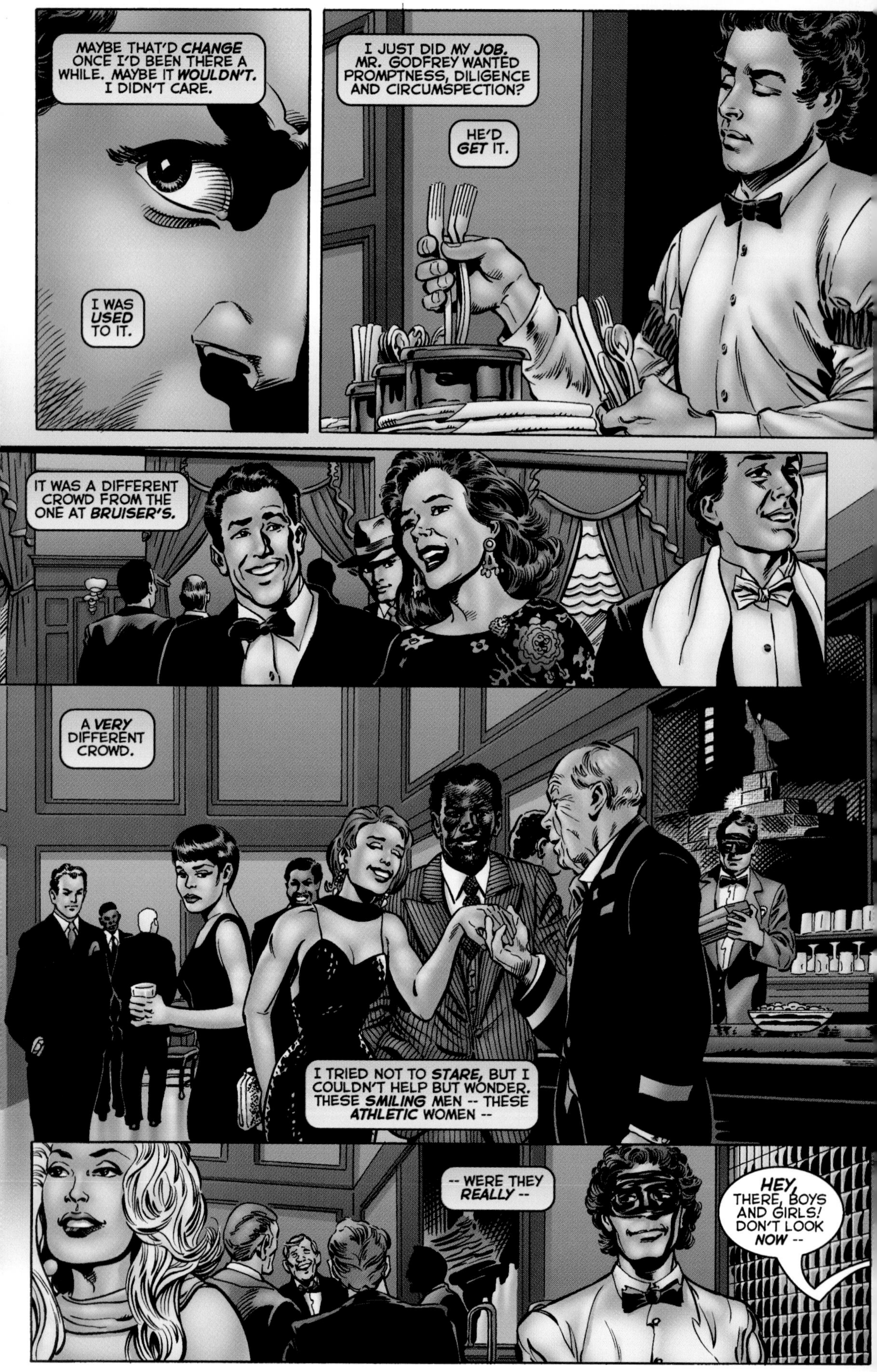

MAYBE THAT'D CHANGE ONCE I'D BEEN THERE A WHILE. MAYBE IT WOULDN'T. I DIDN'T CARE.
I WAS USED TO IT.
I JUST DID MY JOB. MR. GODFREY WANTED PROMPTNESS, DILIGENCE AND CIRCUMSPECTION?
HE'D GET IT.
IT WAS A DIFFERENT CROWD FROM THE ONE AT BRUISER'S.
A VERY DIFFERENT CROWD.
I TRIED NOT TO STARE, BUT I COULDN'T HELP BUT WONDER. THESE SMILING MEN -- THESE ATHLETIC WOMEN --
-- WERE THEY REALLY --
HEY, THERE, BOYS AND GIRLS! DON'T LOOK NOW --

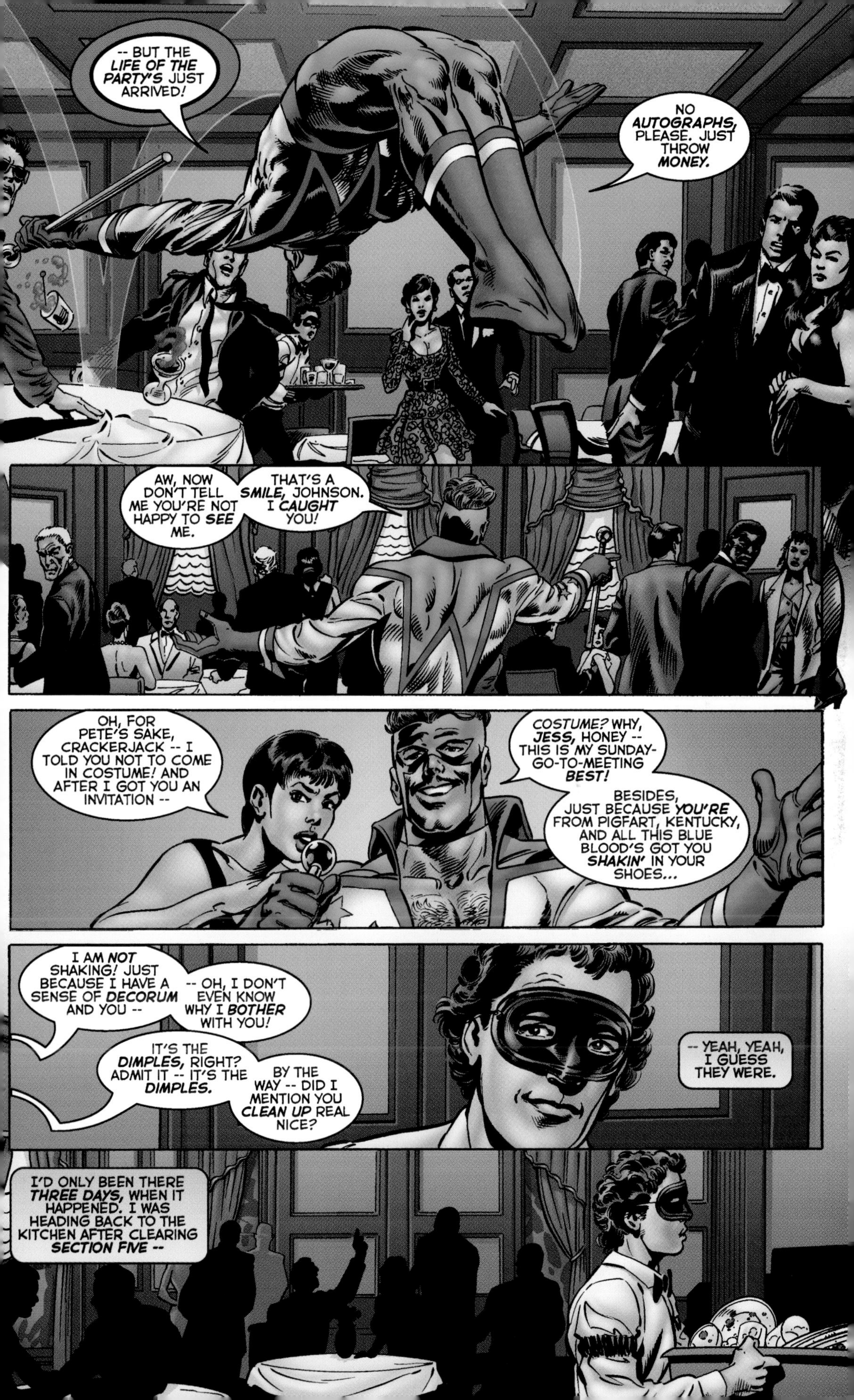

-- BUT THE LIFE OF THE PARTY'S JUST ARRIVED!
NO AUTOGRAPHS, PLEASE. JUST THROW MONEY.
AW, NOW DON'T TELL ME YOU'RE NOT HAPPY TO SEE ME.
THAT'S A SMILE, JOHNSON. I CAUGHT YOU!
OH, FOR PETE'S SAKE, CRACKERJACK -- I TOLD YOU NOT TO COME IN COSTUME! AND AFTER I GOT YOU AN INVITATION --
COSTUME? WHY, JESS, HONEY -- THIS IS MY SUNDAY-GO-TO-MEETING BEST!
BESIDES, JUST BECAUSE YOU'RE FROM PIGFART, KENTUCKY, AND ALL THIS BLUE BLOOD'S GOT YOU SHAKIN' IN YOUR SHOES...
I AM NOT SHAKING! JUST BECAUSE I HAVE A SENSE OF DECORUM AND YOU --
-- OH, I DON'T EVEN KNOW WHY I BOTHER WITH YOU!
IT'S THE DIMPLES, RIGHT? ADMIT IT -- IT'S THE DIMPLES.
BY THE WAY -- DID I MENTION YOU CLEAN UP REAL NICE?
-- YEAH, YEAH, I GUESS THEY WERE.
I'D ONLY BEEN THERE THREE DAYS, WHEN IT HAPPENED. I WAS HEADING BACK TO THE KITCHEN AFTER CLEARING SECTION FIVE --

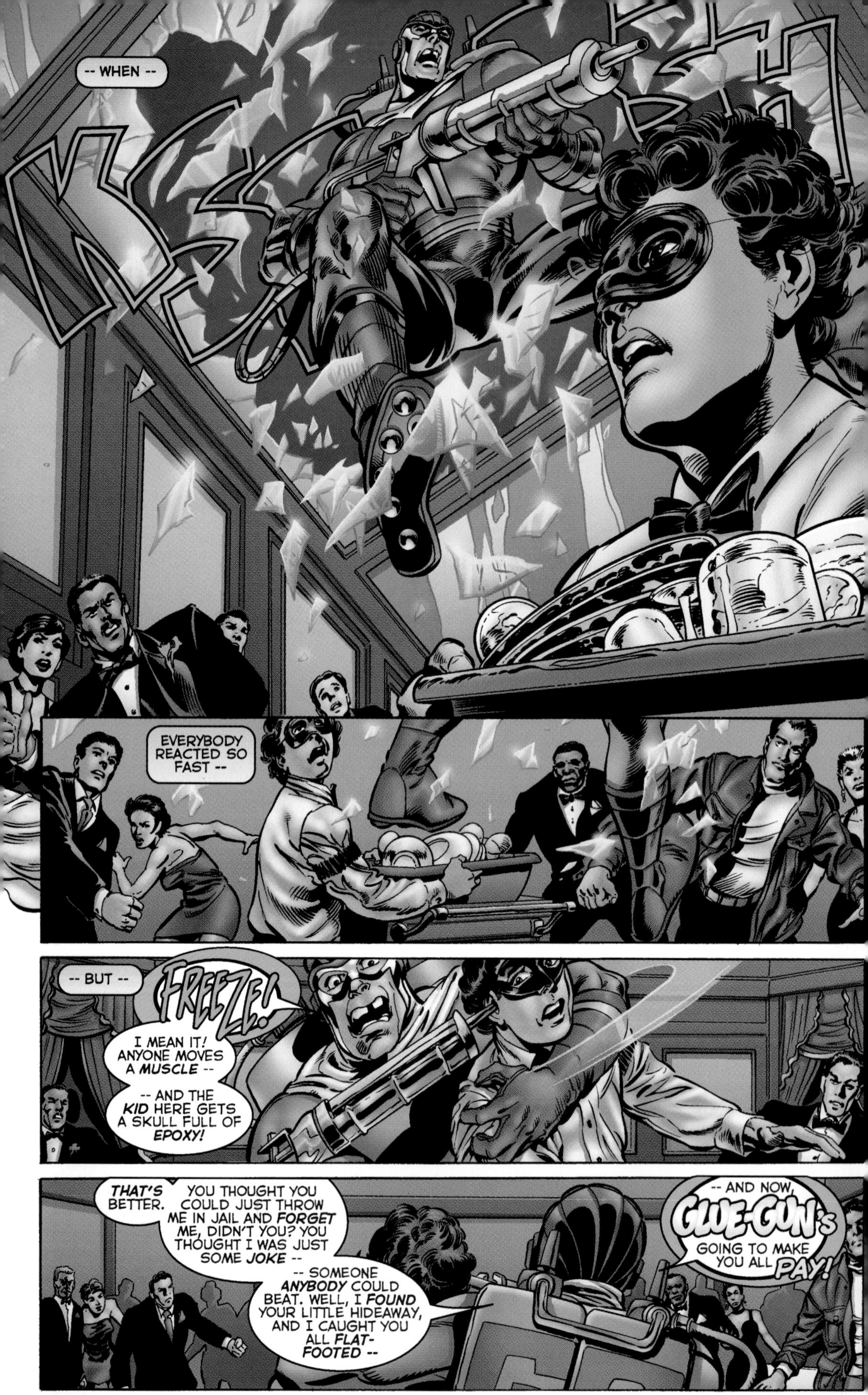
-- WHEN --
KRASH
EVERYBODY REACTED SO FAST --
-- BUT --
FREEZE!
I MEAN IT! ANYONE MOVES A MUSCLE --
-- AND THE KID HERE GETS A SKULL FULL OF EPOXY!
THAT'S BETTER.
YOU THOUGHT YOU COULD JUST THROW ME IN JAIL AND FORGET ME, DIDN'T YOU? YOU THOUGHT I WAS JUST SOME JOKE --
-- SOMEONE ANYBODY COULD BEAT. WELL, I FOUND YOUR LITTLE HIDEAWAY, AND I CAUGHT YOU ALL FLAT-FOOTED --
-- AND NOW, GLUE-GUN'S GOING TO MAKE YOU ALL PAY!

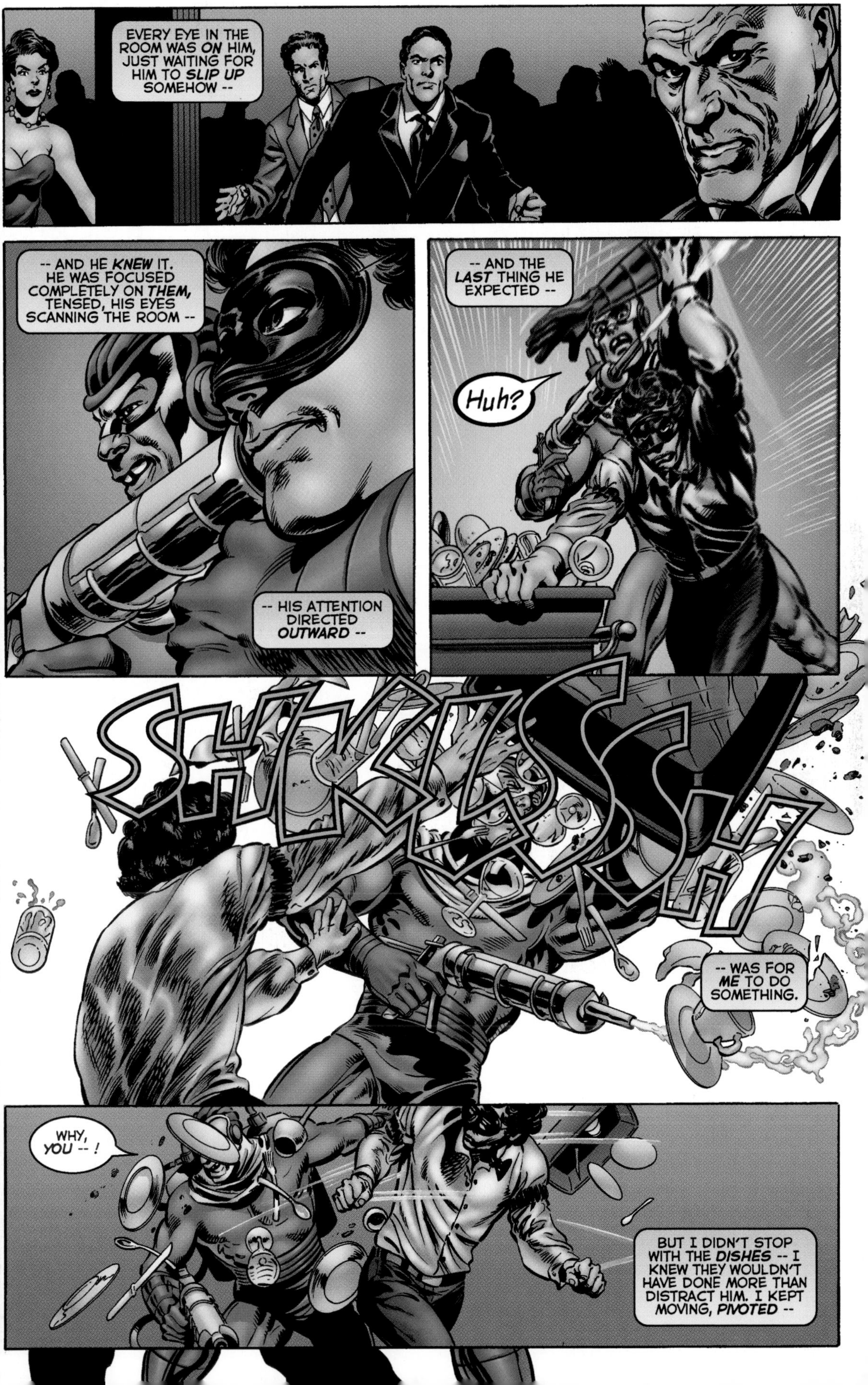
EVERY EYE IN THE ROOM WAS ON HIM, JUST WAITING FOR HIM TO SLIP UP SOMEHOW --
-- AND HE KNEW IT. HE WAS FOCUSED COMPLETELY ON THEM, TENSED, HIS EYES SCANNING THE ROOM --
-- HIS ATTENTION DIRECTED OUTWARD --
-- AND THE LAST THING HE EXPECTED --
Huh?
SHKLSSH
-- WAS FOR ME TO DO SOMETHING.
WHY, YOU -- !
BUT I DIDN'T STOP WITH THE DISHES -- I KNEW THEY WOULDN'T HAVE DONE MORE THAN DISTRACT HIM. I KEPT MOVING, PIVOTED --

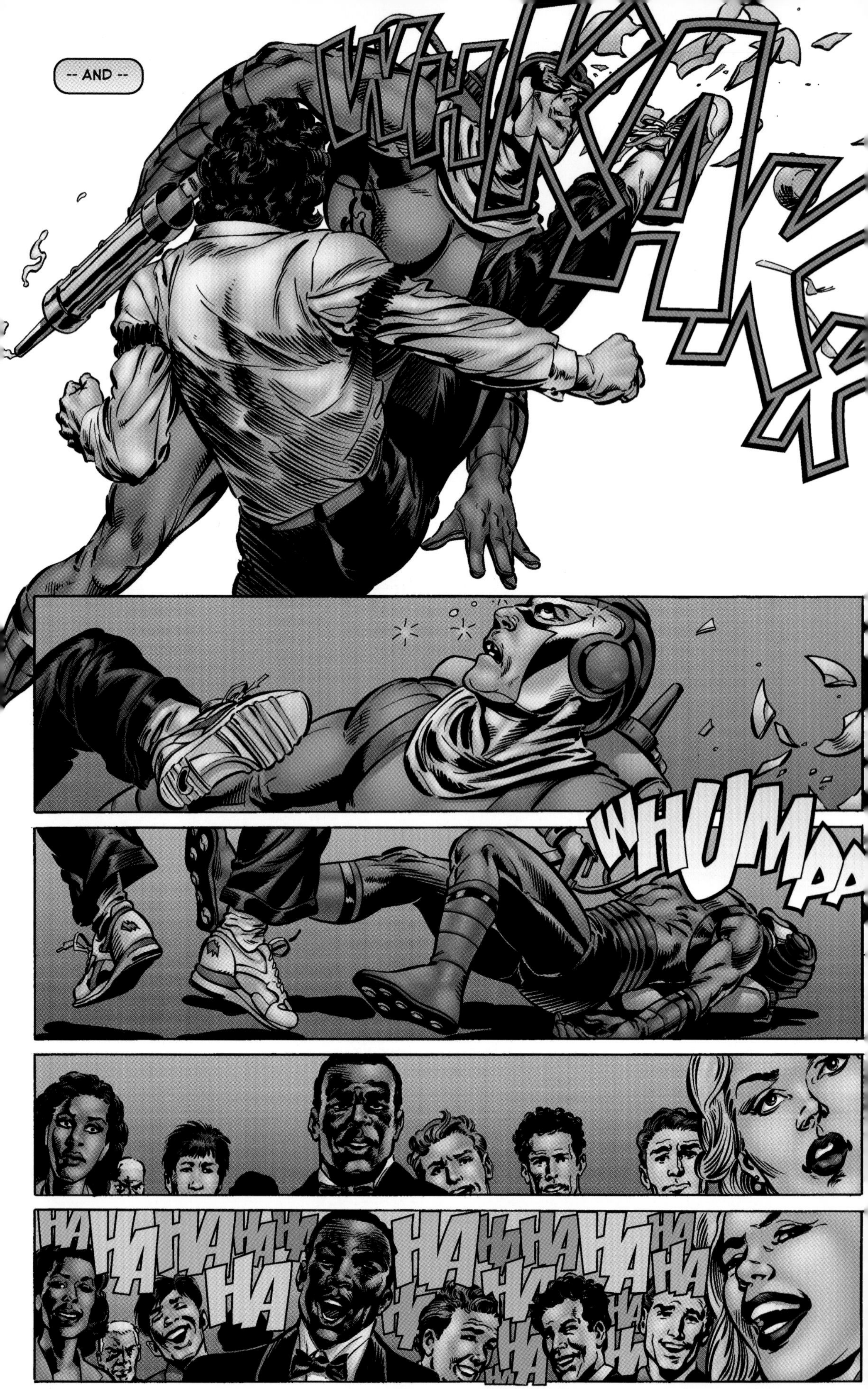
-- AND --
WHUMP
HA HA HA HA HA HA HA HA HA HA HA HA HA

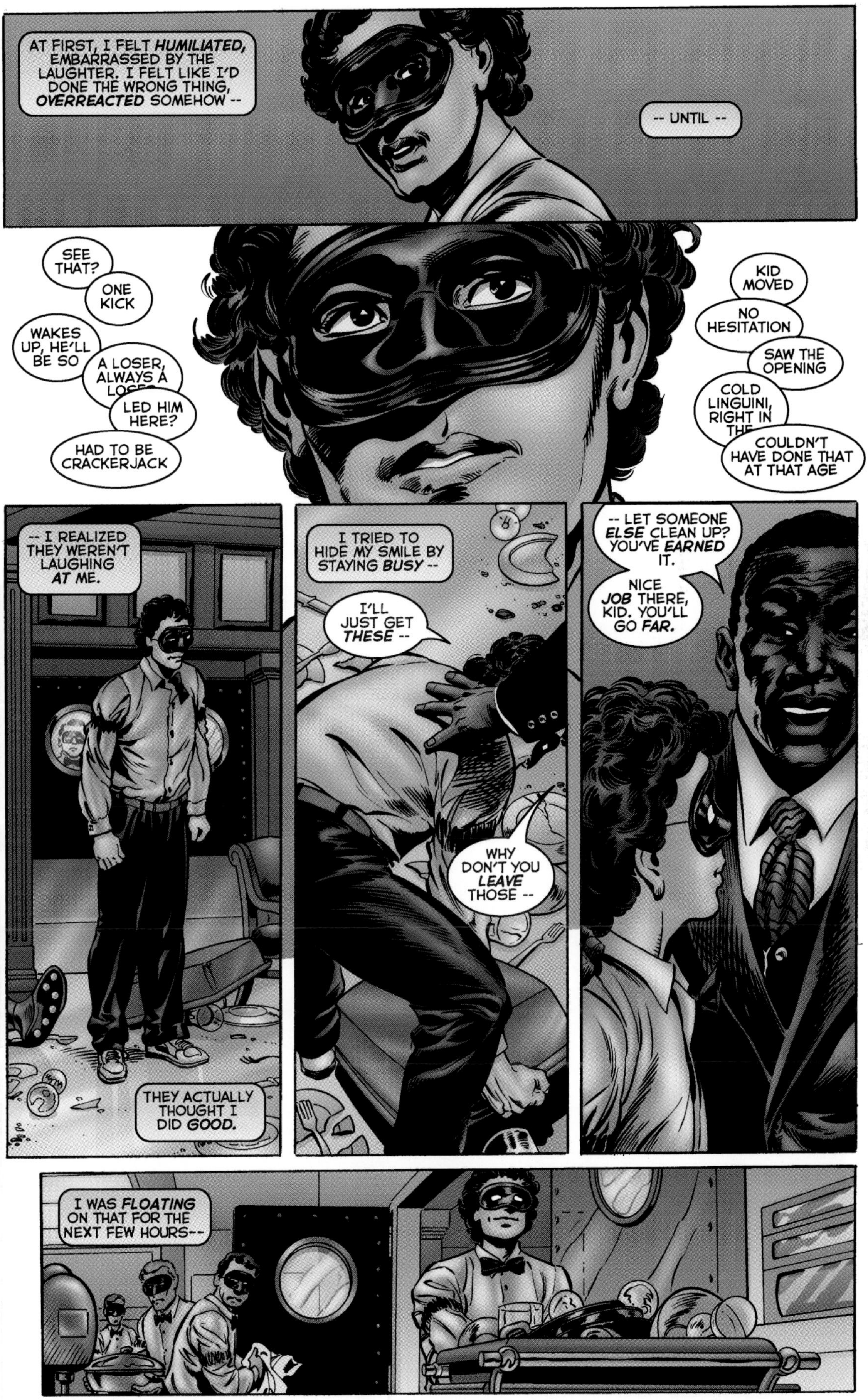
AT FIRST, I FELT HUMILIATED, EMBARRASSED BY THE LAUGHTER. I FELT LIKE I'D DONE THE WRONG THING, OVERREACTED SOMEHOW --
-- UNTIL --
SEE THAT?
ONE KICK
WAKES UP, HE'LL BE SO
A LOSER, ALWAYS A
LED HIM HERE?
HAD TO BE CRACKERJACK
KID MOVED
NO HESITATION
SAW THE OPENING
COLD LINGUINI, RIGHT IN
COULDN'T HAVE DONE THAT AT THAT AGE
-- I REALIZED THEY WEREN'T LAUGHING AT ME.
THEY ACTUALLY THOUGHT I DID GOOD.
I TRIED TO HIDE MY SMILE BY STAYING BUSY --
I'LL JUST GET THESE --
WHY DON'T YOU LEAVE THOSE --
-- LET SOMEONE ELSE CLEAN UP? YOU'VE EARNED IT.
NICE JOB THERE, KID. YOU'LL GO FAR.
I WAS FLOATING ON THAT FOR THE NEXT FEW HOURS--

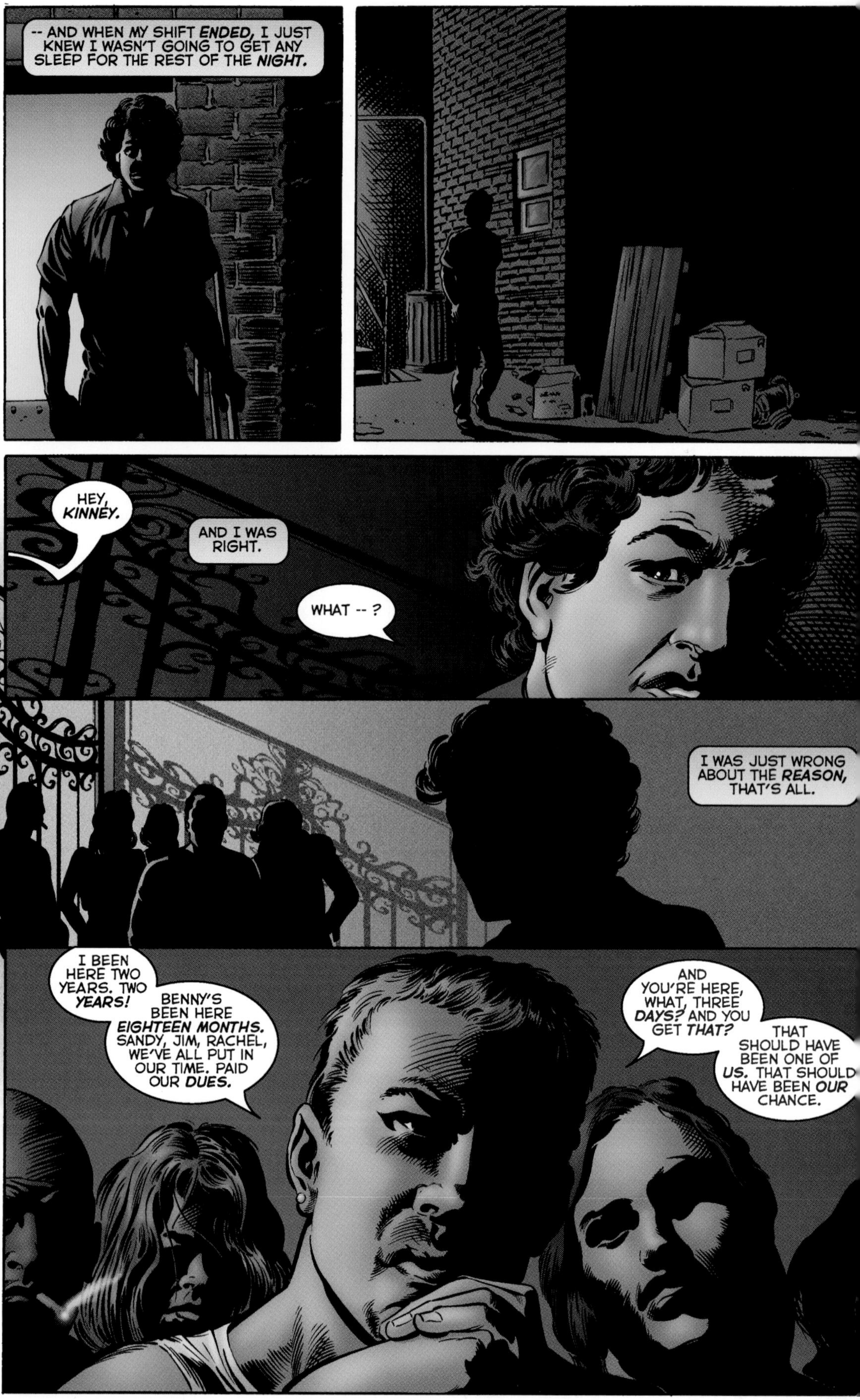
-- AND WHEN MY SHIFT *ENDED,* I JUST KNEW I WASN'T GOING TO GET ANY SLEEP FOR THE REST OF THE *NIGHT.*
HEY, *KINNEY.*
AND I WAS RIGHT.
WHAT -- ?
I WAS JUST WRONG ABOUT THE *REASON,* THAT'S ALL.
I BEEN HERE TWO YEARS. TWO *YEARS!*
BENNY'S BEEN HERE *EIGHTEEN MONTHS.* SANDY, JIM, RACHEL, WE'VE ALL PUT IN OUR TIME. PAID OUR *DUES.*
AND YOU'RE HERE, WHAT, THREE *DAYS?* AND YOU GET *THAT?*
THAT SHOULD HAVE BEEN ONE OF *US.* THAT SHOULD HAVE BEEN *OUR* CHANCE.

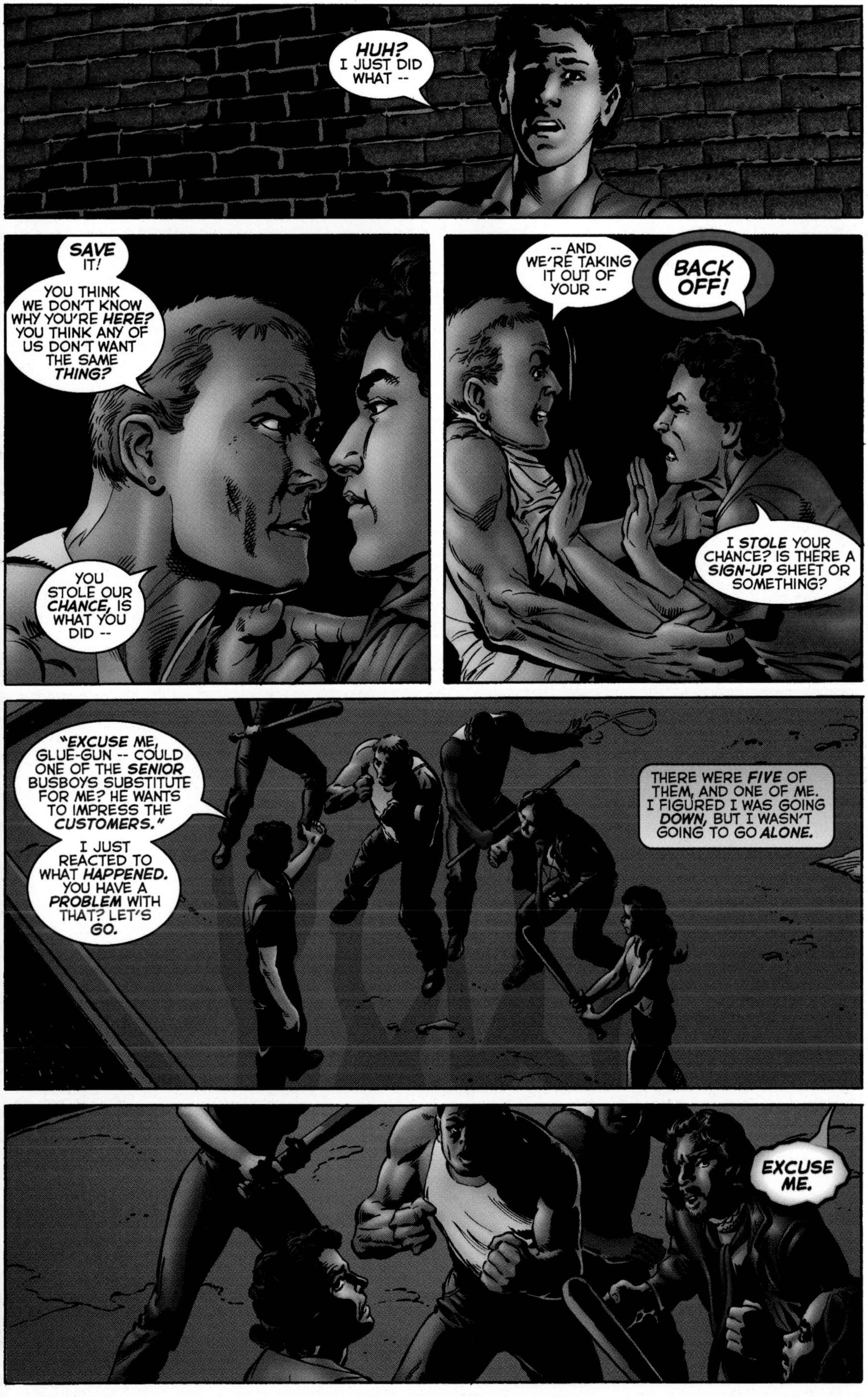
HUH? I JUST DID WHAT --
SAVE IT!
YOU THINK WE DON'T KNOW WHY YOU'RE HERE? YOU THINK ANY OF US DON'T WANT THE SAME THING?
YOU STOLE OUR CHANCE, IS WHAT YOU DID --
-- AND WE'RE TAKING IT OUT OF YOUR --
BACK OFF!
I STOLE YOUR CHANCE? IS THERE A SIGN-UP SHEET OR SOMETHING?
"EXCUSE ME, GLUE-GUN -- COULD ONE OF THE SENIOR BUSBOYS SUBSTITUTE FOR ME? HE WANTS TO IMPRESS THE CUSTOMERS."
I JUST REACTED TO WHAT HAPPENED. YOU HAVE A PROBLEM WITH THAT? LET'S GO.
THERE WERE FIVE OF THEM, AND ONE OF ME. I FIGURED I WAS GOING DOWN, BUT I WASN'T GOING TO GO ALONE.
EXCUSE ME.

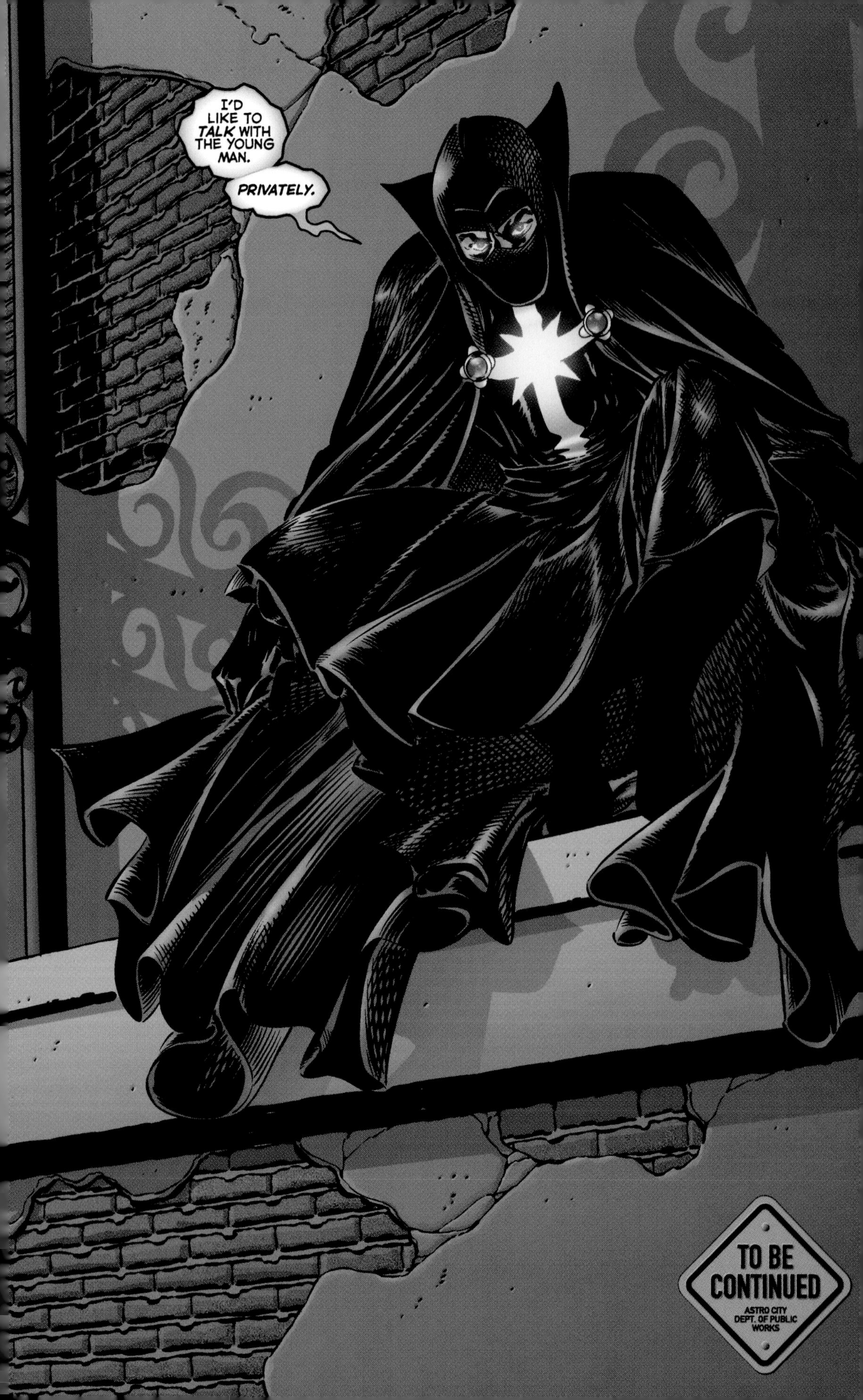
I'D LIKE TO TALK WITH THE YOUNG MAN.
PRIVATELY.
TO BE CONTINUED
ASTRO CITY DEPT. OF PUBLIC WORKS

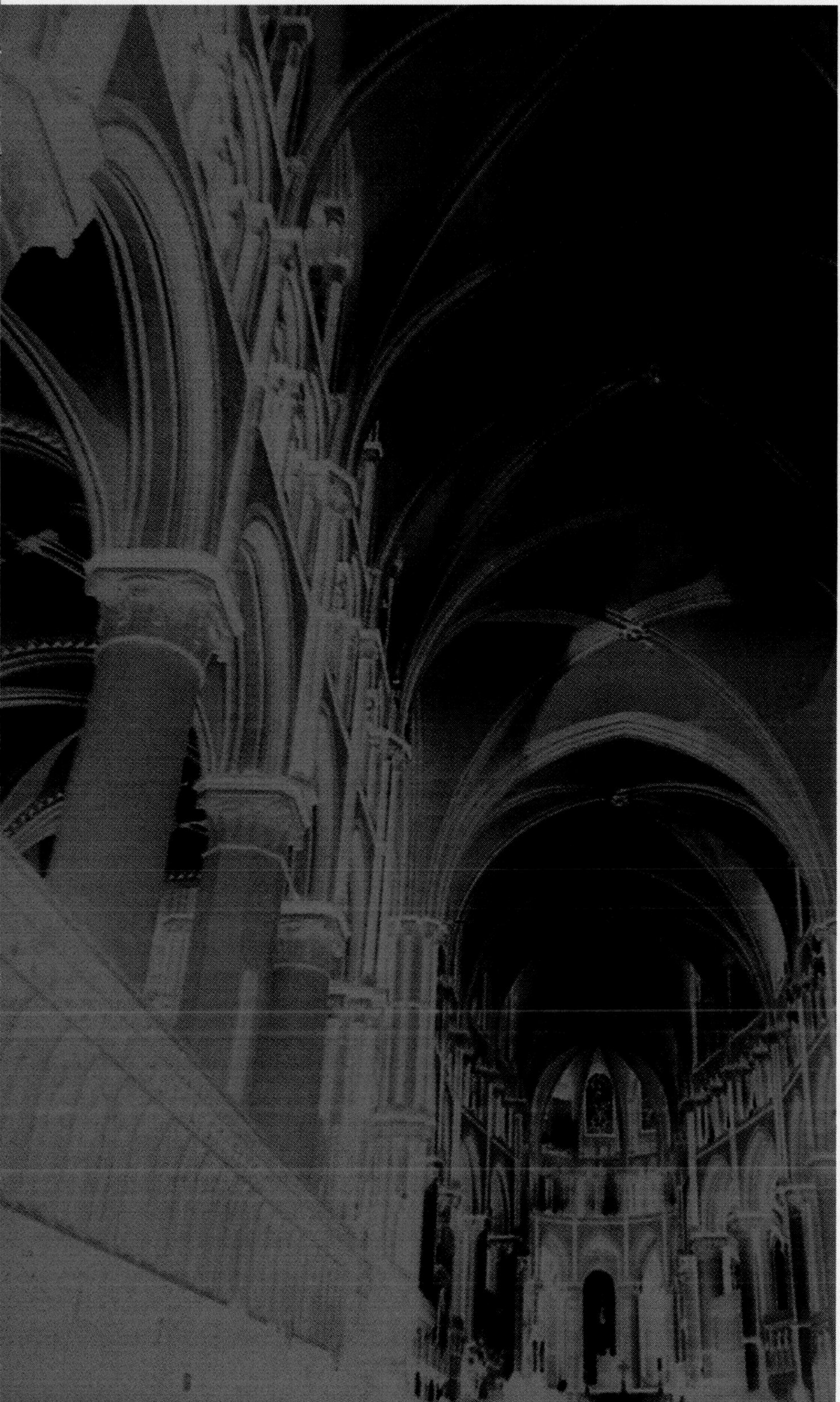

CHAPTER 2

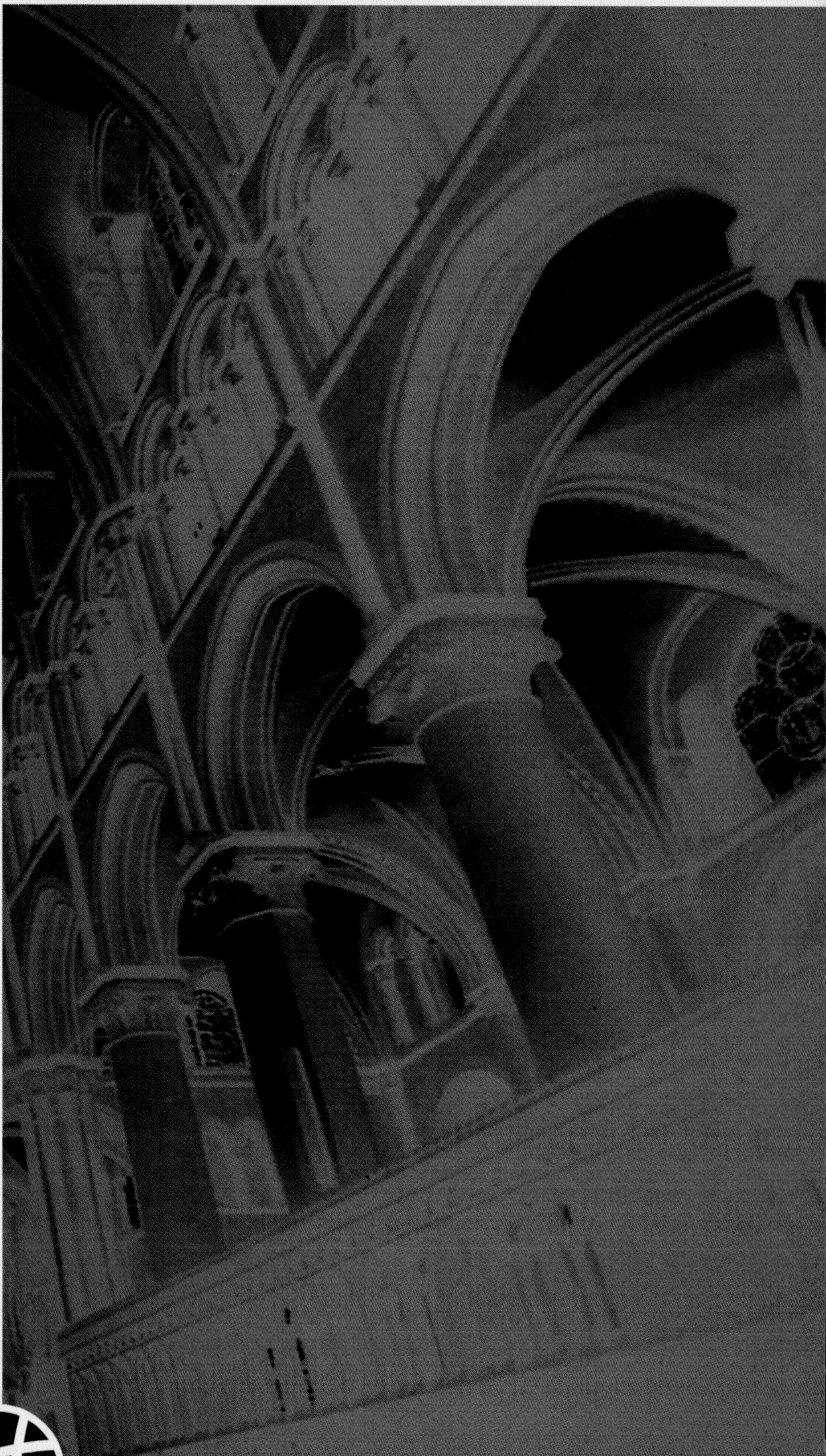

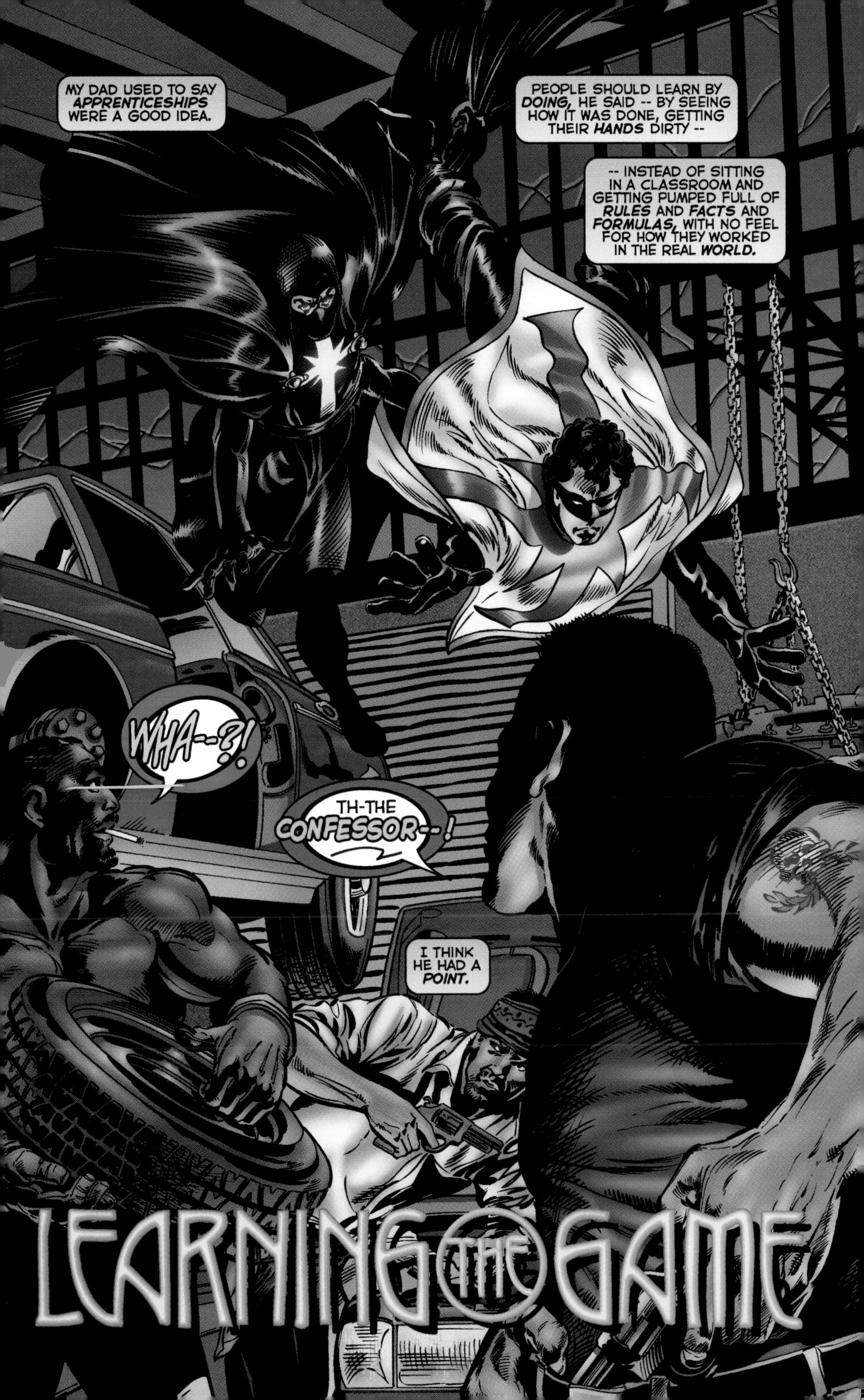
MY DAD USED TO SAY APPRENTICESHIPS WERE A GOOD IDEA.
PEOPLE SHOULD LEARN BY DOING, HE SAID -- BY SEEING HOW IT WAS DONE, GETTING THEIR HANDS DIRTY --
-- INSTEAD OF SITTING IN A CLASSROOM AND GETTING PUMPED FULL OF RULES AND FACTS AND FORMULAS, WITH NO FEEL FOR HOW THEY WORKED IN THE REAL WORLD.
WHA--?!
TH-THE CONFESSOR--!
I THINK HE HAD A POINT.
LEARNING THE GAME

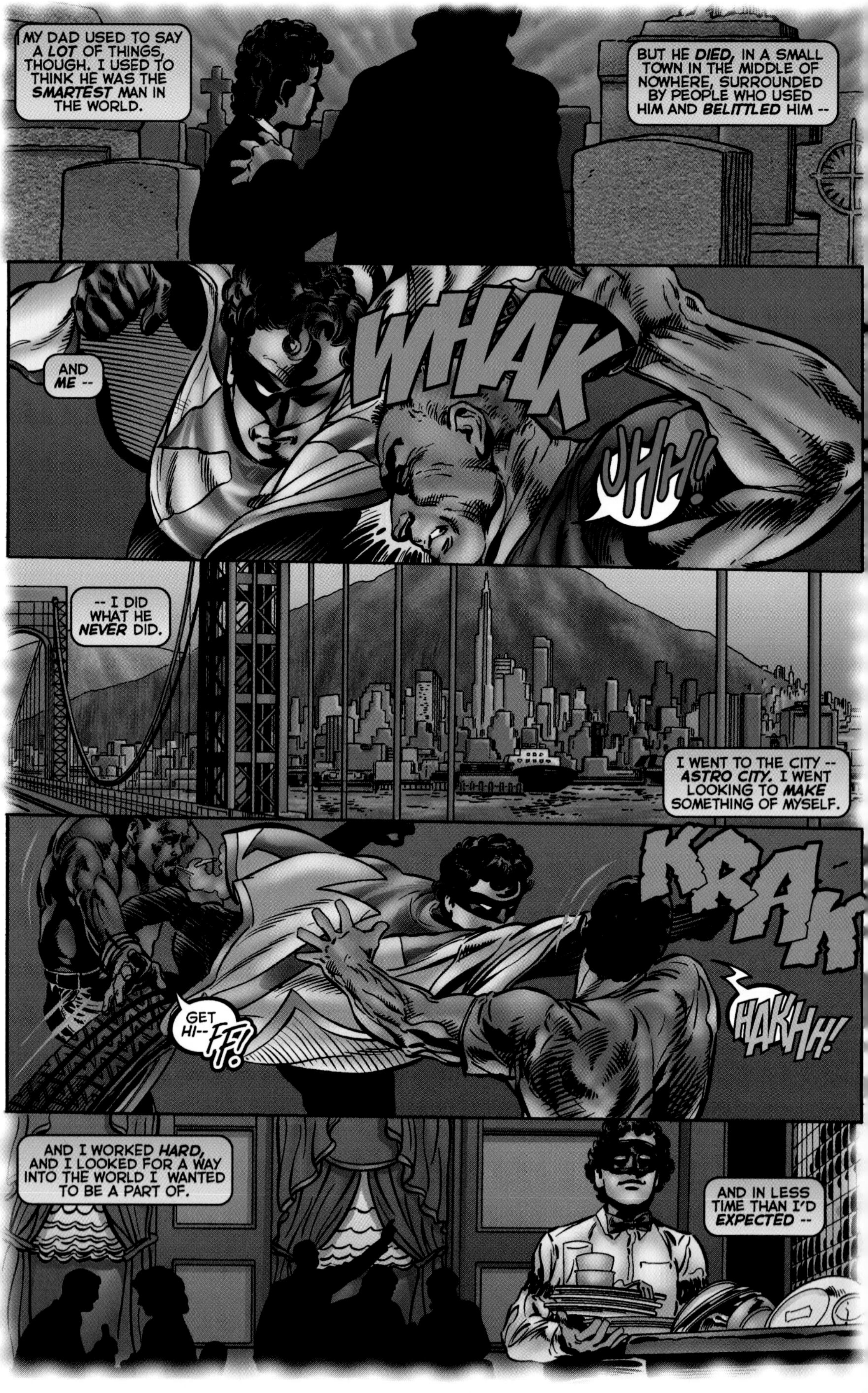
MY DAD USED TO SAY A LOT OF THINGS, THOUGH. I USED TO THINK HE WAS THE SMARTEST MAN IN THE WORLD.
BUT HE DIED, IN A SMALL TOWN IN THE MIDDLE OF NOWHERE, SURROUNDED BY PEOPLE WHO USED HIM AND BELITTLED HIM --
AND ME --
WHAK
UHH!
-- I DID WHAT HE NEVER DID.
I WENT TO THE CITY -- ASTRO CITY. I WENT LOOKING TO MAKE SOMETHING OF MYSELF.
KRAK
GET HI--FF!
HAKHH!
AND I WORKED HARD, AND I LOOKED FOR A WAY INTO THE WORLD I WANTED TO BE A PART OF.
AND IN LESS TIME THAN I'D EXPECTED --

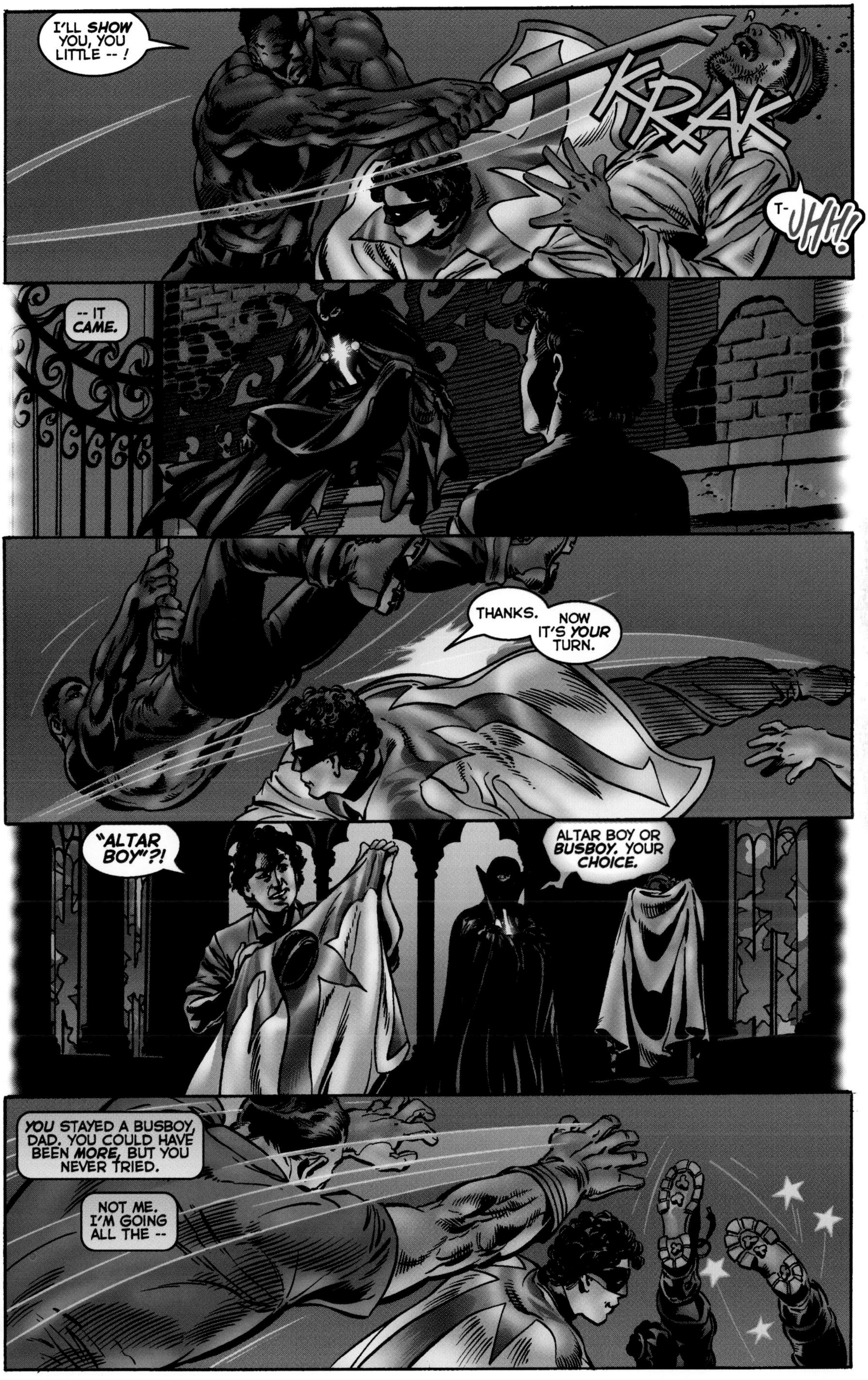

I'LL SHOW YOU, YOU LITTLE -- !
KRAK
T-UHH!
-- IT CAME.
THANKS.
NOW IT'S YOUR TURN.
"ALTAR BOY"?!
ALTAR BOY OR BUSBOY. YOUR CHOICE.
YOU STAYED A BUSBOY, DAD. YOU COULD HAVE BEEN MORE, BUT YOU NEVER TRIED.
NOT ME. I'M GOING ALL THE --

KRAK

BEHIND YOU. ALWAYS KEEP A SENSE OF WHERE *EVERYONE* IS. FOCUS IN ONE DIRECTION, AND YOU'LL *LOSE*.

UH, *THANKS!* I'LL REMEMBER THAT NEXT --

--TÍÍ--!

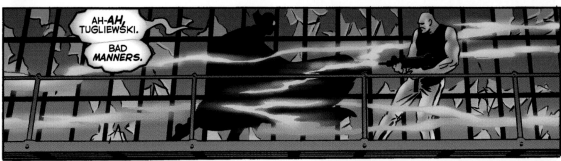

AH-*AH*, TUGLIEWSKI. BAD *MANNERS*.

WHAK

HUH? HOW DID YOU --?!

THE COSTUME WORKED OUT *WELL?* THE WEIGHTED HEM OF THE SURPLICE KEPT IT OUT OF YOUR *WAY?*

AND THE LOW-FRICTION COATING KEPT THEM FROM *GRABBING* YOU BY IT?

UH, YEAH, I *GUESS*. BUT HOW --

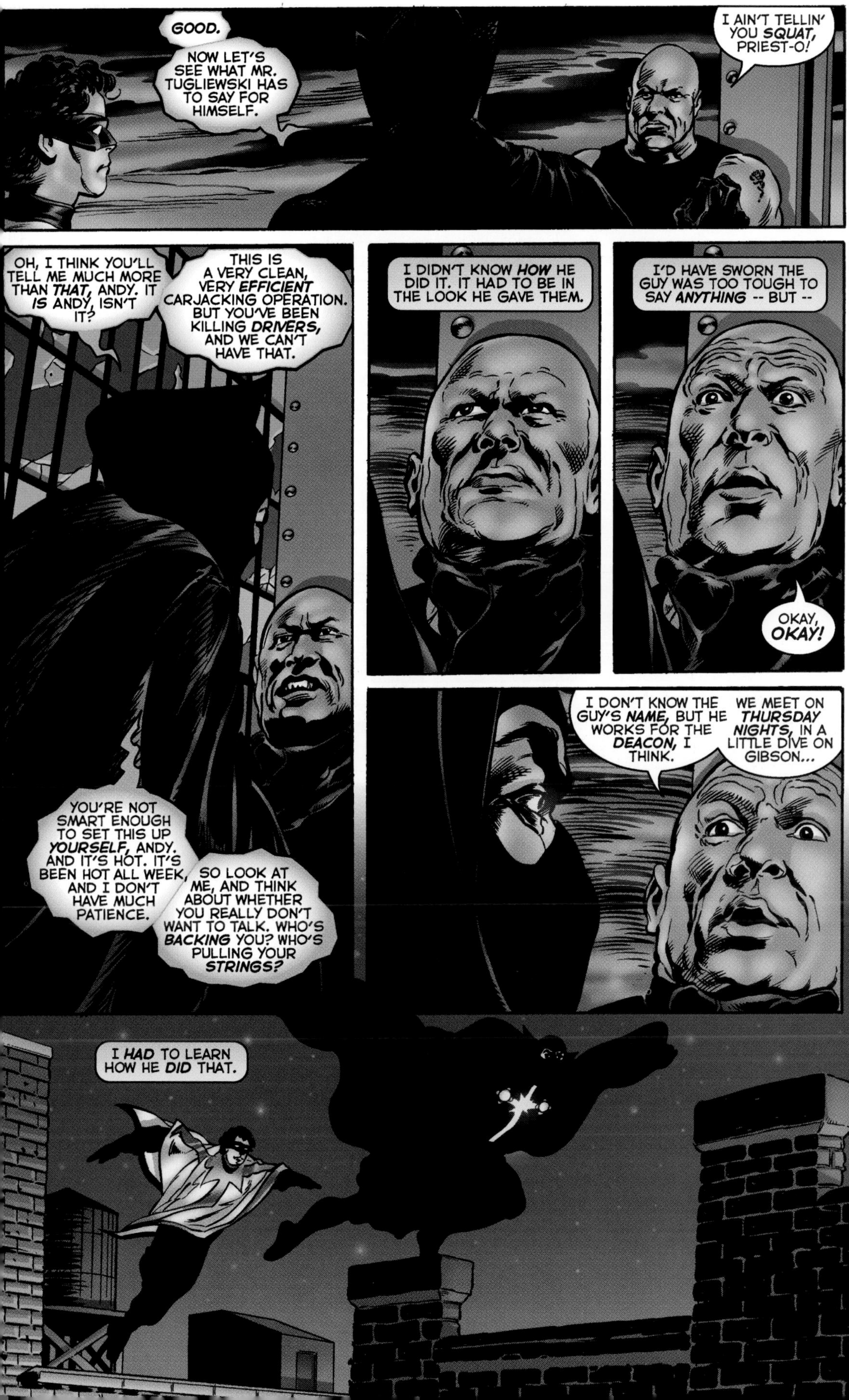
GOOD.
NOW LET'S SEE WHAT MR. TUGLIEWSKI HAS TO SAY FOR HIMSELF.
I AIN'T TELLIN' YOU SQUAT, PRIEST-O!
OH, I THINK YOU'LL TELL ME MUCH MORE THAN THAT, ANDY. IT IS ANDY, ISN'T IT?
THIS IS A VERY CLEAN, VERY EFFICIENT CARJACKING OPERATION. BUT YOU'VE BEEN KILLING DRIVERS, AND WE CAN'T HAVE THAT.
YOU'RE NOT SMART ENOUGH TO SET THIS UP YOURSELF, ANDY. AND IT'S HOT. IT'S BEEN HOT ALL WEEK, AND I DON'T HAVE MUCH PATIENCE.
SO LOOK AT ME, AND THINK ABOUT WHETHER YOU REALLY DON'T WANT TO TALK. WHO'S BACKING YOU? WHO'S PULLING YOUR STRINGS?
I DIDN'T KNOW HOW HE DID IT. IT HAD TO BE IN THE LOOK HE GAVE THEM.
I'D HAVE SWORN THE GUY WAS TOO TOUGH TO SAY ANYTHING -- BUT --
OKAY, OKAY!
I DON'T KNOW THE GUY'S NAME, BUT HE WORKS FOR THE DEACON, I THINK.
WE MEET ON THURSDAY NIGHTS, IN A LITTLE DIVE ON GIBSON...
I HAD TO LEARN HOW HE DID THAT.

-- AMBASSADOR WAS RESCUED AND THE PYRAMID ASSAULT TEAM CAPTURED BY **HONOR GUARD**, AFTER A PITCHED BATTLE.

WITNESSES STATE THAT IF NOT FOR HONOR GUARD'S INTERVENTION, HALF OF THE **SECURITY COUNCIL** WOULD HAVE BEEN WIPED OUT.

BUT LOCALLY, SUPERHERO APPROVAL RATINGS HAVE TAKEN A **DIP** --

-- AMID REPORTS OF CRACKERJACK **ROBBING THE FASS GARDENS BRANCH** OF ASTROBANK --

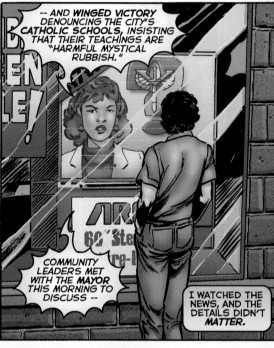

-- AND **WINGED VICTORY** DENOUNCING THE CITY'S **CATHOLIC SCHOOLS**, INSISTING THAT THEIR TEACHINGS ARE "HARMFUL MYSTICAL RUBBISH."

COMMUNITY LEADERS MET WITH THE **MAYOR** THIS MORNING TO DISCUSS --

I WATCHED THE NEWS, AND THE DETAILS DIDN'T **MATTER.**

THERE WAS ALWAYS A HERO OR TWO ON THE OUTS WITH THE **PUBLIC**, AND IT USUALLY TURNED OUT TO BE NOTHING.

WHAT WAS **IMPORTANT** -- AT LEAST TO ME -- WAS THAT I LOOKED AT THOSE IMAGES AND I THOUGHT OF THEM AS "US."

I WAS **ONE** OF THEM.

I HAD A SECRET FROM THE PEOPLE **AROUND** ME. I WAS SOMETHING SPECIAL.

AND I COULDN'T **RESIST** --

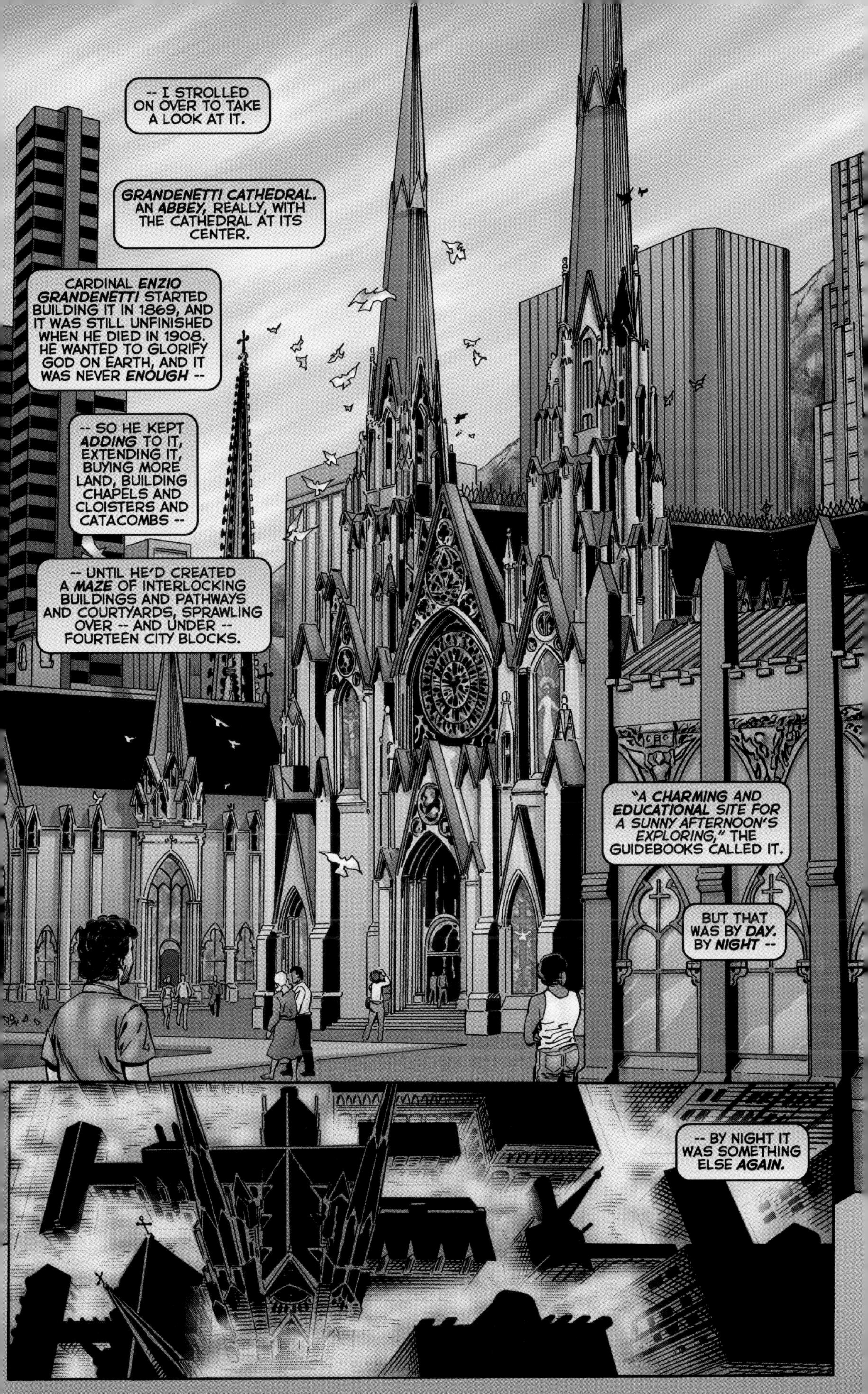
-- I STROLLED ON OVER TO TAKE A LOOK AT IT.
GRANDENETTI CATHEDRAL. AN ABBEY, REALLY, WITH THE CATHEDRAL AT ITS CENTER.
CARDINAL ENZIO GRANDENETTI STARTED BUILDING IT IN 1869, AND IT WAS STILL UNFINISHED WHEN HE DIED IN 1908. HE WANTED TO GLORIFY GOD ON EARTH, AND IT WAS NEVER ENOUGH --
-- SO HE KEPT ADDING TO IT, EXTENDING IT, BUYING MORE LAND, BUILDING CHAPELS AND CLOISTERS AND CATACOMBS --
-- UNTIL HE'D CREATED A MAZE OF INTERLOCKING BUILDINGS AND PATHWAYS AND COURTYARDS, SPRAWLING OVER -- AND UNDER -- FOURTEEN CITY BLOCKS.
"A CHARMING AND EDUCATIONAL SITE FOR A SUNNY AFTERNOON'S EXPLORING," THE GUIDEBOOKS CALLED IT.
BUT THAT WAS BY DAY. BY NIGHT --
-- BY NIGHT IT WAS SOMETHING ELSE AGAIN.

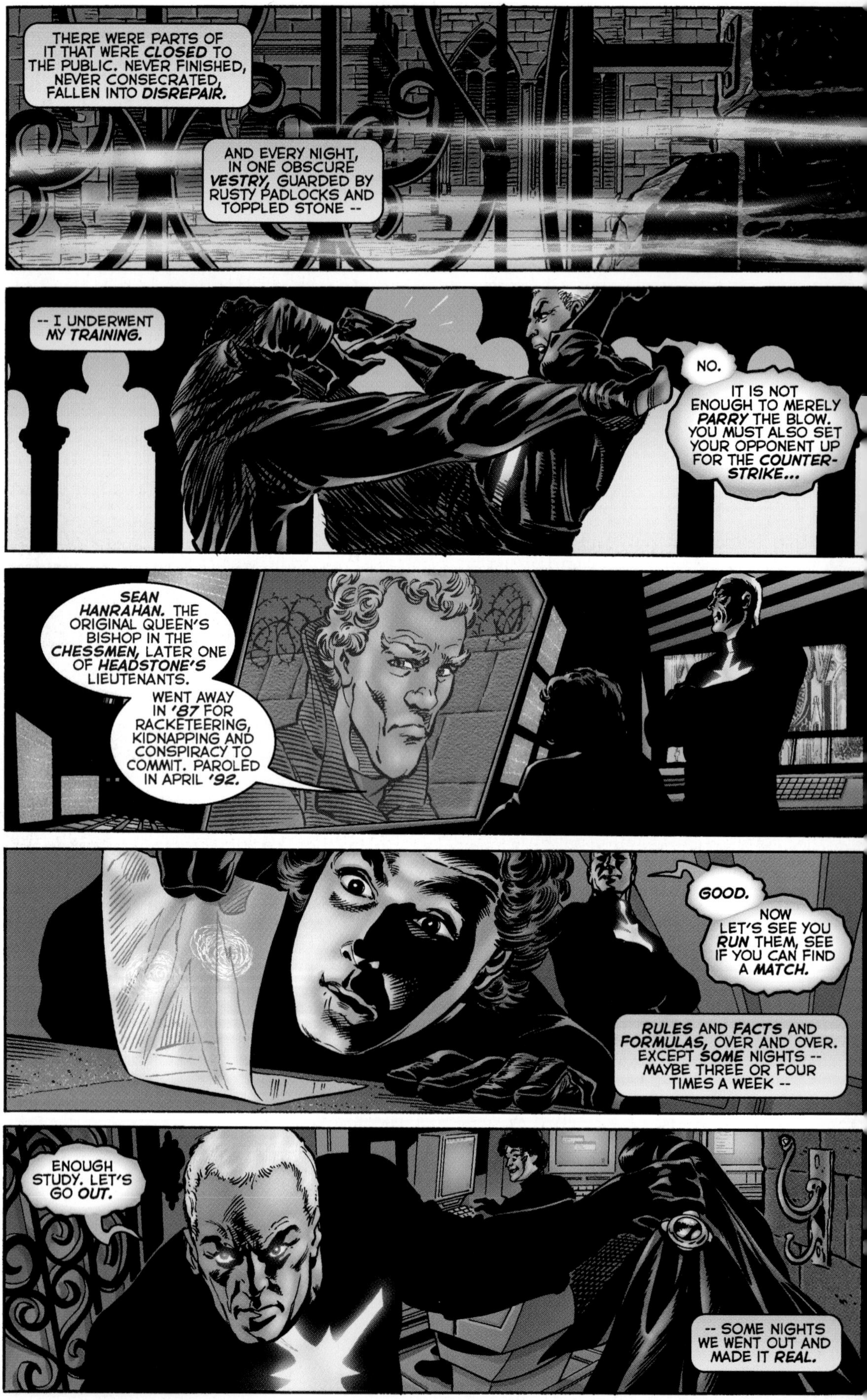
THERE WERE PARTS OF IT THAT WERE CLOSED TO THE PUBLIC. NEVER FINISHED, NEVER CONSECRATED, FALLEN INTO DISREPAIR.
AND EVERY NIGHT, IN ONE OBSCURE VESTRY, GUARDED BY RUSTY PADLOCKS AND TOPPLED STONE --
-- I UNDERWENT MY TRAINING.
NO.
IT IS NOT ENOUGH TO MERELY PARRY THE BLOW. YOU MUST ALSO SET YOUR OPPONENT UP FOR THE COUNTER-STRIKE...
SEAN HANRAHAN. THE ORIGINAL QUEEN'S BISHOP IN THE CHESSMEN, LATER ONE OF HEADSTONE'S LIEUTENANTS.
WENT AWAY IN '87 FOR RACKETEERING, KIDNAPPING AND CONSPIRACY TO COMMIT. PAROLED IN APRIL '92.
GOOD.
NOW LET'S SEE YOU RUN THEM, SEE IF YOU CAN FIND A MATCH.
RULES AND FACTS AND FORMULAS, OVER AND OVER. EXCEPT SOME NIGHTS -- MAYBE THREE OR FOUR TIMES A WEEK --
ENOUGH STUDY. LET'S GO OUT.
-- SOME NIGHTS WE WENT OUT AND MADE IT REAL.

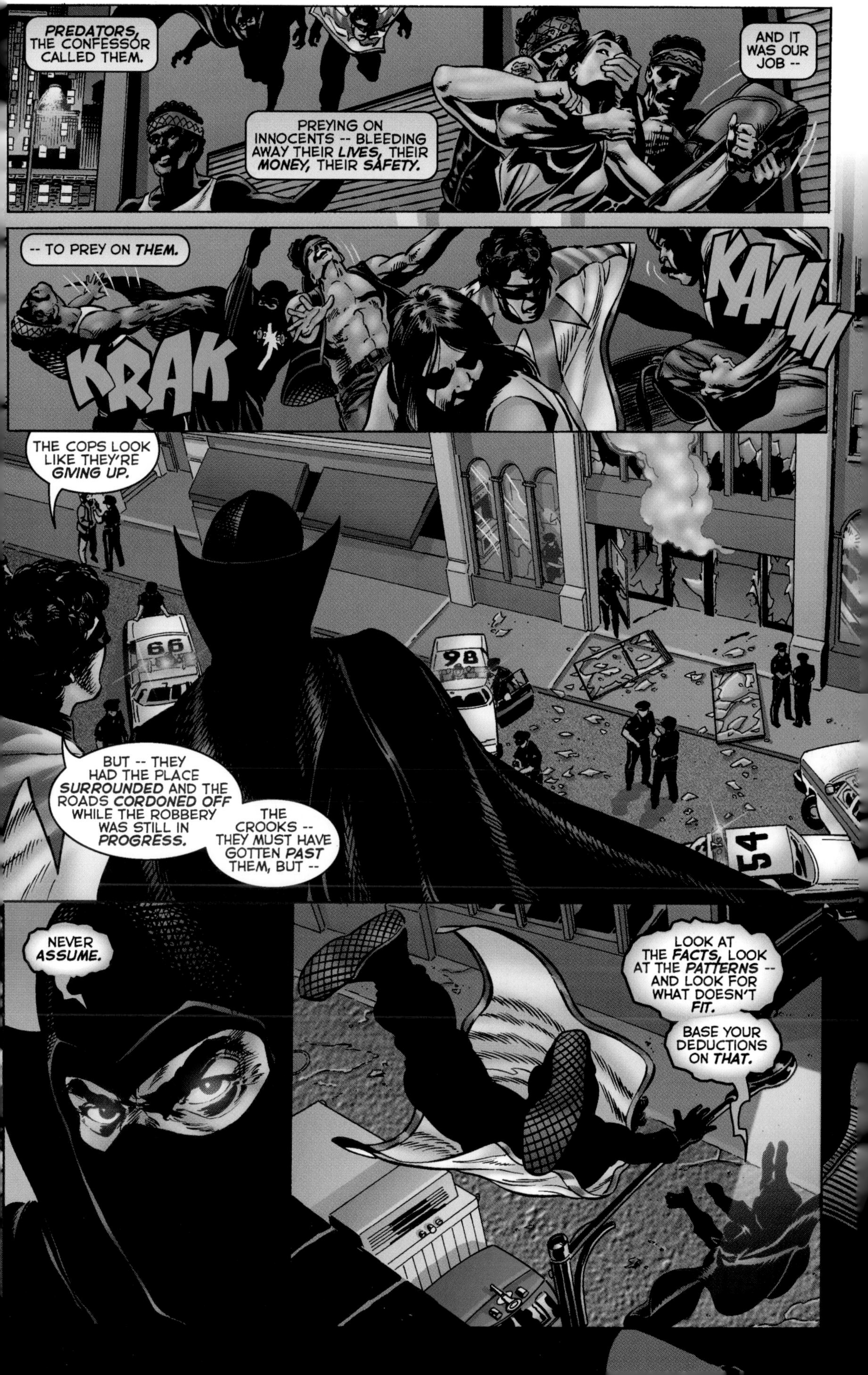
PREDATORS, THE CONFESSOR CALLED THEM.
PREYING ON INNOCENTS -- BLEEDING AWAY THEIR LIVES, THEIR MONEY, THEIR SAFETY.
AND IT WAS OUR JOB --
-- TO PREY ON THEM.
KRAK
KAMM
THE COPS LOOK LIKE THEY'RE GIVING UP.
BUT -- THEY HAD THE PLACE SURROUNDED AND THE ROADS CORDONED OFF WHILE THE ROBBERY WAS STILL IN PROGRESS.
THE CROOKS -- THEY MUST HAVE GOTTEN PAST THEM, BUT --
NEVER ASSUME.
LOOK AT THE FACTS, LOOK AT THE PATTERNS -- AND LOOK FOR WHAT DOESN'T FIT.
BASE YOUR DEDUCTIONS ON THAT.

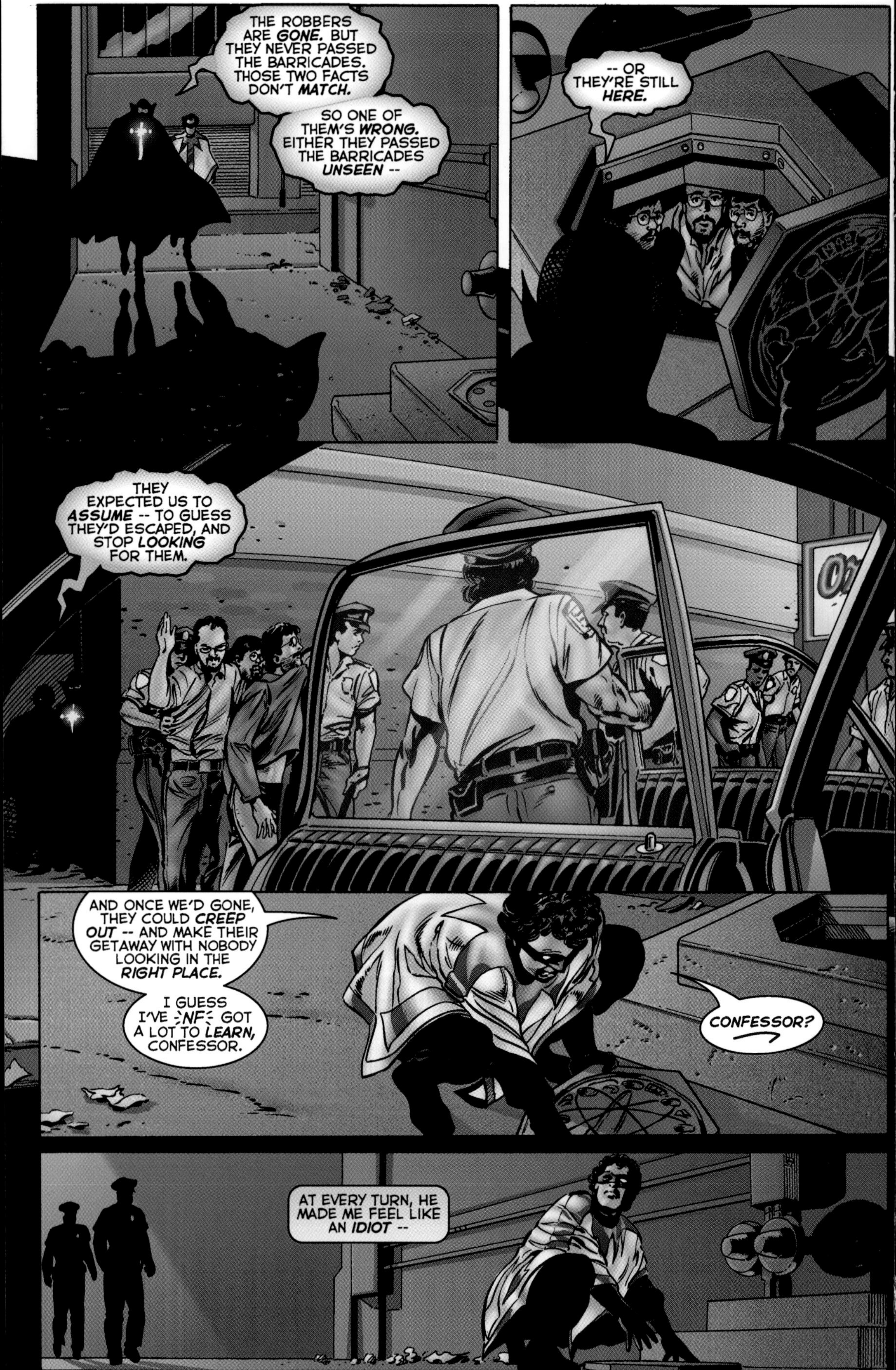
THE ROBBERS ARE GONE. BUT THEY NEVER PASSED THE BARRICADES. THOSE TWO FACTS DON'T MATCH.
SO ONE OF THEM'S WRONG. EITHER THEY PASSED THE BARRICADES UNSEEN --
-- OR THEY'RE STILL HERE.
THEY EXPECTED US TO ASSUME -- TO GUESS THEY'D ESCAPED, AND STOP LOOKING FOR THEM.
AND ONCE WE'D GONE, THEY COULD CREEP OUT -- AND MAKE THEIR GETAWAY WITH NOBODY LOOKING IN THE RIGHT PLACE.
I GUESS I'VE NF GOT A LOT TO LEARN, CONFESSOR.
CONFESSOR?
AT EVERY TURN, HE MADE ME FEEL LIKE AN IDIOT --

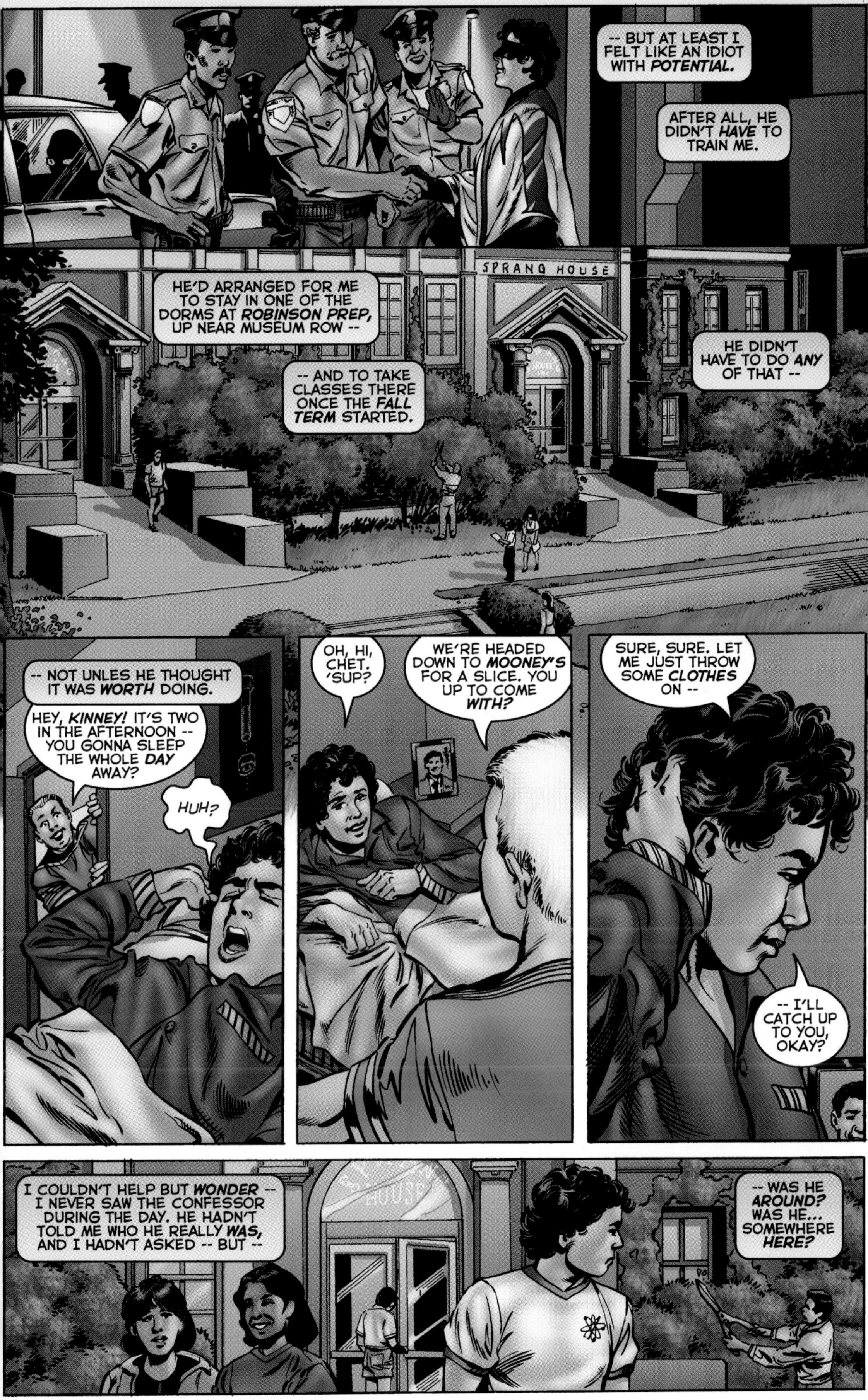
-- BUT AT LEAST I FELT LIKE AN IDIOT WITH *POTENTIAL.*
AFTER ALL, HE DIDN'T *HAVE* TO TRAIN ME.
SPRANG HOUSE
HE'D ARRANGED FOR ME TO STAY IN ONE OF THE DORMS AT *ROBINSON PREP,* UP NEAR MUSEUM ROW --
-- AND TO TAKE CLASSES THERE ONCE THE *FALL TERM* STARTED.
HE DIDN'T HAVE TO DO *ANY* OF THAT --
-- NOT UNLES HE THOUGHT IT WAS *WORTH* DOING.
HEY, *KINNEY!* IT'S TWO IN THE AFTERNOON -- YOU GONNA SLEEP THE WHOLE *DAY* AWAY?
HUH?
OH, HI, CHET. 'SUP?
WE'RE HEADED DOWN TO *MOONEY'S* FOR A SLICE. YOU UP TO COME *WITH?*
SURE, SURE. LET ME JUST THROW SOME *CLOTHES* ON --
-- I'LL CATCH UP TO YOU, OKAY?
I COULDN'T HELP BUT *WONDER* -- I NEVER SAW THE CONFESSOR DURING THE DAY. HE HADN'T TOLD ME WHO HE REALLY *WAS,* AND I HADN'T ASKED -- BUT --
-- WAS HE *AROUND?* WAS HE... SOMEWHERE *HERE?*

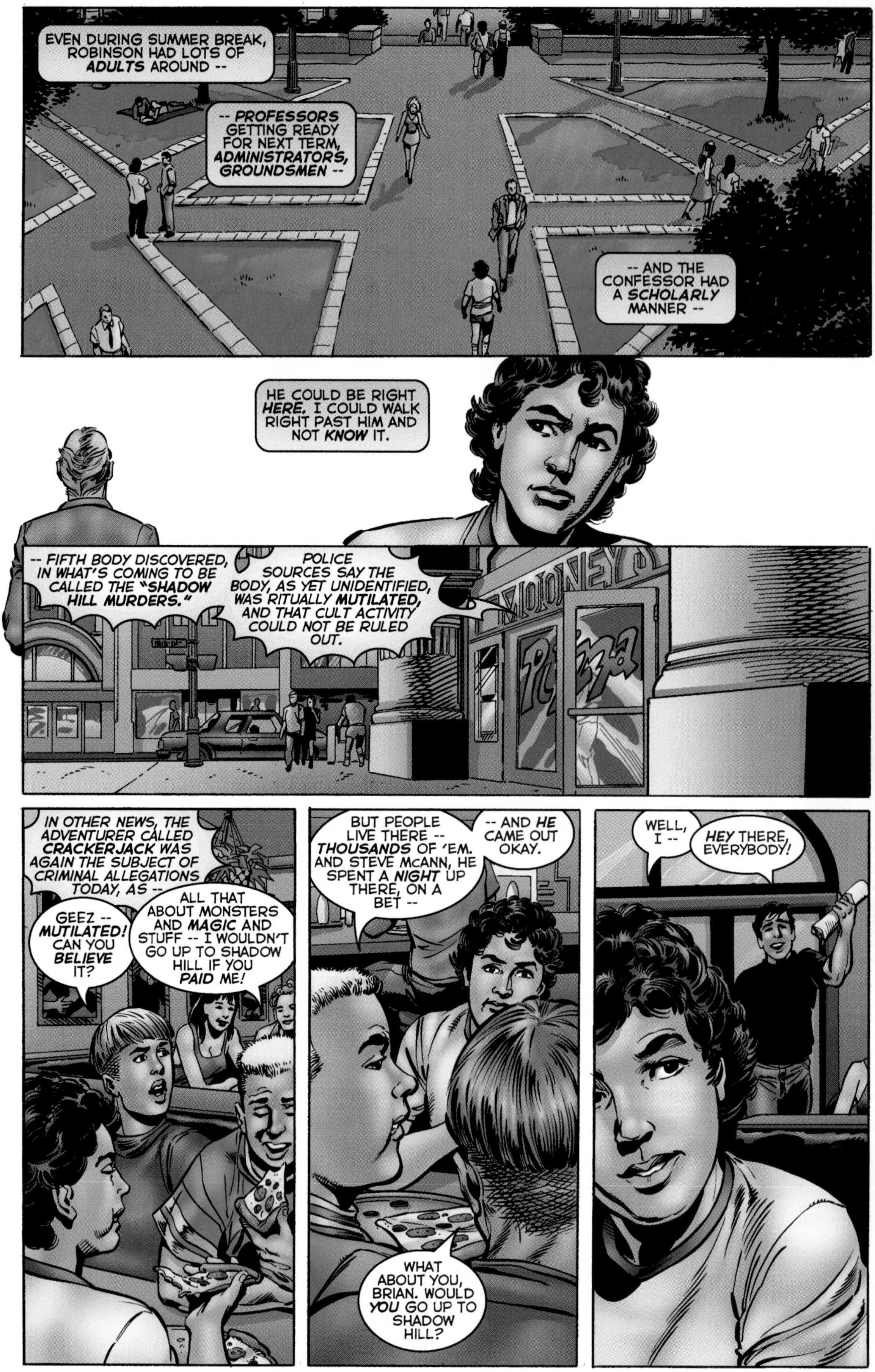

EVEN DURING SUMMER BREAK, ROBINSON HAD LOTS OF *ADULTS* AROUND --
-- *PROFESSORS* GETTING READY FOR NEXT TERM, *ADMINISTRATORS, GROUNDSMEN* --
-- AND THE CONFESSOR HAD A *SCHOLARLY* MANNER --
HE COULD BE RIGHT *HERE.* I COULD WALK RIGHT PAST HIM AND NOT *KNOW* IT.
-- FIFTH BODY DISCOVERED, IN WHAT'S COMING TO BE CALLED THE *"SHADOW HILL MURDERS."*
POLICE SOURCES SAY THE BODY, AS YET UNIDENTIFIED, WAS RITUALLY *MUTILATED,* AND THAT CULT ACTIVITY COULD NOT BE RULED OUT.
MOONEY'S
Pizza
IN OTHER NEWS, THE ADVENTURER CALLED *CRACKERJACK* WAS AGAIN THE SUBJECT OF CRIMINAL ALLEGATIONS TODAY, AS --
GEEZ -- *MUTILATED!* CAN YOU *BELIEVE* IT?
ALL THAT ABOUT MONSTERS AND *MAGIC* AND STUFF -- I WOULDN'T GO UP TO SHADOW HILL IF YOU *PAID* ME!
BUT PEOPLE LIVE THERE -- *THOUSANDS* OF 'EM. AND STEVE McCANN, HE SPENT A *NIGHT* UP THERE, ON A BET --
-- AND *HE* CAME OUT OKAY.
WHAT ABOUT YOU, BRIAN. WOULD *YOU* GO UP TO SHADOW HILL?
WELL, I --
HEY THERE, EVERYBODY!

TAKE A LOOK -- THE NEW ISSUE OF *CURRENT*.

PICTURES OF *ALTAR BOY*.

ALTAR BOY? THE NEW GUY WHO'S HANGING AROUND WITH THE *CONFESSOR*?

COOL.

ltar Boy, newest crime-fighter in Astro City, caught in th ct of apprehending members of the Chester A artnered with the myster tle is k

FEATURE New in

YOU NOTICE THEY NEVER GET ANY PICTURES OF THE CONFESSOR *HIMSELF*. I SAW AN *'ARTIST'S RENDERING'* ONCE, BUT THAT'S IT.

YEAH, HE STAYS OUT'VE THE *LIMELIGHT*. I GUESS HE HASN'T TAUGHT THE KID HOW TO *DO* THAT YET...

HE LOOKS LIKE HE'S ABOUT OUR AGE. MAN, THAT MUST BE GREAT.

SURE, BUT *"ALTAR BOY"*? IT'S A PRETTY DUMB *NAME*, DON'T YOU THINK?

WHO CARES? I THINK HE'S *CUTE*. LOOK AT THAT *SMILE*...

YOU THINK HE'S CUTE? *REALLY?*

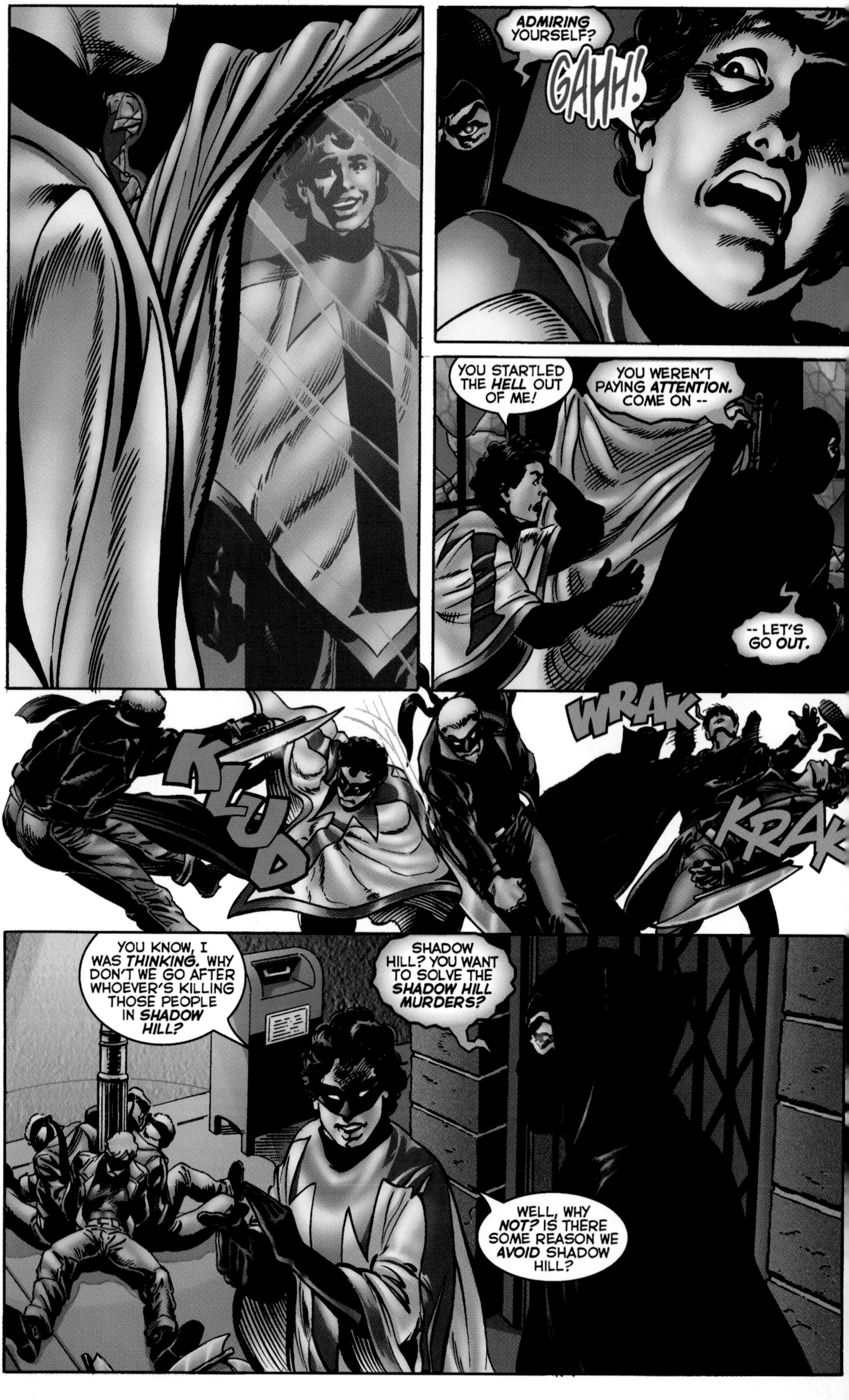
ADMIRING YOURSELF?
GAHH!
YOU STARTLED THE HELL OUT OF ME!
YOU WEREN'T PAYING ATTENTION. COME ON --
-- LET'S GO OUT.
KLUD
WRAK
KRAK
YOU KNOW, I WAS THINKING. WHY DON'T WE GO AFTER WHOEVER'S KILLING THOSE PEOPLE IN SHADOW HILL?
SHADOW HILL? YOU WANT TO SOLVE THE SHADOW HILL MURDERS?
WELL, WHY NOT? IS THERE SOME REASON WE AVOID SHADOW HILL?

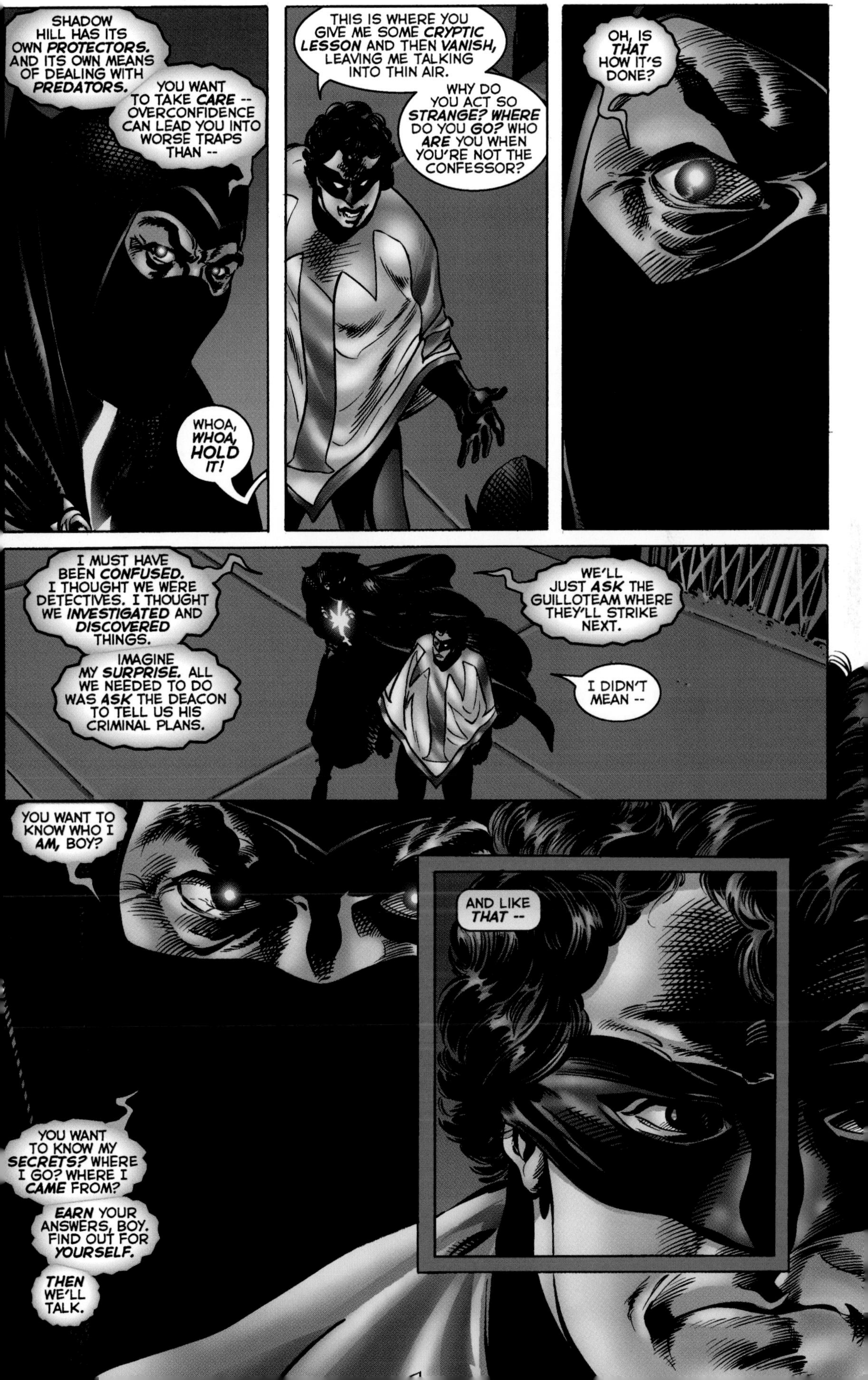
SHADOW HILL HAS ITS OWN PROTECTORS. AND ITS OWN MEANS OF DEALING WITH PREDATORS.
YOU WANT TO TAKE CARE -- OVERCONFIDENCE CAN LEAD YOU INTO WORSE TRAPS THAN --
WHOA, WHOA, HOLD IT!
THIS IS WHERE YOU GIVE ME SOME CRYPTIC LESSON AND THEN VANISH, LEAVING ME TALKING INTO THIN AIR.
WHY DO YOU ACT SO STRANGE? WHERE DO YOU GO? WHO ARE YOU WHEN YOU'RE NOT THE CONFESSOR?
OH, IS THAT HOW IT'S DONE?
I MUST HAVE BEEN CONFUSED. I THOUGHT WE WERE DETECTIVES. I THOUGHT WE INVESTIGATED AND DISCOVERED THINGS.
IMAGINE MY SURPRISE. ALL WE NEEDED TO DO WAS ASK THE DEACON TO TELL US HIS CRIMINAL PLANS.
WE'LL JUST ASK THE GUILLOTEAM WHERE THEY'LL STRIKE NEXT.
I DIDN'T MEAN --
YOU WANT TO KNOW WHO I AM, BOY?
YOU WANT TO KNOW MY SECRETS? WHERE I GO? WHERE I CAME FROM?
EARN YOUR ANSWERS, BOY. FIND OUT FOR YOURSELF.
THEN WE'LL TALK.
AND LIKE THAT --

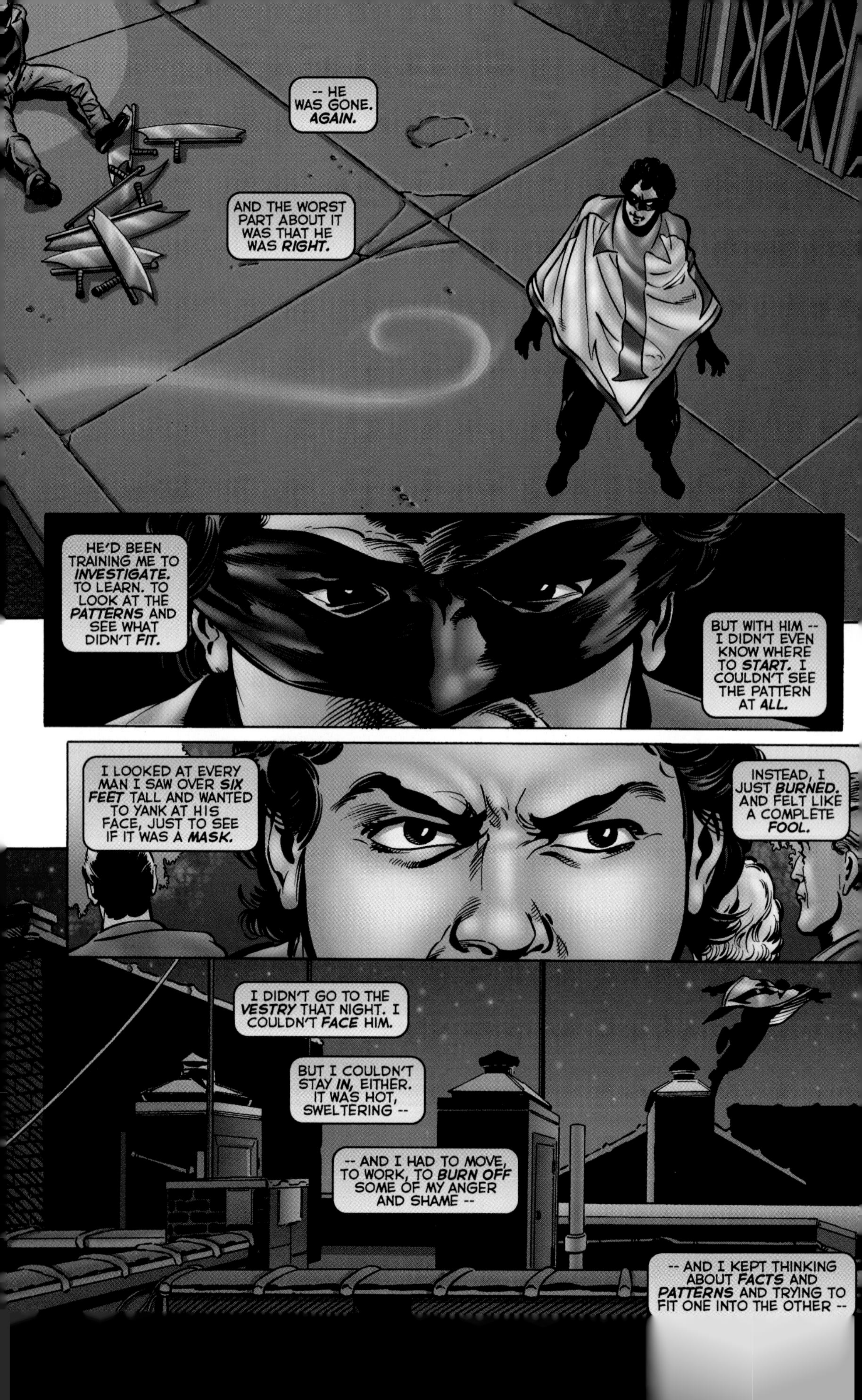
-- HE WAS GONE. AGAIN.
AND THE WORST PART ABOUT IT WAS THAT HE WAS RIGHT.
HE'D BEEN TRAINING ME TO INVESTIGATE. TO LEARN. TO LOOK AT THE PATTERNS AND SEE WHAT DIDN'T FIT.
BUT WITH HIM -- I DIDN'T EVEN KNOW WHERE TO START. I COULDN'T SEE THE PATTERN AT ALL.
I LOOKED AT EVERY MAN I SAW OVER SIX FEET TALL AND WANTED TO YANK AT HIS FACE, JUST TO SEE IF IT WAS A MASK.
INSTEAD, I JUST BURNED. AND FELT LIKE A COMPLETE FOOL.
I DIDN'T GO TO THE VESTRY THAT NIGHT. I COULDN'T FACE HIM.
BUT I COULDN'T STAY IN, EITHER. IT WAS HOT, SWELTERING --
-- AND I HAD TO MOVE, TO WORK, TO BURN OFF SOME OF MY ANGER AND SHAME --
-- AND I KEPT THINKING ABOUT FACTS AND PATTERNS AND TRYING TO FIT ONE INTO THE OTHER --

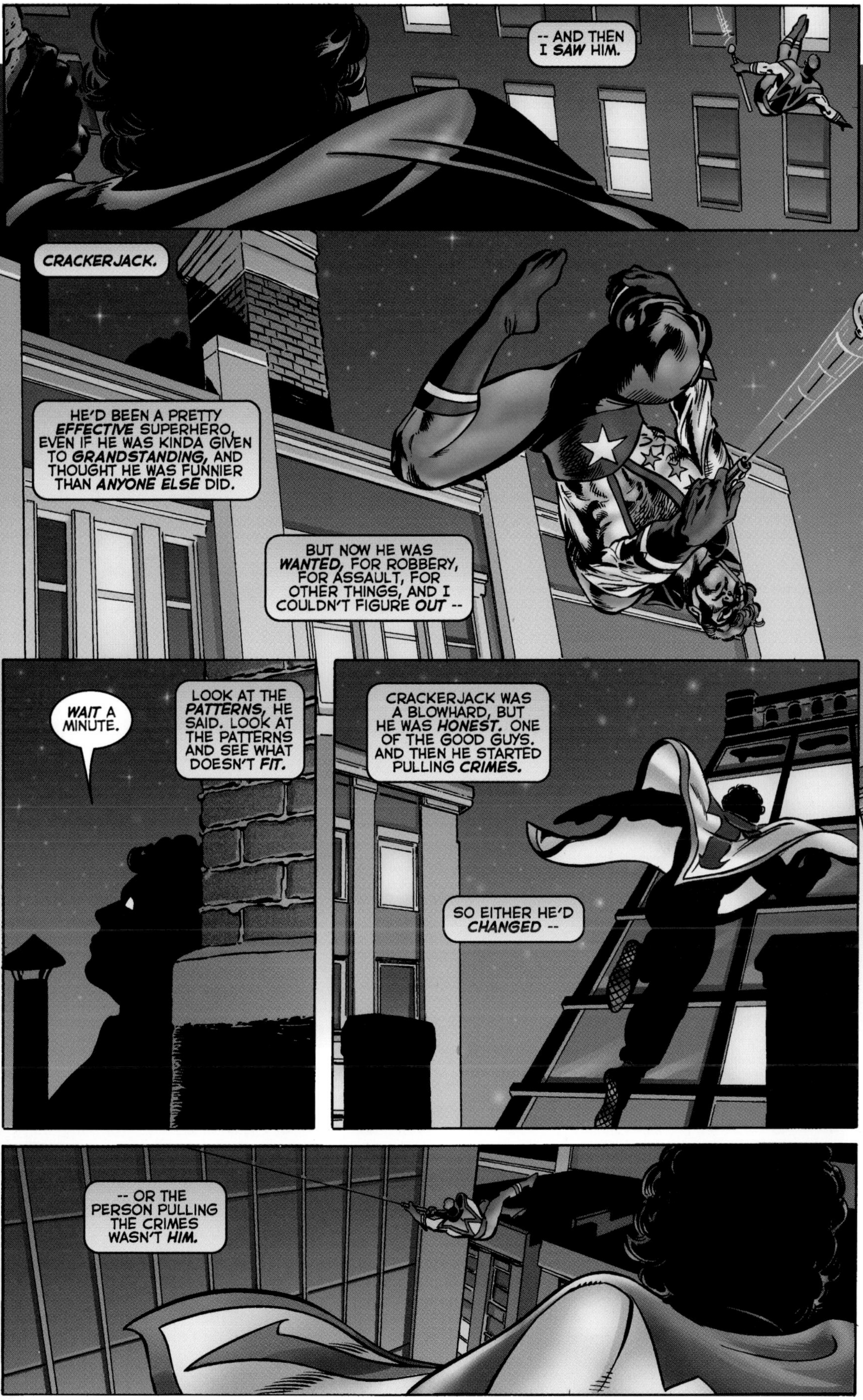

-- AND THEN I SAW HIM.
CRACKERJACK.
HE'D BEEN A PRETTY EFFECTIVE SUPERHERO, EVEN IF HE WAS KINDA GIVEN TO GRANDSTANDING, AND THOUGHT HE WAS FUNNIER THAN ANYONE ELSE DID.
BUT NOW HE WAS WANTED, FOR ROBBERY, FOR ASSAULT, FOR OTHER THINGS, AND I COULDN'T FIGURE OUT --
WAIT A MINUTE.
LOOK AT THE PATTERNS, HE SAID. LOOK AT THE PATTERNS AND SEE WHAT DOESN'T FIT.
CRACKERJACK WAS A BLOWHARD, BUT HE WAS HONEST. ONE OF THE GOOD GUYS. AND THEN HE STARTED PULLING CRIMES.
SO EITHER HE'D CHANGED --
-- OR THE PERSON PULLING THE CRIMES WASN'T HIM.

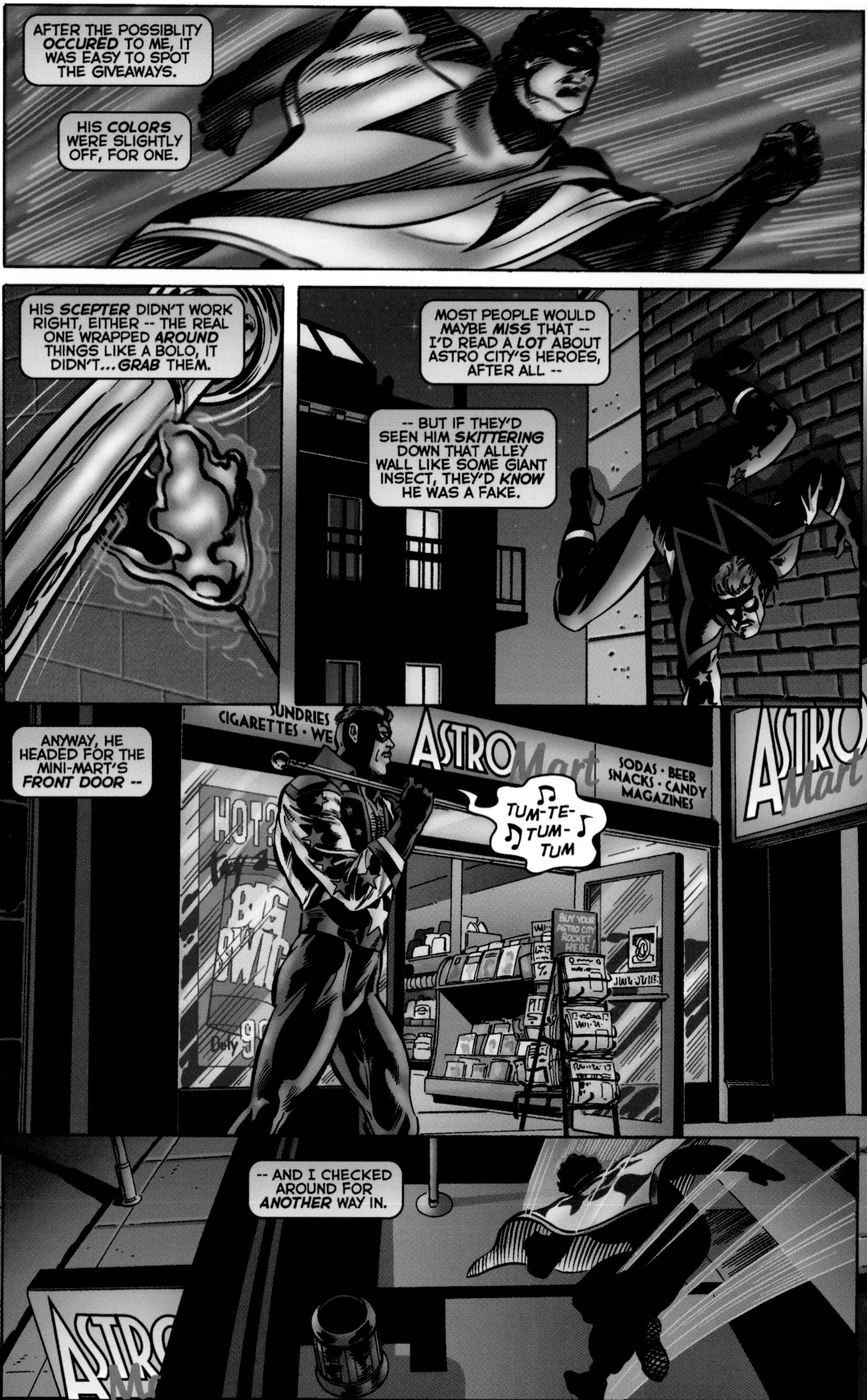
AFTER THE POSSIBLITY OCCURED TO ME, IT WAS EASY TO SPOT THE GIVEAWAYS.
HIS COLORS WERE SLIGHTLY OFF, FOR ONE.
HIS SCEPTER DIDN'T WORK RIGHT, EITHER -- THE REAL ONE WRAPPED AROUND THINGS LIKE A BOLO, IT DIDN'T... GRAB THEM.
MOST PEOPLE WOULD MAYBE MISS THAT -- I'D READ A LOT ABOUT ASTRO CITY'S HEROES, AFTER ALL --
-- BUT IF THEY'D SEEN HIM SKITTERING DOWN THAT ALLEY WALL LIKE SOME GIANT INSECT, THEY'D KNOW HE WAS A FAKE.
ANYWAY, HE HEADED FOR THE MINI-MART'S FRONT DOOR --
SUNDRIES
CIGARETTES · WE
ASTRO Mart
SODAS · BEER
SNACKS · CANDY
MAGAZINES
HOT?
BUY YOUR ASTRO CITY ROCKET HERE!
TUM-TE-TUM-TUM
ASTRO Mart
-- AND I CHECKED AROUND FOR ANOTHER WAY IN.

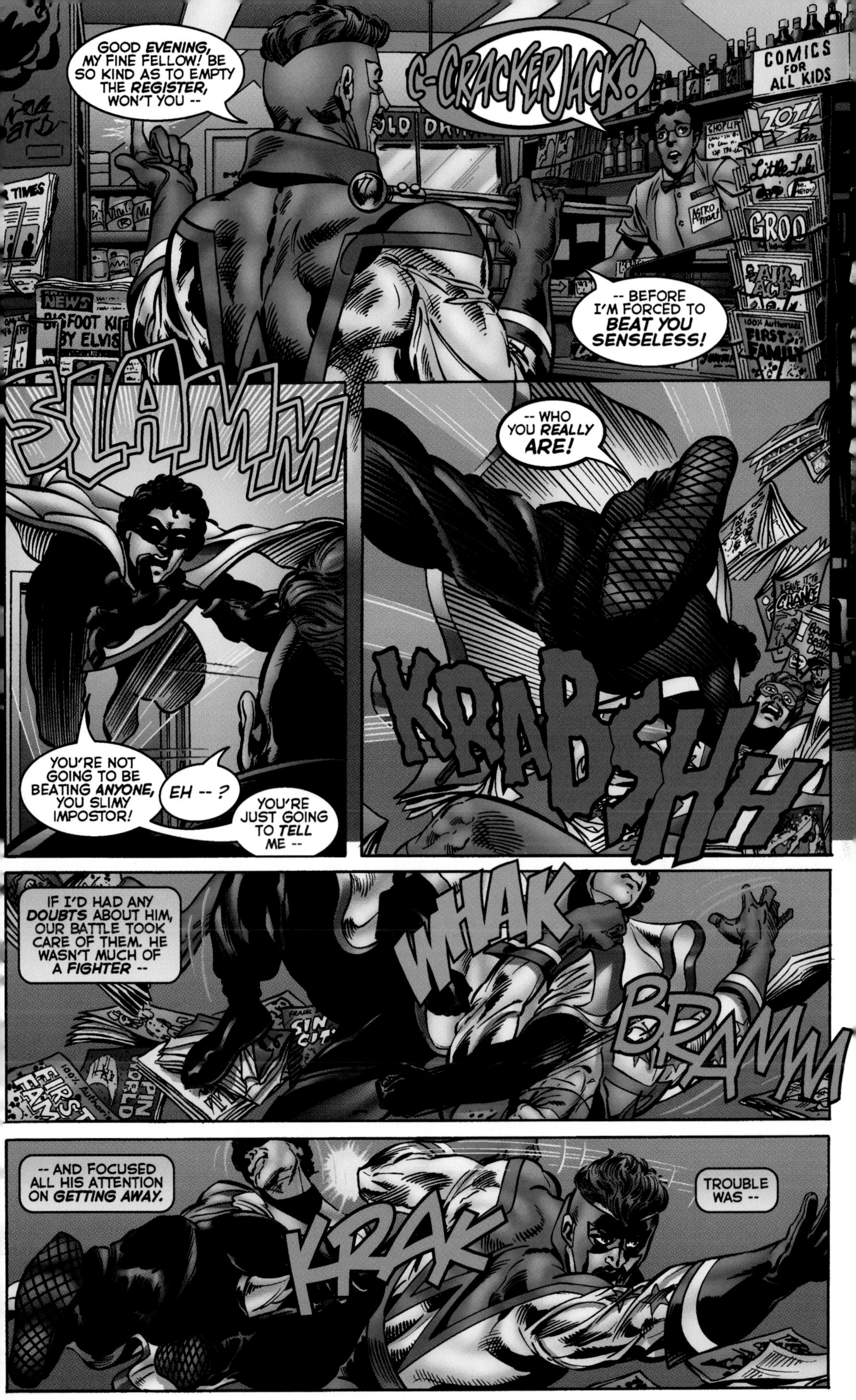
GOOD EVENING, MY FINE FELLOW! BE SO KIND AS TO EMPTY THE REGISTER, WON'T YOU --
C-CRACKERJACK!
COMICS FOR ALL KIDS
-- BEFORE I'M FORCED TO BEAT YOU SENSELESS!
SLAMM
YOU'RE NOT GOING TO BE BEATING ANYONE, YOU SLIMY IMPOSTOR!
EH -- ?
YOU'RE JUST GOING TO TELL ME --
-- WHO YOU REALLY ARE!
KRABASHH
IF I'D HAD ANY DOUBTS ABOUT HIM, OUR BATTLE TOOK CARE OF THEM. HE WASN'T MUCH OF A FIGHTER --
WHAK
BRAMM
-- AND FOCUSED ALL HIS ATTENTION ON GETTING AWAY.
KRAK
TROUBLE WAS --

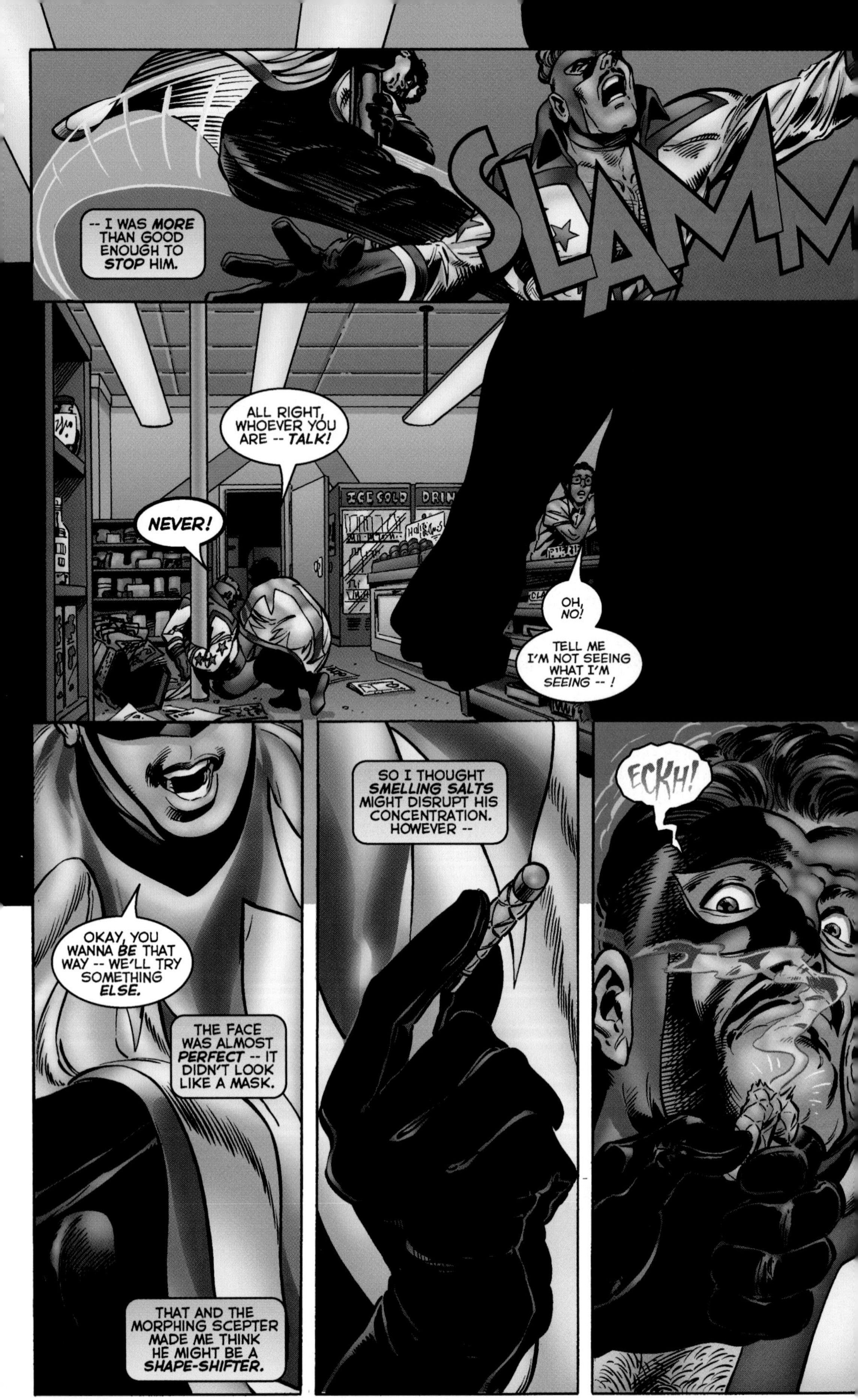
-- I WAS MORE THAN GOOD ENOUGH TO STOP HIM.
SLAMM
ALL RIGHT, WHOEVER YOU ARE -- TALK!
NEVER!
OH, NO!
TELL ME I'M NOT SEEING WHAT I'M SEEING -- !
OKAY, YOU WANNA BE THAT WAY -- WE'LL TRY SOMETHING ELSE.
THE FACE WAS ALMOST PERFECT -- IT DIDN'T LOOK LIKE A MASK.
THAT AND THE MORPHING SCEPTER MADE ME THINK HE MIGHT BE A SHAPE-SHIFTER.
SO I THOUGHT SMELLING SALTS MIGHT DISRUPT HIS CONCENTRATION. HOWEVER --
ECKH!

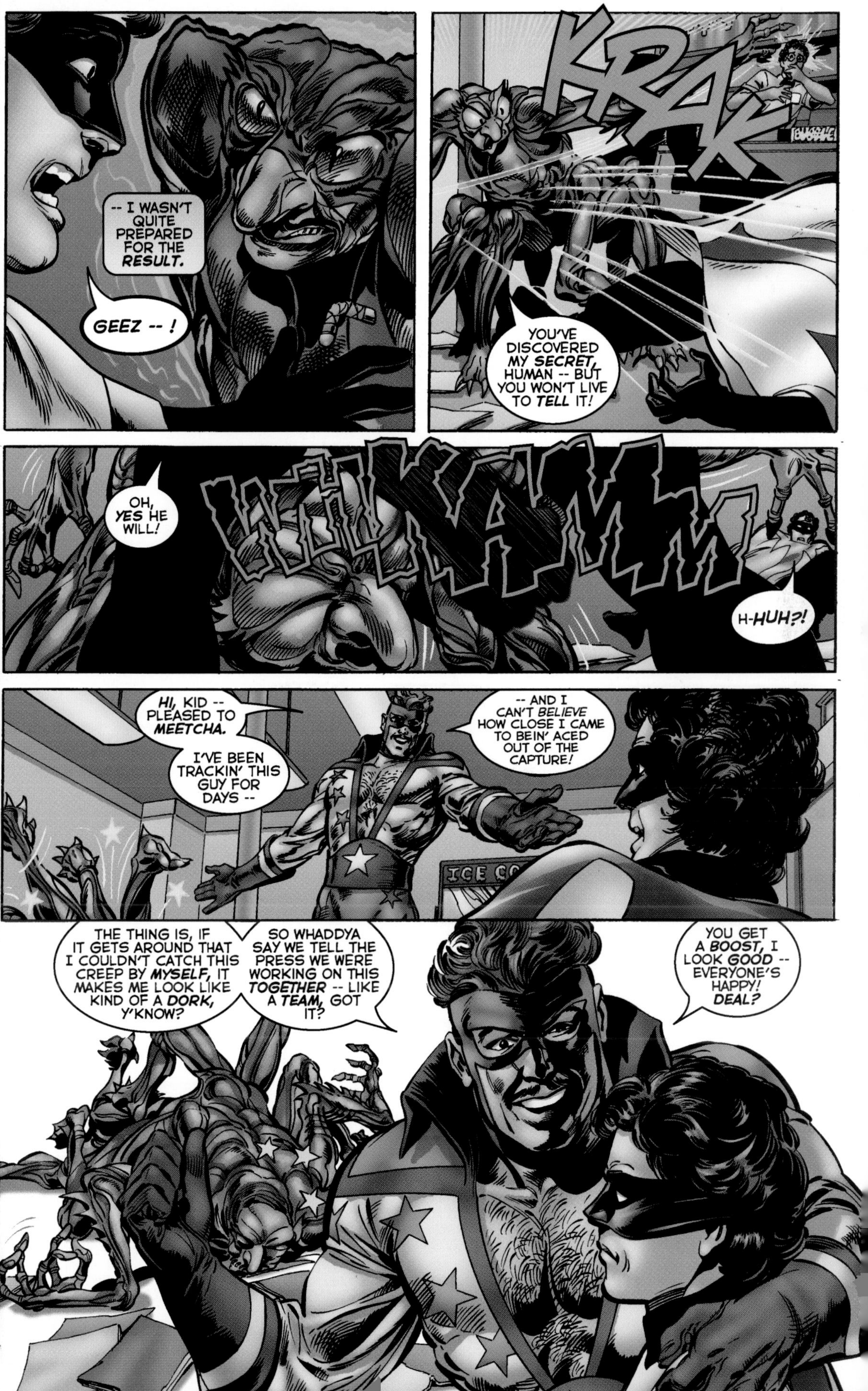
-- I WASN'T QUITE PREPARED FOR THE RESULT.
GEEZ -- !
KRAK
YOU'VE DISCOVERED MY SECRET, HUMAN -- BUT YOU WON'T LIVE TO TELL IT!
OH, YES HE WILL!
WHHAMM
H-HUH?!
HI, KID -- PLEASED TO MEETCHA.
I'VE BEEN TRACKIN' THIS GUY FOR DAYS --
-- AND I CAN'T BELIEVE HOW CLOSE I CAME TO BEIN' ACED OUT OF THE CAPTURE!
ICE CO
THE THING IS, IF IT GETS AROUND THAT I COULDN'T CATCH THIS CREEP BY MYSELF, IT MAKES ME LOOK LIKE KIND OF A DORK, Y'KNOW?
SO WHADDYA SAY WE TELL THE PRESS WE WERE WORKING ON THIS TOGETHER -- LIKE A TEAM, GOT IT?
YOU GET A BOOST, I LOOK GOOD -- EVERYONE'S HAPPY! DEAL?

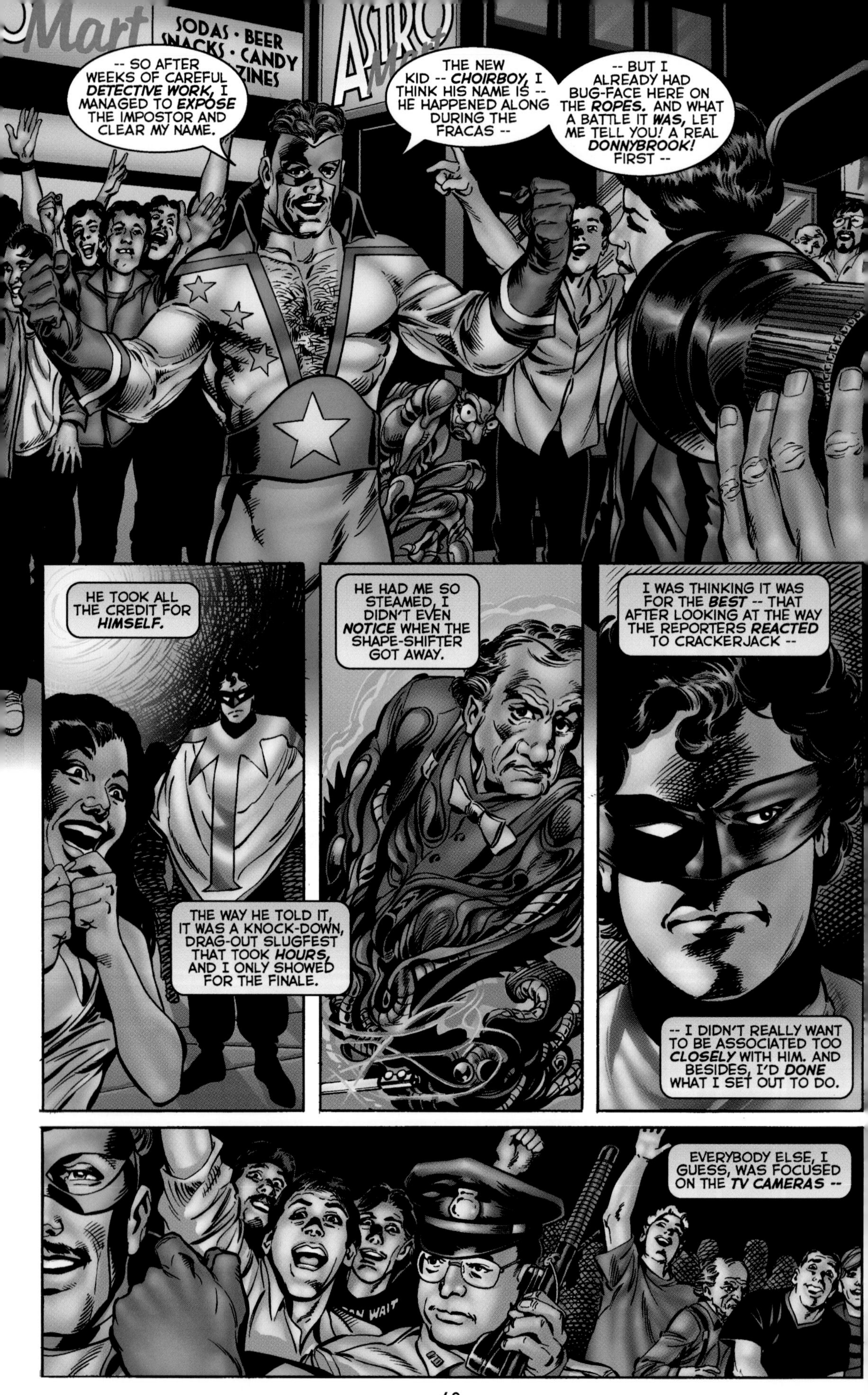

Mart
SODAS · BEER
SNACKS · CANDY
ZINES
ASTRO
Mart
-- SO AFTER WEEKS OF CAREFUL DETECTIVE WORK, I MANAGED TO EXPOSE THE IMPOSTOR AND CLEAR MY NAME.
THE NEW KID -- CHOIRBOY, I THINK HIS NAME IS -- HE HAPPENED ALONG DURING THE FRACAS --
-- BUT I ALREADY HAD BUG-FACE HERE ON THE ROPES. AND WHAT A BATTLE IT WAS, LET ME TELL YOU! A REAL DONNYBROOK! FIRST --
HE TOOK ALL THE CREDIT FOR HIMSELF.
THE WAY HE TOLD IT, IT WAS A KNOCK-DOWN, DRAG-OUT SLUGFEST THAT TOOK HOURS, AND I ONLY SHOWED FOR THE FINALE.
HE HAD ME SO STEAMED, I DIDN'T EVEN NOTICE WHEN THE SHAPE-SHIFTER GOT AWAY.
I WAS THINKING IT WAS FOR THE BEST -- THAT AFTER LOOKING AT THE WAY THE REPORTERS REACTED TO CRACKERJACK --
-- I DIDN'T REALLY WANT TO BE ASSOCIATED TOO CLOSELY WITH HIM. AND BESIDES, I'D DONE WHAT I SET OUT TO DO.
EVERYBODY ELSE, I GUESS, WAS FOCUSED ON THE TV CAMERAS --

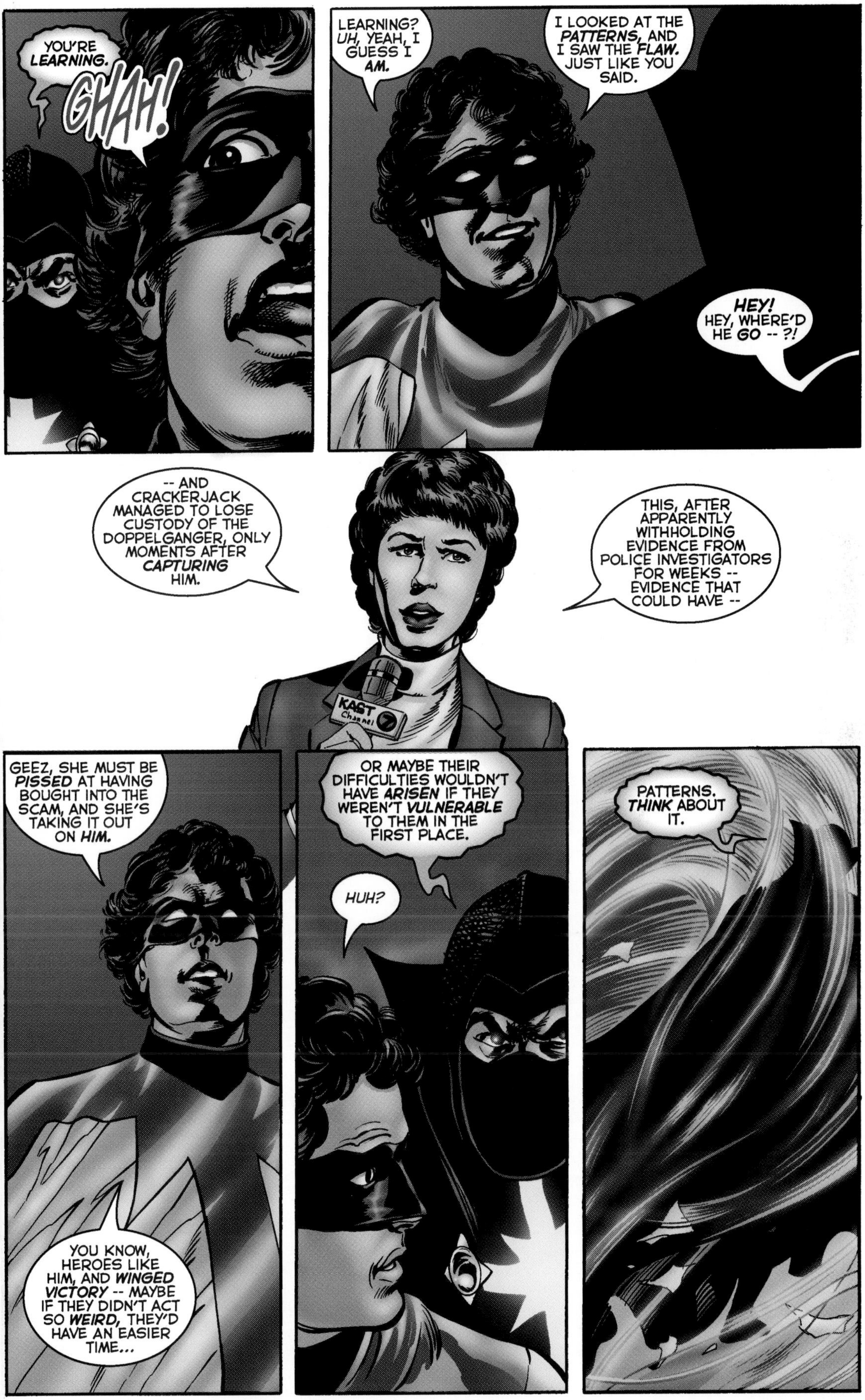

YOU'RE LEARNING.
GHAH!
LEARNING? UH, YEAH, I GUESS I AM.
I LOOKED AT THE PATTERNS, AND I SAW THE FLAW. JUST LIKE YOU SAID.
HEY! HEY, WHERE'D HE GO -- ?!
-- AND CRACKERJACK MANAGED TO LOSE CUSTODY OF THE DOPPELGANGER, ONLY MOMENTS AFTER CAPTURING HIM.
THIS, AFTER APPARENTLY WITHHOLDING EVIDENCE FROM POLICE INVESTIGATORS FOR WEEKS -- EVIDENCE THAT COULD HAVE --
KAST Channel 7
GEEZ, SHE MUST BE PISSED AT HAVING BOUGHT INTO THE SCAM, AND SHE'S TAKING IT OUT ON HIM.
YOU KNOW, HEROES LIKE HIM, AND WINGED VICTORY -- MAYBE IF THEY DIDN'T ACT SO WEIRD, THEY'D HAVE AN EASIER TIME...
OR MAYBE THEIR DIFFICULTIES WOULDN'T HAVE ARISEN IF THEY WEREN'T VULNERABLE TO THEM IN THE FIRST PLACE.
HUH?
PATTERNS. THINK ABOUT IT.

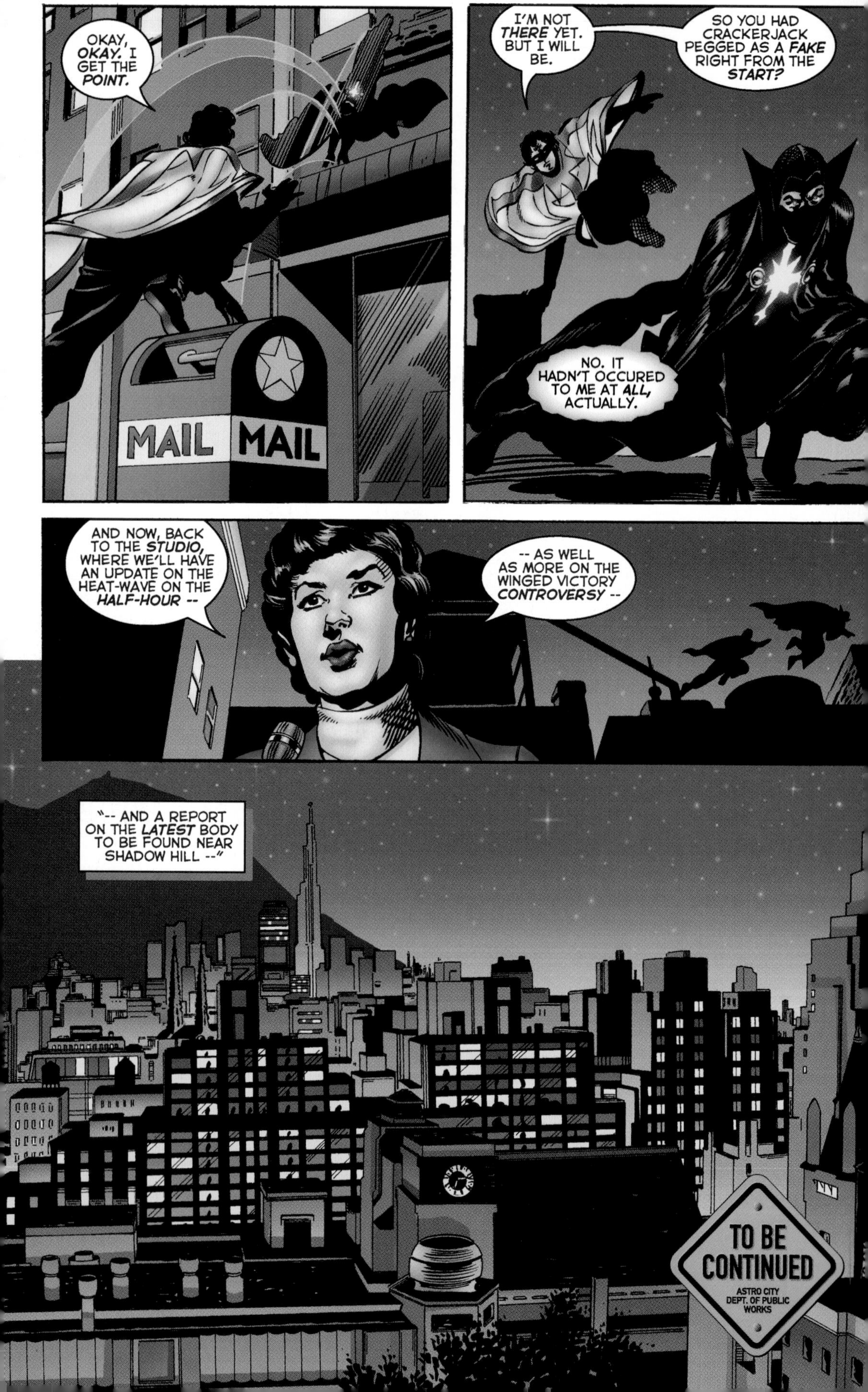
OKAY, OKAY. I GET THE POINT.
I'M NOT THERE YET. BUT I WILL BE.
SO YOU HAD CRACKERJACK PEGGED AS A FAKE RIGHT FROM THE START?
NO. IT HADN'T OCCURED TO ME AT ALL, ACTUALLY.
MAIL
MAIL
AND NOW, BACK TO THE STUDIO, WHERE WE'LL HAVE AN UPDATE ON THE HEAT-WAVE ON THE HALF-HOUR --
-- AS WELL AS MORE ON THE WINGED VICTORY CONTROVERSY --
"-- AND A REPORT ON THE LATEST BODY TO BE FOUND NEAR SHADOW HILL --"
TO BE CONTINUED
ASTRO CITY DEPT. OF PUBLIC WORKS

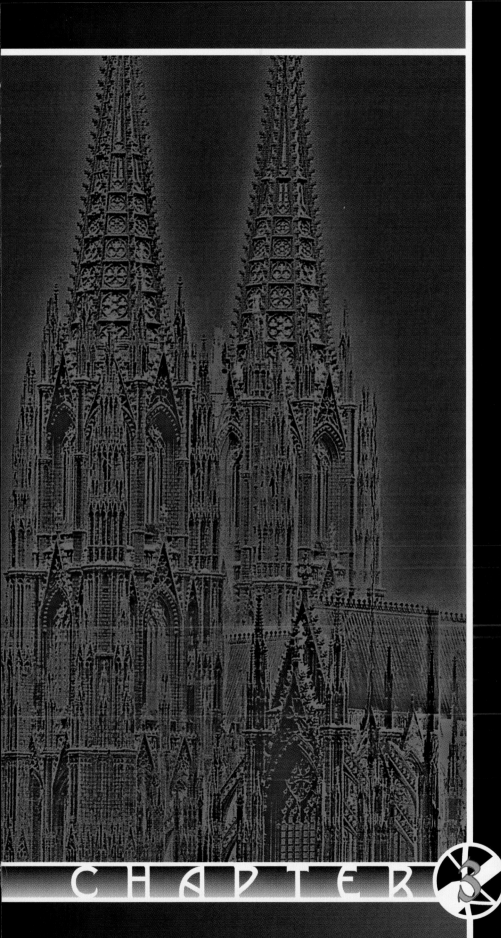

CHAPTER 3

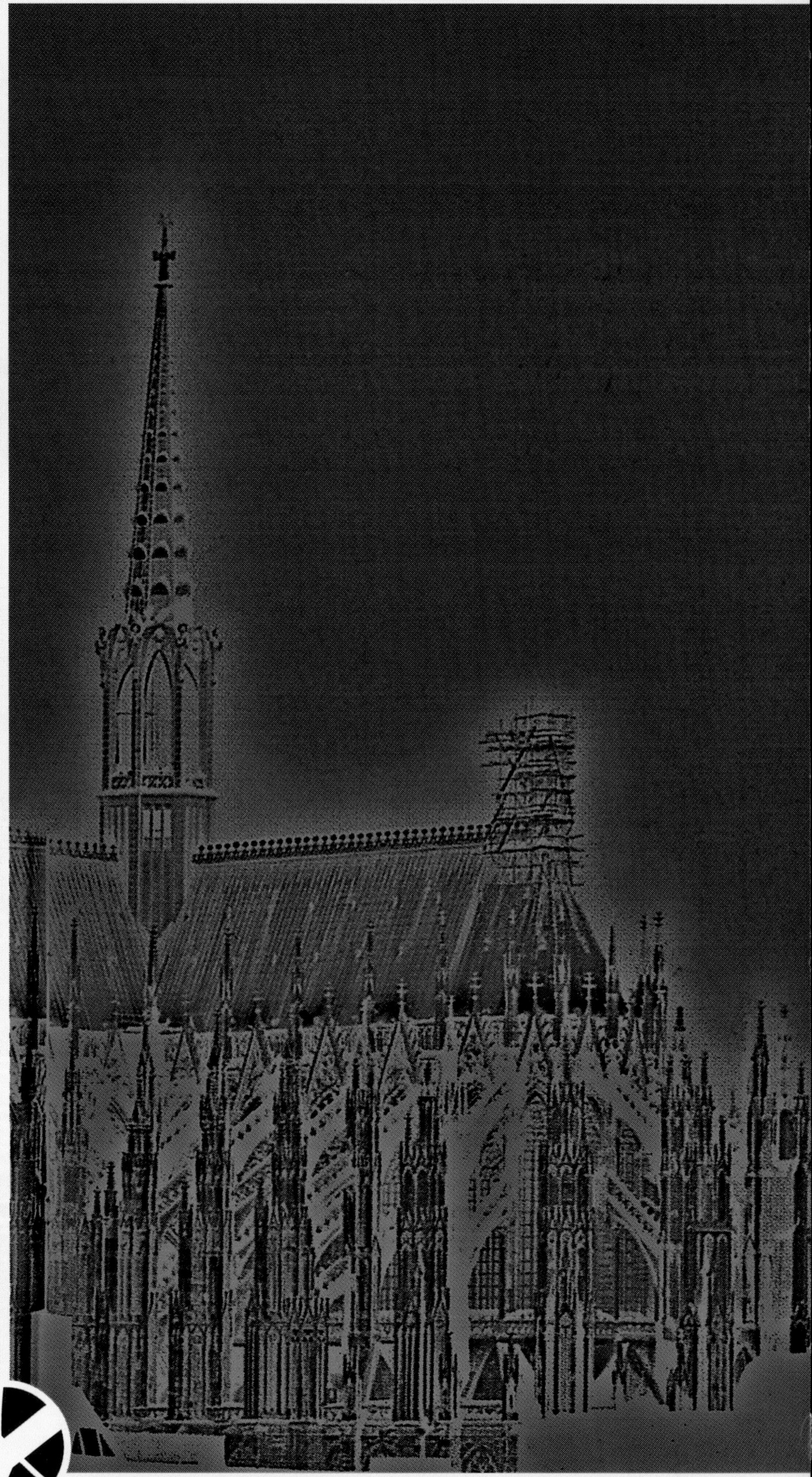

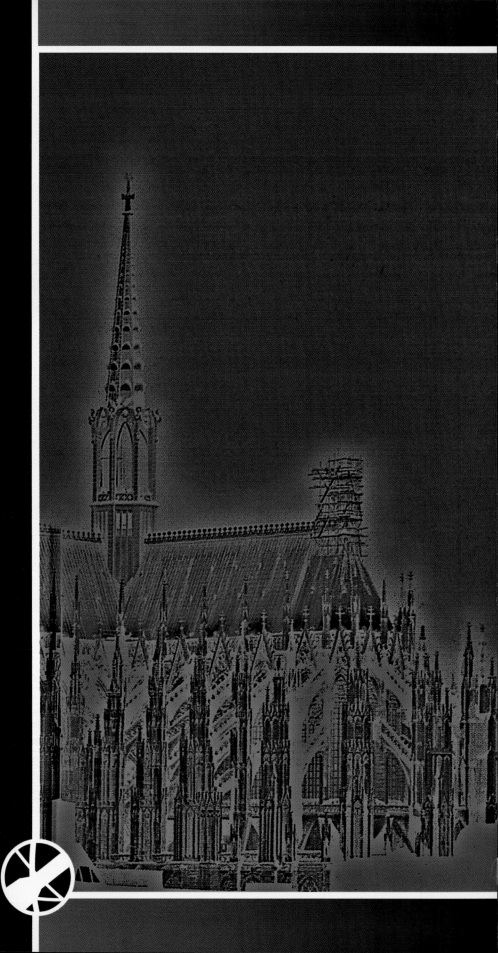

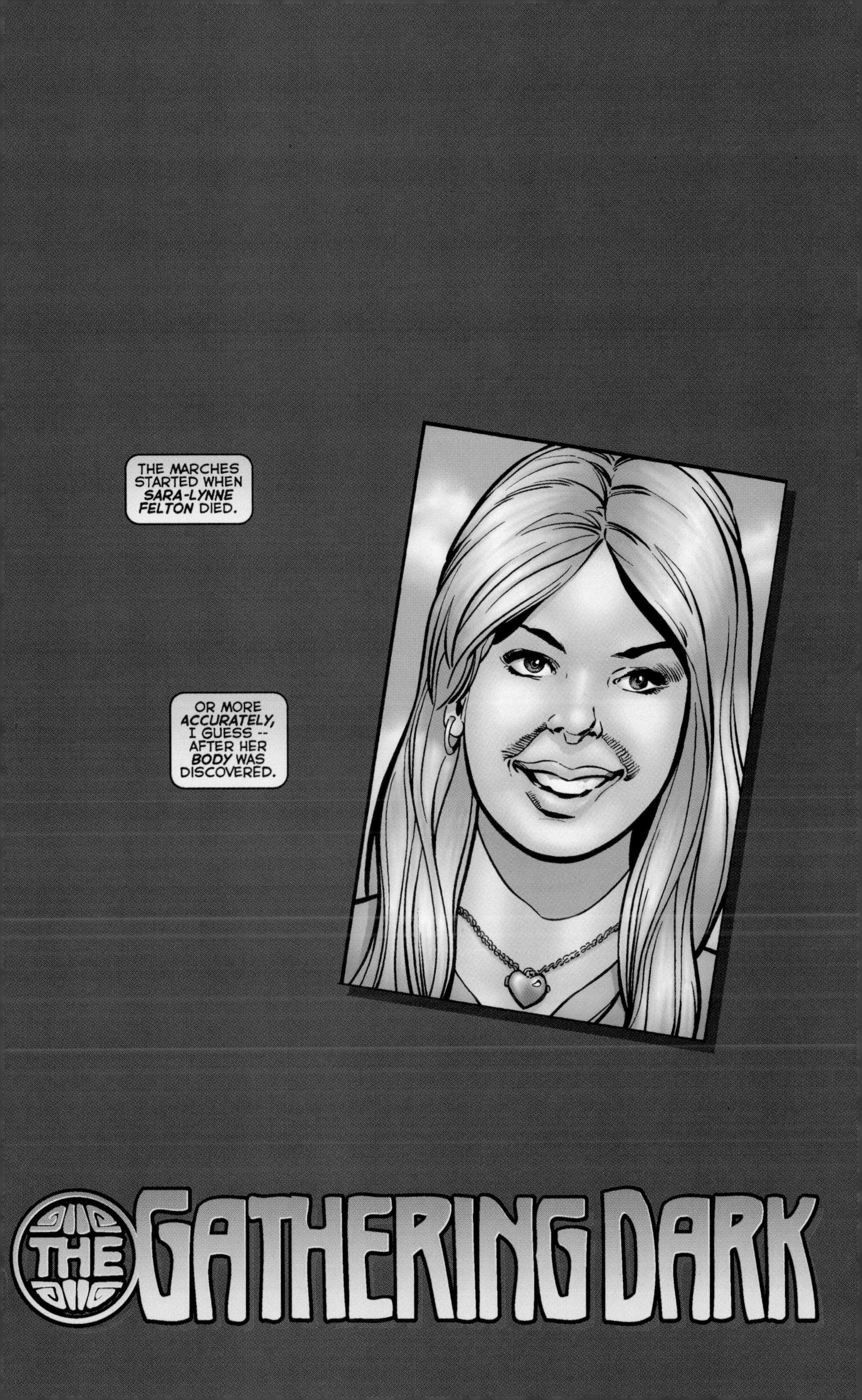
THE MARCHES STARTED WHEN SARA-LYNNE FELTON DIED.
OR MORE ACCURATELY, I GUESS -- AFTER HER BODY WAS DISCOVERED.
THE GATHERING DARK

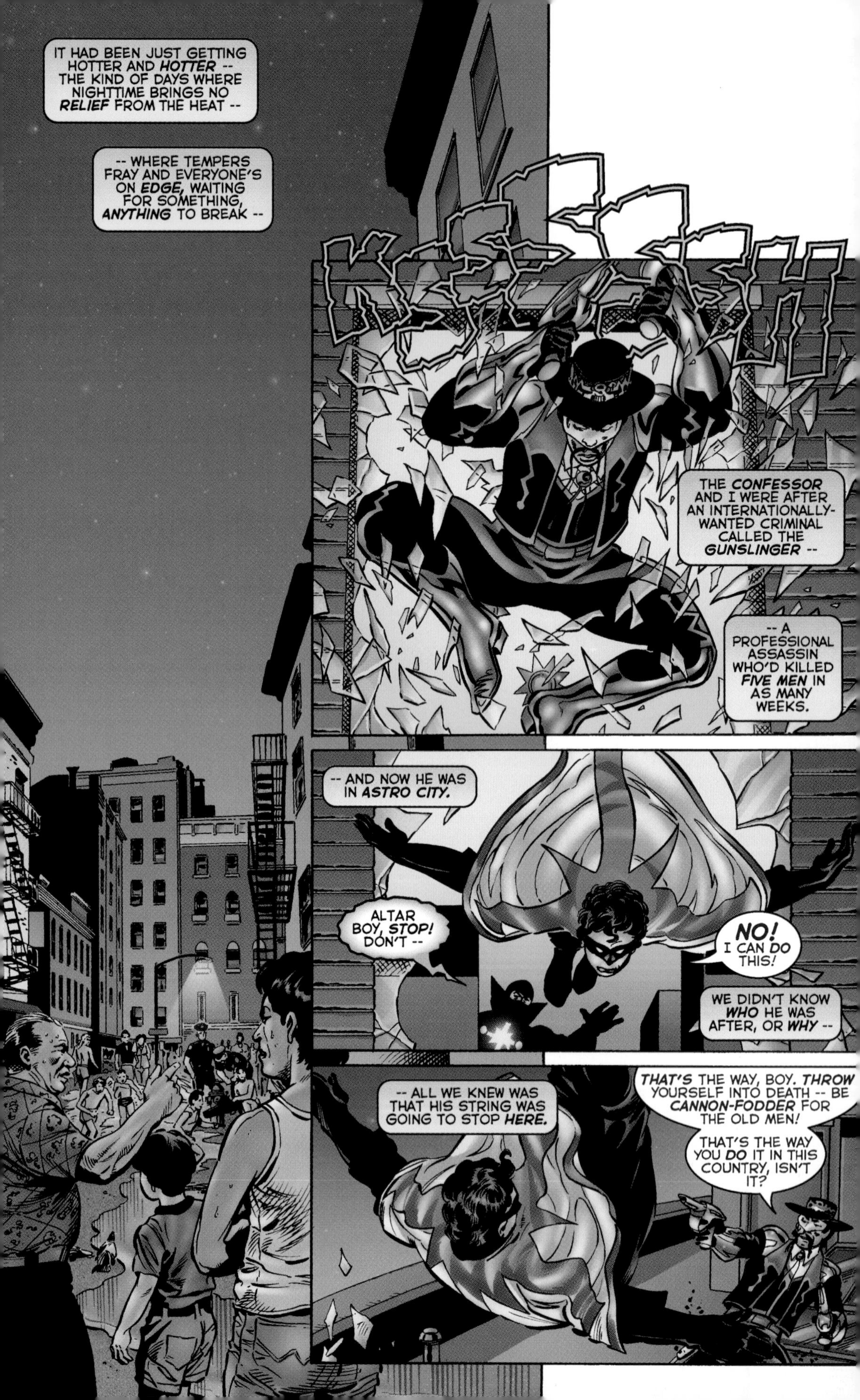
IT HAD BEEN JUST GETTING HOTTER AND HOTTER -- THE KIND OF DAYS WHERE NIGHTTIME BRINGS NO RELIEF FROM THE HEAT --
-- WHERE TEMPERS FRAY AND EVERYONE'S ON EDGE, WAITING FOR SOMETHING, ANYTHING TO BREAK --
THE CONFESSOR AND I WERE AFTER AN INTERNATIONALLY-WANTED CRIMINAL CALLED THE GUNSLINGER --
-- A PROFESSIONAL ASSASSIN WHO'D KILLED FIVE MEN IN AS MANY WEEKS.
-- AND NOW HE WAS IN ASTRO CITY.
ALTAR BOY, STOP! DON'T --
NO! I CAN DO THIS!
WE DIDN'T KNOW WHO HE WAS AFTER, OR WHY --
-- ALL WE KNEW WAS THAT HIS STRING WAS GOING TO STOP HERE.
THAT'S THE WAY, BOY. THROW YOURSELF INTO DEATH -- BE CANNON-FODDER FOR THE OLD MEN!
THAT'S THE WAY YOU DO IT IN THIS COUNTRY, ISN'T IT?

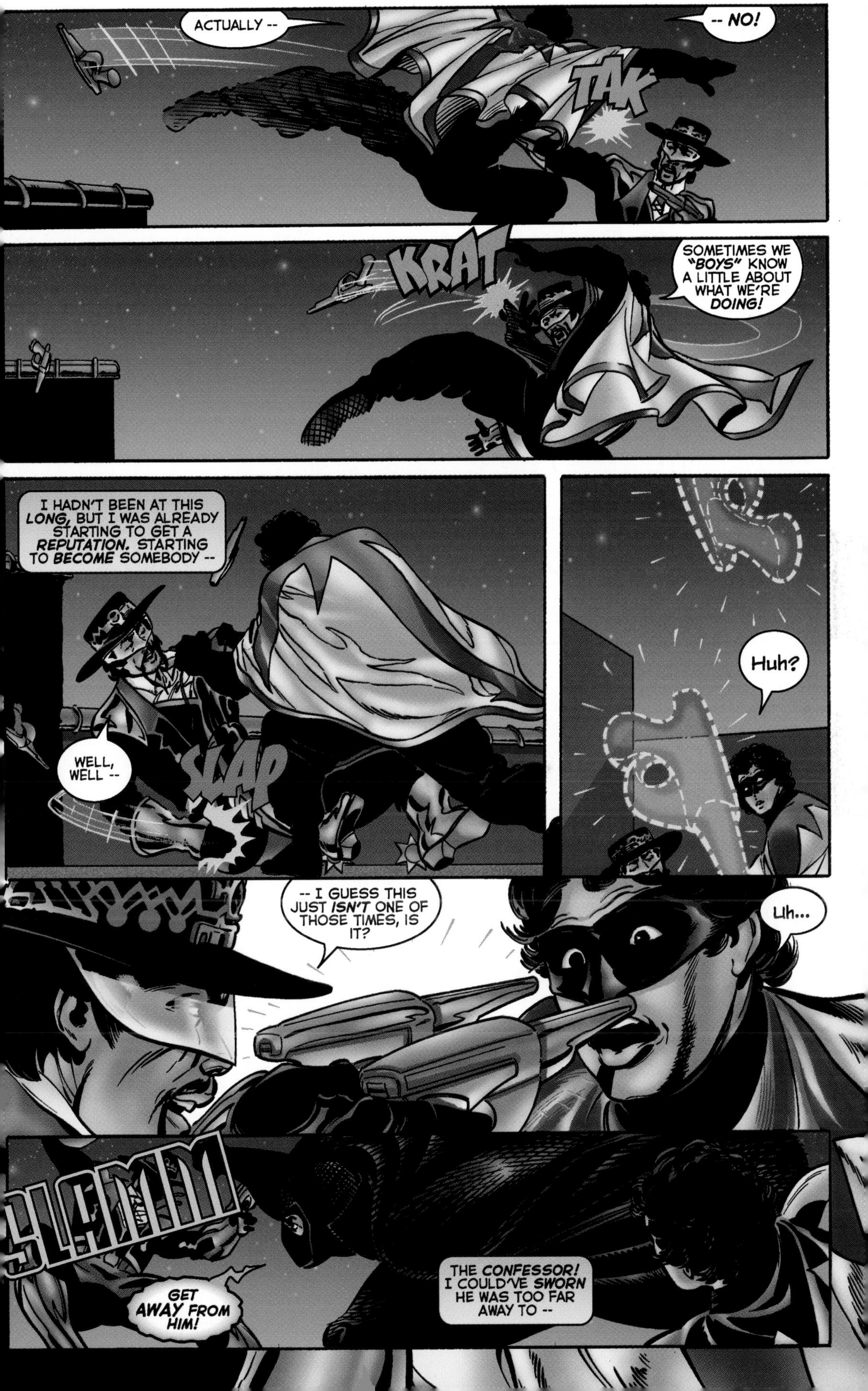
ACTUALLY --
-- NO!
TAK
KRAT
SOMETIMES WE "BOYS" KNOW A LITTLE ABOUT WHAT WE'RE DOING!
I HADN'T BEEN AT THIS LONG, BUT I WAS ALREADY STARTING TO GET A REPUTATION. STARTING TO BECOME SOMEBODY --
WELL, WELL --
SLAP
Huh?
-- I GUESS THIS JUST ISN'T ONE OF THOSE TIMES, IS IT?
Uh...
SLAMM
GET AWAY FROM HIM!
THE CONFESSOR! I COULD'VE SWORN HE WAS TOO FAR AWAY TO --

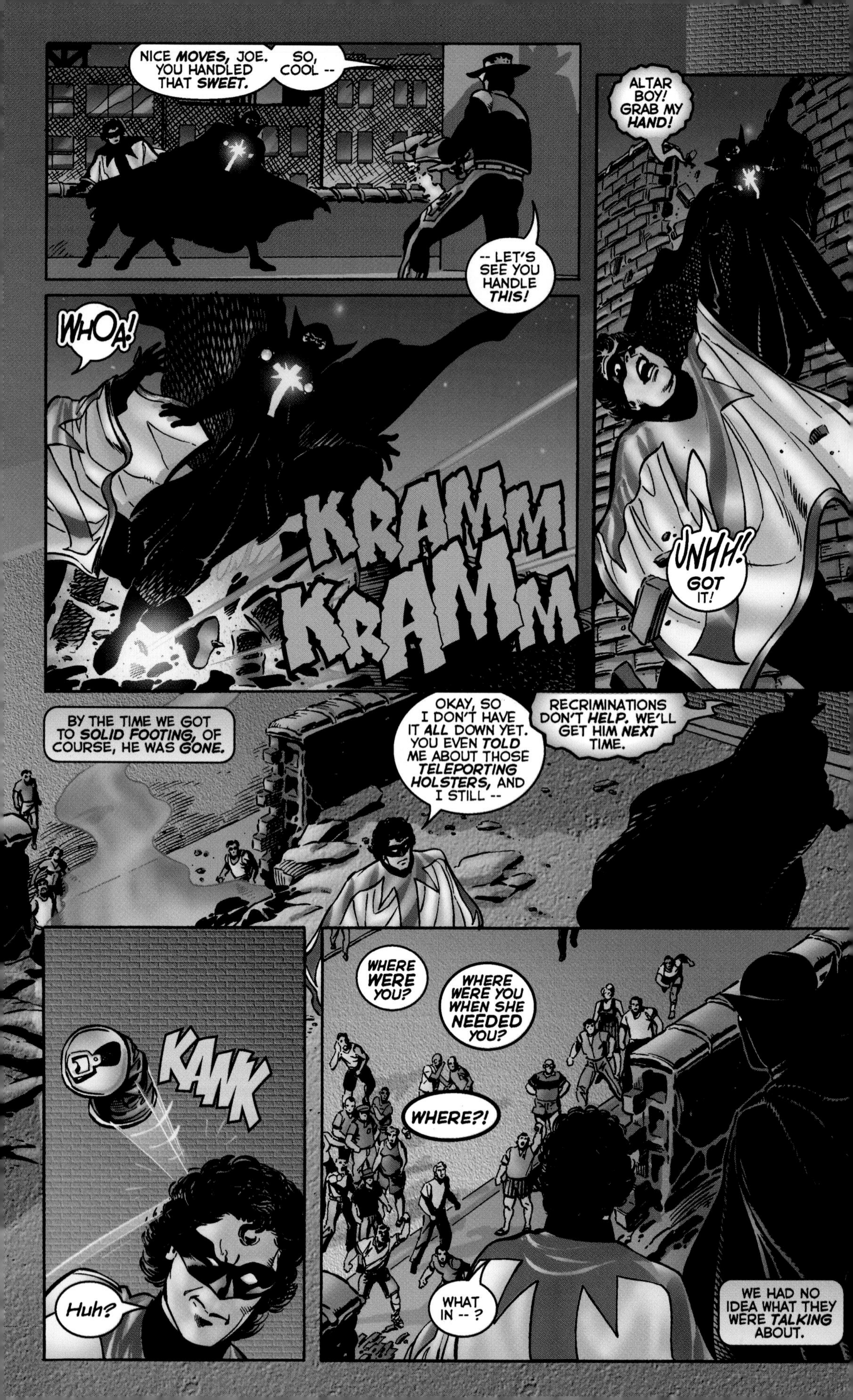

NICE *MOVES,* JOE. YOU HANDLED THAT *SWEET.*
SO, COOL --
-- LET'S SEE YOU HANDLE *THIS!*
ALTAR BOY! GRAB MY *HAND!*
WHOA!
KRAMM KRAMM
UNHH! GOT IT!
BY THE TIME WE GOT TO *SOLID FOOTING,* OF COURSE, HE WAS *GONE.*
OKAY, SO I DON'T HAVE IT *ALL* DOWN YET. YOU EVEN *TOLD* ME ABOUT THOSE *TELEPORTING HOLSTERS,* AND I STILL --
RECRIMINATIONS DON'T *HELP.* WE'LL GET HIM *NEXT* TIME.
KANK
Huh?
WHERE WERE YOU?
WHERE WERE YOU WHEN SHE NEEDED YOU?
WHERE?!
WHAT IN -- ?
WE HAD NO IDEA WHAT THEY WERE *TALKING* ABOUT.

BUT WE *FOUND OUT*, AS SOON AS WE GOT BACK TO THE CATACOMBS BENEATH THE *ABANDONED VESTRY* THE CONFESSOR USED AS A BASE.

IT WAS HARD TO *MISS* IT. IT WAS ALL OVER THE NEWS.

SARA-LYNNE FELTON WAS A PRETTY, POPULAR EIGHTH-GRADER -- UNTIL SHE BECAME JUST ANOTHER NAME ON A *POLICE BLOTTER.*

WE WERE WALKING *HOME* -- SHE WANTED TO GO BUY A MAGAZINE -- THAT'S THE LAST TIME WE *SAW* HER --

IT'S A *TERRIBLE* THING -- A *TERRIBLE, TERRIBLE* THING -- !

IT WAS THE *SHADOW HILL KILLER.*

SHE WAS THE *EIGHTH* TO BE FOUND. THE EIGHTH KILLED, THE EIGHTH *RITUALLY MUTILATED* --

-- ALL IN THE NEIGHBORHOODS SURROUNDING SHADOW HILL. BUT SHE WAS ALSO THE *LAST STRAW.*

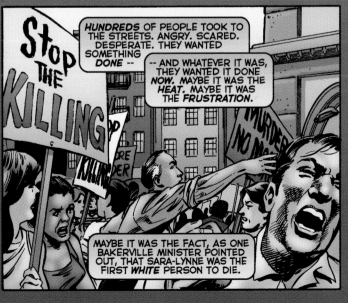

HUNDREDS OF PEOPLE TOOK TO THE STREETS. ANGRY. SCARED. DESPERATE. THEY WANTED SOMETHING *DONE* --

-- AND WHATEVER IT WAS, THEY WANTED IT DONE *NOW.* MAYBE IT WAS THE *HEAT.* MAYBE IT WAS THE *FRUSTRATION.*

STOP THE KILLING

MAYBE IT WAS THE FACT, AS ONE BAKERVILLE MINISTER POINTED OUT, THAT SARA-LYNNE WAS THE FIRST *WHITE* PERSON TO DIE.

BUT WHATEVER IT WAS, *I* FELT IT TOO.

WE COULD *PATROL* -- INVESTIGATE -- STAKE THE AREA *OUT* --

THERE'S GOT TO BE *SOMETHING* WE CAN DO -- !

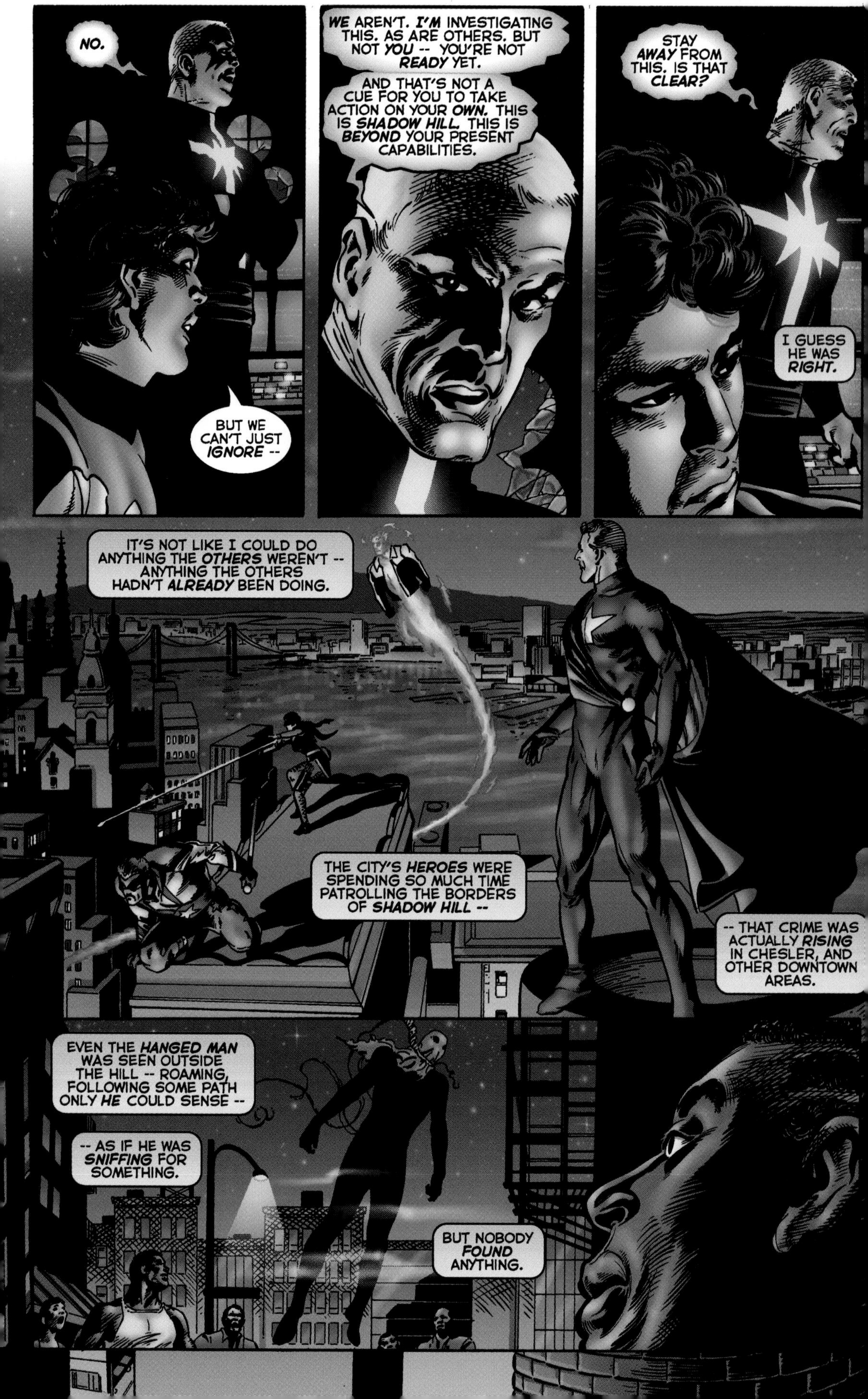
NO.
BUT WE CAN'T JUST IGNORE --
WE AREN'T. I'M INVESTIGATING THIS. AS ARE OTHERS. BUT NOT YOU -- YOU'RE NOT READY YET.
AND THAT'S NOT A CUE FOR YOU TO TAKE ACTION ON YOUR OWN. THIS IS SHADOW HILL. THIS IS BEYOND YOUR PRESENT CAPABILITIES.
STAY AWAY FROM THIS. IS THAT CLEAR?
I GUESS HE WAS RIGHT.
IT'S NOT LIKE I COULD DO ANYTHING THE OTHERS WEREN'T -- ANYTHING THE OTHERS HADN'T ALREADY BEEN DOING.
THE CITY'S HEROES WERE SPENDING SO MUCH TIME PATROLLING THE BORDERS OF SHADOW HILL --
-- THAT CRIME WAS ACTUALLY RISING IN CHESLER, AND OTHER DOWNTOWN AREAS.
EVEN THE HANGED MAN WAS SEEN OUTSIDE THE HILL -- ROAMING, FOLLOWING SOME PATH ONLY HE COULD SENSE --
-- AS IF HE WAS SNIFFING FOR SOMETHING.
BUT NOBODY FOUND ANYTHING.

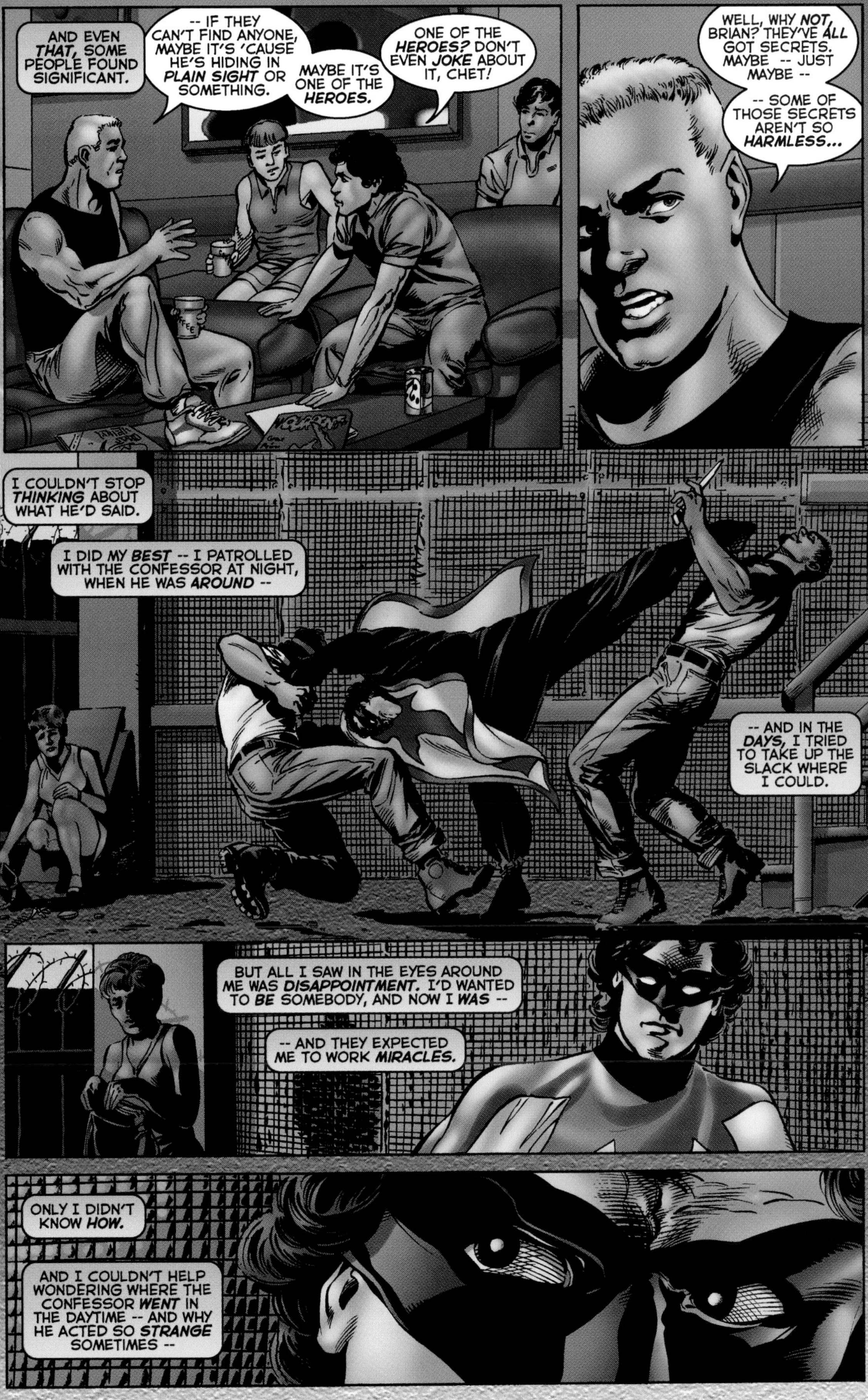
AND EVEN THAT, SOME PEOPLE FOUND SIGNIFICANT.
-- IF THEY CAN'T FIND ANYONE, MAYBE IT'S 'CAUSE HE'S HIDING IN PLAIN SIGHT OR SOMETHING.
MAYBE IT'S ONE OF THE HEROES.
ONE OF THE HEROES? DON'T EVEN JOKE ABOUT IT, CHET!
WELL, WHY NOT, BRIAN? THEY'VE ALL GOT SECRETS. MAYBE -- JUST MAYBE --
-- SOME OF THOSE SECRETS AREN'T SO HARMLESS...
I COULDN'T STOP THINKING ABOUT WHAT HE'D SAID.
I DID MY BEST -- I PATROLLED WITH THE CONFESSOR AT NIGHT, WHEN HE WAS AROUND --
-- AND IN THE DAYS, I TRIED TO TAKE UP THE SLACK WHERE I COULD.
BUT ALL I SAW IN THE EYES AROUND ME WAS DISAPPOINTMENT. I'D WANTED TO BE SOMEBODY, AND NOW I WAS --
-- AND THEY EXPECTED ME TO WORK MIRACLES.
ONLY I DIDN'T KNOW HOW.
AND I COULDN'T HELP WONDERING WHERE THE CONFESSOR WENT IN THE DAYTIME -- AND WHY HE ACTED SO STRANGE SOMETIMES --

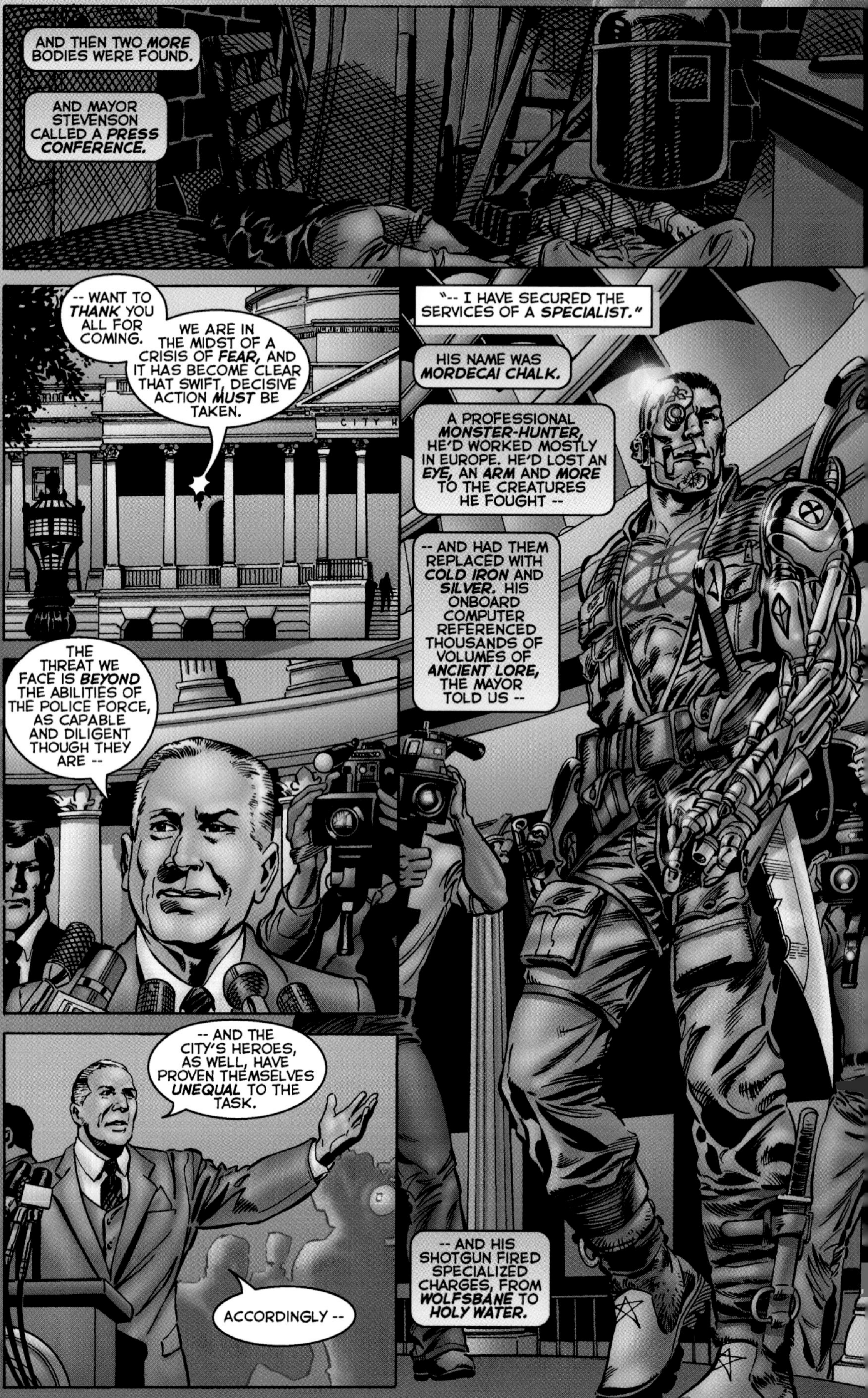
AND THEN TWO MORE BODIES WERE FOUND.
AND MAYOR STEVENSON CALLED A PRESS CONFERENCE.
-- WANT TO THANK YOU ALL FOR COMING.
WE ARE IN THE MIDST OF A CRISIS OF FEAR, AND IT HAS BECOME CLEAR THAT SWIFT, DECISIVE ACTION MUST BE TAKEN.
CITY H
THE THREAT WE FACE IS BEYOND THE ABILITIES OF THE POLICE FORCE, AS CAPABLE AND DILIGENT THOUGH THEY ARE --
-- AND THE CITY'S HEROES, AS WELL, HAVE PROVEN THEMSELVES UNEQUAL TO THE TASK.
ACCORDINGLY --
"-- I HAVE SECURED THE SERVICES OF A SPECIALIST."
HIS NAME WAS MORDECAI CHALK.
A PROFESSIONAL MONSTER-HUNTER, HE'D WORKED MOSTLY IN EUROPE. HE'D LOST AN EYE, AN ARM AND MORE TO THE CREATURES HE FOUGHT --
-- AND HAD THEM REPLACED WITH COLD IRON AND SILVER. HIS ONBOARD COMPUTER REFERENCED THOUSANDS OF VOLUMES OF ANCIENT LORE, THE MAYOR TOLD US --
-- AND HIS SHOTGUN FIRED SPECIALIZED CHARGES, FROM WOLFSBANE TO HOLY WATER.

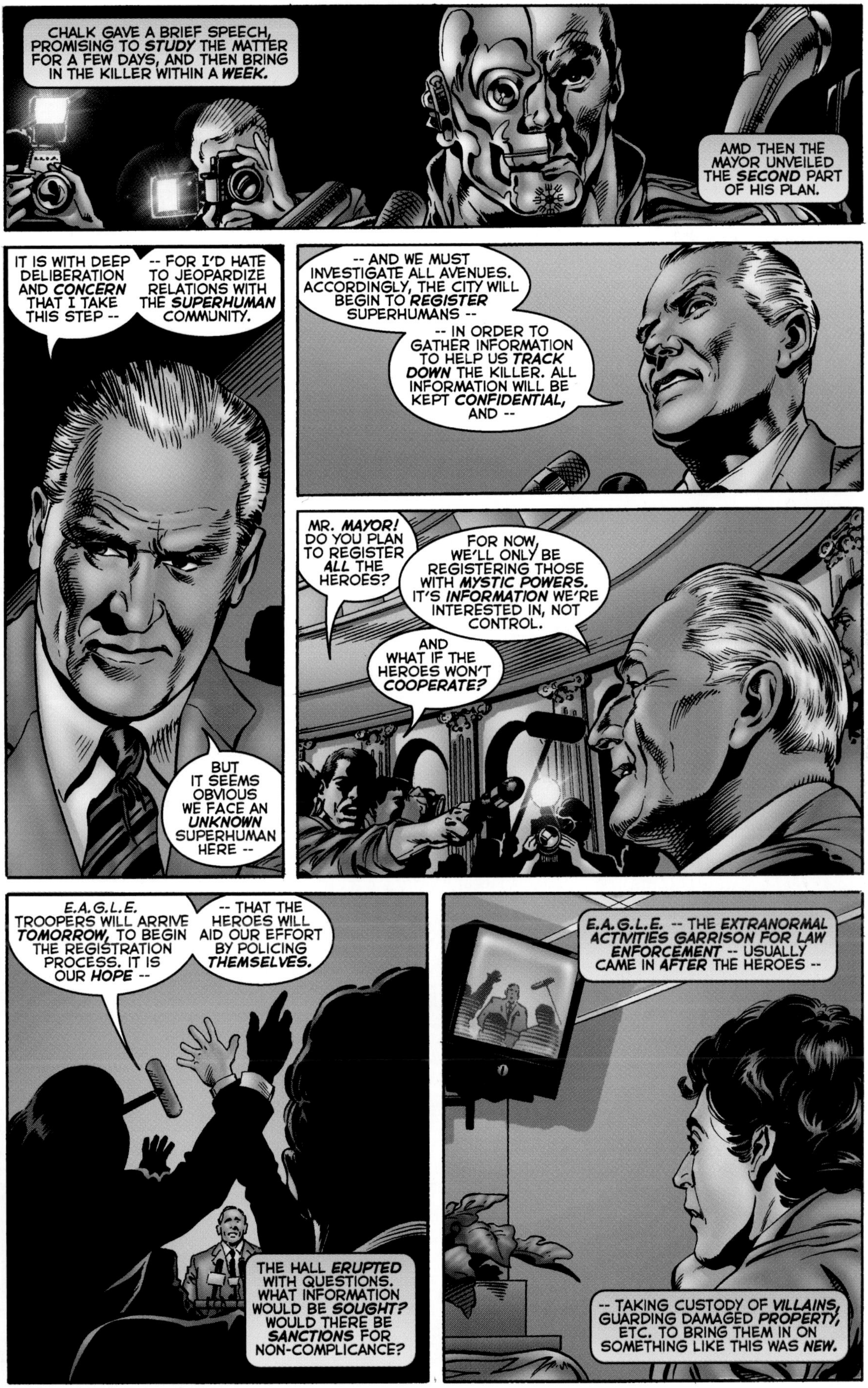
CHALK GAVE A BRIEF SPEECH, PROMISING TO STUDY THE MATTER FOR A FEW DAYS, AND THEN BRING IN THE KILLER WITHIN A WEEK.
AMD THEN THE MAYOR UNVEILED THE SECOND PART OF HIS PLAN.
IT IS WITH DEEP DELIBERATION AND CONCERN THAT I TAKE THIS STEP --
-- FOR I'D HATE TO JEOPARDIZE RELATIONS WITH THE SUPERHUMAN COMMUNITY.
BUT IT SEEMS OBVIOUS WE FACE AN UNKNOWN SUPERHUMAN HERE --
-- AND WE MUST INVESTIGATE ALL AVENUES. ACCORDINGLY, THE CITY WILL BEGIN TO REGISTER SUPERHUMANS --
-- IN ORDER TO GATHER INFORMATION TO HELP US TRACK DOWN THE KILLER. ALL INFORMATION WILL BE KEPT CONFIDENTIAL, AND --
MR. MAYOR! DO YOU PLAN TO REGISTER ALL THE HEROES?
FOR NOW, WE'LL ONLY BE REGISTERING THOSE WITH MYSTIC POWERS. IT'S INFORMATION WE'RE INTERESTED IN, NOT CONTROL.
AND WHAT IF THE HEROES WON'T COOPERATE?
E.A.G.L.E. TROOPERS WILL ARRIVE TOMORROW, TO BEGIN THE REGISTRATION PROCESS. IT IS OUR HOPE --
-- THAT THE HEROES WILL AID OUR EFFORT BY POLICING THEMSELVES.
THE HALL ERUPTED WITH QUESTIONS. WHAT INFORMATION WOULD BE SOUGHT? WOULD THERE BE SANCTIONS FOR NON-COMPLIANCE?
E.A.G.L.E. -- THE EXTRANORMAL ACTIVITIES GARRISON FOR LAW ENFORCEMENT -- USUALLY CAME IN AFTER THE HEROES --
-- TAKING CUSTODY OF VILLAINS, GUARDING DAMAGED PROPERTY, ETC. TO BRING THEM IN ON SOMETHING LIKE THIS WAS NEW.

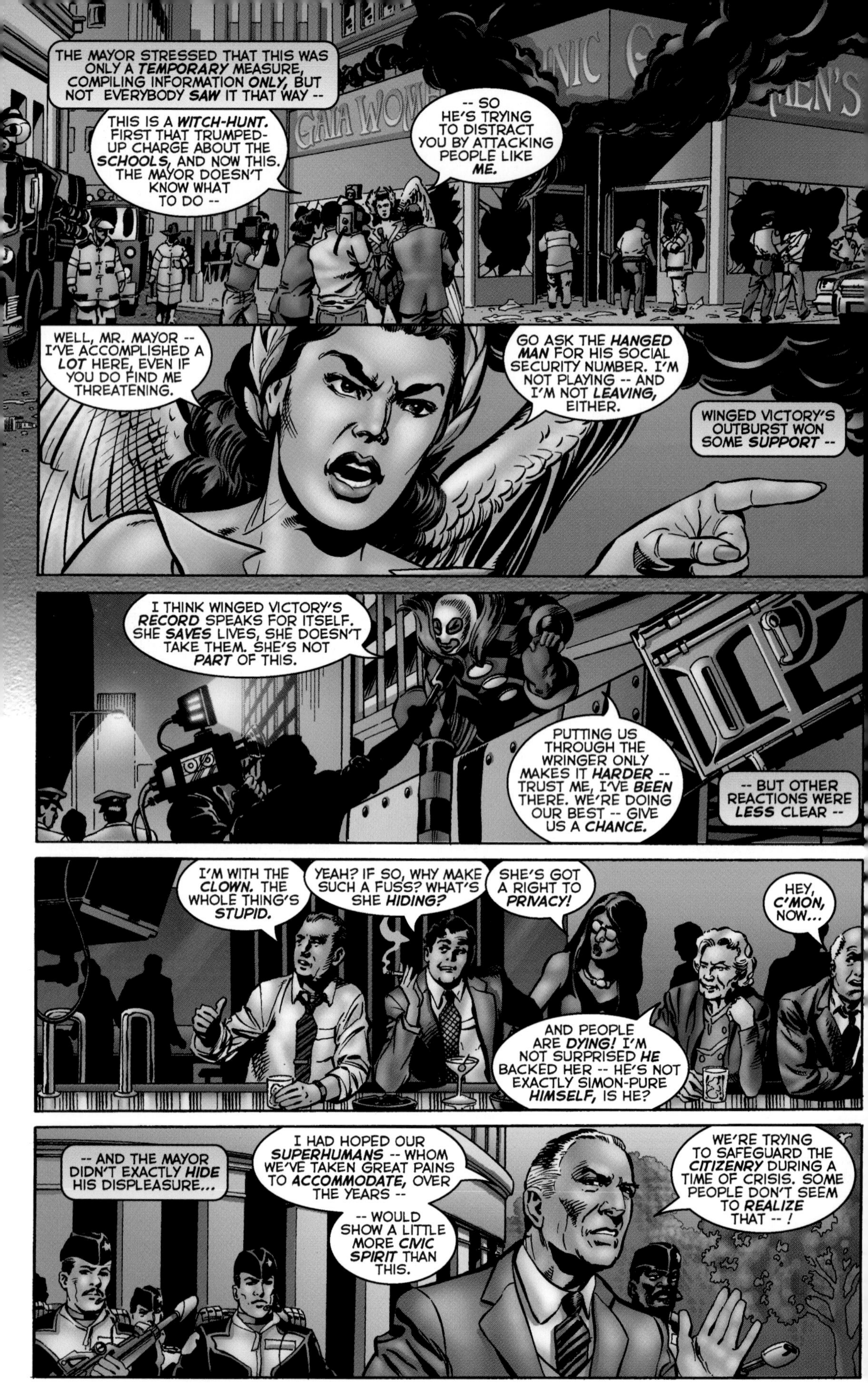

THE MAYOR STRESSED THAT THIS WAS ONLY A TEMPORARY MEASURE, COMPILING INFORMATION ONLY, BUT NOT EVERYBODY SAW IT THAT WAY --
THIS IS A WITCH-HUNT. FIRST THAT TRUMPED-UP CHARGE ABOUT THE SCHOOLS, AND NOW THIS. THE MAYOR DOESN'T KNOW WHAT TO DO --
-- SO HE'S TRYING TO DISTRACT YOU BY ATTACKING PEOPLE LIKE ME.
GAIA WOM
MEN'S
WELL, MR. MAYOR -- I'VE ACCOMPLISHED A LOT HERE, EVEN IF YOU DO FIND ME THREATENING.
GO ASK THE HANGED MAN FOR HIS SOCIAL SECURITY NUMBER. I'M NOT PLAYING -- AND I'M NOT LEAVING, EITHER.
WINGED VICTORY'S OUTBURST WON SOME SUPPORT --
I THINK WINGED VICTORY'S RECORD SPEAKS FOR ITSELF. SHE SAVES LIVES, SHE DOESN'T TAKE THEM. SHE'S NOT PART OF THIS.
PUTTING US THROUGH THE WRINGER ONLY MAKES IT HARDER -- TRUST ME, I'VE BEEN THERE. WE'RE DOING OUR BEST -- GIVE US A CHANCE.
-- BUT OTHER REACTIONS WERE LESS CLEAR --
I'M WITH THE CLOWN. THE WHOLE THING'S STUPID.
YEAH? IF SO, WHY MAKE SUCH A FUSS? WHAT'S SHE HIDING?
SHE'S GOT A RIGHT TO PRIVACY!
HEY, C'MON, NOW...
AND PEOPLE ARE DYING! I'M NOT SURPRISED HE BACKED HER -- HE'S NOT EXACTLY SIMON-PURE HIMSELF, IS HE?
-- AND THE MAYOR DIDN'T EXACTLY HIDE HIS DISPLEASURE...
I HAD HOPED OUR SUPERHUMANS -- WHOM WE'VE TAKEN GREAT PAINS TO ACCOMMODATE, OVER THE YEARS --
-- WOULD SHOW A LITTLE MORE CIVIC SPIRIT THAN THIS.
WE'RE TRYING TO SAFEGUARD THE CITIZENRY DURING A TIME OF CRISIS. SOME PEOPLE DON'T SEEM TO REALIZE THAT -- !

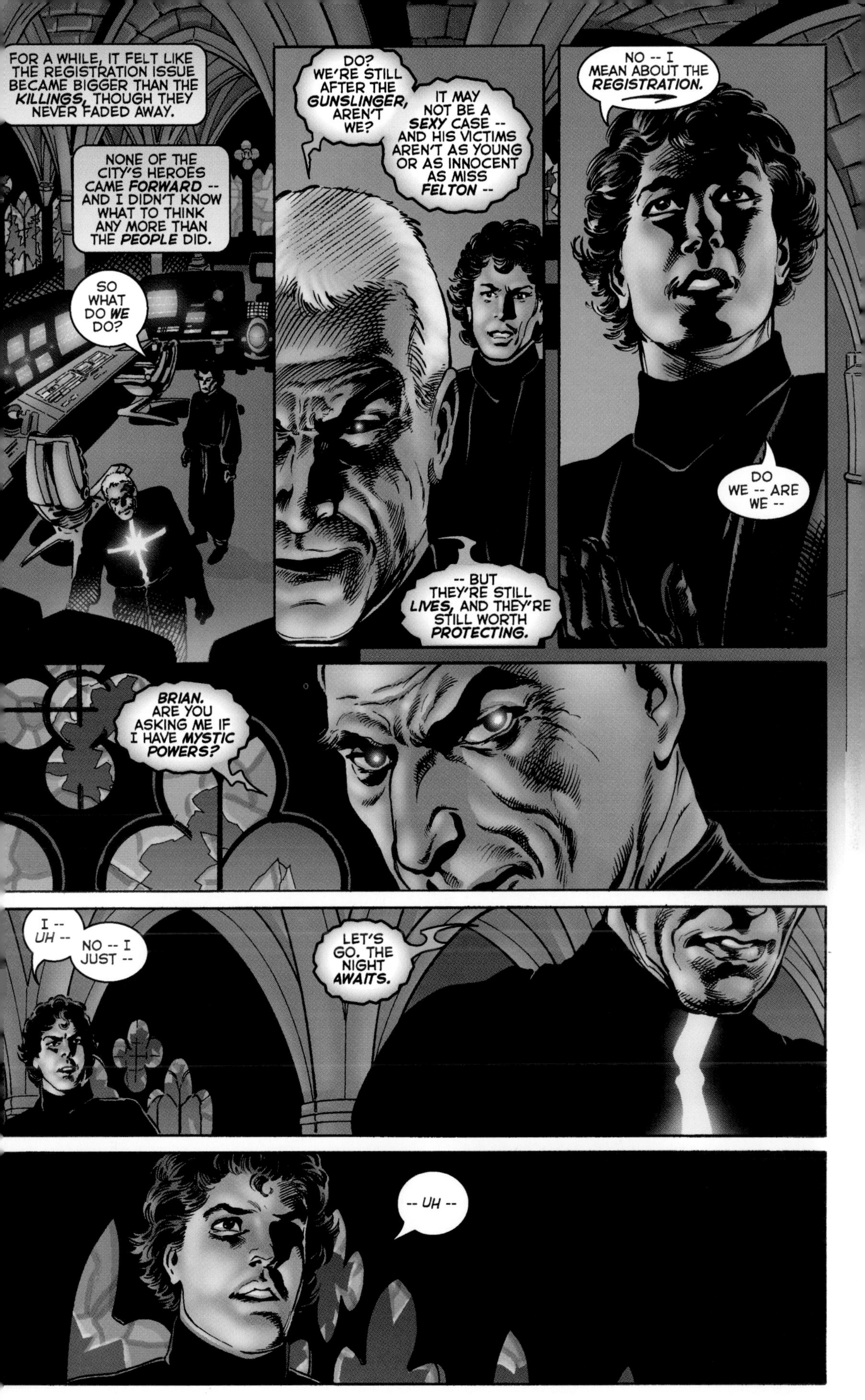
FOR A WHILE, IT FELT LIKE THE REGISTRATION ISSUE BECAME BIGGER THAN THE KILLINGS, THOUGH THEY NEVER FADED AWAY.
NONE OF THE CITY'S HEROES CAME FORWARD -- AND I DIDN'T KNOW WHAT TO THINK ANY MORE THAN THE PEOPLE DID.
SO WHAT DO WE DO?
DO? WE'RE STILL AFTER THE GUNSLINGER, AREN'T WE?
IT MAY NOT BE A SEXY CASE -- AND HIS VICTIMS AREN'T AS YOUNG OR AS INNOCENT AS MISS FELTON --
-- BUT THEY'RE STILL LIVES, AND THEY'RE STILL WORTH PROTECTING.
NO -- I MEAN ABOUT THE REGISTRATION.
DO WE -- ARE WE --
BRIAN. ARE YOU ASKING ME IF I HAVE MYSTIC POWERS?
I -- UH --
NO -- I JUST --
LET'S GO. THE NIGHT AWAITS.
-- UH --

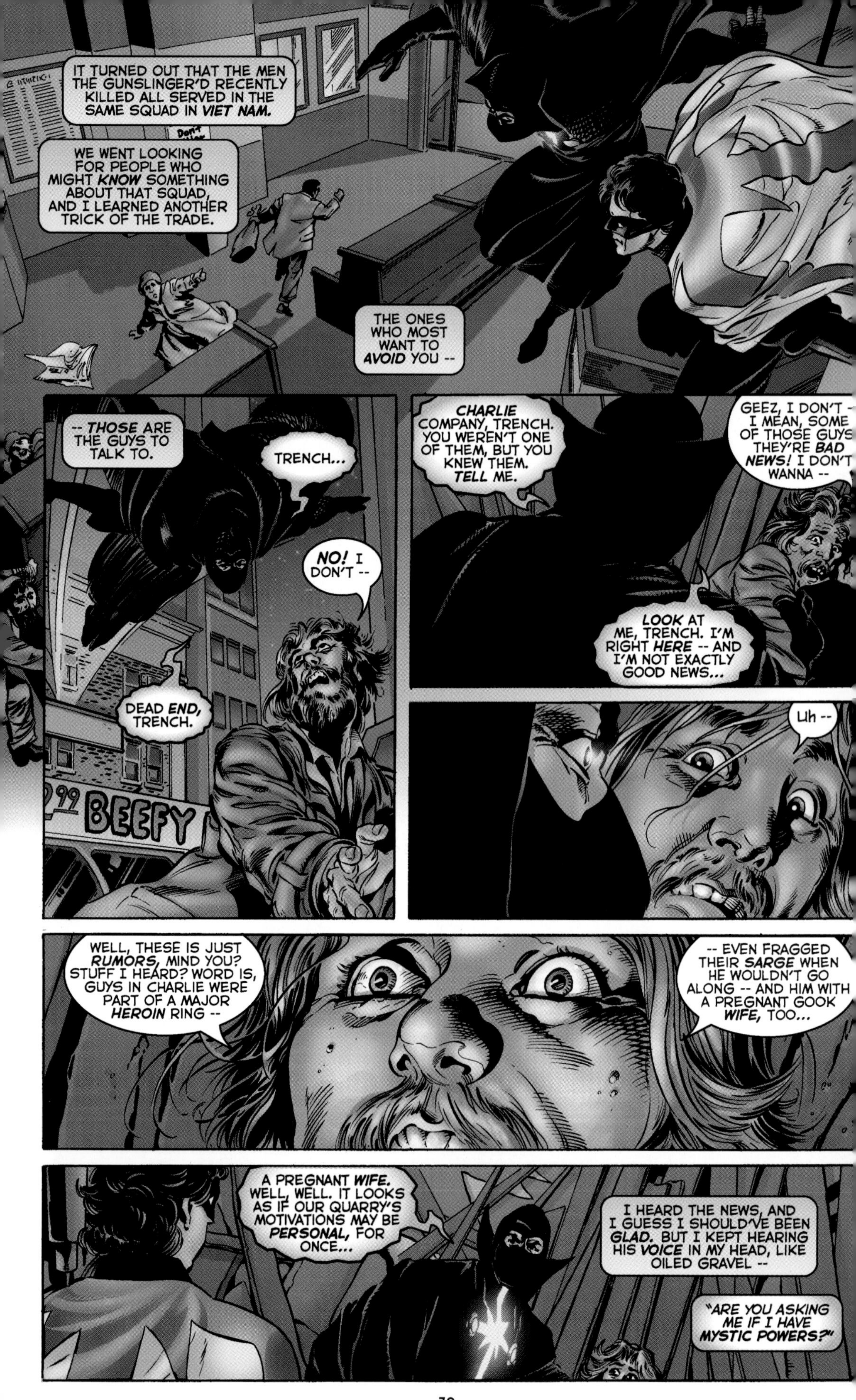
IT TURNED OUT THAT THE MEN THE GUNSLINGER'D RECENTLY KILLED ALL SERVED IN THE SAME SQUAD IN VIET NAM.
WE WENT LOOKING FOR PEOPLE WHO MIGHT KNOW SOMETHING ABOUT THAT SQUAD, AND I LEARNED ANOTHER TRICK OF THE TRADE.
THE ONES WHO MOST WANT TO AVOID YOU --
-- THOSE ARE THE GUYS TO TALK TO.
TRENCH...
NO! I DON'T --
DEAD END, TRENCH.
2.99 BEEFY
CHARLIE COMPANY, TRENCH. YOU WEREN'T ONE OF THEM, BUT YOU KNEW THEM. TELL ME.
GEEZ, I DON'T -- I MEAN, SOME OF THOSE GUYS THEY'RE BAD NEWS! I DON'T WANNA --
LOOK AT ME, TRENCH. I'M RIGHT HERE -- AND I'M NOT EXACTLY GOOD NEWS...
Uh --
WELL, THESE IS JUST RUMORS, MIND YOU? STUFF I HEARD? WORD IS, GUYS IN CHARLIE WERE PART OF A MAJOR HEROIN RING --
-- EVEN FRAGGED THEIR SARGE WHEN HE WOULDN'T GO ALONG -- AND HIM WITH A PREGNANT GOOK WIFE, TOO...
A PREGNANT WIFE. WELL, WELL. IT LOOKS AS IF OUR QUARRY'S MOTIVATIONS MAY BE PERSONAL, FOR ONCE...
I HEARD THE NEWS, AND I GUESS I SHOULD'VE BEEN GLAD. BUT I KEPT HEARING HIS VOICE IN MY HEAD, LIKE OILED GRAVEL --
"ARE YOU ASKING ME IF I HAVE MYSTIC POWERS?"

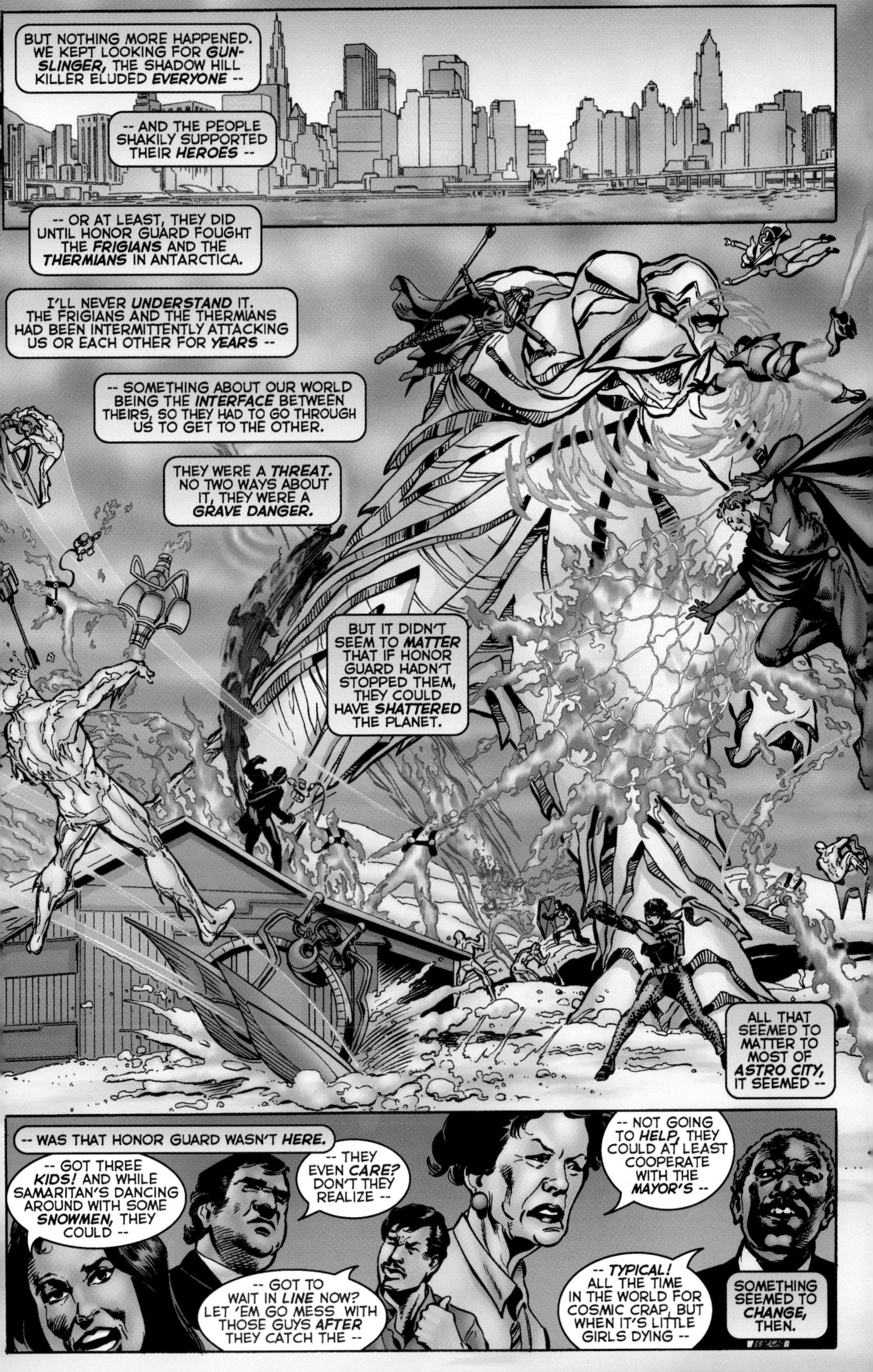
BUT NOTHING MORE HAPPENED. WE KEPT LOOKING FOR GUN-SLINGER, THE SHADOW HILL KILLER ELUDED EVERYONE --
-- AND THE PEOPLE SHAKILY SUPPORTED THEIR HEROES --
-- OR AT LEAST, THEY DID UNTIL HONOR GUARD FOUGHT THE FRIGIANS AND THE THERMIANS IN ANTARCTICA.
I'LL NEVER UNDERSTAND IT. THE FRIGIANS AND THE THERMIANS HAD BEEN INTERMITTENTLY ATTACKING US OR EACH OTHER FOR YEARS --
-- SOMETHING ABOUT OUR WORLD BEING THE INTERFACE BETWEEN THEIRS, SO THEY HAD TO GO THROUGH US TO GET TO THE OTHER.
THEY WERE A THREAT. NO TWO WAYS ABOUT IT, THEY WERE A GRAVE DANGER.
BUT IT DIDN'T SEEM TO MATTER THAT IF HONOR GUARD HADN'T STOPPED THEM, THEY COULD HAVE SHATTERED THE PLANET.
ALL THAT SEEMED TO MATTER TO MOST OF ASTRO CITY, IT SEEMED --
-- WAS THAT HONOR GUARD WASN'T HERE.
-- GOT THREE KIDS! AND WHILE SAMARITAN'S DANCING AROUND WITH SOME SNOWMEN, THEY COULD --
-- THEY EVEN CARE? DON'T THEY REALIZE --
-- NOT GOING TO HELP, THEY COULD AT LEAST COOPERATE WITH THE MAYOR'S --
-- GOT TO WAIT IN LINE NOW? LET 'EM GO MESS WITH THOSE GUYS AFTER THEY CATCH THE --
-- TYPICAL! ALL THE TIME IN THE WORLD FOR COSMIC CRAP, BUT WHEN IT'S LITTLE GIRLS DYING --
SOMETHING SEEMED TO CHANGE, THEN.

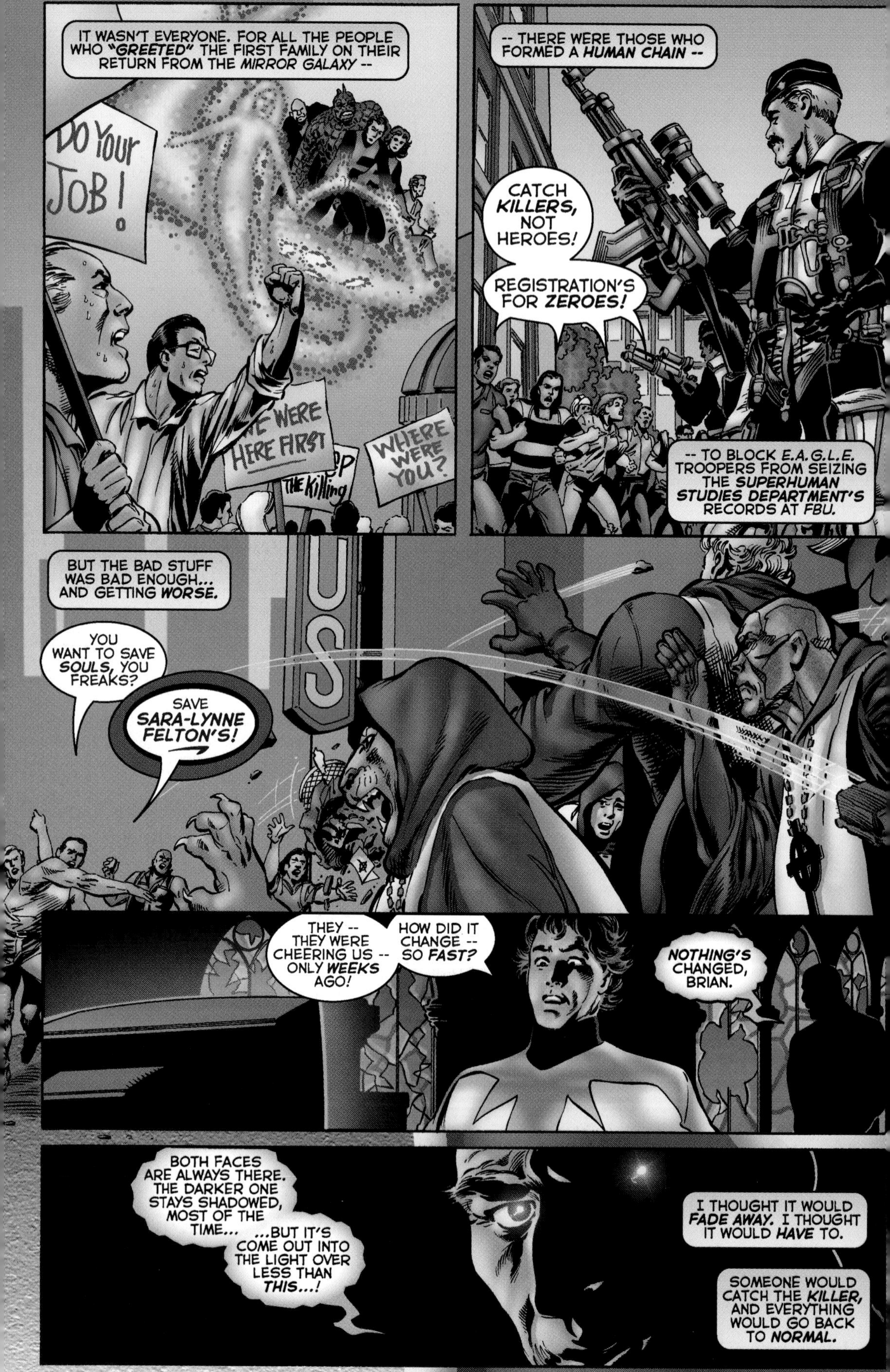
IT WASN'T EVERYONE. FOR ALL THE PEOPLE WHO "GREETED" THE FIRST FAMILY ON THEIR RETURN FROM THE MIRROR GALAXY --
DO YOUR JOB!
WHERE WERE YOU?
-- THERE WERE THOSE WHO FORMED A HUMAN CHAIN --
CATCH KILLERS, NOT HEROES!
REGISTRATION'S FOR ZEROES!
-- TO BLOCK E.A.G.L.E. TROOPERS FROM SEIZING THE SUPERHUMAN STUDIES DEPARTMENT'S RECORDS AT FBU.
BUT THE BAD STUFF WAS BAD ENOUGH... AND GETTING WORSE.
YOU WANT TO SAVE SOULS, YOU FREAKS?
SAVE SARA-LYNNE FELTON'S!
THEY -- THEY WERE CHEERING US -- ONLY WEEKS AGO!
HOW DID IT CHANGE -- SO FAST?
NOTHING'S CHANGED, BRIAN.
BOTH FACES ARE ALWAYS THERE. THE DARKER ONE STAYS SHADOWED, MOST OF THE TIME...
...BUT IT'S COME OUT INTO THE LIGHT OVER LESS THAN THIS...!
I THOUGHT IT WOULD FADE AWAY. I THOUGHT IT WOULD HAVE TO.
SOMEONE WOULD CATCH THE KILLER, AND EVERYTHING WOULD GO BACK TO NORMAL.

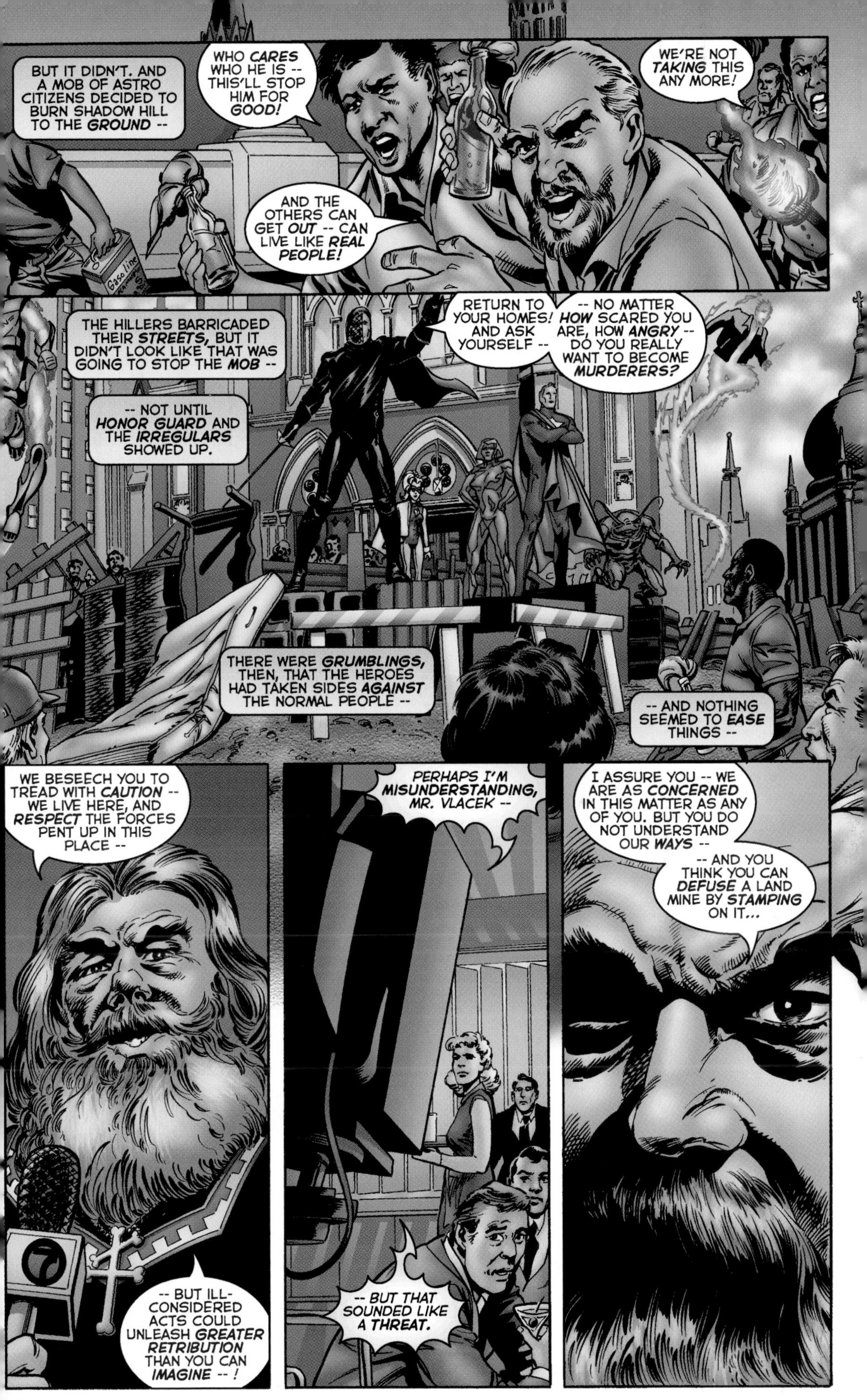
BUT IT DIDN'T. AND A MOB OF ASTRO CITIZENS DECIDED TO BURN SHADOW HILL TO THE GROUND --
WHO CARES WHO HE IS -- THIS'LL STOP HIM FOR GOOD!
WE'RE NOT TAKING THIS ANY MORE!
AND THE OTHERS CAN GET OUT -- CAN LIVE LIKE REAL PEOPLE!
Gasoline
THE HILLERS BARRICADED THEIR STREETS, BUT IT DIDN'T LOOK LIKE THAT WAS GOING TO STOP THE MOB --
-- NOT UNTIL HONOR GUARD AND THE IRREGULARS SHOWED UP.
RETURN TO YOUR HOMES! AND ASK YOURSELF --
-- NO MATTER HOW SCARED YOU ARE, HOW ANGRY -- DO YOU REALLY WANT TO BECOME MURDERERS?
THERE WERE GRUMBLINGS, THEN, THAT THE HEROES HAD TAKEN SIDES AGAINST THE NORMAL PEOPLE --
-- AND NOTHING SEEMED TO EASE THINGS --
WE BESEECH YOU TO TREAD WITH CAUTION -- WE LIVE HERE, AND RESPECT THE FORCES PENT UP IN THIS PLACE --
-- BUT ILL-CONSIDERED ACTS COULD UNLEASH GREATER RETRIBUTION THAN YOU CAN IMAGINE -- !
7
PERHAPS I'M MISUNDERSTANDING, MR. VLACEK --
-- BUT THAT SOUNDED LIKE A THREAT.
I ASSURE YOU -- WE ARE AS CONCERNED IN THIS MATTER AS ANY OF YOU. BUT YOU DO NOT UNDERSTAND OUR WAYS --
-- AND YOU THINK YOU CAN DEFUSE A LAND MINE BY STAMPING ON IT...

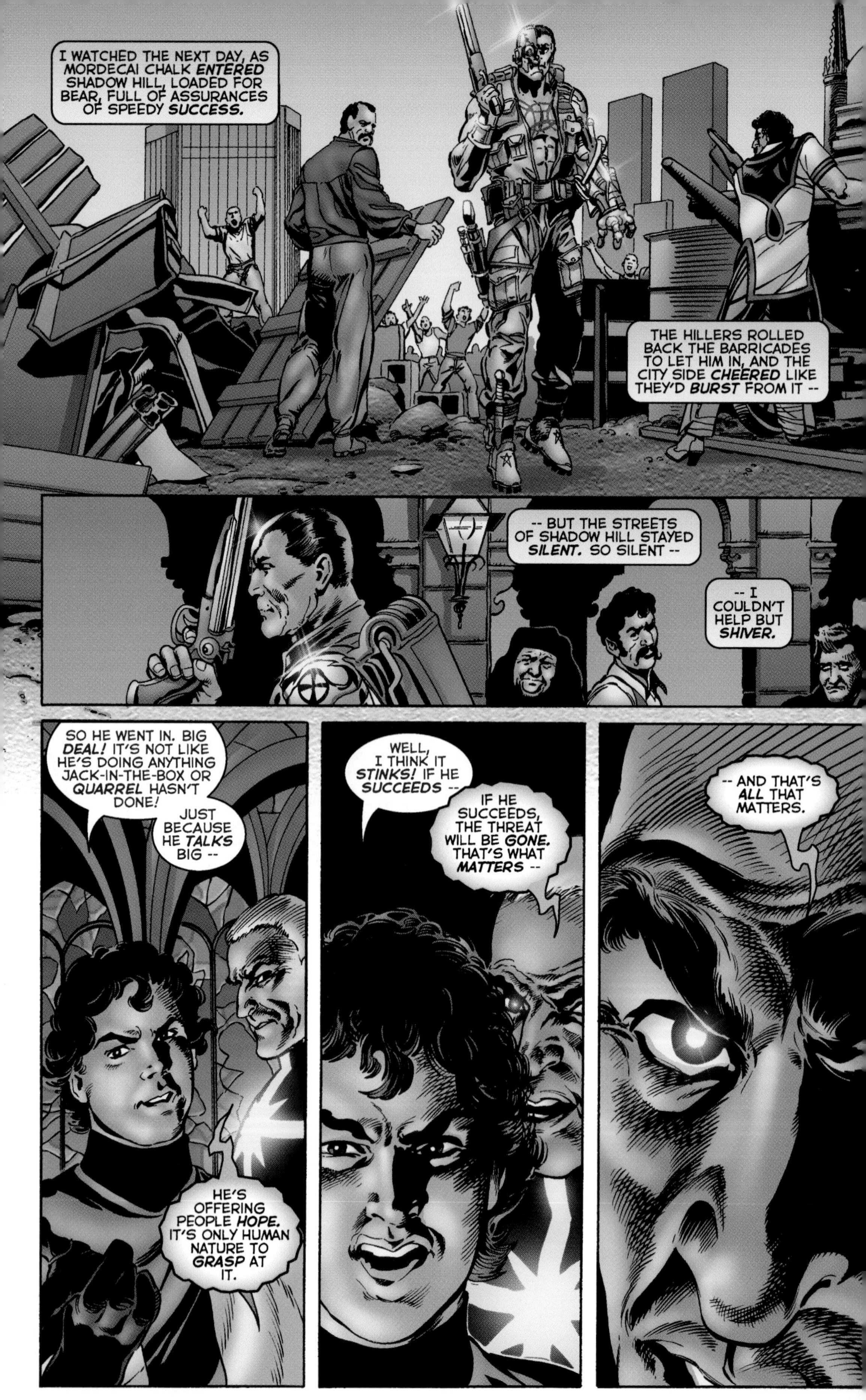
I WATCHED THE NEXT DAY, AS MORDECAI CHALK ENTERED SHADOW HILL, LOADED FOR BEAR, FULL OF ASSURANCES OF SPEEDY SUCCESS.
THE HILLERS ROLLED BACK THE BARRICADES TO LET HIM IN, AND THE CITY SIDE CHEERED LIKE THEY'D BURST FROM IT --
-- BUT THE STREETS OF SHADOW HILL STAYED SILENT. SO SILENT --
-- I COULDN'T HELP BUT SHIVER.
SO HE WENT IN. BIG DEAL! IT'S NOT LIKE HE'S DOING ANYTHING JACK-IN-THE-BOX OR QUARREL HASN'T DONE!
JUST BECAUSE HE TALKS BIG --
HE'S OFFERING PEOPLE HOPE. IT'S ONLY HUMAN NATURE TO GRASP AT IT.
WELL, I THINK IT STINKS! IF HE SUCCEEDS --
IF HE SUCCEEDS, THE THREAT WILL BE GONE. THAT'S WHAT MATTERS --
-- AND THAT'S ALL THAT MATTERS.

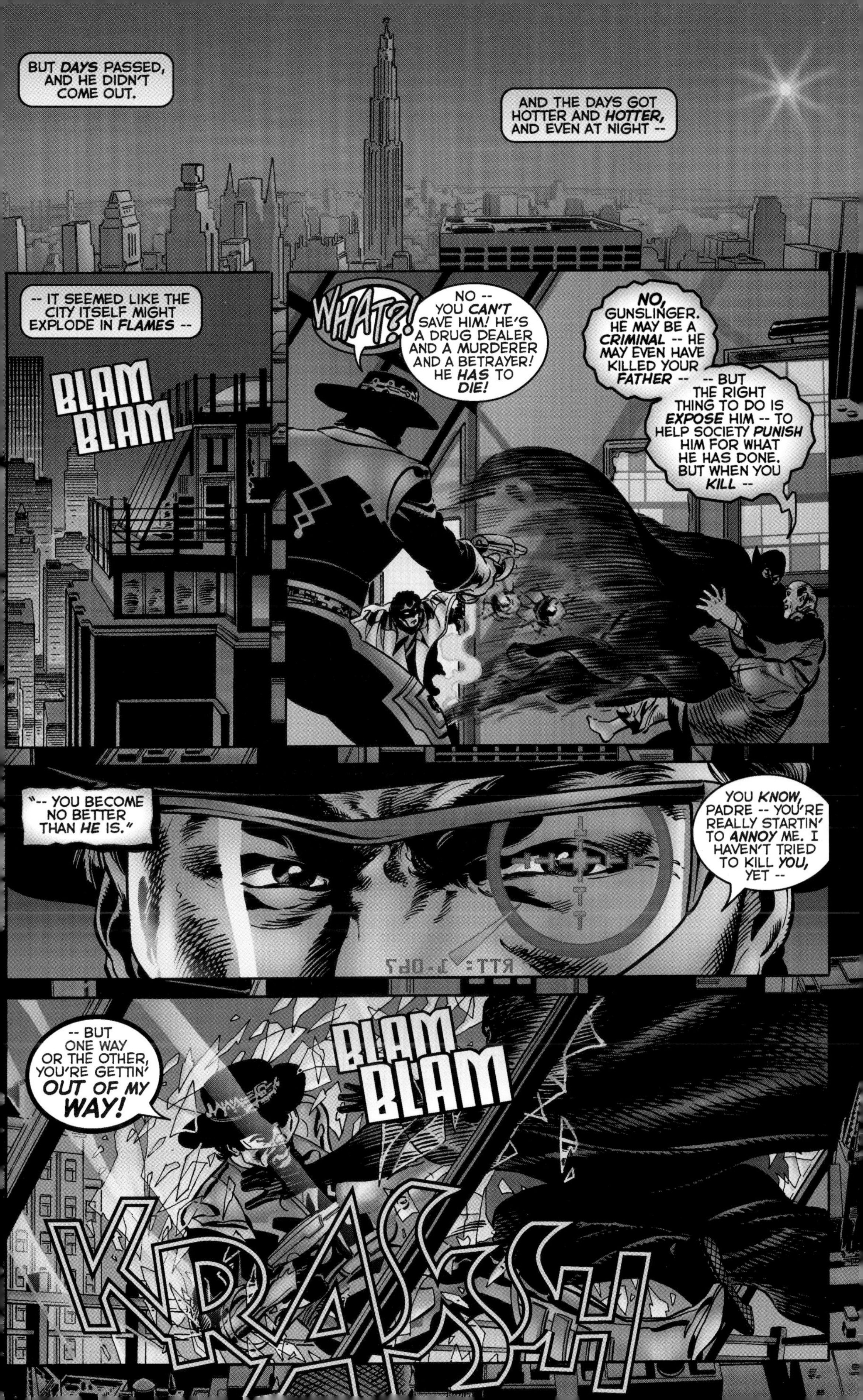

BUT DAYS PASSED, AND HE DIDN'T COME OUT.
AND THE DAYS GOT HOTTER AND HOTTER, AND EVEN AT NIGHT --
-- IT SEEMED LIKE THE CITY ITSELF MIGHT EXPLODE IN FLAMES --
BLAM BLAM
WHAT?!
NO -- YOU CAN'T SAVE HIM! HE'S A DRUG DEALER AND A MURDERER AND A BETRAYER! HE HAS TO DIE!
NO, GUNSLINGER. HE MAY BE A CRIMINAL -- HE MAY EVEN HAVE KILLED YOUR FATHER --
-- BUT THE RIGHT THING TO DO IS EXPOSE HIM -- TO HELP SOCIETY PUNISH HIM FOR WHAT HE HAS DONE. BUT WHEN YOU KILL --
"-- YOU BECOME NO BETTER THAN HE IS."
YOU KNOW, PADRE -- YOU'RE REALLY STARTIN' TO ANNOY ME. I HAVEN'T TRIED TO KILL YOU, YET --
-- BUT ONE WAY OR THE OTHER, YOU'RE GETTIN' OUT OF MY WAY!
BLAM BLAM
KRASSH

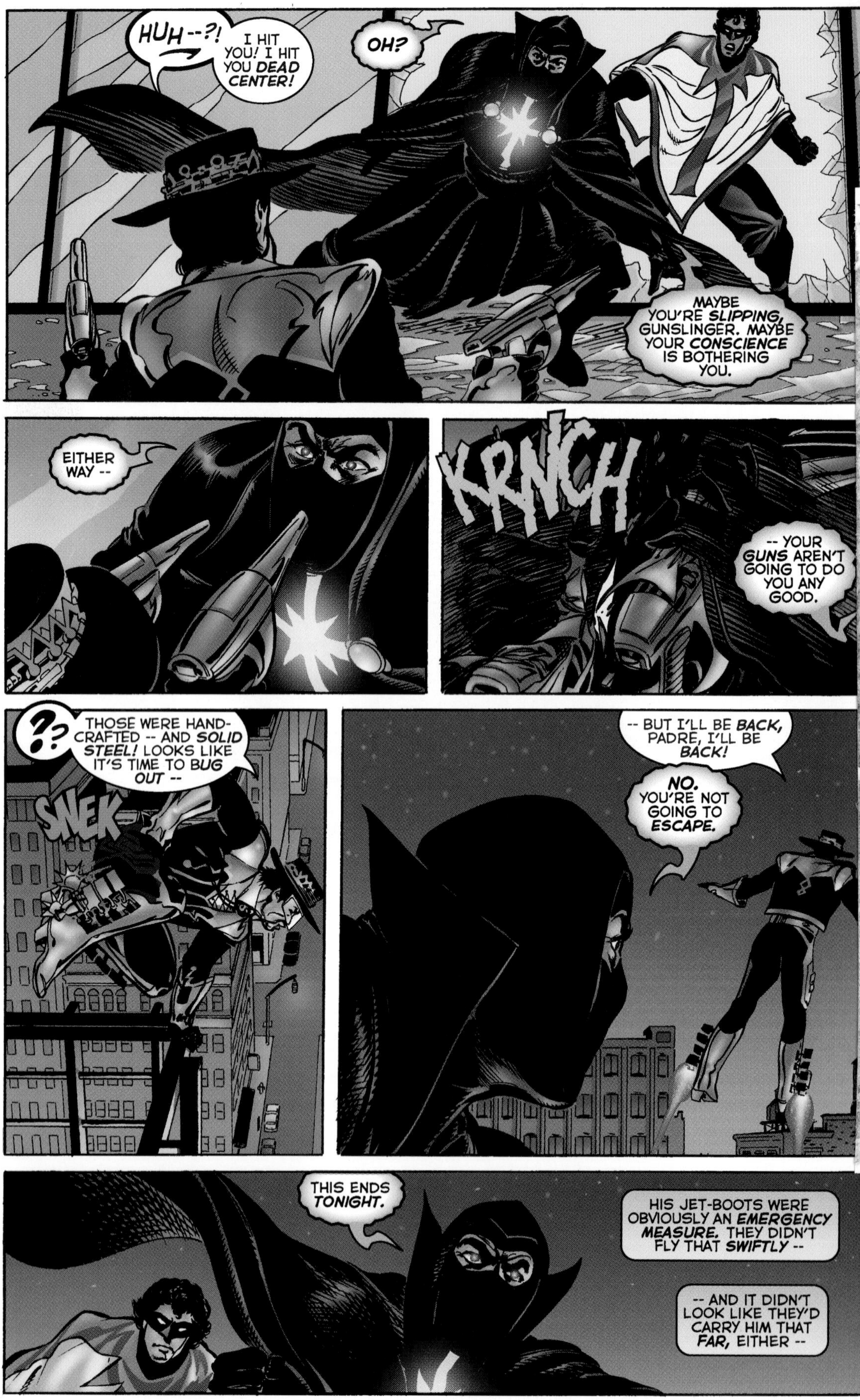
HUH --?!
I HIT YOU! I HIT YOU DEAD CENTER!
OH?
MAYBE YOU'RE SLIPPING, GUNSLINGER. MAYBE YOUR CONSCIENCE IS BOTHERING YOU.
EITHER WAY --
KRNCH
-- YOUR GUNS AREN'T GOING TO DO YOU ANY GOOD.
??
THOSE WERE HAND-CRAFTED -- AND SOLID STEEL! LOOKS LIKE IT'S TIME TO BUG OUT --
SWEK
-- BUT I'LL BE BACK, PADRE, I'LL BE BACK!
NO. YOU'RE NOT GOING TO ESCAPE.
THIS ENDS TONIGHT.
HIS JET-BOOTS WERE OBVIOUSLY AN EMERGENCY MEASURE. THEY DIDN'T FLY THAT SWIFTLY --
-- AND IT DIDN'T LOOK LIKE THEY'D CARRY HIM THAT FAR, EITHER --

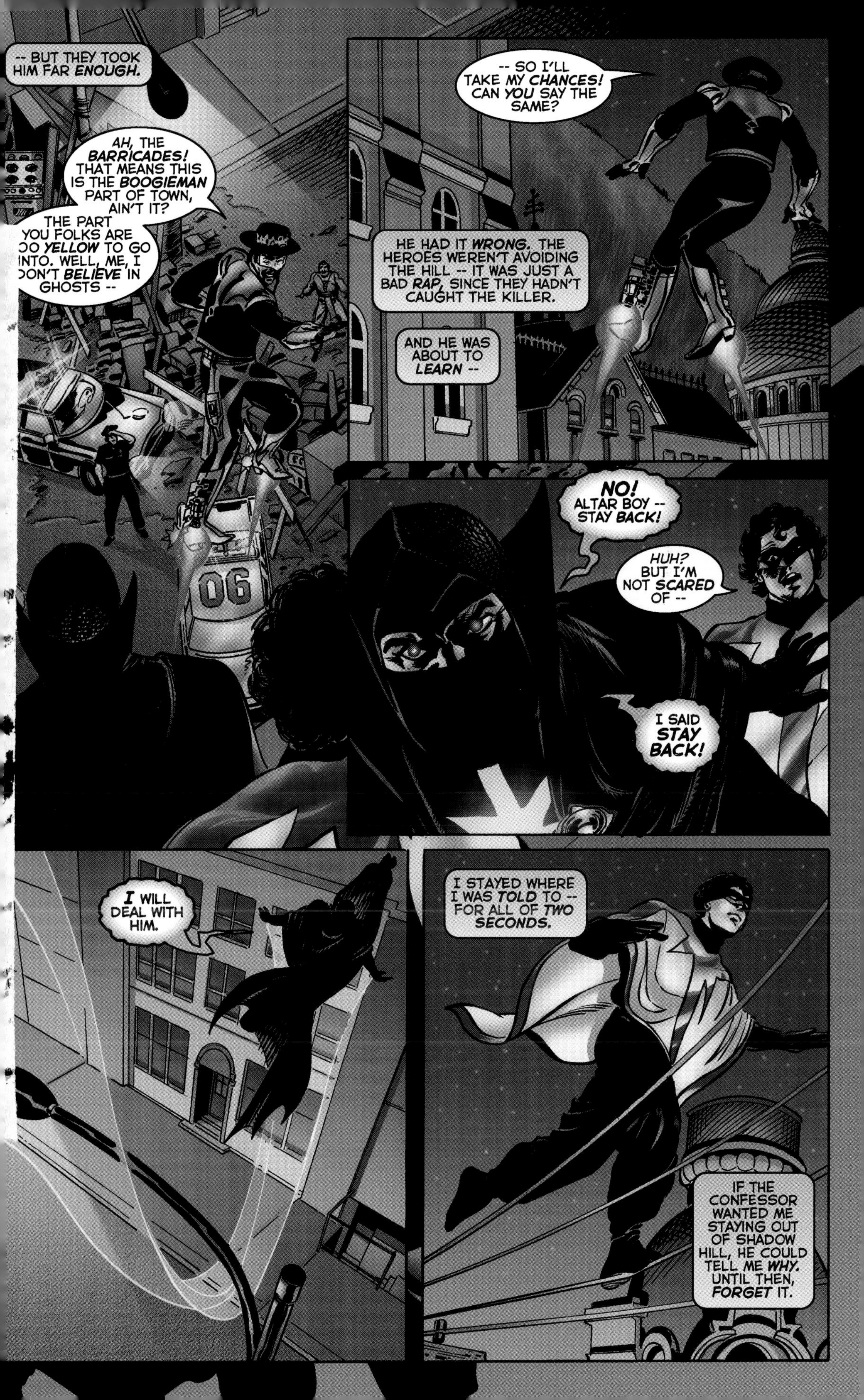
-- BUT THEY TOOK HIM FAR ENOUGH.
AH, THE BARRICADES! THAT MEANS THIS IS THE BOOGIEMAN PART OF TOWN, AIN'T IT?
THE PART YOU FOLKS ARE TOO YELLOW TO GO INTO. WELL, ME, I DON'T BELIEVE IN GHOSTS --
-- SO I'LL TAKE MY CHANCES! CAN YOU SAY THE SAME?
HE HAD IT WRONG. THE HEROES WEREN'T AVOIDING THE HILL -- IT WAS JUST A BAD RAP, SINCE THEY HADN'T CAUGHT THE KILLER.
AND HE WAS ABOUT TO LEARN --
06
NO! ALTAR BOY -- STAY BACK!
HUH? BUT I'M NOT SCARED OF --
I SAID STAY BACK!
I WILL DEAL WITH HIM.
I STAYED WHERE I WAS TOLD TO -- FOR ALL OF TWO SECONDS.
IF THE CONFESSOR WANTED ME STAYING OUT OF SHADOW HILL, HE COULD TELL ME WHY. UNTIL THEN, FORGET IT.

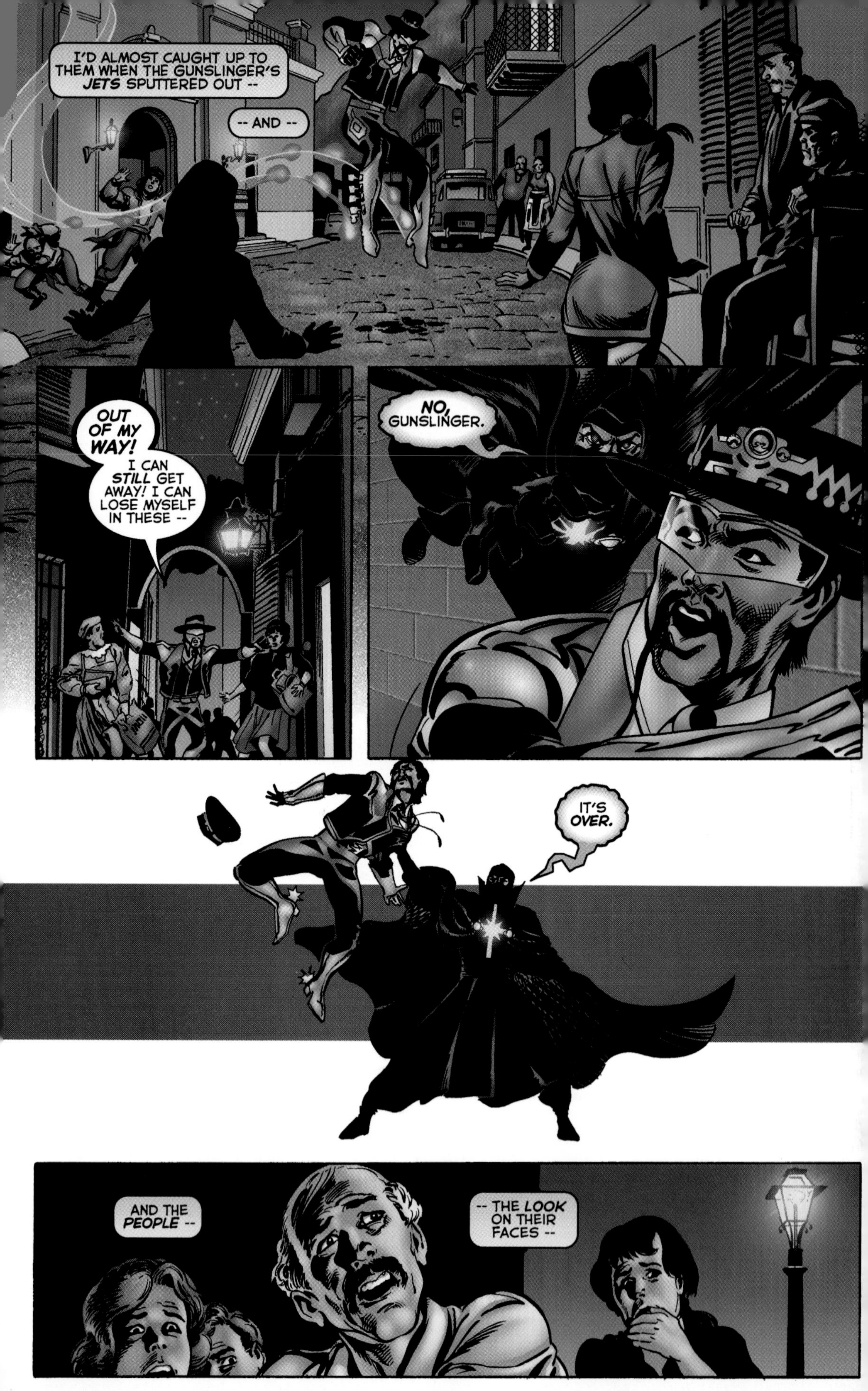
I'D ALMOST CAUGHT UP TO THEM WHEN THE GUNSLINGER'S *JETS* SPUTTERED OUT --
-- AND --
OUT OF MY WAY! I CAN *STILL* GET AWAY! I CAN LOSE MYSELF IN THESE --
NO, GUNSLINGER.
IT'S *OVER.*
AND THE *PEOPLE* --
-- THE *LOOK* ON THEIR FACES --

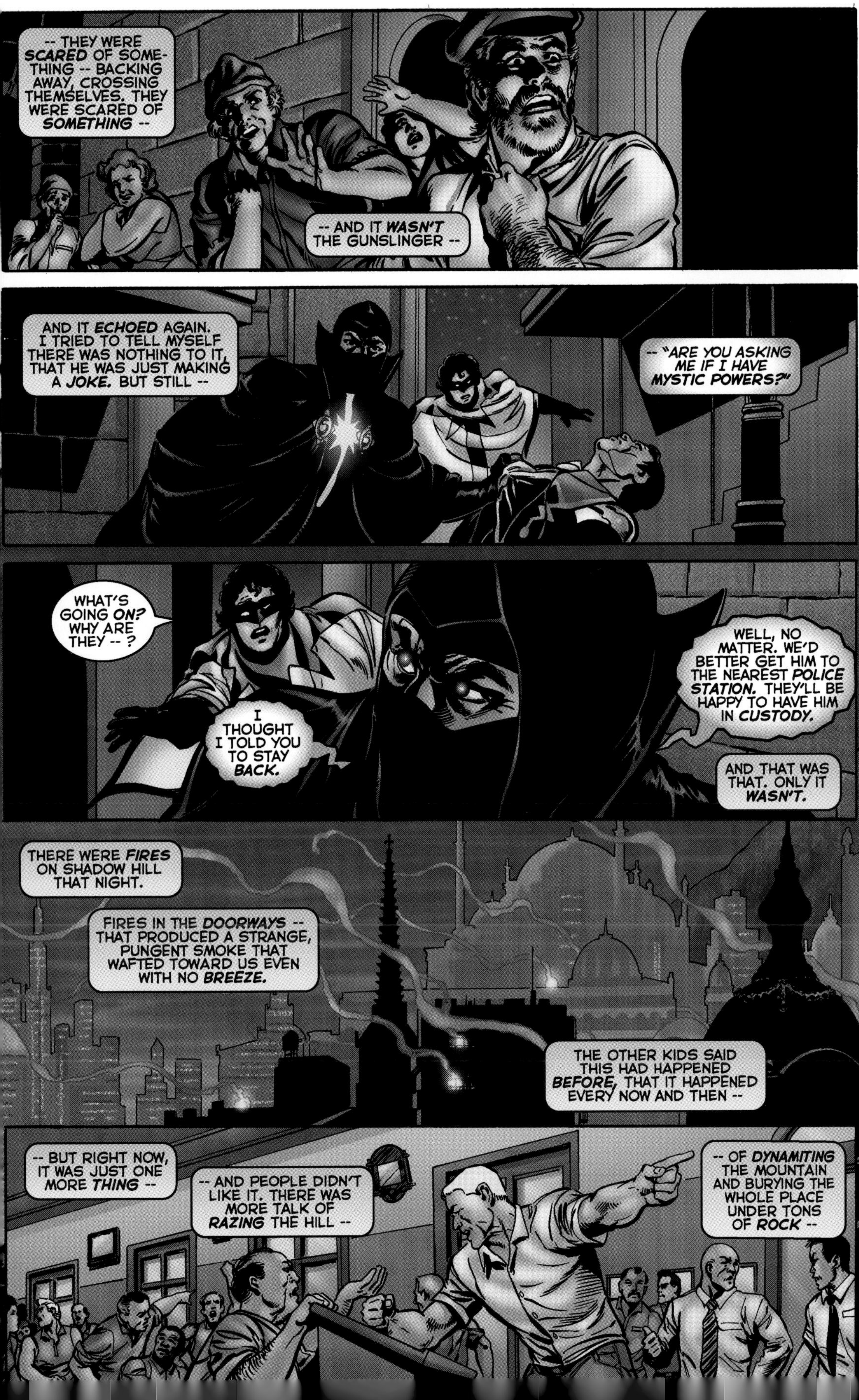
-- THEY WERE SCARED OF SOMETHING -- BACKING AWAY, CROSSING THEMSELVES. THEY WERE SCARED OF SOMETHING --
-- AND IT WASN'T THE GUNSLINGER --
AND IT ECHOED AGAIN. I TRIED TO TELL MYSELF THERE WAS NOTHING TO IT, THAT HE WAS JUST MAKING A JOKE. BUT STILL --
-- "ARE YOU ASKING ME IF I HAVE MYSTIC POWERS?"
WHAT'S GOING ON? WHY ARE THEY -- ?
I THOUGHT I TOLD YOU TO STAY BACK.
WELL, NO MATTER. WE'D BETTER GET HIM TO THE NEAREST POLICE STATION. THEY'LL BE HAPPY TO HAVE HIM IN CUSTODY.
AND THAT WAS THAT. ONLY IT WASN'T.
THERE WERE FIRES ON SHADOW HILL THAT NIGHT.
FIRES IN THE DOORWAYS -- THAT PRODUCED A STRANGE, PUNGENT SMOKE THAT WAFTED TOWARD US EVEN WITH NO BREEZE.
THE OTHER KIDS SAID THIS HAD HAPPENED BEFORE, THAT IT HAPPENED EVERY NOW AND THEN --
-- BUT RIGHT NOW, IT WAS JUST ONE MORE THING --
-- AND PEOPLE DIDN'T LIKE IT. THERE WAS MORE TALK OF RAZING THE HILL --
-- OF DYNAMITING THE MOUNTAIN AND BURYING THE WHOLE PLACE UNDER TONS OF ROCK --

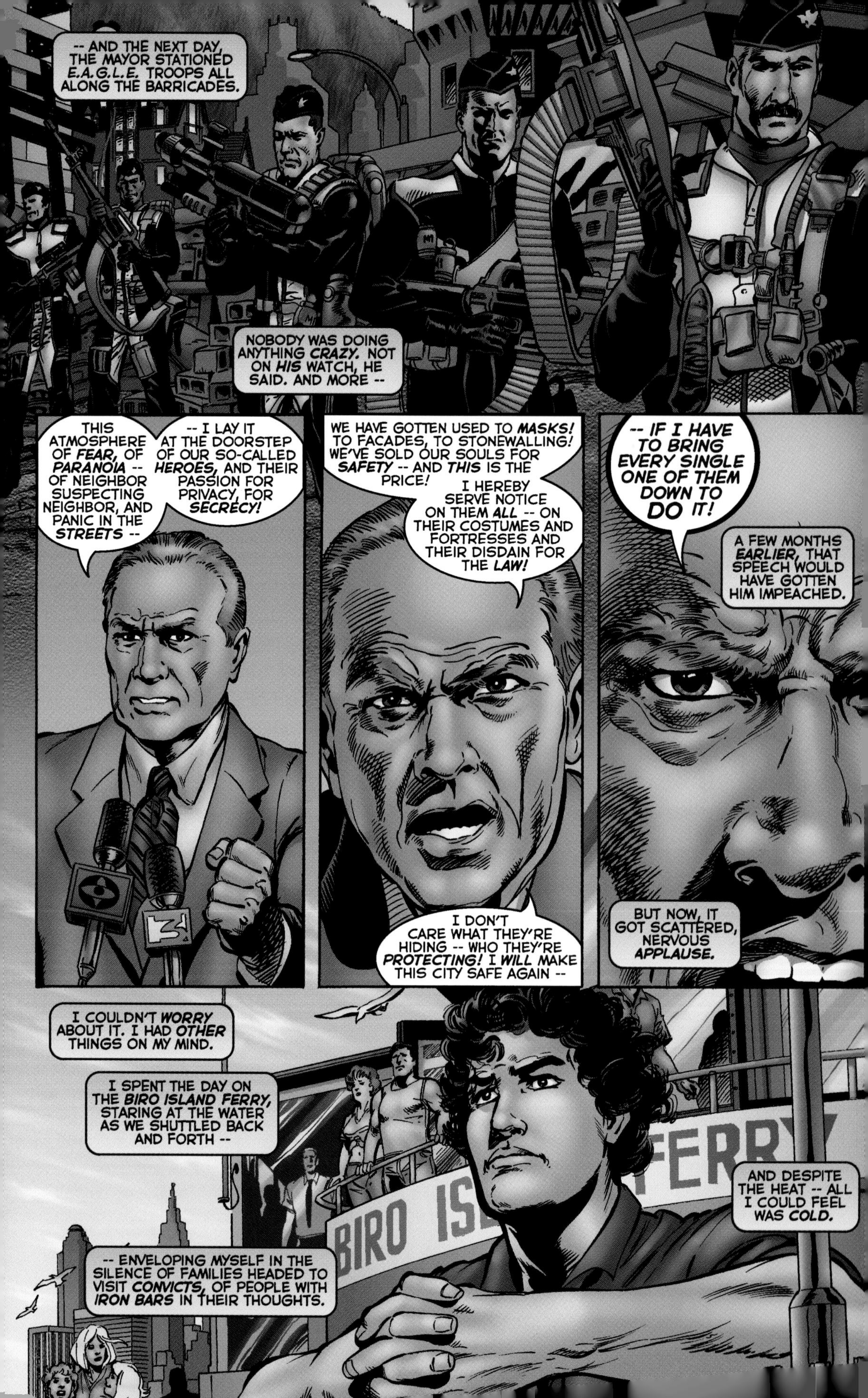
-- AND THE NEXT DAY, THE MAYOR STATIONED E.A.G.L.E. TROOPS ALL ALONG THE BARRICADES.
NOBODY WAS DOING ANYTHING CRAZY. NOT ON HIS WATCH, HE SAID. AND MORE --
THIS ATMOSPHERE OF FEAR, OF PARANOIA -- OF NEIGHBOR SUSPECTING NEIGHBOR, AND PANIC IN THE STREETS --
-- I LAY IT AT THE DOORSTEP OF OUR SO-CALLED HEROES, AND THEIR PASSION FOR PRIVACY, FOR SECRECY!
WE HAVE GOTTEN USED TO MASKS! TO FACADES, TO STONEWALLING! WE'VE SOLD OUR SOULS FOR SAFETY -- AND THIS IS THE PRICE!
I HEREBY SERVE NOTICE ON THEM ALL -- ON THEIR COSTUMES AND FORTRESSES AND THEIR DISDAIN FOR THE LAW!
I DON'T CARE WHAT THEY'RE HIDING -- WHO THEY'RE PROTECTING! I WILL MAKE THIS CITY SAFE AGAIN --
-- IF I HAVE TO BRING EVERY SINGLE ONE OF THEM DOWN TO DO IT!
A FEW MONTHS EARLIER, THAT SPEECH WOULD HAVE GOTTEN HIM IMPEACHED.
BUT NOW, IT GOT SCATTERED, NERVOUS APPLAUSE.
I COULDN'T WORRY ABOUT IT. I HAD OTHER THINGS ON MY MIND.
I SPENT THE DAY ON THE BIRO ISLAND FERRY, STARING AT THE WATER AS WE SHUTTLED BACK AND FORTH --
-- ENVELOPING MYSELF IN THE SILENCE OF FAMILIES HEADED TO VISIT CONVICTS, OF PEOPLE WITH IRON BARS IN THEIR THOUGHTS.
AND DESPITE THE HEAT -- ALL I COULD FEEL WAS COLD.

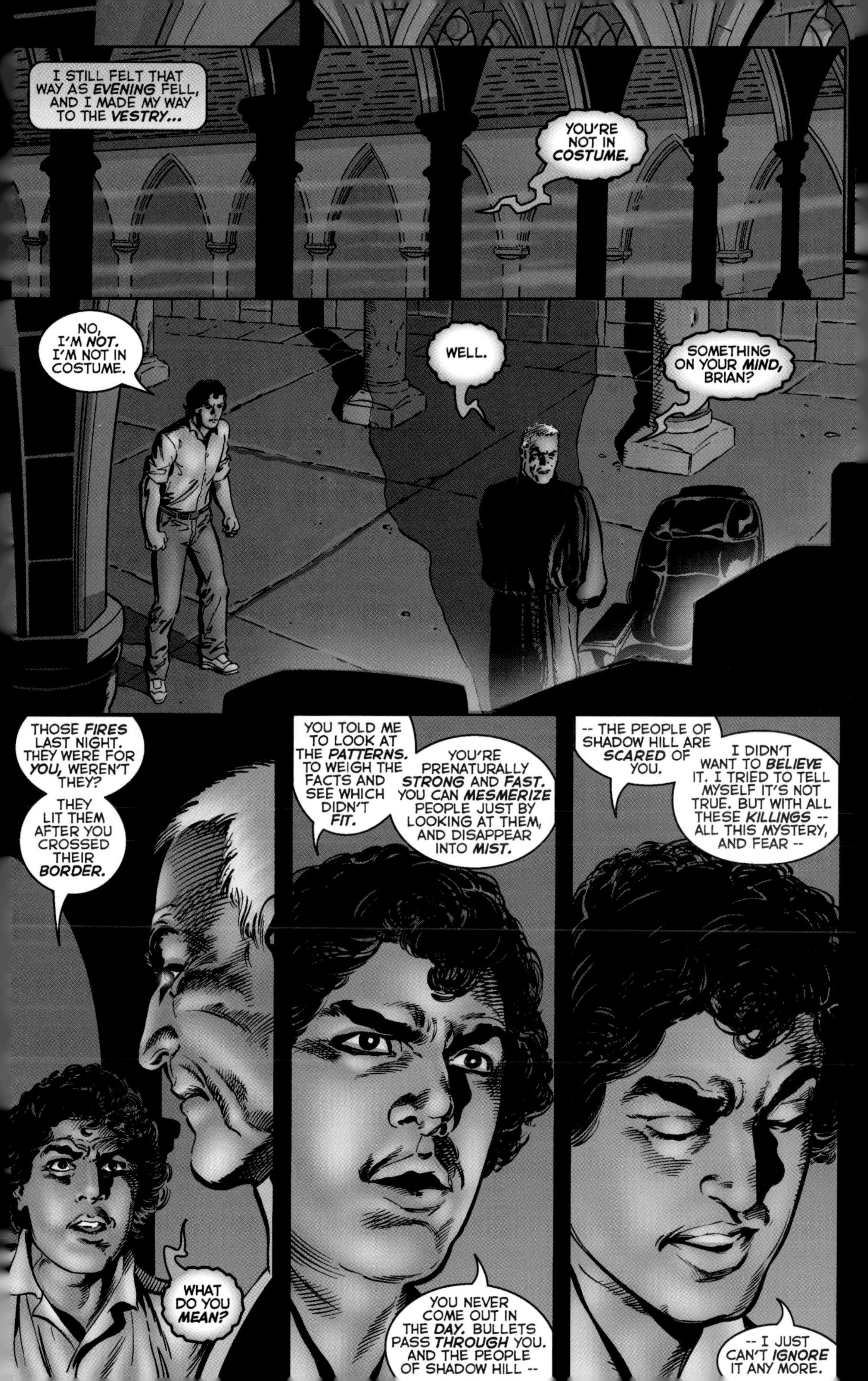
I STILL FELT THAT WAY AS EVENING FELL, AND I MADE MY WAY TO THE VESTRY...
YOU'RE NOT IN COSTUME.
NO, I'M NOT. I'M NOT IN COSTUME.
WELL.
SOMETHING ON YOUR MIND, BRIAN?
THOSE FIRES LAST NIGHT. THEY WERE FOR YOU, WEREN'T THEY?
THEY LIT THEM AFTER YOU CROSSED THEIR BORDER.
WHAT DO YOU MEAN?
YOU TOLD ME TO LOOK AT THE PATTERNS. TO WEIGH THE FACTS AND SEE WHICH DIDN'T FIT.
YOU'RE PRENATURALLY STRONG AND FAST. YOU CAN MESMERIZE PEOPLE JUST BY LOOKING AT THEM, AND DISAPPEAR INTO MIST.
YOU NEVER COME OUT IN THE DAY. BULLETS PASS THROUGH YOU. AND THE PEOPLE OF SHADOW HILL --
-- THE PEOPLE OF SHADOW HILL ARE SCARED OF YOU.
I DIDN'T WANT TO BELIEVE IT. I TRIED TO TELL MYSELF IT'S NOT TRUE. BUT WITH ALL THESE KILLINGS -- ALL THIS MYSTERY, AND FEAR --
-- I JUST CAN'T IGNORE IT ANY MORE.

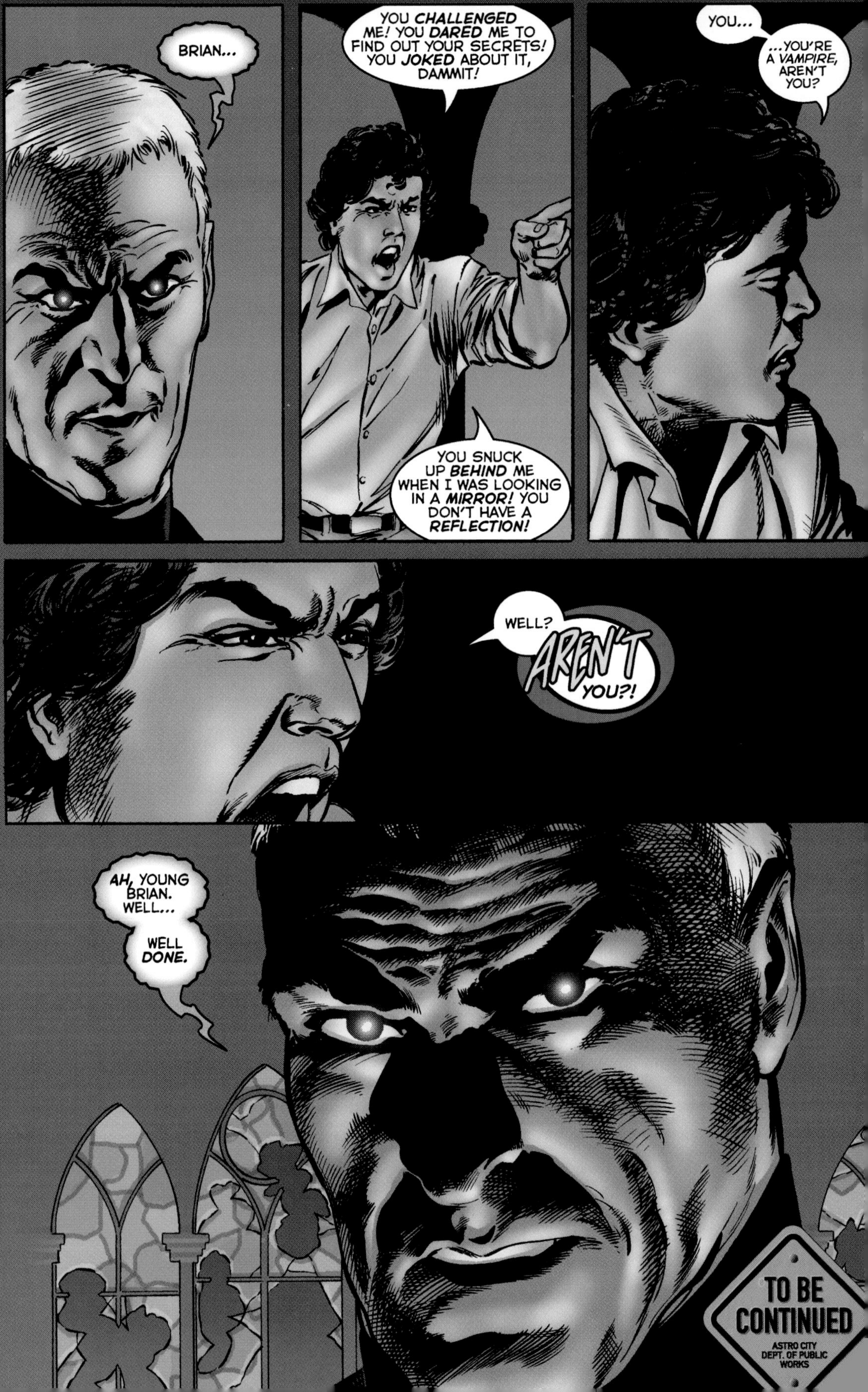
BRIAN...
YOU CHALLENGED ME! YOU DARED ME TO FIND OUT YOUR SECRETS! YOU JOKED ABOUT IT, DAMMIT!
YOU SNUCK UP BEHIND ME WHEN I WAS LOOKING IN A MIRROR! YOU DON'T HAVE A REFLECTION!
YOU...
...YOU'RE A VAMPIRE, AREN'T YOU?
WELL?
AREN'T YOU?!
AH, YOUNG BRIAN. WELL...
WELL DONE.
TO BE CONTINUED
ASTRO CITY DEPT. OF PUBLIC WORKS

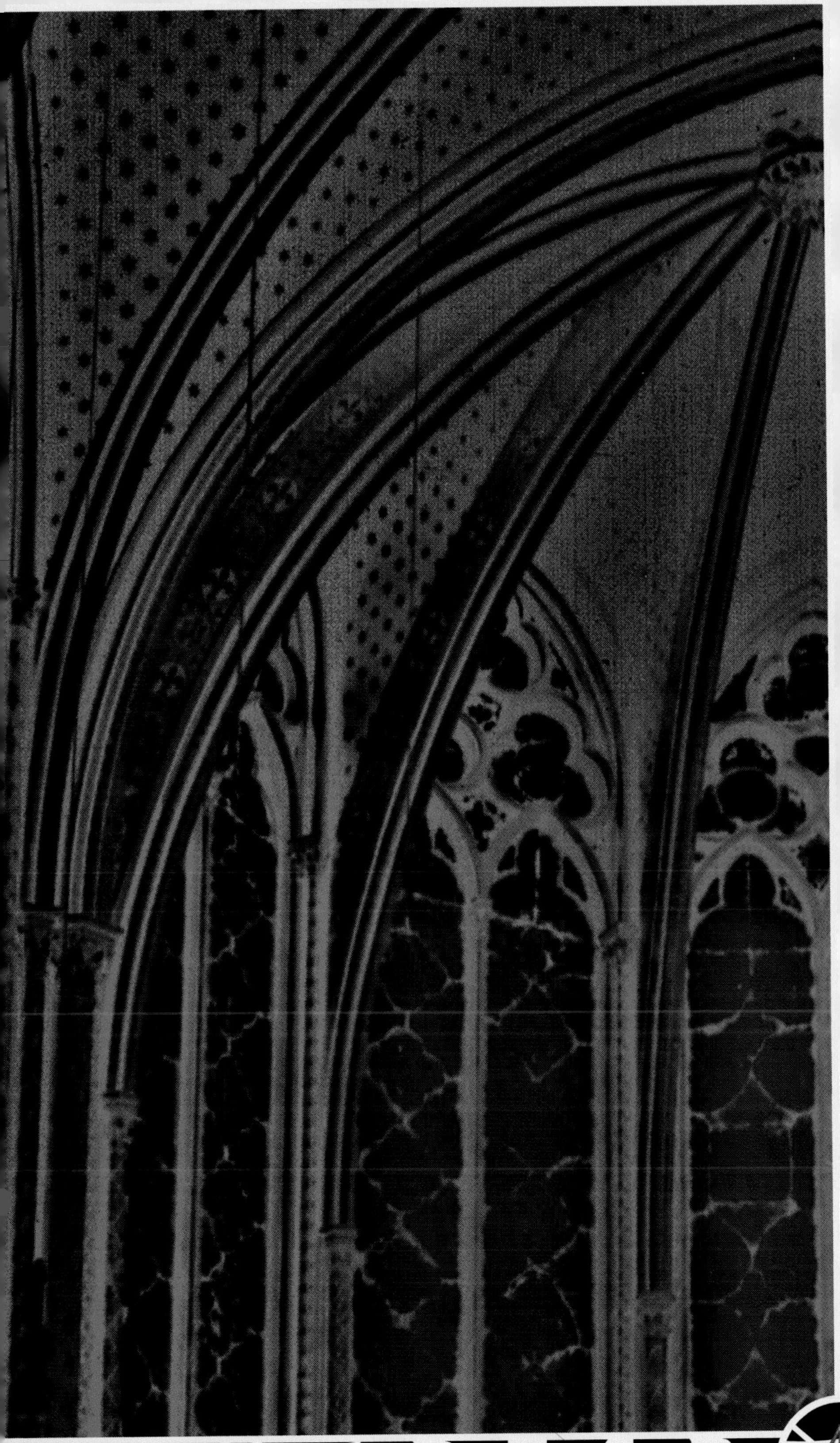

CHAPTER

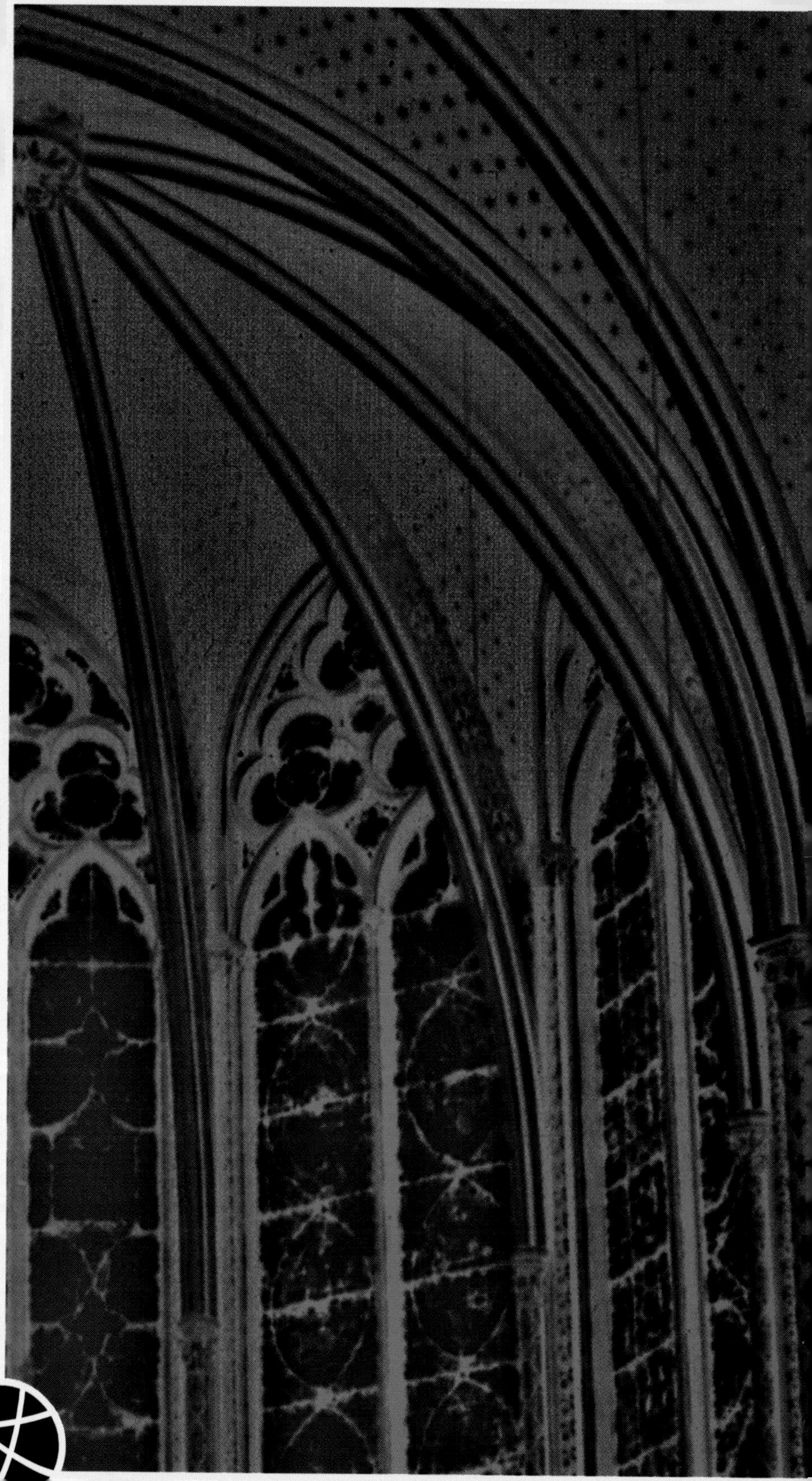

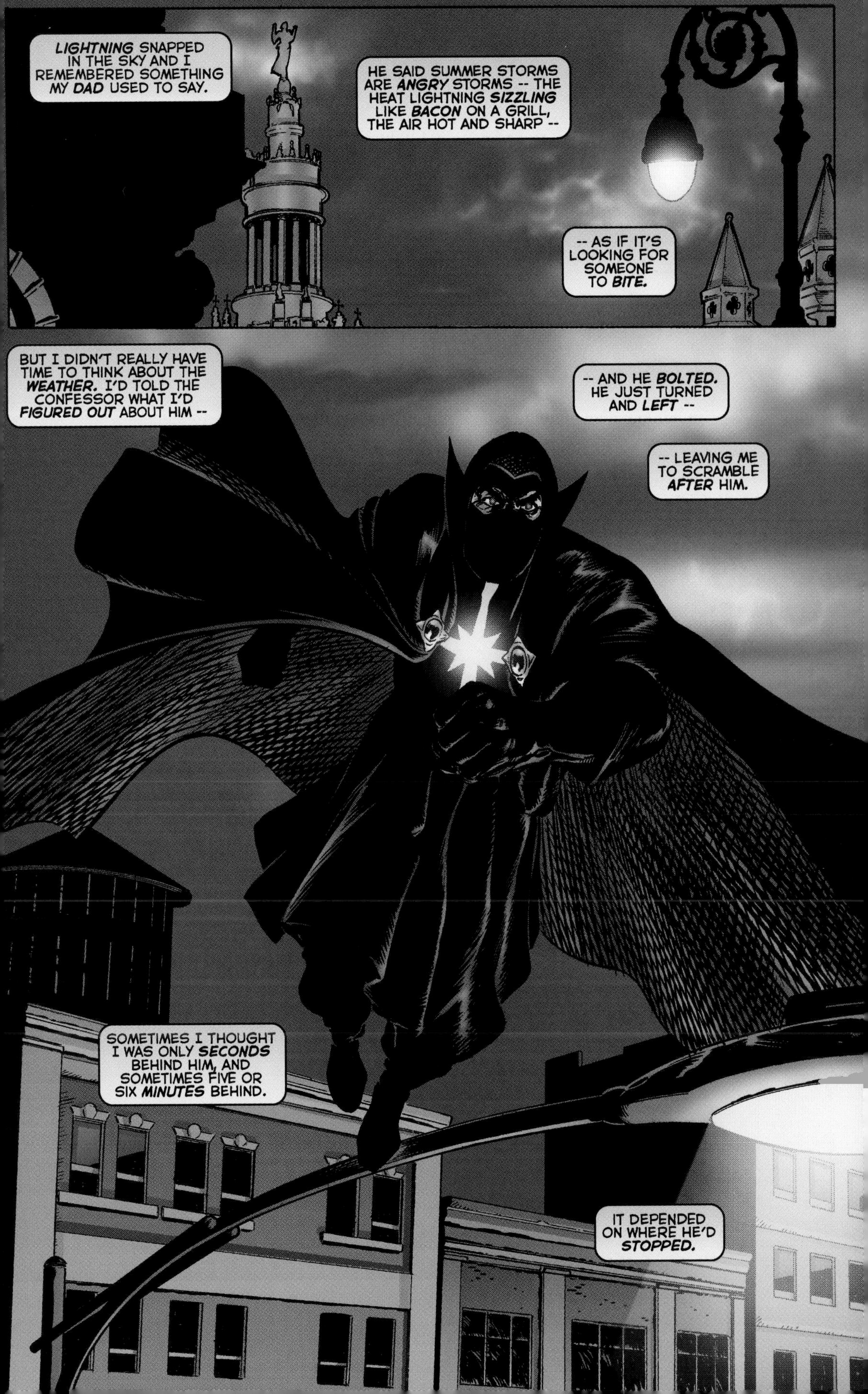
LIGHTNING SNAPPED IN THE SKY AND I REMEMBERED SOMETHING MY DAD USED TO SAY.
HE SAID SUMMER STORMS ARE ANGRY STORMS -- THE HEAT LIGHTNING SIZZLING LIKE BACON ON A GRILL, THE AIR HOT AND SHARP --
-- AS IF IT'S LOOKING FOR SOMEONE TO BITE.
BUT I DIDN'T REALLY HAVE TIME TO THINK ABOUT THE WEATHER. I'D TOLD THE CONFESSOR WHAT I'D FIGURED OUT ABOUT HIM --
-- AND HE BOLTED. HE JUST TURNED AND LEFT --
-- LEAVING ME TO SCRAMBLE AFTER HIM.
SOMETIMES I THOUGHT I WAS ONLY SECONDS BEHIND HIM, AND SOMETIMES FIVE OR SIX MINUTES BEHIND.
IT DEPENDED ON WHERE HE'D STOPPED.

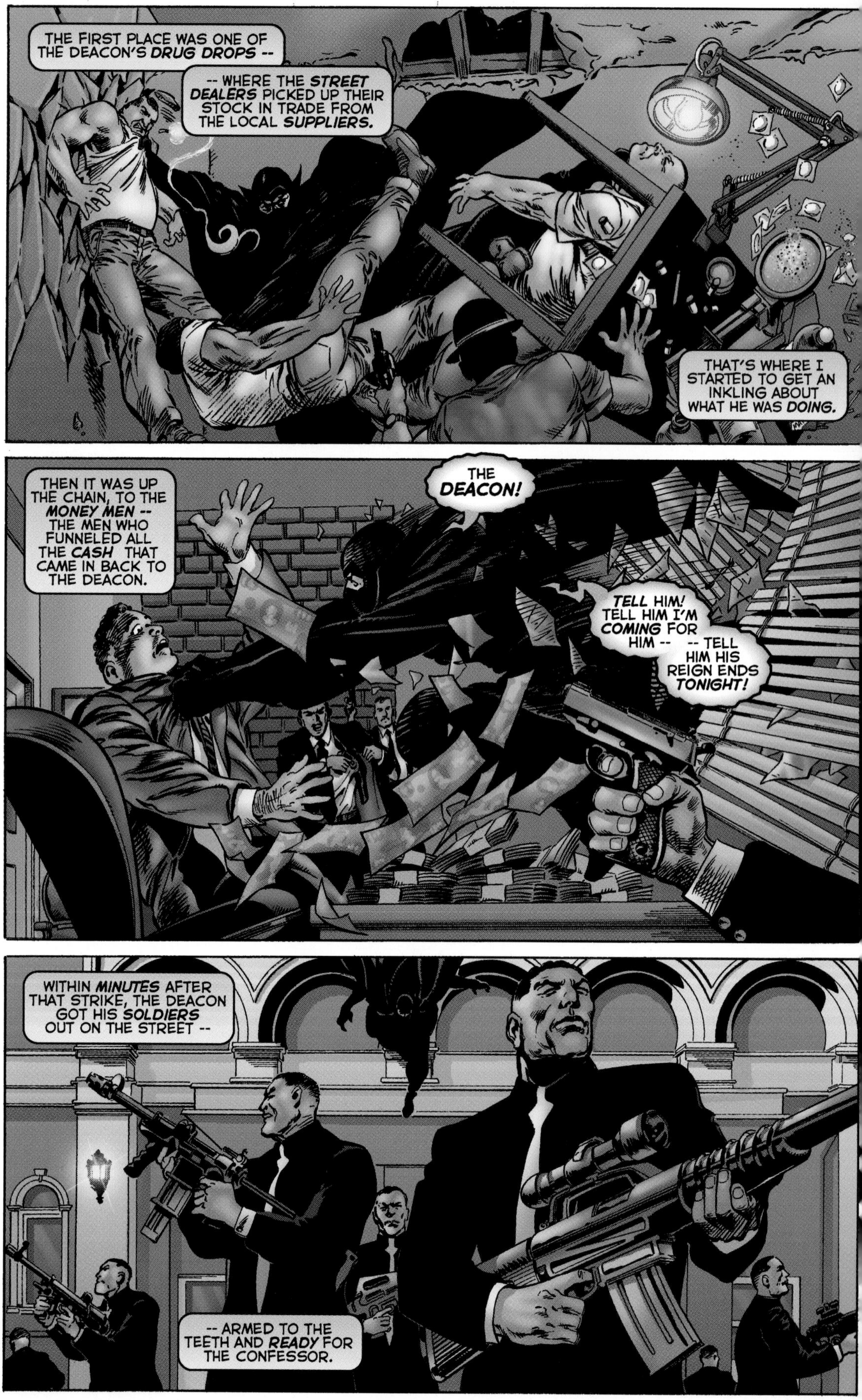
THE FIRST PLACE WAS ONE OF THE DEACON'S DRUG DROPS --
-- WHERE THE STREET DEALERS PICKED UP THEIR STOCK IN TRADE FROM THE LOCAL SUPPLIERS.
THAT'S WHERE I STARTED TO GET AN INKLING ABOUT WHAT HE WAS DOING.
THEN IT WAS UP THE CHAIN, TO THE MONEY MEN -- THE MEN WHO FUNNELED ALL THE CASH THAT CAME IN BACK TO THE DEACON.
THE DEACON!
TELL HIM! TELL HIM I'M COMING FOR HIM --
-- TELL HIM HIS REIGN ENDS TONIGHT!
WITHIN MINUTES AFTER THAT STRIKE, THE DEACON GOT HIS SOLDIERS OUT ON THE STREET --
-- ARMED TO THE TEETH AND READY FOR THE CONFESSOR.

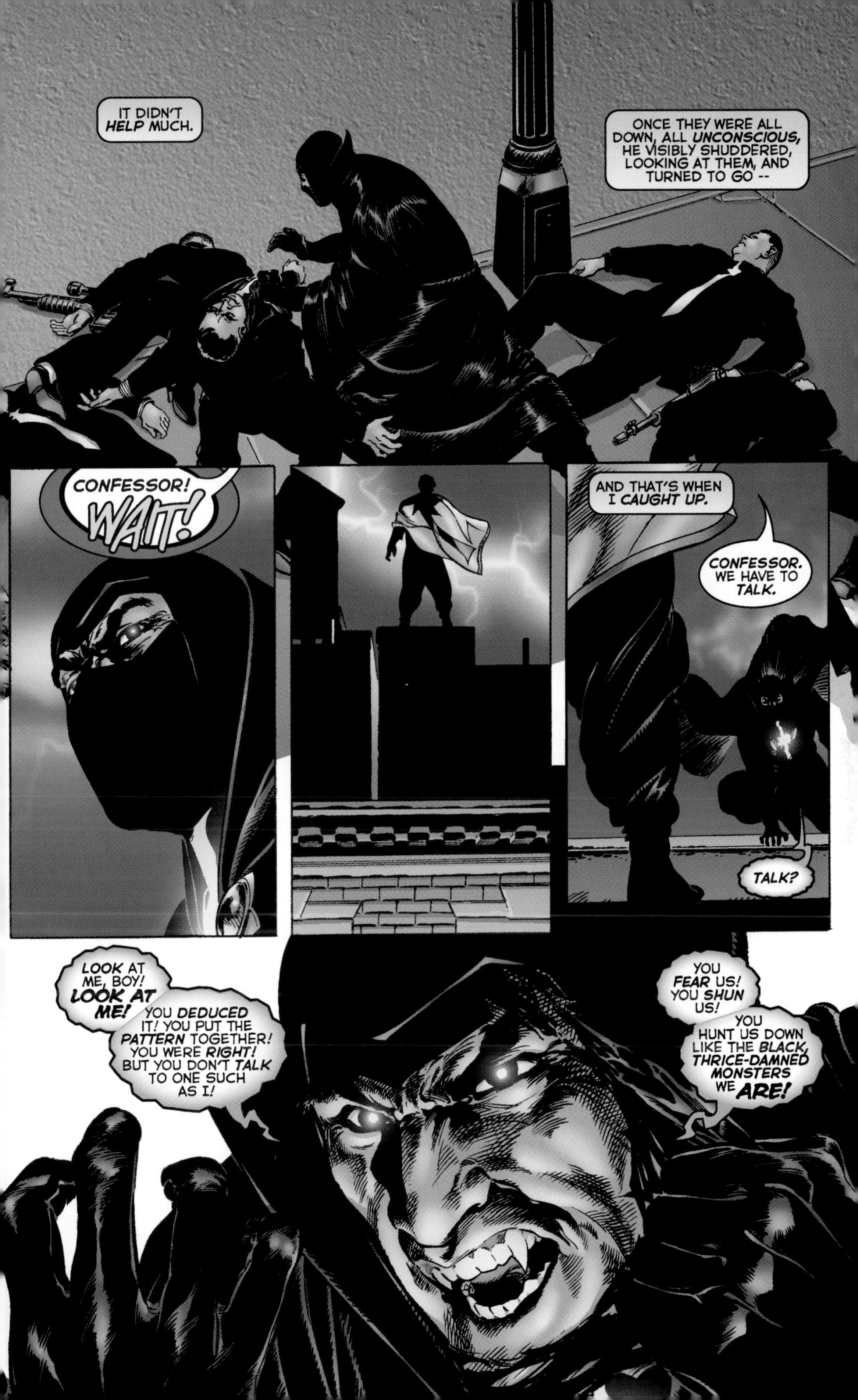
IT DIDN'T HELP MUCH.
ONCE THEY WERE ALL DOWN, ALL UNCONSCIOUS, HE VISIBLY SHUDDERED, LOOKING AT THEM, AND TURNED TO GO --
CONFESSOR! WAIT!
AND THAT'S WHEN I CAUGHT UP.
CONFESSOR. WE HAVE TO TALK.
TALK?
LOOK AT ME, BOY! LOOK AT ME!
YOU DEDUCED IT! YOU PUT THE PATTERN TOGETHER! YOU WERE RIGHT! BUT YOU DON'T TALK TO ONE SUCH AS I!
YOU FEAR US! YOU SHUN US!
YOU HUNT US DOWN LIKE THE BLACK, THRICE-DAMNED MONSTERS WE ARE!

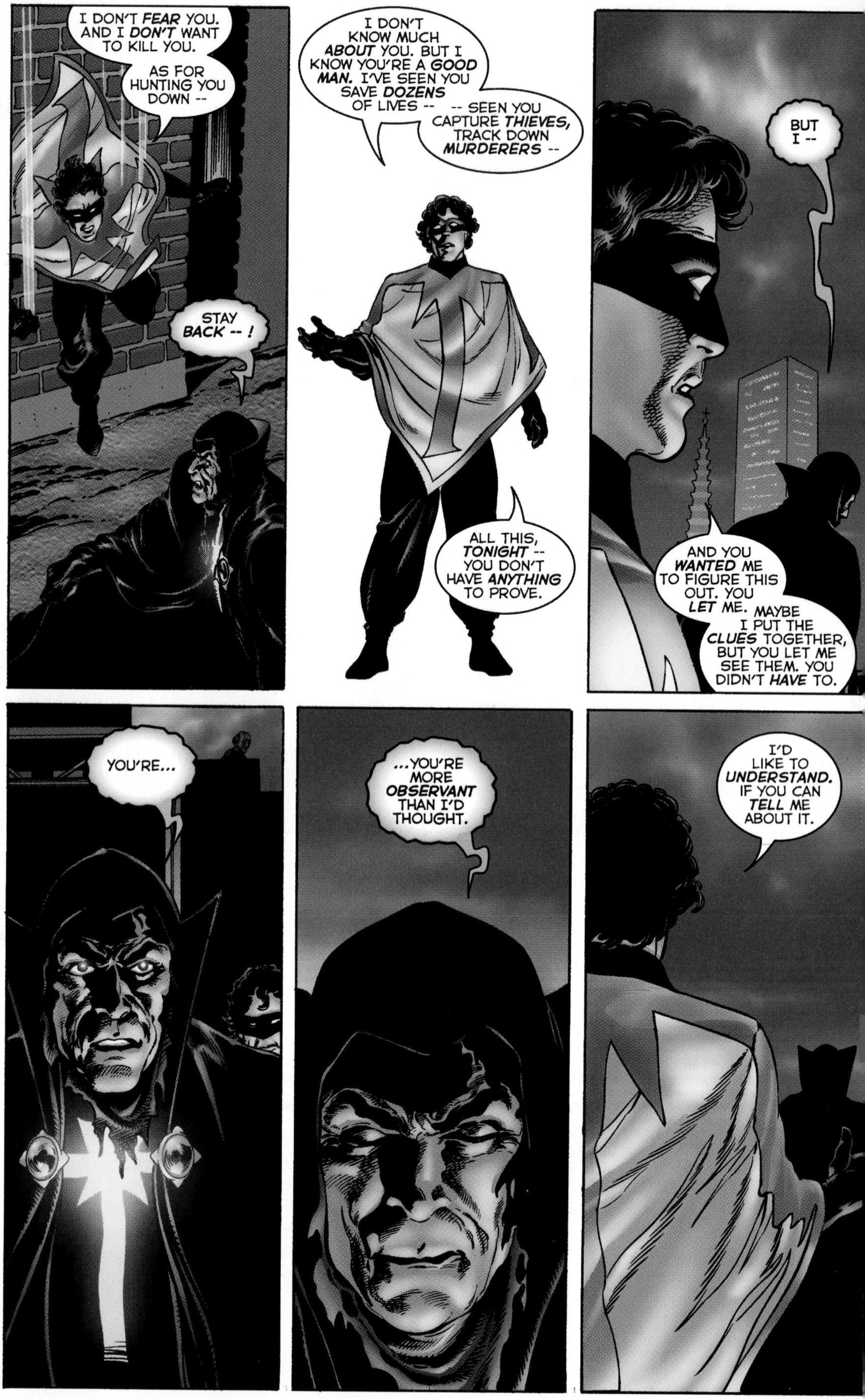
I DON'T FEAR YOU. AND I DON'T WANT TO KILL YOU.
AS FOR HUNTING YOU DOWN --
STAY BACK -- !
I DON'T KNOW MUCH ABOUT YOU. BUT I KNOW YOU'RE A GOOD MAN. I'VE SEEN YOU SAVE DOZENS OF LIVES --
-- SEEN YOU CAPTURE THIEVES, TRACK DOWN MURDERERS --
ALL THIS, TONIGHT -- YOU DON'T HAVE ANYTHING TO PROVE.
BUT I --
AND YOU WANTED ME TO FIGURE THIS OUT. YOU LET ME.
MAYBE I PUT THE CLUES TOGETHER, BUT YOU LET ME SEE THEM. YOU DIDN'T HAVE TO.
YOU'RE...
...YOU'RE MORE OBSERVANT THAN I'D THOUGHT.
I'D LIKE TO UNDERSTAND. IF YOU CAN TELL ME ABOUT IT.

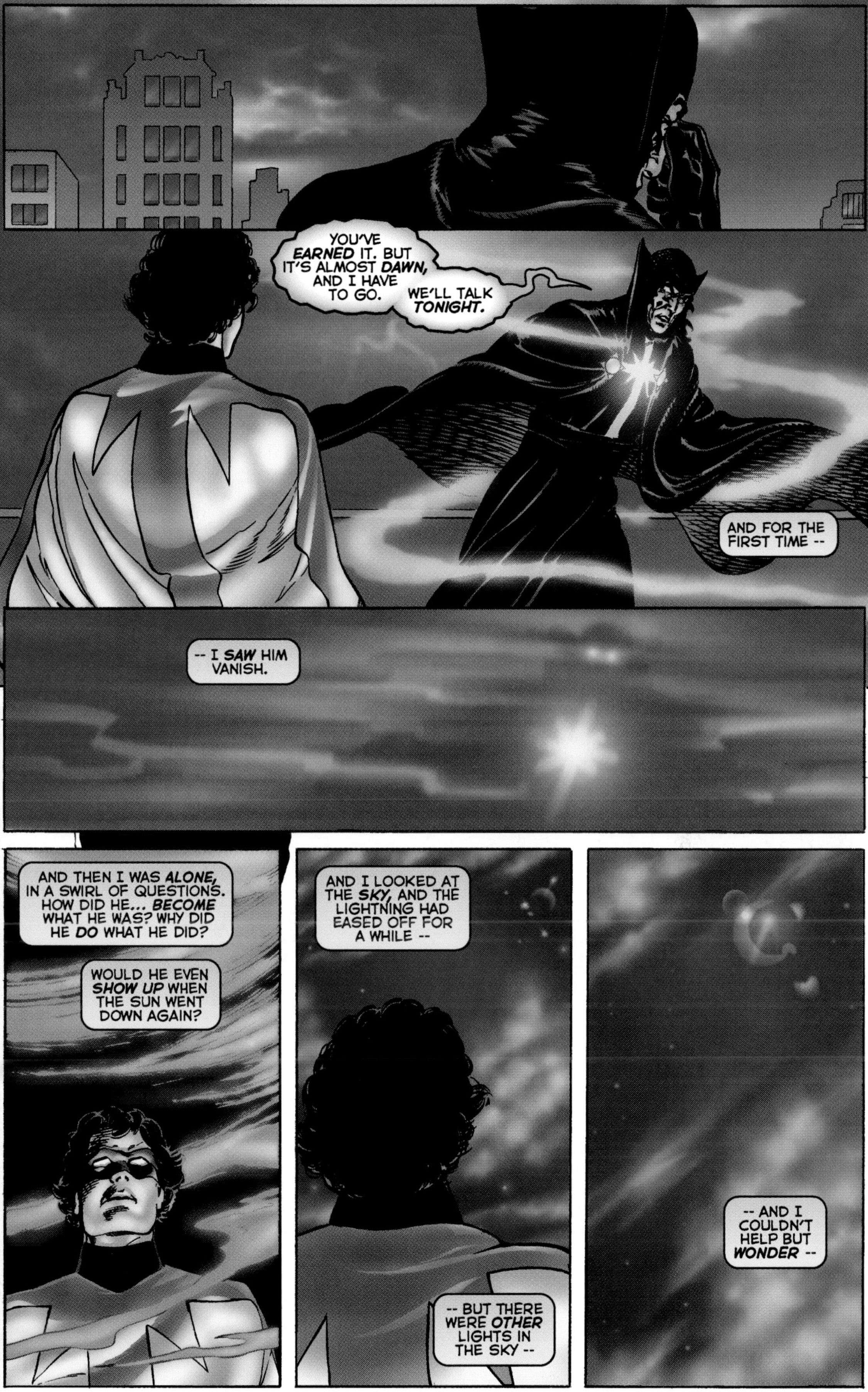
YOU'VE EARNED IT. BUT IT'S ALMOST DAWN, AND I HAVE TO GO.
WE'LL TALK TONIGHT.
AND FOR THE FIRST TIME --
-- I SAW HIM VANISH.
AND THEN I WAS ALONE, IN A SWIRL OF QUESTIONS. HOW DID HE... BECOME WHAT HE WAS? WHY DID HE DO WHAT HE DID?
WOULD HE EVEN SHOW UP WHEN THE SUN WENT DOWN AGAIN?
AND I LOOKED AT THE SKY, AND THE LIGHTNING HAD EASED OFF FOR A WHILE --
-- BUT THERE WERE OTHER LIGHTS IN THE SKY --
-- AND I COULDN'T HELP BUT WONDER --

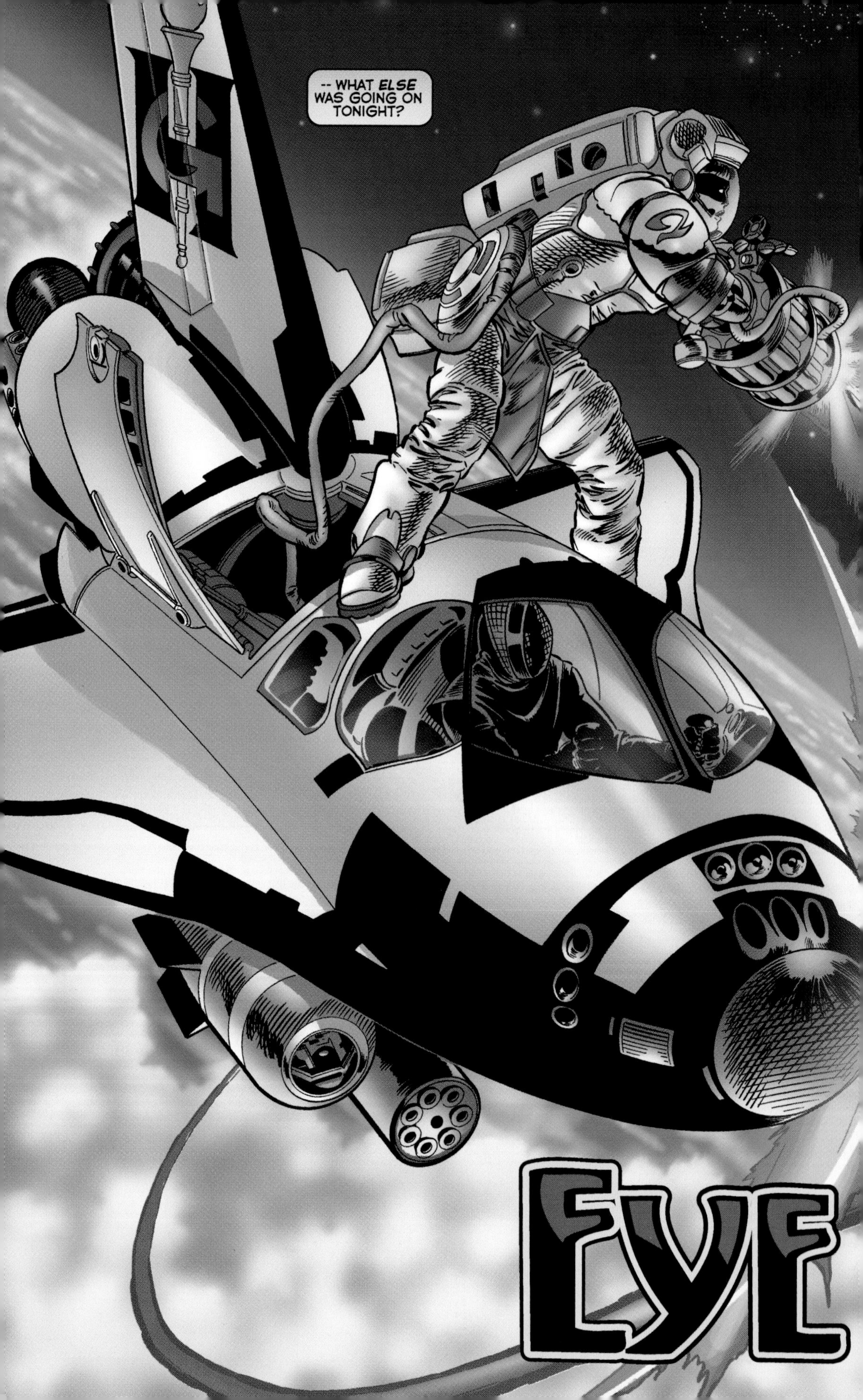
-- WHAT ELSE WAS GOING ON TONIGHT?
EYE

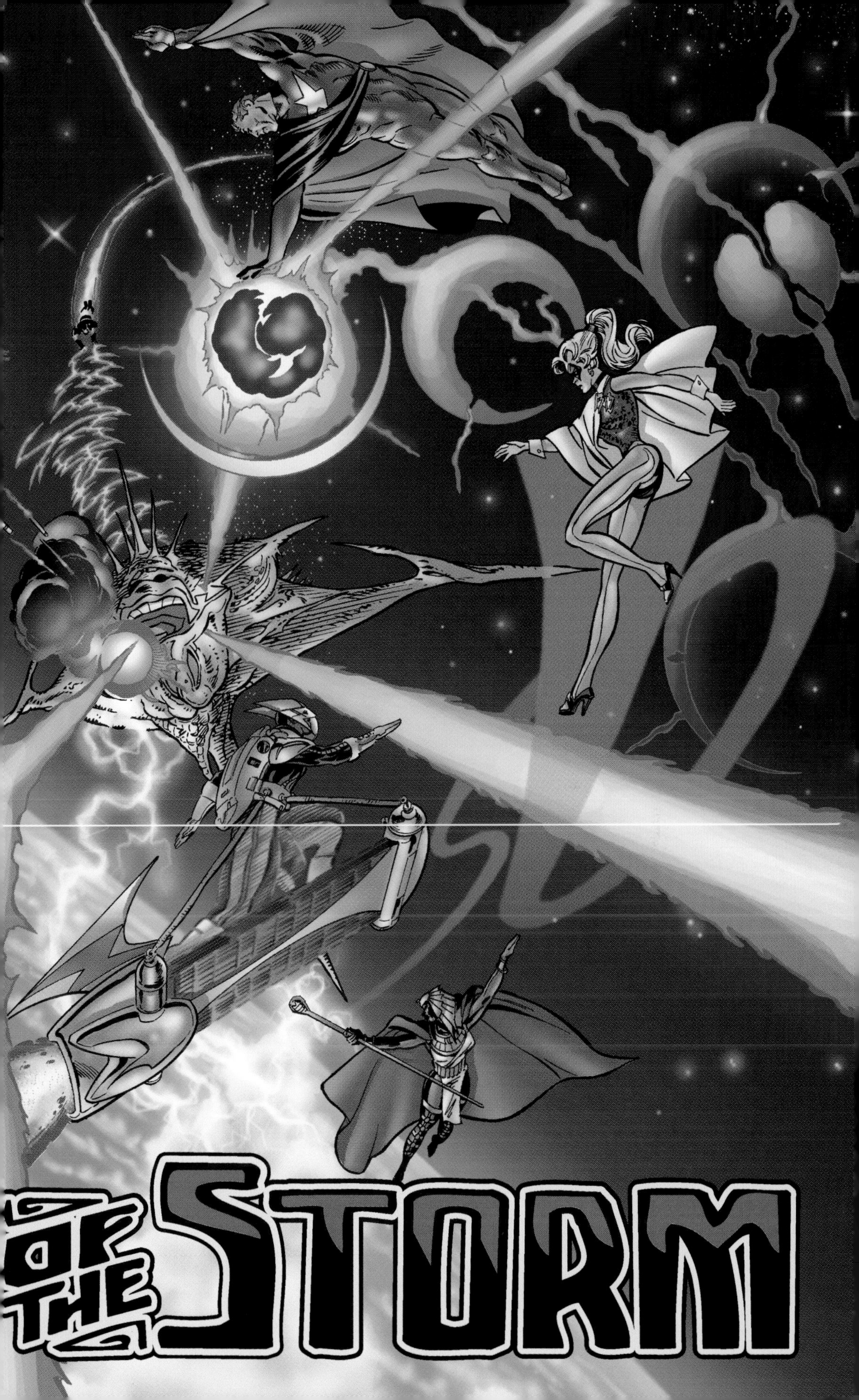
OF THE STORM

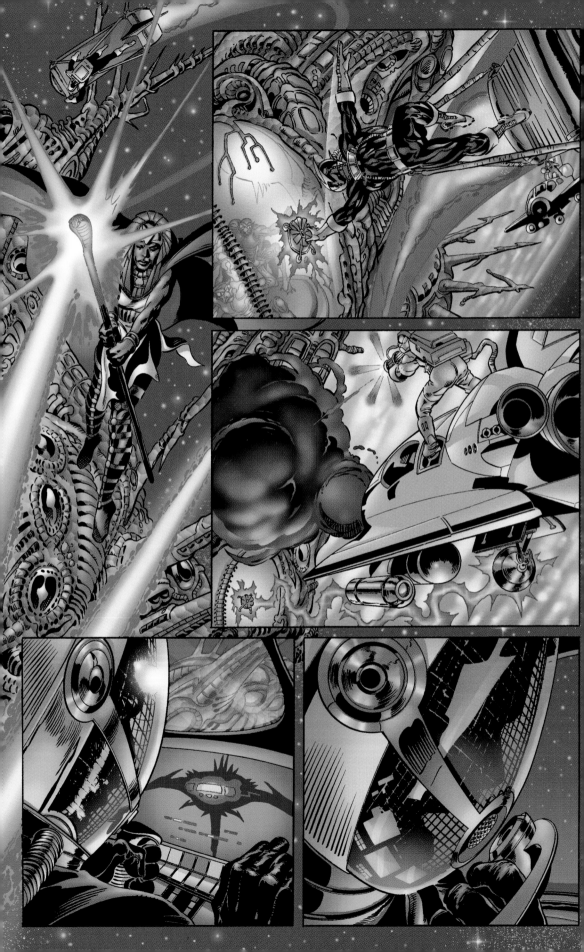

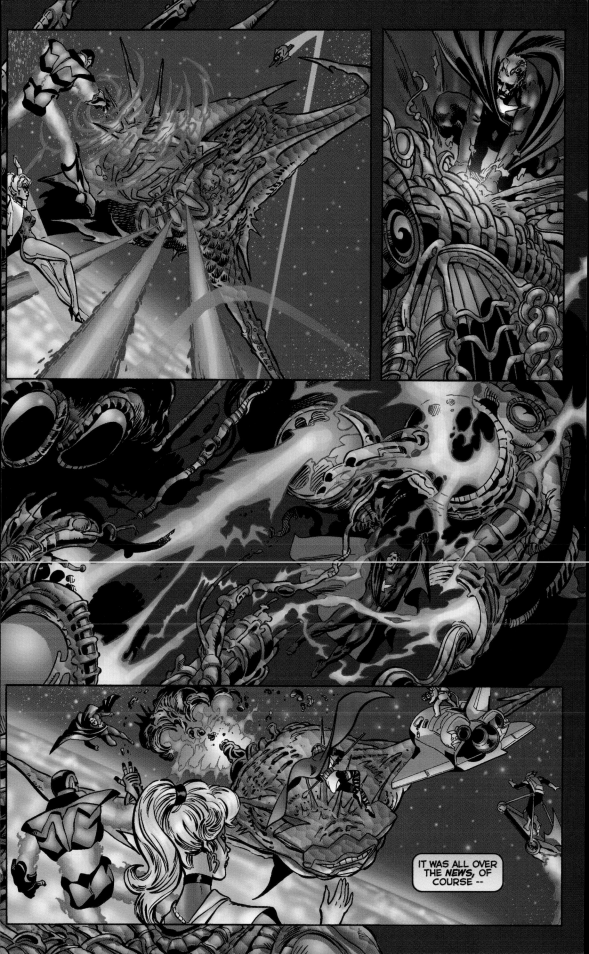

IT WAS ALL OVER
THE *NEWS*, OF
COURSE --

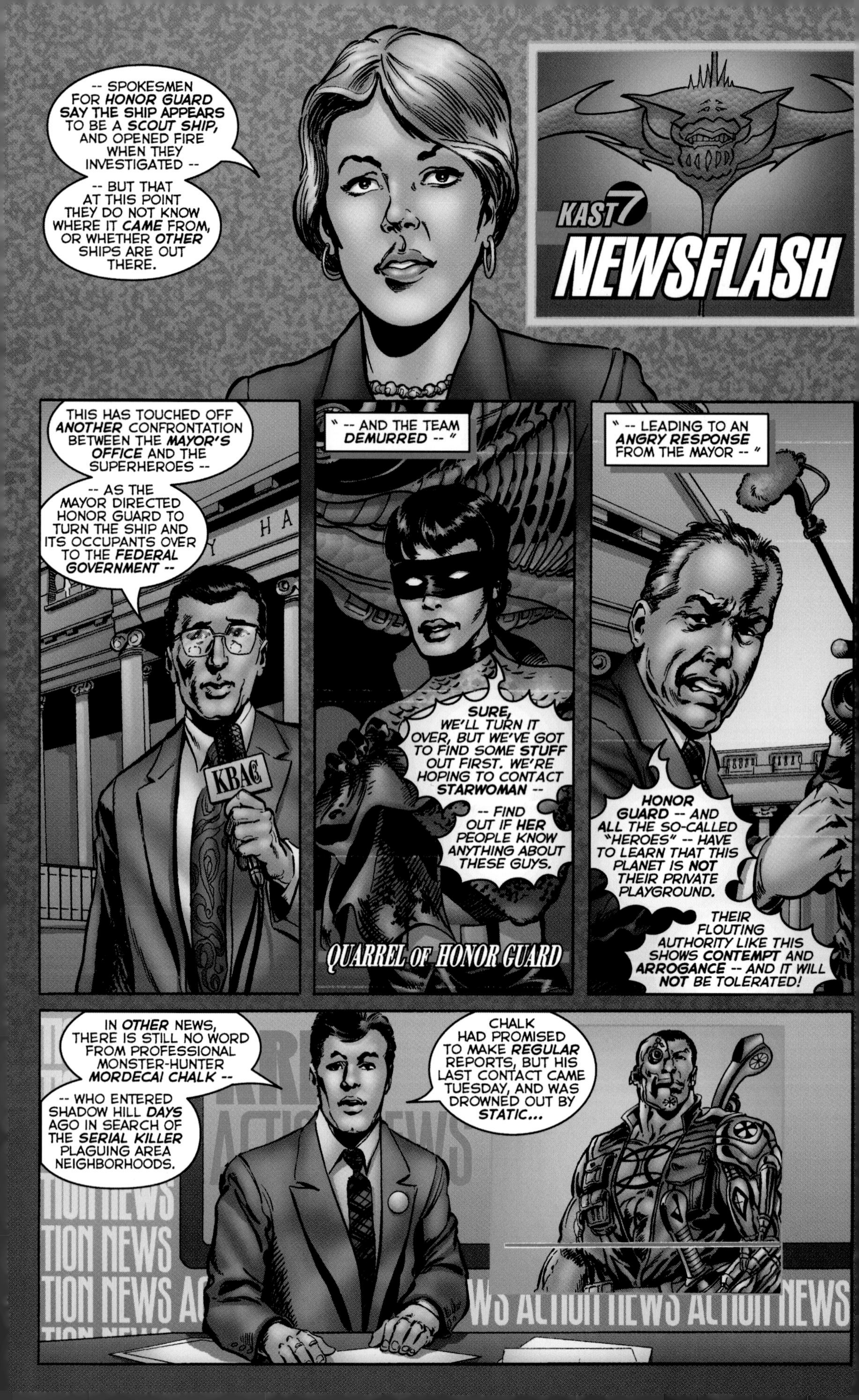

-- SPOKESMEN FOR HONOR GUARD SAY THE SHIP APPEARS TO BE A SCOUT SHIP, AND OPENED FIRE WHEN THEY INVESTIGATED --
-- BUT THAT AT THIS POINT THEY DO NOT KNOW WHERE IT CAME FROM, OR WHETHER OTHER SHIPS ARE OUT THERE.
KAST 7
NEWSFLASH
THIS HAS TOUCHED OFF ANOTHER CONFRONTATION BETWEEN THE MAYOR'S OFFICE AND THE SUPERHEROES --
-- AS THE MAYOR DIRECTED HONOR GUARD TO TURN THE SHIP AND ITS OCCUPANTS OVER TO THE FEDERAL GOVERNMENT --
KBAC
" -- AND THE TEAM DEMURRED -- "
SURE, WE'LL TURN IT OVER, BUT WE'VE GOT TO FIND SOME STUFF OUT FIRST. WE'RE HOPING TO CONTACT STARWOMAN --
-- FIND OUT IF HER PEOPLE KNOW ANYTHING ABOUT THESE GUYS.
QUARREL OF HONOR GUARD
" -- LEADING TO AN ANGRY RESPONSE FROM THE MAYOR -- "
HONOR GUARD -- AND ALL THE SO-CALLED "HEROES" -- HAVE TO LEARN THAT THIS PLANET IS NOT THEIR PRIVATE PLAYGROUND.
THEIR FLOUTING AUTHORITY LIKE THIS SHOWS CONTEMPT AND ARROGANCE -- AND IT WILL NOT BE TOLERATED!
IN OTHER NEWS, THERE IS STILL NO WORD FROM PROFESSIONAL MONSTER-HUNTER MORDECAI CHALK --
-- WHO ENTERED SHADOW HILL DAYS AGO IN SEARCH OF THE SERIAL KILLER PLAGUING AREA NEIGHBORHOODS.
CHALK HAD PROMISED TO MAKE REGULAR REPORTS, BUT HIS LAST CONTACT CAME TUESDAY, AND WAS DROWNED OUT BY STATIC...
TION NEWS
TION NEWS
TION NEWS AC
WS ACTION NEWS ACTION NEWS

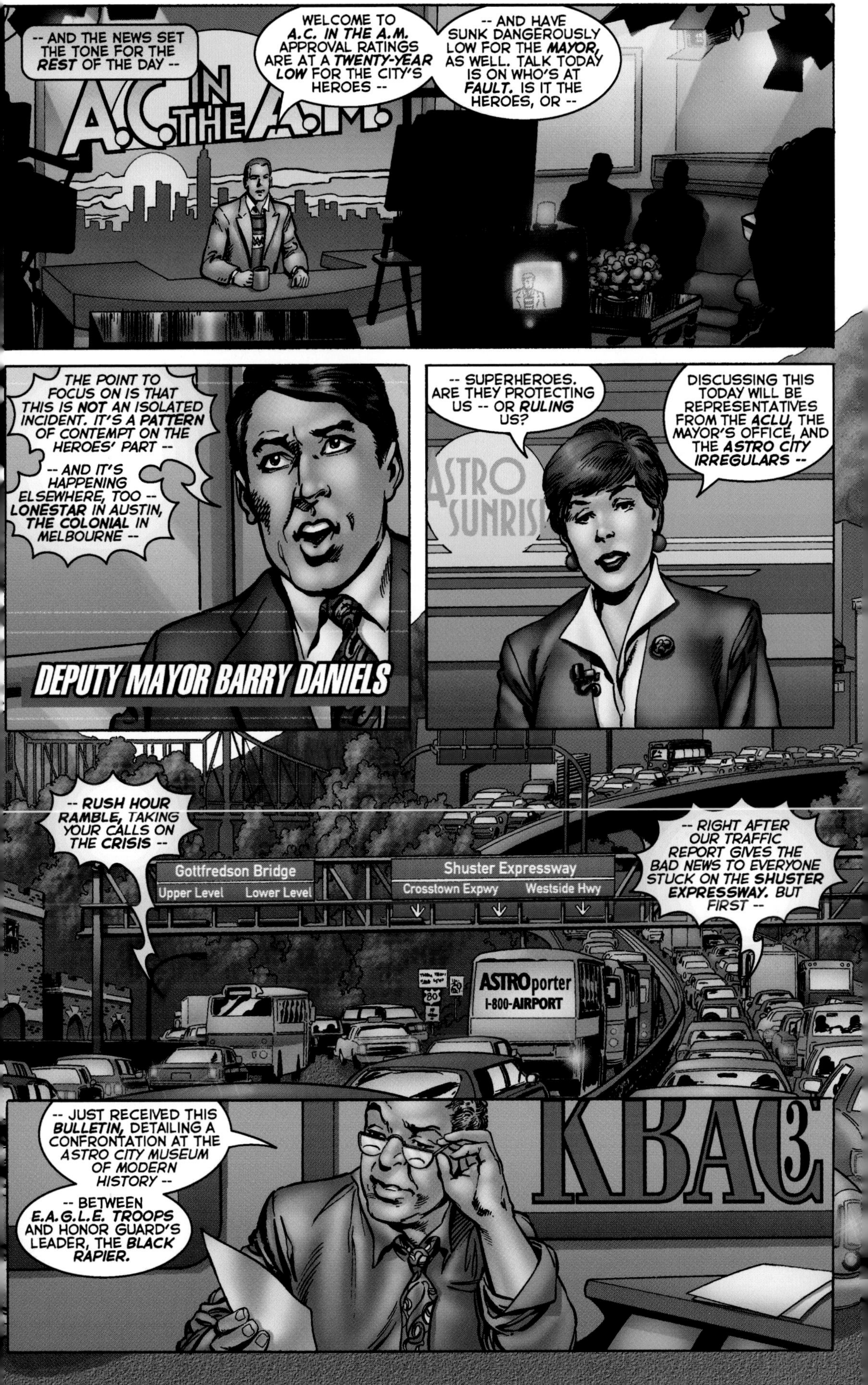
-- AND THE NEWS SET THE TONE FOR THE REST OF THE DAY --
A.C. IN THE A.M.
WELCOME TO A.C. IN THE A.M. APPROVAL RATINGS ARE AT A TWENTY-YEAR LOW FOR THE CITY'S HEROES --
-- AND HAVE SUNK DANGEROUSLY LOW FOR THE MAYOR, AS WELL. TALK TODAY IS ON WHO'S AT FAULT. IS IT THE HEROES, OR --
THE POINT TO FOCUS ON IS THAT THIS IS NOT AN ISOLATED INCIDENT. IT'S A PATTERN OF CONTEMPT ON THE HEROES' PART --
-- AND IT'S HAPPENING ELSEWHERE, TOO -- LONESTAR IN AUSTIN, THE COLONIAL IN MELBOURNE --
DEPUTY MAYOR BARRY DANIELS
-- SUPERHEROES. ARE THEY PROTECTING US -- OR RULING US?
DISCUSSING THIS TODAY WILL BE REPRESENTATIVES FROM THE ACLU, THE MAYOR'S OFFICE, AND THE ASTRO CITY IRREGULARS --
ASTRO SUNRISE
-- RUSH HOUR RAMBLE, TAKING YOUR CALLS ON THE CRISIS --
Gottfredson Bridge
Upper Level Lower Level
Shuster Expressway
Crosstown Expwy Westside Hwy
-- RIGHT AFTER OUR TRAFFIC REPORT GIVES THE BAD NEWS TO EVERYONE STUCK ON THE SHUSTER EXPRESSWAY. BUT FIRST --
ASTROporter
1-800-AIRPORT
-- JUST RECEIVED THIS BULLETIN, DETAILING A CONFRONTATION AT THE ASTRO CITY MUSEUM OF MODERN HISTORY --
-- BETWEEN E.A.G.L.E. TROOPS AND HONOR GUARD'S LEADER, THE BLACK RAPIER.
KBAC 3

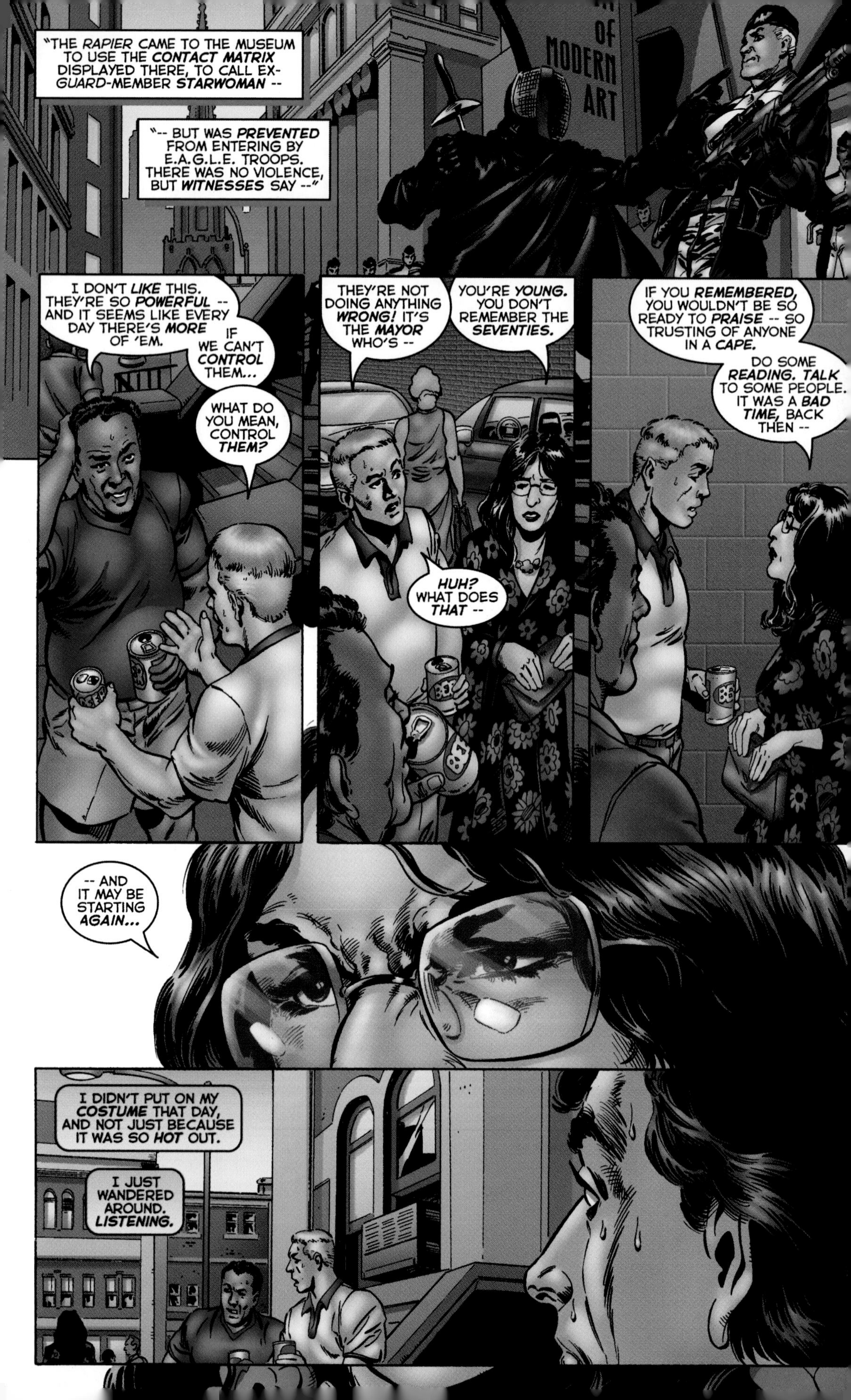
"THE RAPIER CAME TO THE MUSEUM TO USE THE CONTACT MATRIX DISPLAYED THERE, TO CALL EX-GUARD-MEMBER STARWOMAN --
"-- BUT WAS PREVENTED FROM ENTERING BY E.A.G.L.E. TROOPS. THERE WAS NO VIOLENCE, BUT WITNESSES SAY --"
OF MODERN ART
I DON'T LIKE THIS. THEY'RE SO POWERFUL -- AND IT SEEMS LIKE EVERY DAY THERE'S MORE OF 'EM.
IF WE CAN'T CONTROL THEM...
WHAT DO YOU MEAN, CONTROL THEM?
THEY'RE NOT DOING ANYTHING WRONG! IT'S THE MAYOR WHO'S --
YOU'RE YOUNG. YOU DON'T REMEMBER THE SEVENTIES.
HUH? WHAT DOES THAT --
IF YOU REMEMBERED, YOU WOULDN'T BE SO READY TO PRAISE -- SO TRUSTING OF ANYONE IN A CAPE.
DO SOME READING. TALK TO SOME PEOPLE. IT WAS A BAD TIME, BACK THEN --
-- AND IT MAY BE STARTING AGAIN...
I DIDN'T PUT ON MY COSTUME THAT DAY, AND NOT JUST BECAUSE IT WAS SO HOT OUT.
I JUST WANDERED AROUND. LISTENING.

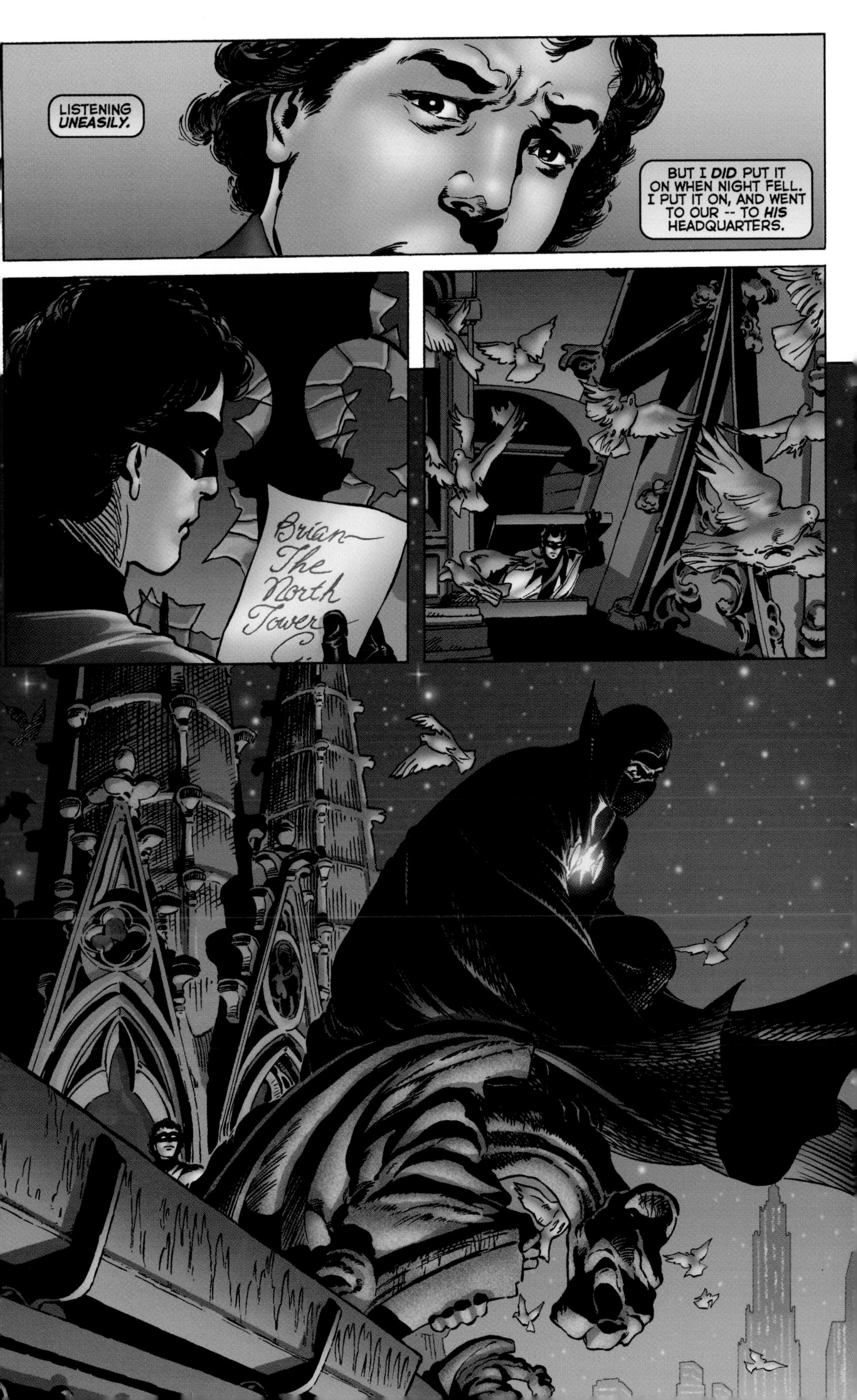
LISTENING UNEASILY.
BUT I DID PUT IT ON WHEN NIGHT FELL. I PUT IT ON, AND WENT TO OUR -- TO HIS HEADQUARTERS.
Brian — The North Tower

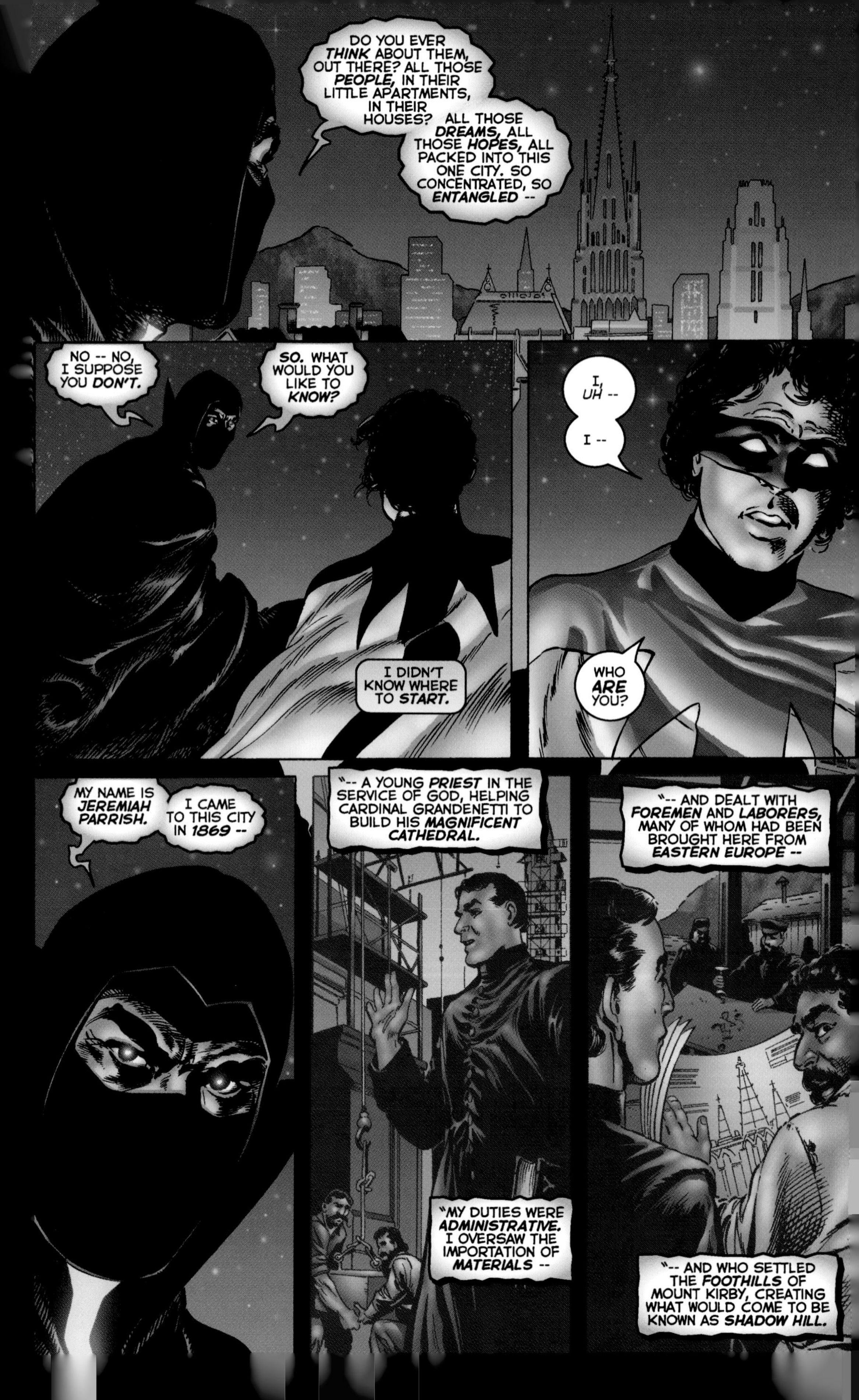
DO YOU EVER THINK ABOUT THEM, OUT THERE? ALL THOSE PEOPLE, IN THEIR LITTLE APARTMENTS, IN THEIR HOUSES?
ALL THOSE DREAMS, ALL THOSE HOPES, ALL PACKED INTO THIS ONE CITY. SO CONCENTRATED, SO ENTANGLED --
NO -- NO, I SUPPOSE YOU DON'T.
SO. WHAT WOULD YOU LIKE TO KNOW?
I DIDN'T KNOW WHERE TO START.
I, UH --
I --
WHO ARE YOU?
MY NAME IS JEREMIAH PARRISH.
I CAME TO THIS CITY IN 1869 --
"-- A YOUNG PRIEST IN THE SERVICE OF GOD, HELPING CARDINAL GRANDENETTI TO BUILD HIS MAGNIFICENT CATHEDRAL.
"MY DUTIES WERE ADMINISTRATIVE. I OVERSAW THE IMPORTATION OF MATERIALS --
"-- AND DEALT WITH FOREMEN AND LABORERS, MANY OF WHOM HAD BEEN BROUGHT HERE FROM EASTERN EUROPE --
"-- AND WHO SETTLED THE FOOTHILLS OF MOUNT KIRBY, CREATING WHAT WOULD COME TO BE KNOWN AS SHADOW HILL.

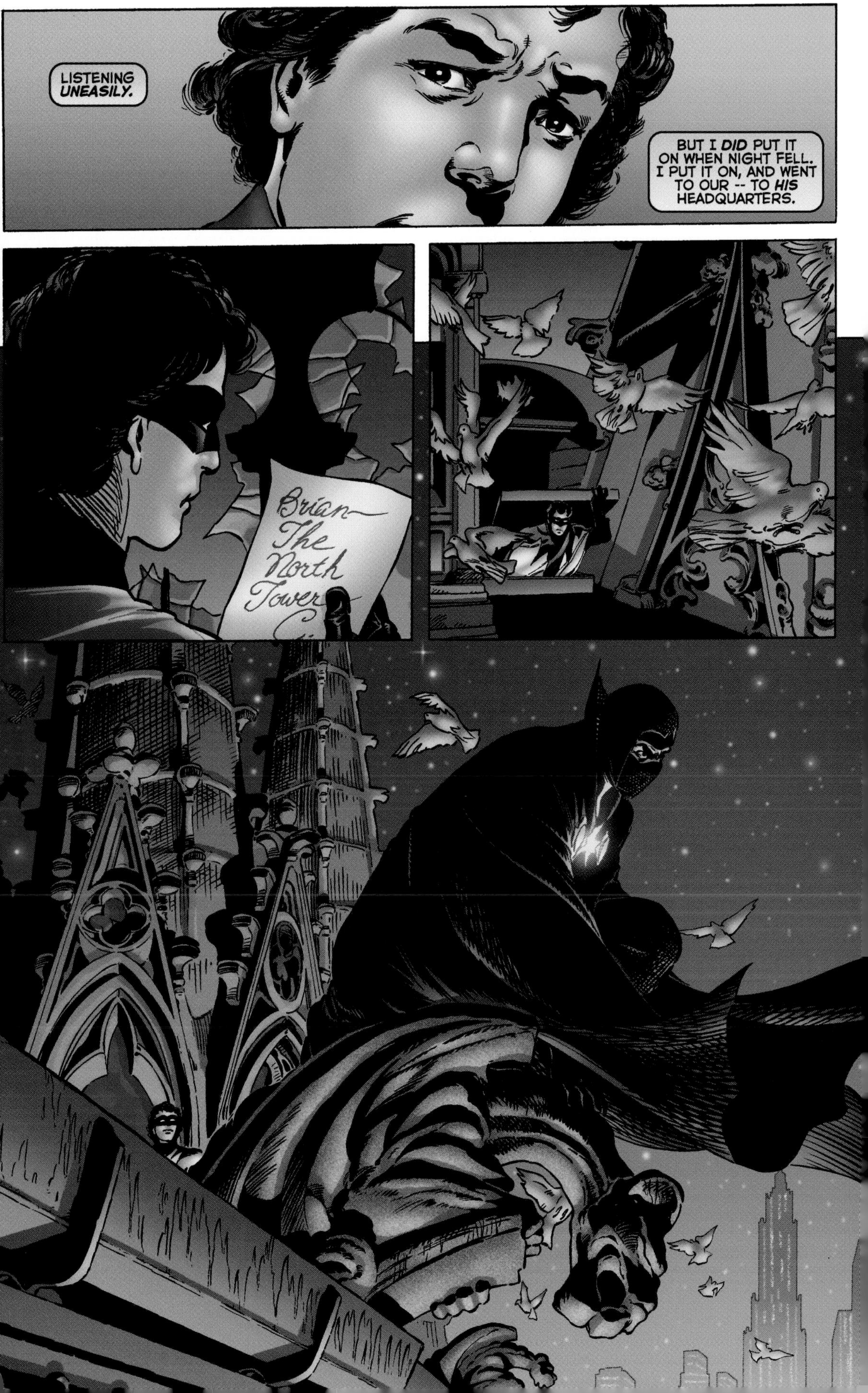
LISTENING UNEASILY.
BUT I DID PUT IT ON WHEN NIGHT FELL. I PUT IT ON, AND WENT TO OUR -- TO HIS HEADQUARTERS.
Brian — The North Tower

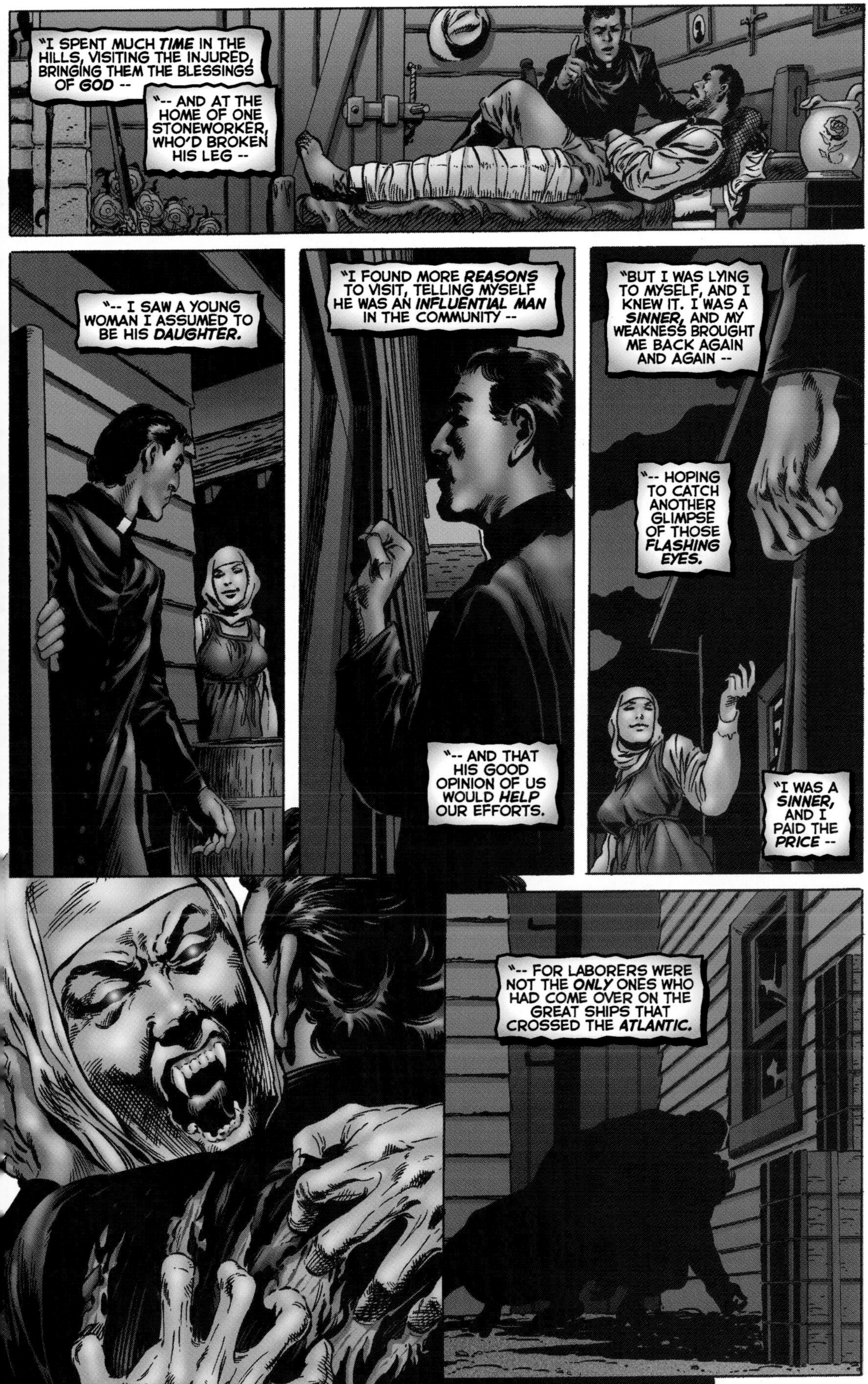
"I SPENT MUCH *TIME* IN THE HILLS, VISITING THE INJURED, BRINGING THEM THE BLESSINGS OF *GOD* --
"-- AND AT THE HOME OF ONE STONEWORKER, WHO'D BROKEN HIS LEG --
"-- I SAW A YOUNG WOMAN I ASSUMED TO BE HIS *DAUGHTER.*
"I FOUND MORE *REASONS* TO VISIT, TELLING MYSELF HE WAS AN *INFLUENTIAL MAN* IN THE COMMUNITY --
"-- AND THAT HIS GOOD OPINION OF US WOULD *HELP* OUR EFFORTS.
"BUT I WAS LYING TO *MYSELF*, AND I KNEW IT. I WAS A *SINNER,* AND MY WEAKNESS BROUGHT ME BACK AGAIN AND AGAIN --
"-- HOPING TO CATCH ANOTHER GLIMPSE OF THOSE *FLASHING EYES.*
"I WAS A *SINNER,* AND I PAID THE *PRICE* --
"-- FOR LABORERS WERE NOT THE *ONLY* ONES WHO HAD COME OVER ON THE GREAT SHIPS THAT CROSSED THE *ATLANTIC.*

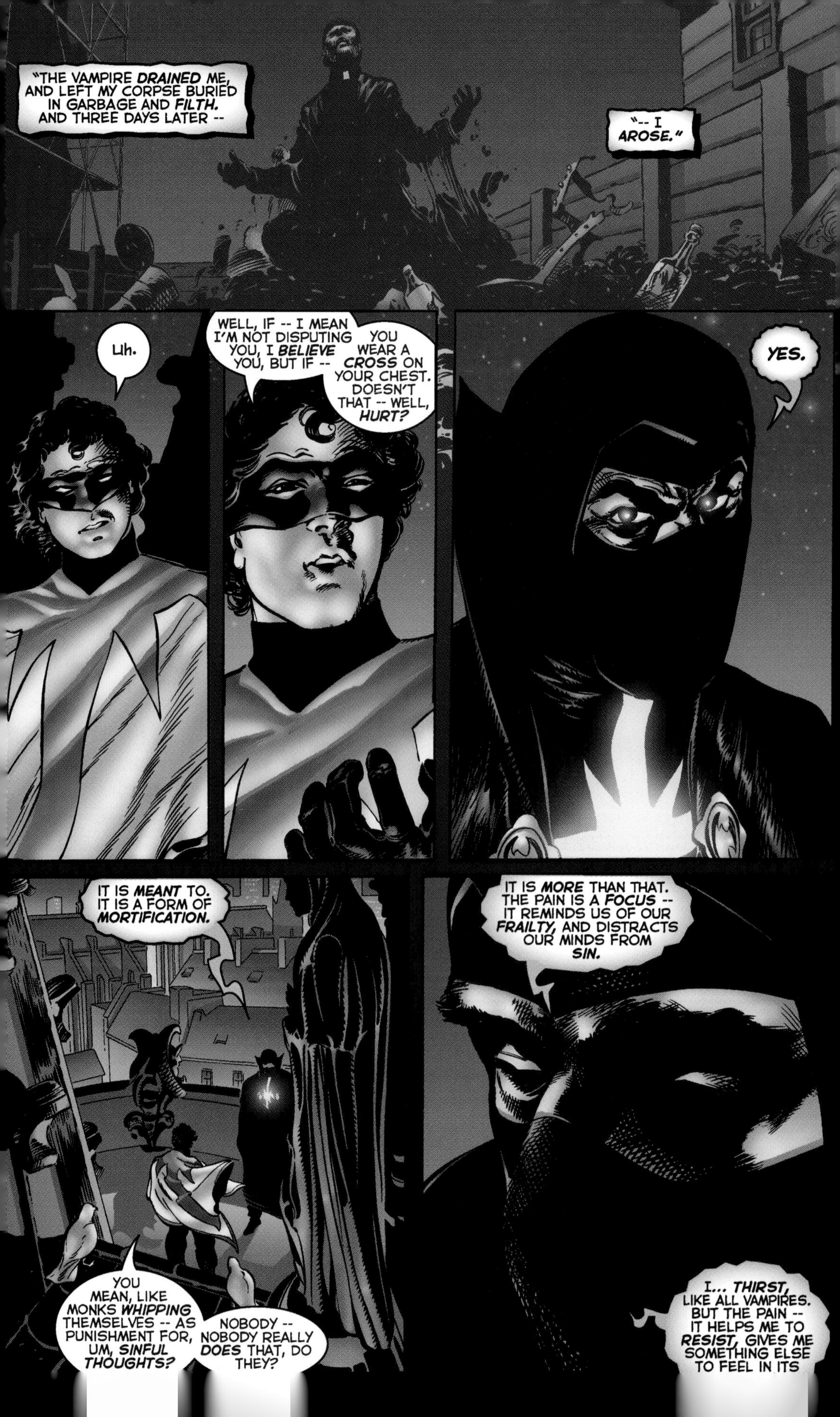
"THE VAMPIRE DRAINED ME, AND LEFT MY CORPSE BURIED IN GARBAGE AND FILTH. AND THREE DAYS LATER --
"-- I AROSE."
UH.
WELL, IF -- I MEAN I'M NOT DISPUTING YOU, I BELIEVE YOU, BUT IF --
YOU WEAR A CROSS ON YOUR CHEST. DOESN'T THAT -- WELL, HURT?
YES.
IT IS MEANT TO. IT IS A FORM OF MORTIFICATION.
YOU MEAN, LIKE MONKS WHIPPING THEMSELVES -- AS PUNISHMENT FOR, UM, SINFUL THOUGHTS?
NOBODY -- NOBODY REALLY DOES THAT, DO THEY?
IT IS MORE THAN THAT. THE PAIN IS A FOCUS -- IT REMINDS US OF OUR FRAILTY, AND DISTRACTS OUR MINDS FROM SIN.
I... THIRST, LIKE ALL VAMPIRES. BUT THE PAIN -- IT HELPS ME TO RESIST, GIVES ME SOMETHING ELSE TO FEEL IN ITS

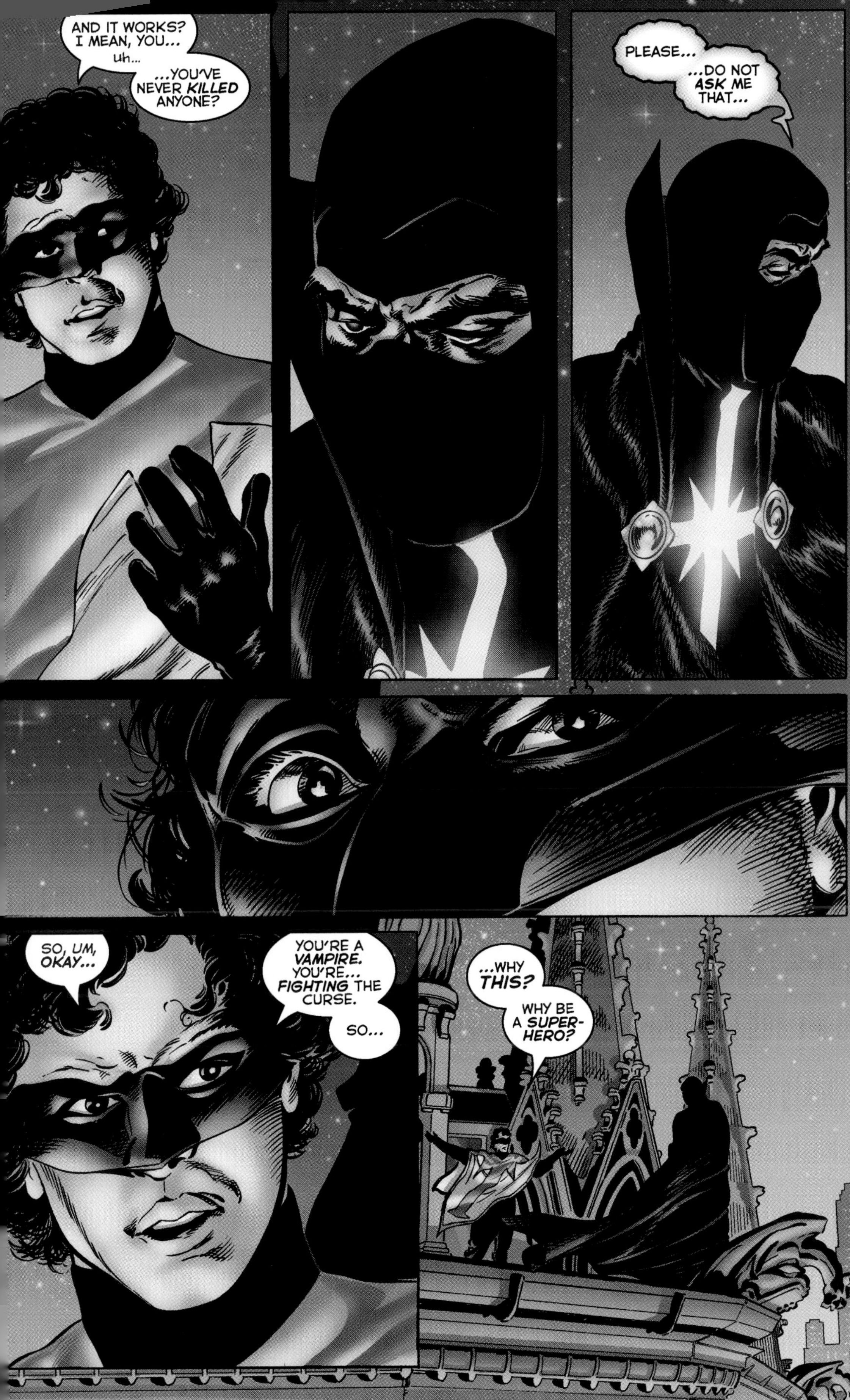
AND IT WORKS? I MEAN, YOU...
uh...
...YOU'VE NEVER KILLED ANYONE?
PLEASE...
...DO NOT ASK ME THAT...
SO, UM, OKAY...
YOU'RE A VAMPIRE. YOU'RE... FIGHTING THE CURSE.
SO...
...WHY THIS?
WHY BE A SUPER-HERO?

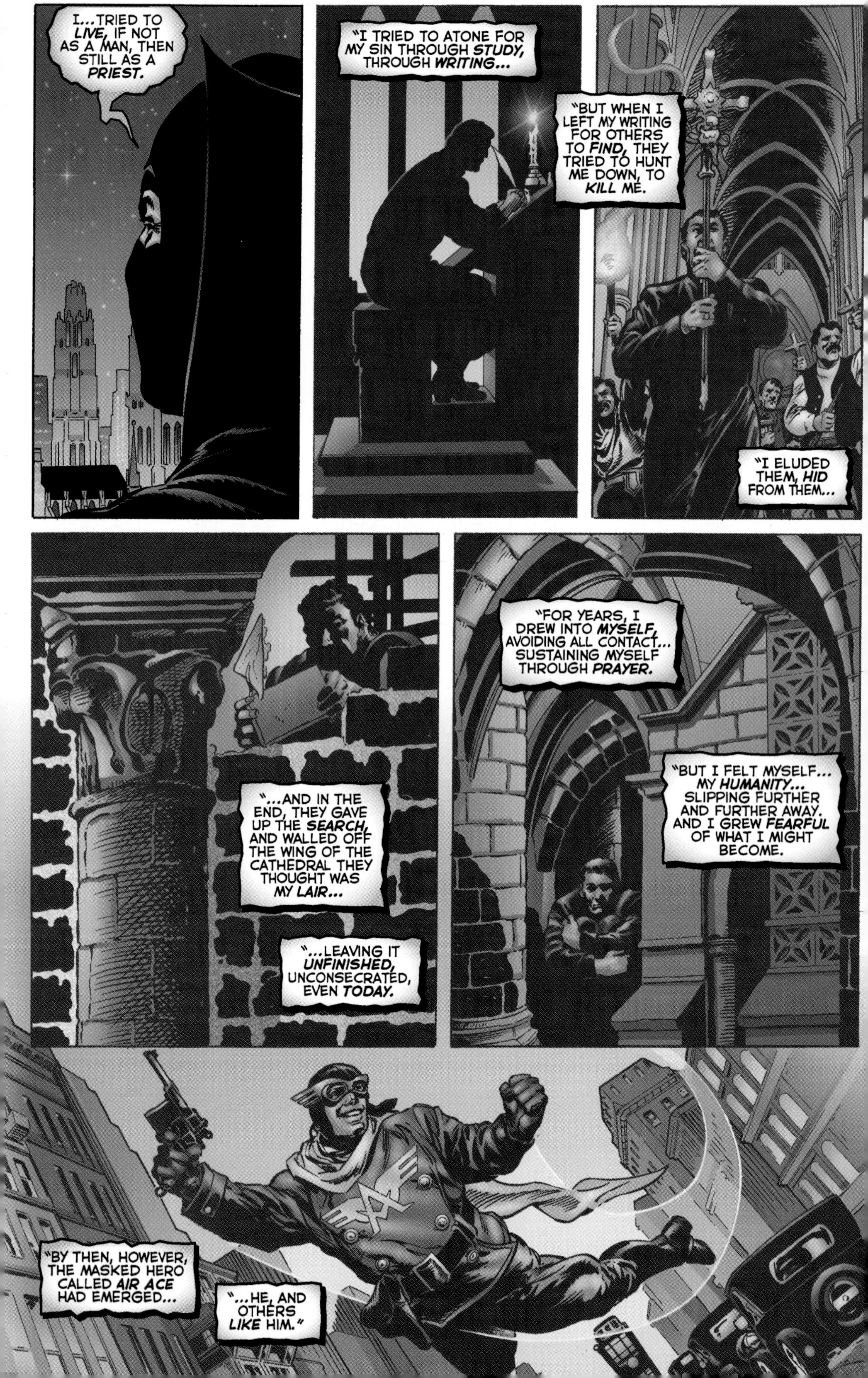
I...TRIED TO LIVE, IF NOT AS A MAN, THEN STILL AS A PRIEST.
"I TRIED TO ATONE FOR MY SIN THROUGH STUDY, THROUGH WRITING...
"BUT WHEN I LEFT MY WRITING FOR OTHERS TO FIND, THEY TRIED TO HUNT ME DOWN, TO KILL ME.
"I ELUDED THEM, HID FROM THEM...
"...AND IN THE END, THEY GAVE UP THE SEARCH, AND WALLED OFF THE WING OF THE CATHEDRAL THEY THOUGHT WAS MY LAIR...
"...LEAVING IT UNFINISHED, UNCONSECRATED, EVEN TODAY.
"FOR YEARS, I DREW INTO MYSELF, AVOIDING ALL CONTACT... SUSTAINING MYSELF THROUGH PRAYER.
"BUT I FELT MYSELF... MY HUMANITY... SLIPPING FURTHER AND FURTHER AWAY. AND I GREW FEARFUL OF WHAT I MIGHT BECOME.
"BY THEN, HOWEVER, THE MASKED HERO CALLED AIR ACE HAD EMERGED...
"...HE, AND OTHERS LIKE HIM."

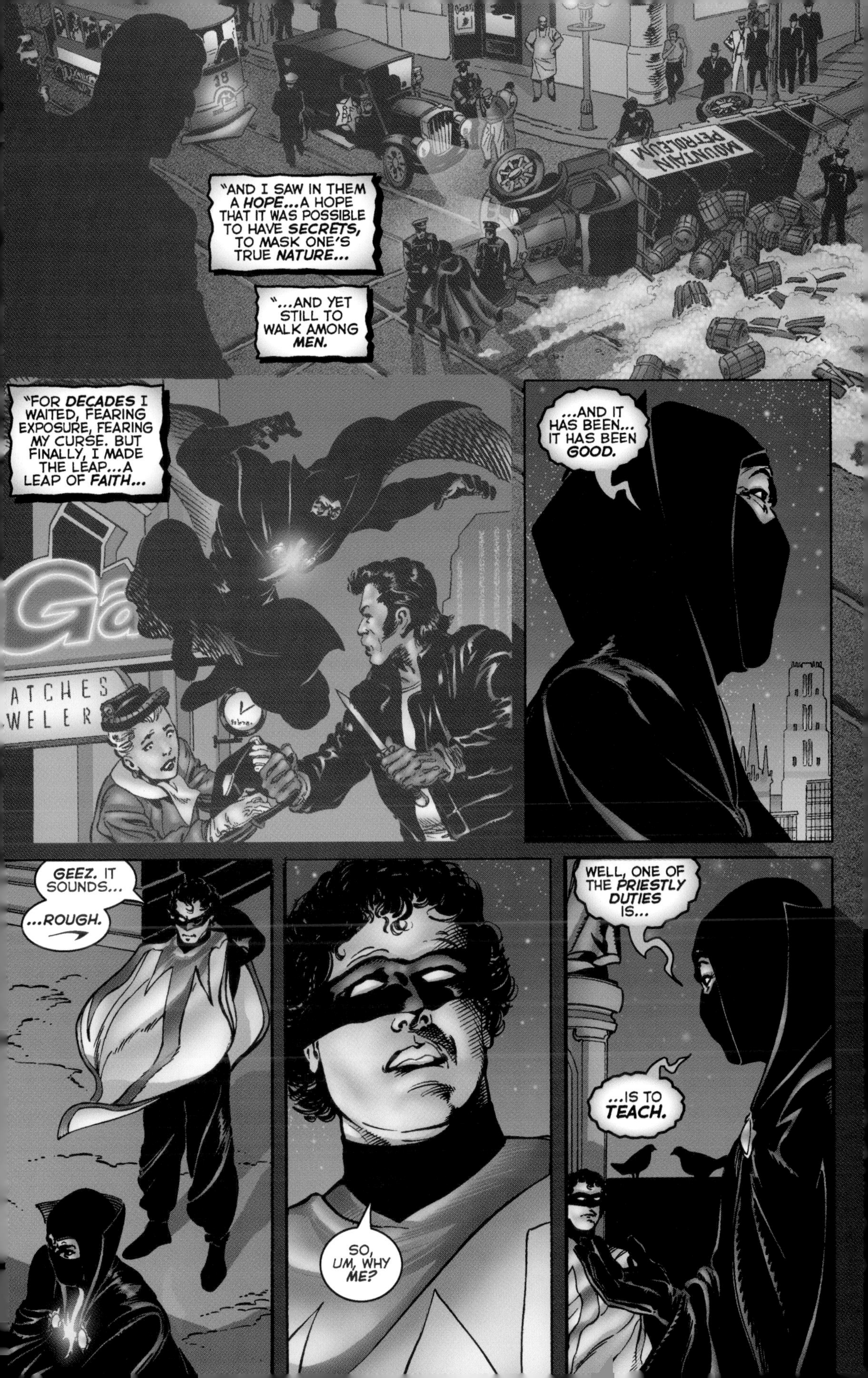
"AND I SAW IN THEM A HOPE...A HOPE THAT IT WAS POSSIBLE TO HAVE SECRETS, TO MASK ONE'S TRUE NATURE...
"...AND YET STILL TO WALK AMONG MEN.
MOUNTAIN PETROLEUM
"FOR DECADES I WAITED, FEARING EXPOSURE, FEARING MY CURSE. BUT FINALLY, I MADE THE LEAP...A LEAP OF FAITH...
ATCHES
WELER
...AND IT HAS BEEN... IT HAS BEEN GOOD.
GEEZ. IT SOUNDS...
...ROUGH.
SO, UM, WHY ME?
WELL, ONE OF THE PRIESTLY DUTIES IS...
...IS TO TEACH.

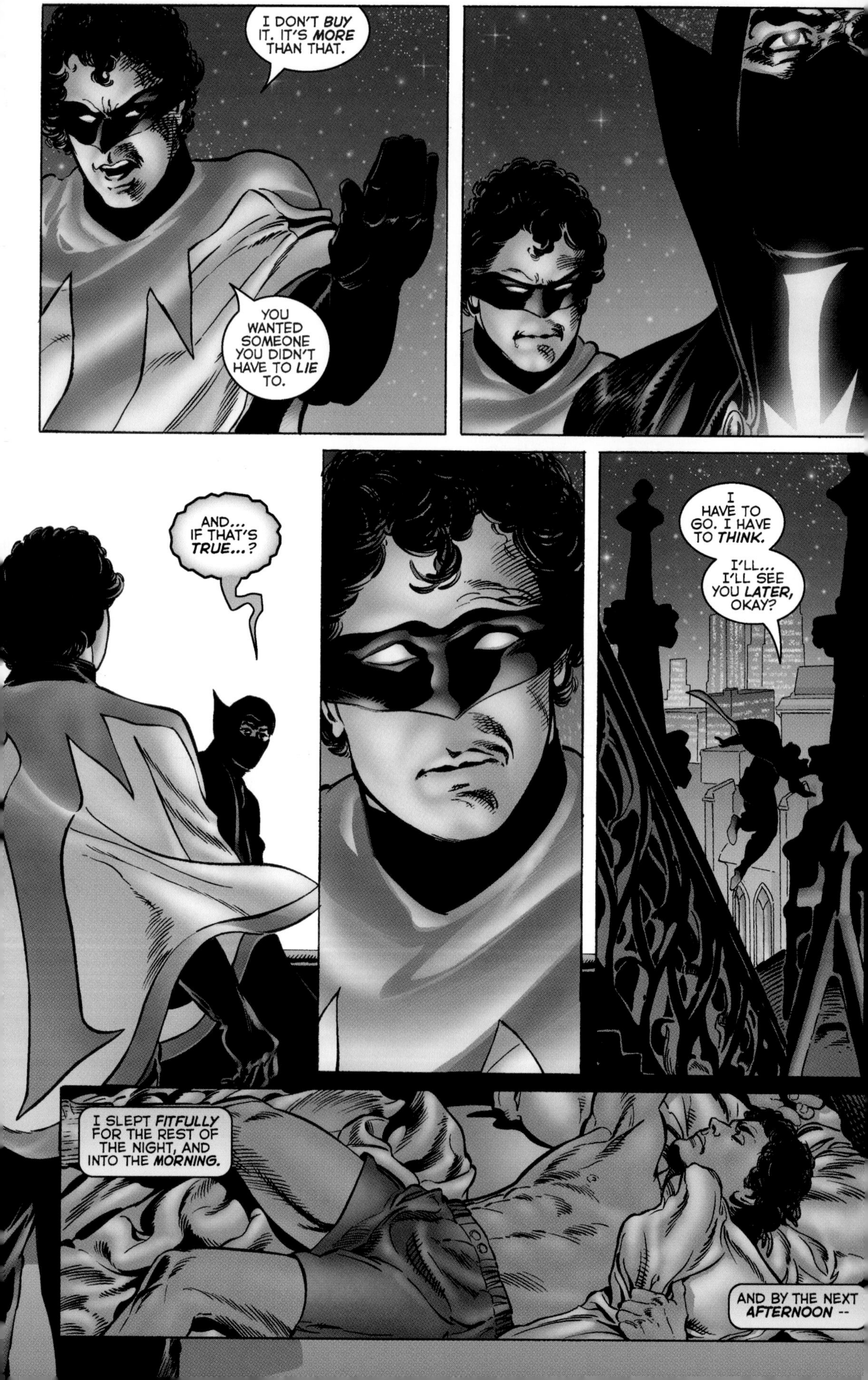
I DON'T BUY IT. IT'S MORE THAN THAT.
YOU WANTED SOMEONE YOU DIDN'T HAVE TO LIE TO.
AND... IF THAT'S TRUE...?
I HAVE TO GO. I HAVE TO THINK.
I'LL... I'LL SEE YOU LATER, OKAY?
I SLEPT FITFULLY FOR THE REST OF THE NIGHT, AND INTO THE MORNING.
AND BY THE NEXT AFTERNOON --

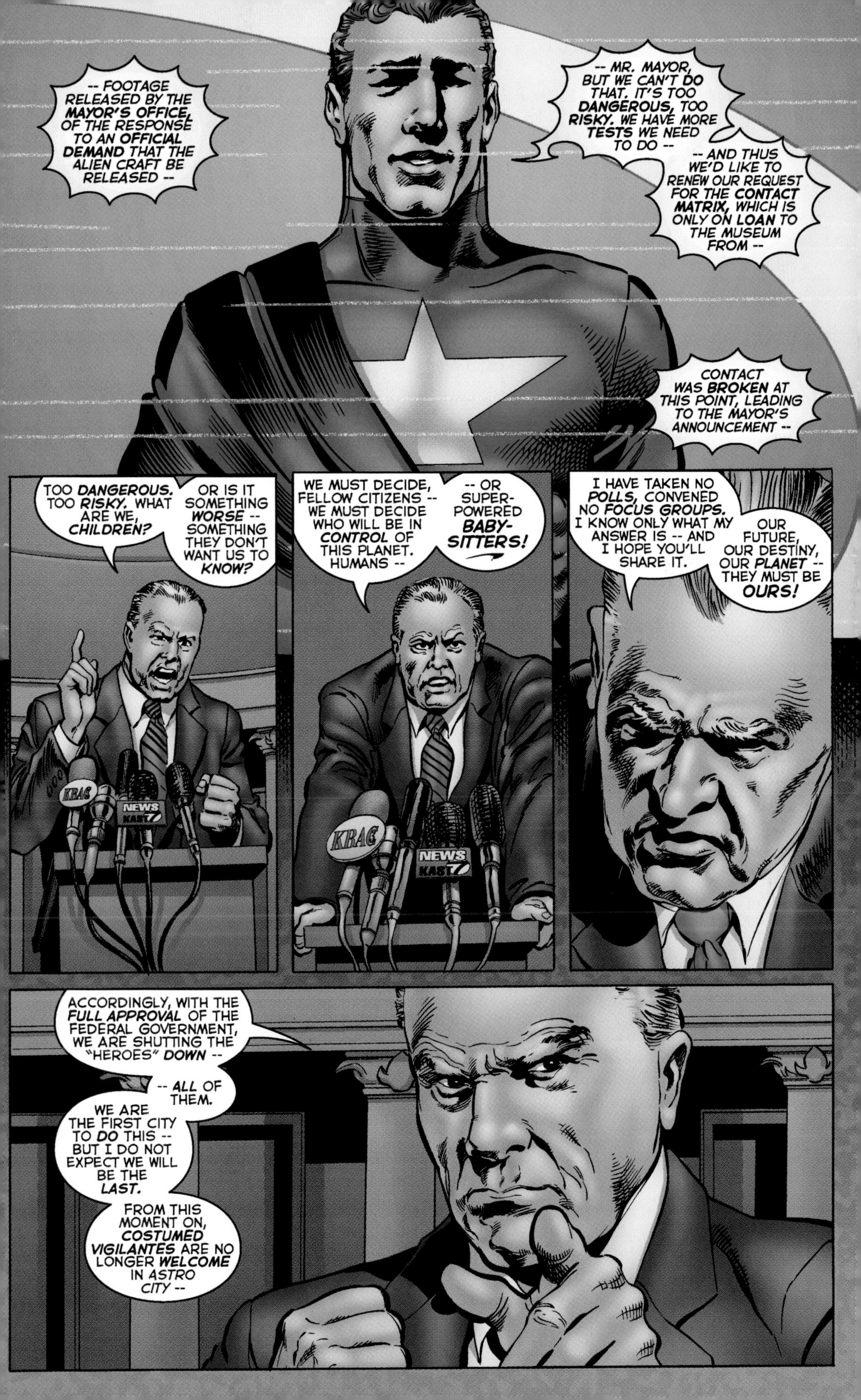
-- FOOTAGE RELEASED BY THE MAYOR'S OFFICE, OF THE RESPONSE TO AN OFFICIAL DEMAND THAT THE ALIEN CRAFT BE RELEASED --
-- MR. MAYOR, BUT WE CAN'T DO THAT. IT'S TOO DANGEROUS, TOO RISKY. WE HAVE MORE TESTS WE NEED TO DO --
-- AND THUS WE'D LIKE TO RENEW OUR REQUEST FOR THE CONTACT MATRIX, WHICH IS ONLY ON LOAN TO THE MUSEUM FROM --
CONTACT WAS BROKEN AT THIS POINT, LEADING TO THE MAYOR'S ANNOUNCEMENT --
TOO DANGEROUS. TOO RISKY. WHAT ARE WE, CHILDREN?
OR IS IT SOMETHING WORSE -- SOMETHING THEY DON'T WANT US TO KNOW?
KBAG
NEWS KAS 7
WE MUST DECIDE, FELLOW CITIZENS -- WE MUST DECIDE WHO WILL BE IN CONTROL OF THIS PLANET. HUMANS --
-- OR SUPER-POWERED BABY-SITTERS!
KBAG
NEWS KAS 7
I HAVE TAKEN NO POLLS, CONVENED NO FOCUS GROUPS. I KNOW ONLY WHAT MY ANSWER IS -- AND I HOPE YOU'LL SHARE IT.
OUR FUTURE, OUR DESTINY, OUR PLANET -- THEY MUST BE OURS!
ACCORDINGLY, WITH THE FULL APPROVAL OF THE FEDERAL GOVERNMENT, WE ARE SHUTTING THE "HEROES" DOWN --
-- ALL OF THEM.
WE ARE THE FIRST CITY TO DO THIS -- BUT I DO NOT EXPECT WE WILL BE THE LAST.
FROM THIS MOMENT ON, COSTUMED VIGILANTES ARE NO LONGER WELCOME IN ASTRO CITY --

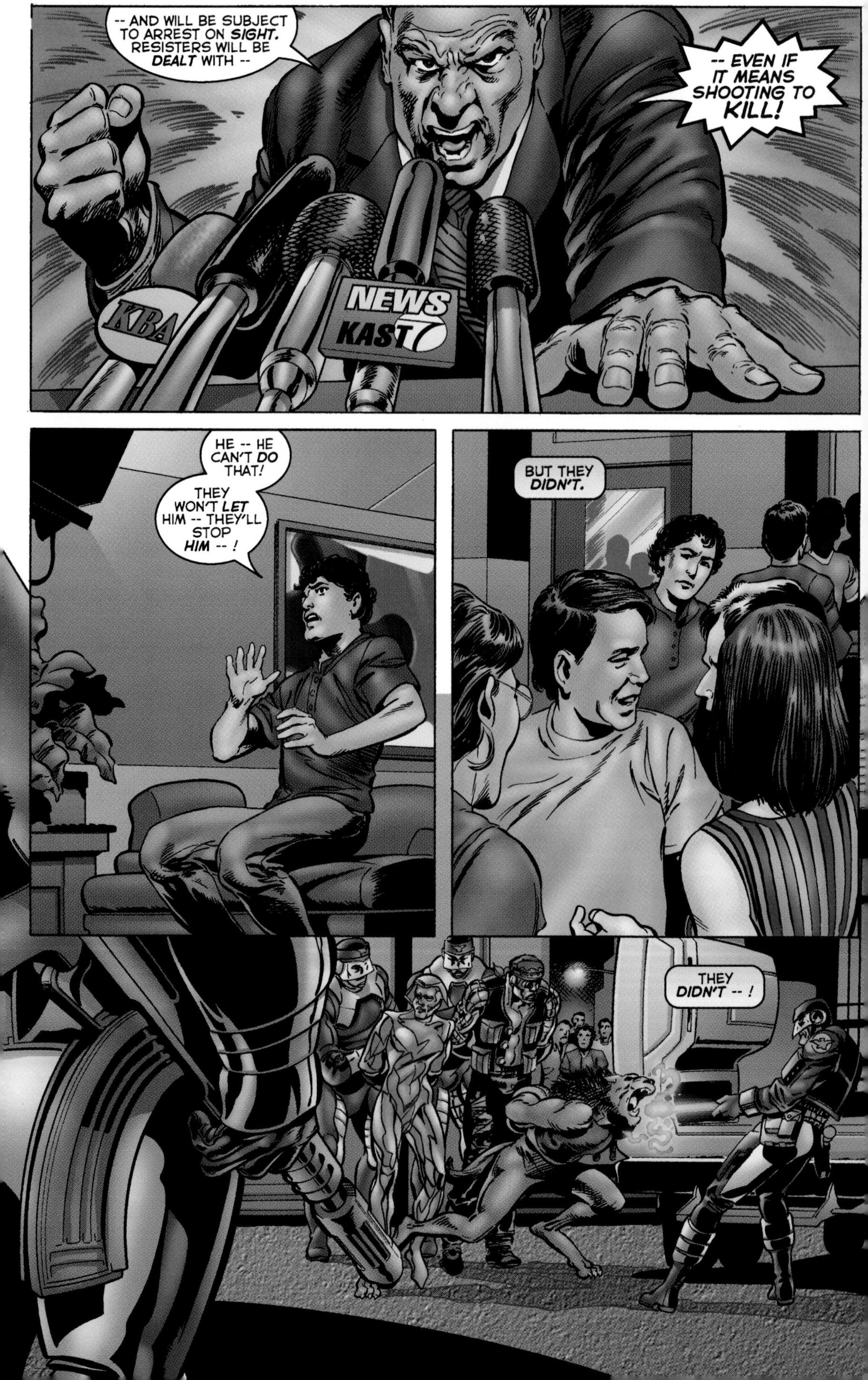

-- AND WILL BE SUBJECT TO ARREST ON SIGHT. RESISTERS WILL BE DEALT WITH --
-- EVEN IF IT MEANS SHOOTING TO KILL!
KBA
NEWS KAST 7
HE -- HE CAN'T DO THAT!
THEY WON'T LET HIM -- THEY'LL STOP HIM -- !
BUT THEY DIDN'T.
THEY DIDN'T -- !

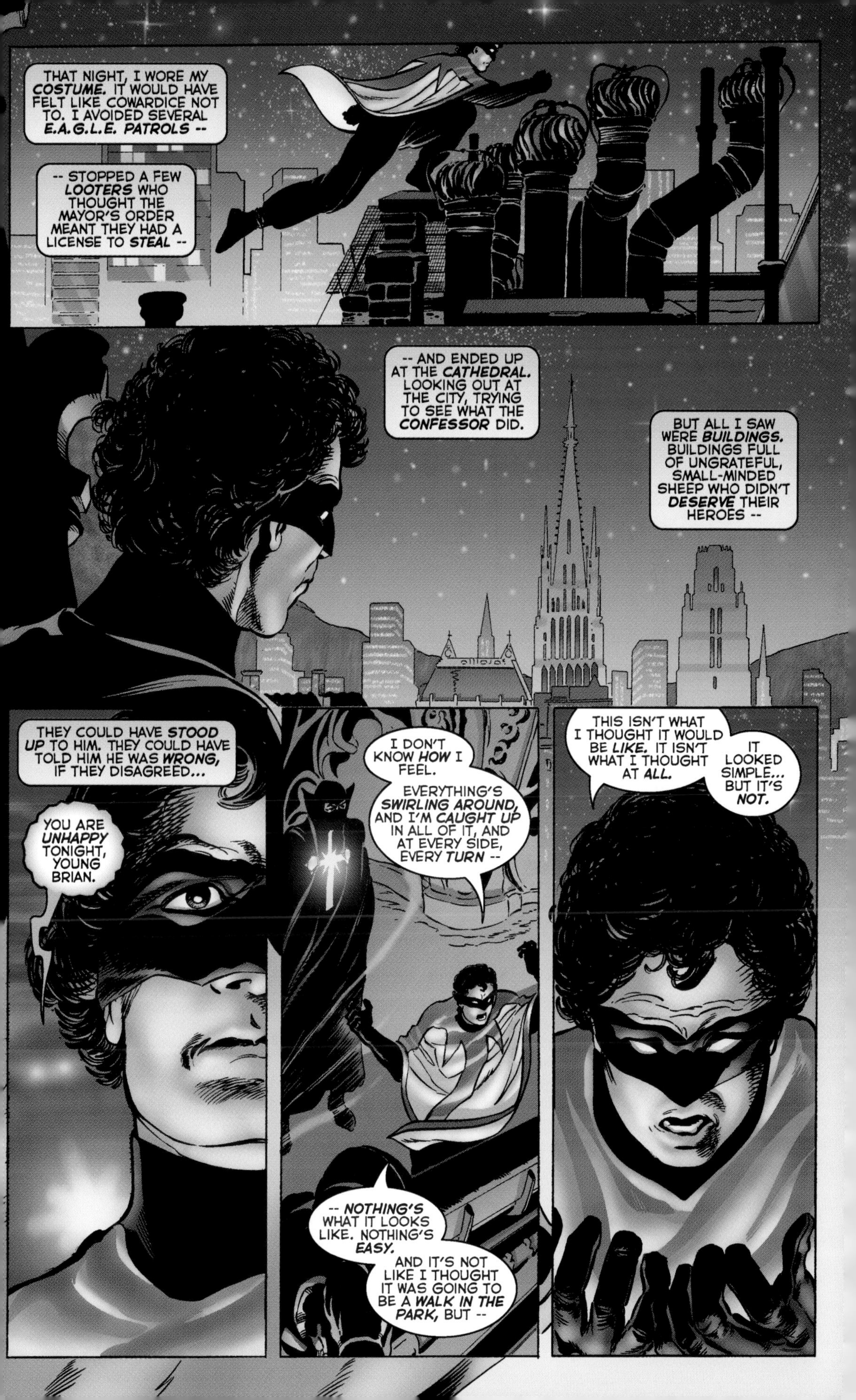
THAT NIGHT, I WORE MY COSTUME. IT WOULD HAVE FELT LIKE COWARDICE NOT TO. I AVOIDED SEVERAL E.A.G.L.E. PATROLS --
-- STOPPED A FEW LOOTERS WHO THOUGHT THE MAYOR'S ORDER MEANT THEY HAD A LICENSE TO STEAL --
-- AND ENDED UP AT THE CATHEDRAL. LOOKING OUT AT THE CITY, TRYING TO SEE WHAT THE CONFESSOR DID.
BUT ALL I SAW WERE BUILDINGS. BUILDINGS FULL OF UNGRATEFUL, SMALL-MINDED SHEEP WHO DIDN'T DESERVE THEIR HEROES --
THEY COULD HAVE STOOD UP TO HIM. THEY COULD HAVE TOLD HIM HE WAS WRONG, IF THEY DISAGREED...
YOU ARE UNHAPPY TONIGHT, YOUNG BRIAN.
I DON'T KNOW HOW I FEEL.
EVERYTHING'S SWIRLING AROUND, AND I'M CAUGHT UP IN ALL OF IT, AND AT EVERY SIDE, EVERY TURN --
-- NOTHING'S WHAT IT LOOKS LIKE. NOTHING'S EASY.
AND IT'S NOT LIKE I THOUGHT IT WAS GOING TO BE A WALK IN THE PARK, BUT --
THIS ISN'T WHAT I THOUGHT IT WOULD BE LIKE. IT ISN'T WHAT I THOUGHT AT ALL.
IT LOOKED SIMPLE... BUT IT'S NOT.

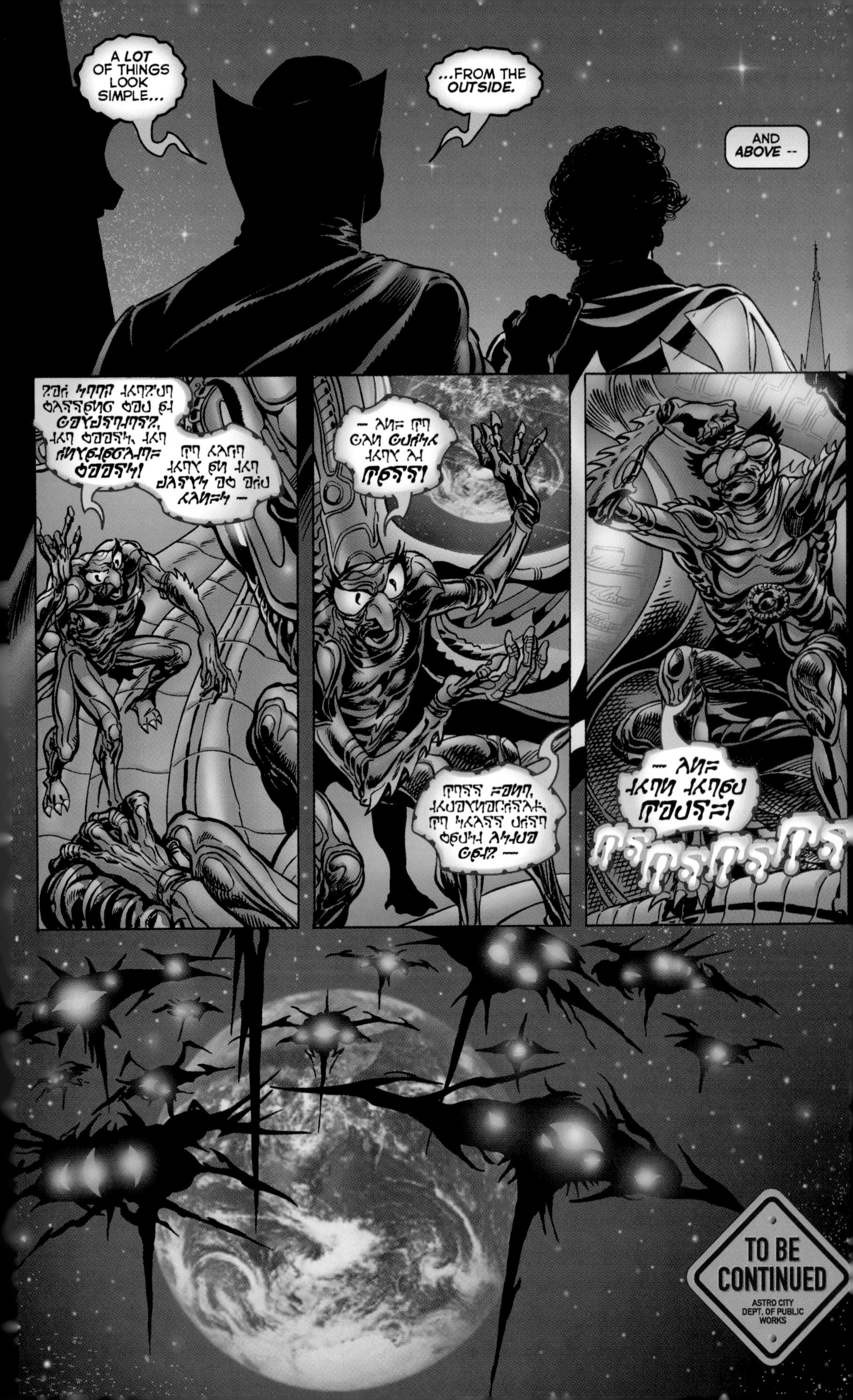
A LOT OF THINGS LOOK SIMPLE...
...FROM THE OUTSIDE.
AND ABOVE --
TO BE CONTINUED
ASTRO CITY DEPT. OF PUBLIC WORKS

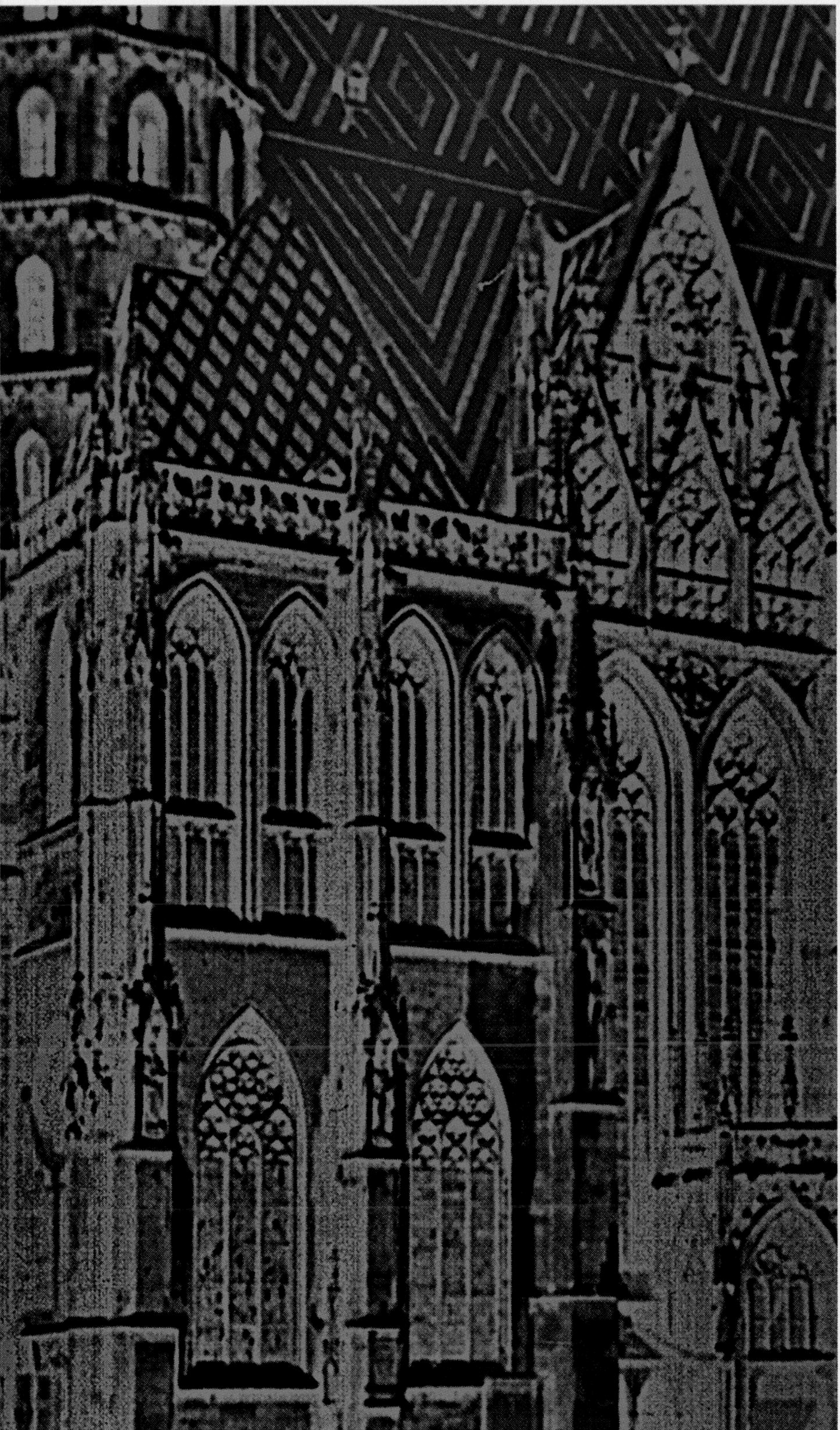

CHAPTER 5

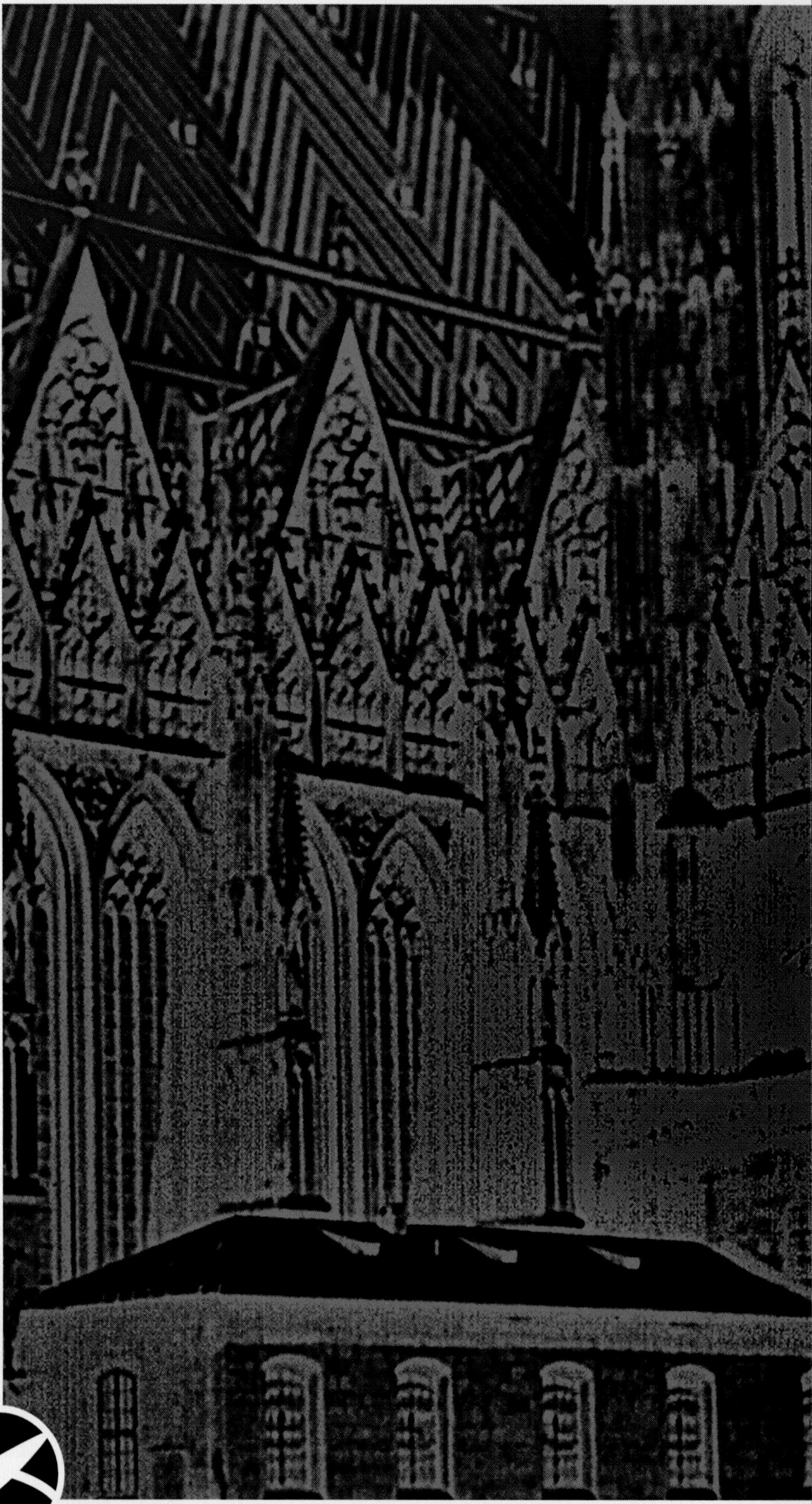

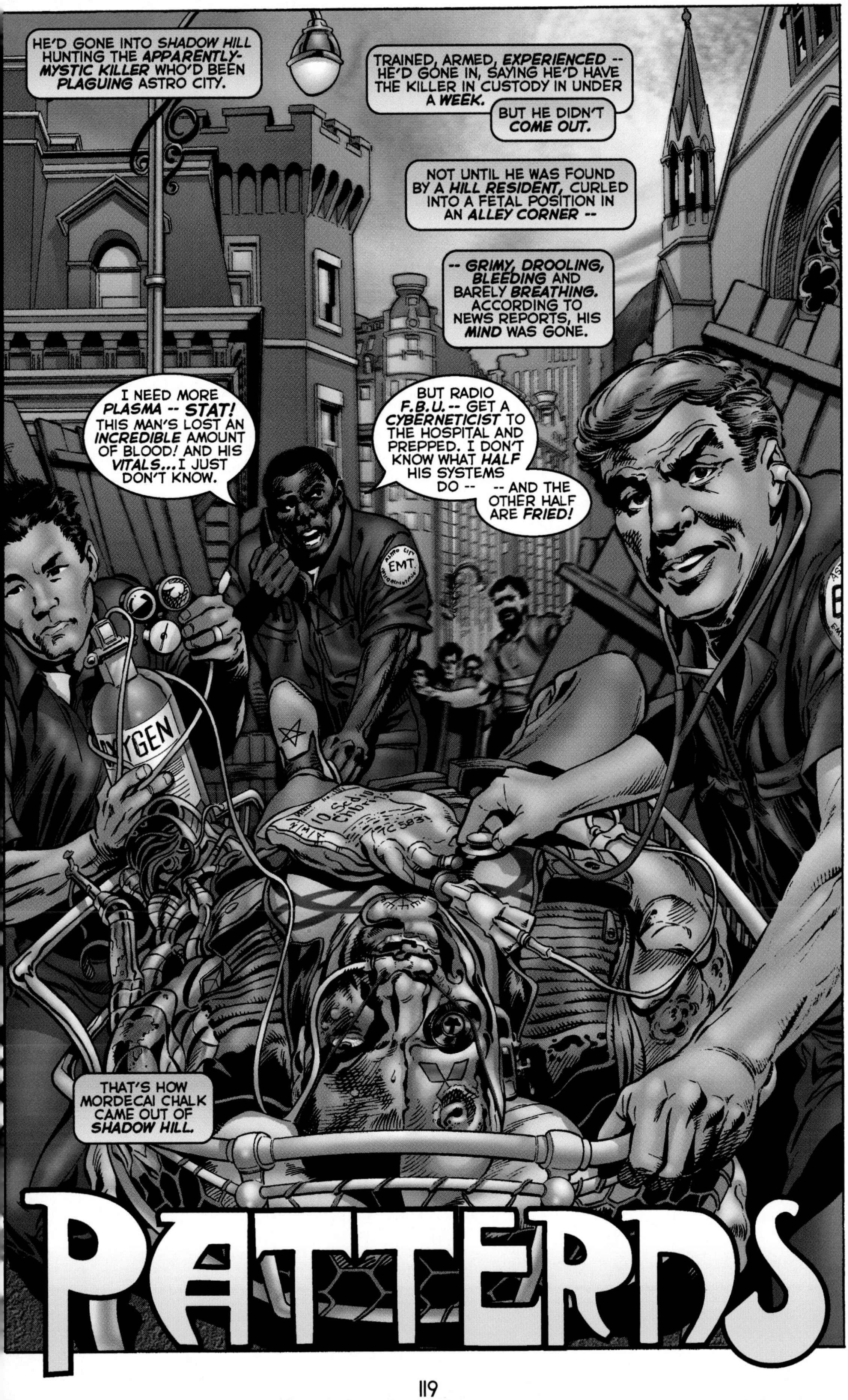
HE'D GONE INTO SHADOW HILL HUNTING THE APPARENTLY-MYSTIC KILLER WHO'D BEEN PLAGUING ASTRO CITY.
TRAINED, ARMED, EXPERIENCED -- HE'D GONE IN, SAYING HE'D HAVE THE KILLER IN CUSTODY IN UNDER A WEEK.
BUT HE DIDN'T COME OUT.
NOT UNTIL HE WAS FOUND BY A HILL RESIDENT, CURLED INTO A FETAL POSITION IN AN ALLEY CORNER --
-- GRIMY, DROOLING, BLEEDING AND BARELY BREATHING. ACCORDING TO NEWS REPORTS, HIS MIND WAS GONE.
I NEED MORE PLASMA -- STAT! THIS MAN'S LOST AN INCREDIBLE AMOUNT OF BLOOD! AND HIS VITALS... I JUST DON'T KNOW.
BUT RADIO F.B.U. -- GET A CYBERNETICIST TO THE HOSPITAL AND PREPPED. I DON'T KNOW WHAT HALF HIS SYSTEMS DO --
-- AND THE OTHER HALF ARE FRIED!
EMT
THAT'S HOW MORDECAI CHALK CAME OUT OF SHADOW HILL.
PATTERNS

SIR!

IS HE -- ?

WHAT'S HIS --

WHAT *WAS* IT? WHAT DID HE *MEET* IN THERE?

I DON'T KNOW. BUT *WHATEVER* IT WAS, HE SURE AS HELL MET *SOMETHING.*

AND THERE YOU HAVE IT. HE MET... *SOMETHING.* AS TO THE *DETAILS* -- AT THIS POINT, ONLY *TIME* WILL TELL.

THE MAYOR ISSUED A *STATEMENT* THIS MORNING, UPON HEARING OF THE *TRAGIC DEVELOPMENTS...*

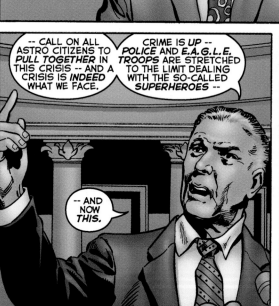

-- CALL ON ALL ASTRO CITIZENS TO *PULL TOGETHER* IN THIS CRISIS -- AND A CRISIS IS *INDEED* WHAT WE FACE.

CRIME IS *UP* -- POLICE AND *E.A.G.L.E.* TROOPS ARE STRETCHED TO THE LIMIT DEALING WITH THE SO-CALLED *SUPERHEROES* --

-- AND NOW *THIS.*

THE BOTTOM LINE IS THE *SAFETY* OF THE CITIZENRY --

-- BUT THE "HEROES" SEEM TO HAVE FORGOTTEN THAT. ONCE AGAIN, I URGE THEM -- HELP US. *WORK WITH US.* YOUR INTRANSIGENCE IS *DIVISIVE* --

-- AND ANYTHING LESS THAN FULL COOPERATION IS HARMFUL TO US ALL.

HE'S A POLITICIAN, WHADDYA *EXPECT?* C'MON, *GILLIGAN'S ISLAND'S* ON.

PSHYEAH, *RIGHT.* HE IS SO FULL OF IT.

THE MAYOR WAS *WRONG.* THE HEROES WERE DOING *FINE* -- OR AT LEAST DOING THEIR *BEST* --

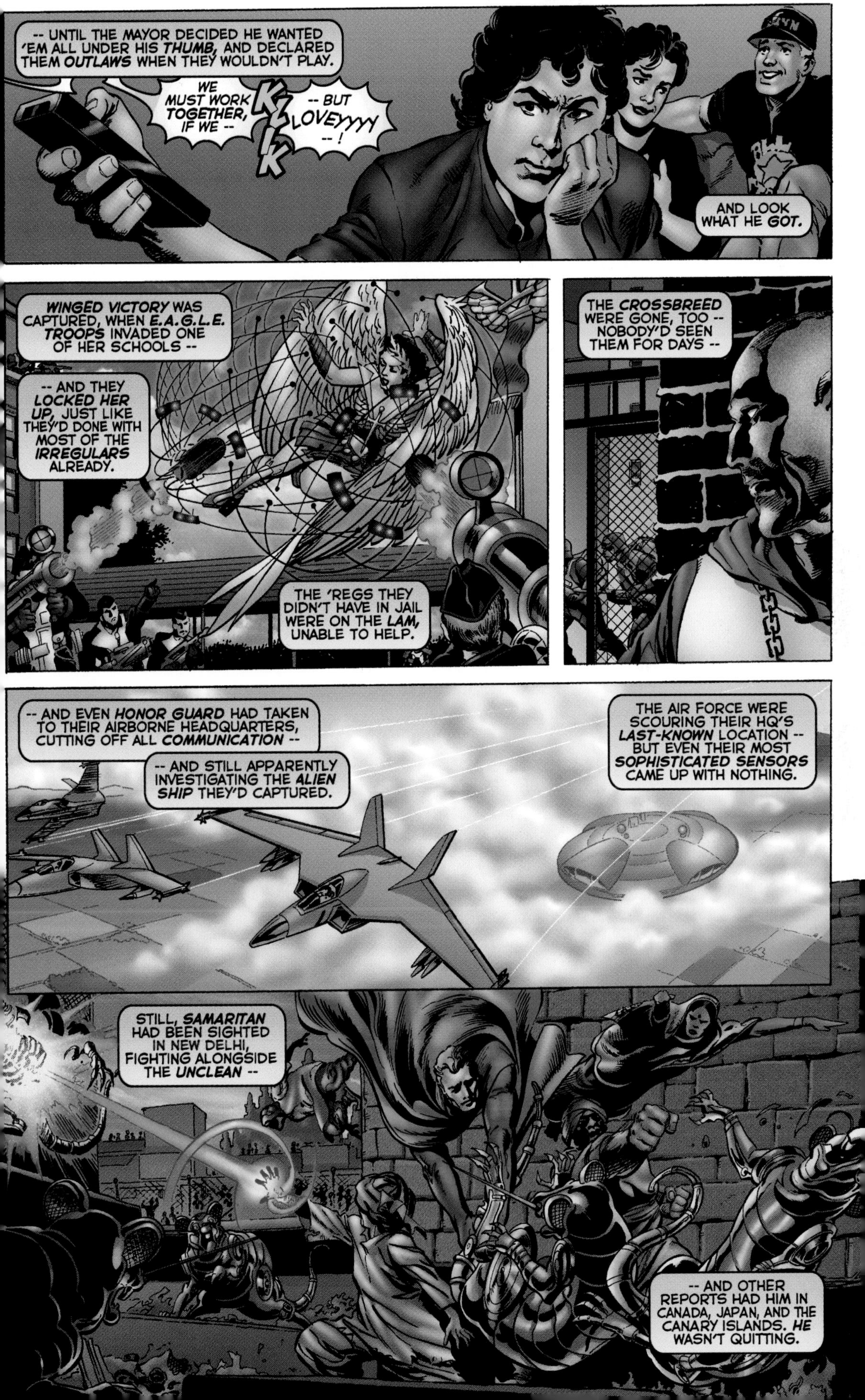
-- UNTIL THE MAYOR DECIDED HE WANTED 'EM ALL UNDER HIS THUMB, AND DECLARED THEM OUTLAWS WHEN THEY WOULDN'T PLAY.
WE MUST WORK TOGETHER, IF WE --
KLIK
-- BUT LOVEYYYY -- !
AND LOOK WHAT HE GOT.
WINGED VICTORY WAS CAPTURED, WHEN E.A.G.L.E. TROOPS INVADED ONE OF HER SCHOOLS --
-- AND THEY LOCKED HER UP, JUST LIKE THEY'D DONE WITH MOST OF THE IRREGULARS ALREADY.
THE 'REGS THEY DIDN'T HAVE IN JAIL WERE ON THE LAM, UNABLE TO HELP.
THE CROSSBREED WERE GONE, TOO -- NOBODY'D SEEN THEM FOR DAYS --
-- AND EVEN HONOR GUARD HAD TAKEN TO THEIR AIRBORNE HEADQUARTERS, CUTTING OFF ALL COMMUNICATION --
-- AND STILL APPARENTLY INVESTIGATING THE ALIEN SHIP THEY'D CAPTURED.
THE AIR FORCE WERE SCOURING THEIR HQ'S LAST-KNOWN LOCATION -- BUT EVEN THEIR MOST SOPHISTICATED SENSORS CAME UP WITH NOTHING.
STILL, SAMARITAN HAD BEEN SIGHTED IN NEW DELHI, FIGHTING ALONGSIDE THE UNCLEAN --
-- AND OTHER REPORTS HAD HIM IN CANADA, JAPAN, AND THE CANARY ISLANDS. HE WASN'T QUITTING.

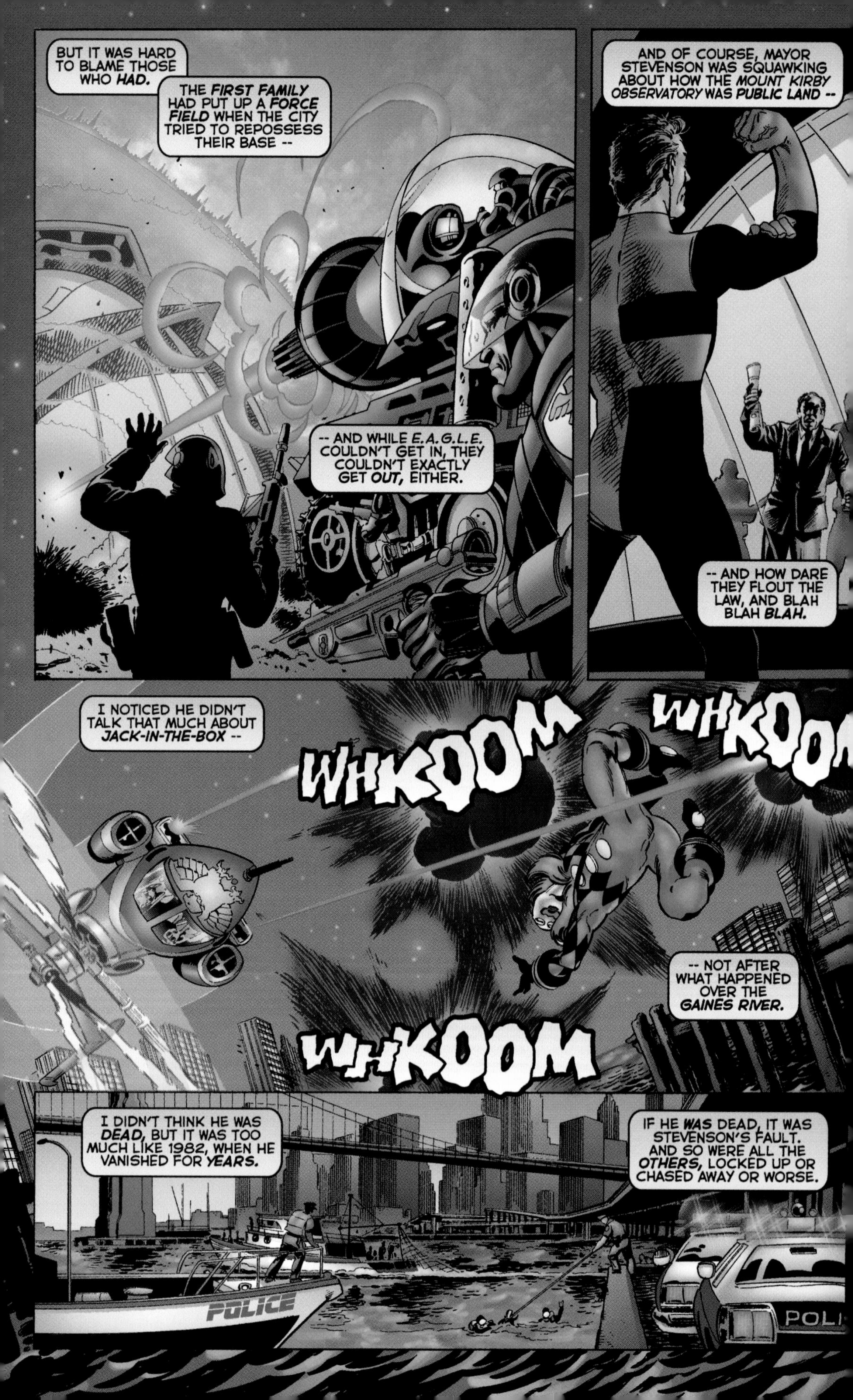
BUT IT WAS HARD TO BLAME THOSE WHO *HAD.*
THE *FIRST FAMILY* HAD PUT UP A *FORCE FIELD* WHEN THE CITY TRIED TO REPOSSESS THEIR BASE --
-- AND WHILE *E.A.G.L.E.* COULDN'T GET IN, THEY COULDN'T EXACTLY GET *OUT,* EITHER.
AND OF COURSE, MAYOR STEVENSON WAS SQUAWKING ABOUT HOW THE *MOUNT KIRBY OBSERVATORY* WAS *PUBLIC LAND* --
-- AND HOW DARE THEY FLOUT THE LAW, AND BLAH BLAH *BLAH.*
I NOTICED HE DIDN'T TALK THAT MUCH ABOUT *JACK-IN-THE-BOX* --
WHKOOM
WHKOOM
-- NOT AFTER WHAT HAPPENED OVER THE *GAINES RIVER.*
WHKOOM
I DIDN'T THINK HE WAS *DEAD,* BUT IT WAS TOO MUCH LIKE 1982, WHEN HE VANISHED FOR *YEARS.*
IF HE *WAS* DEAD, IT WAS STEVENSON'S FAULT. AND SO WERE ALL THE *OTHERS,* LOCKED UP OR CHASED AWAY OR WORSE.
POLICE
POLI

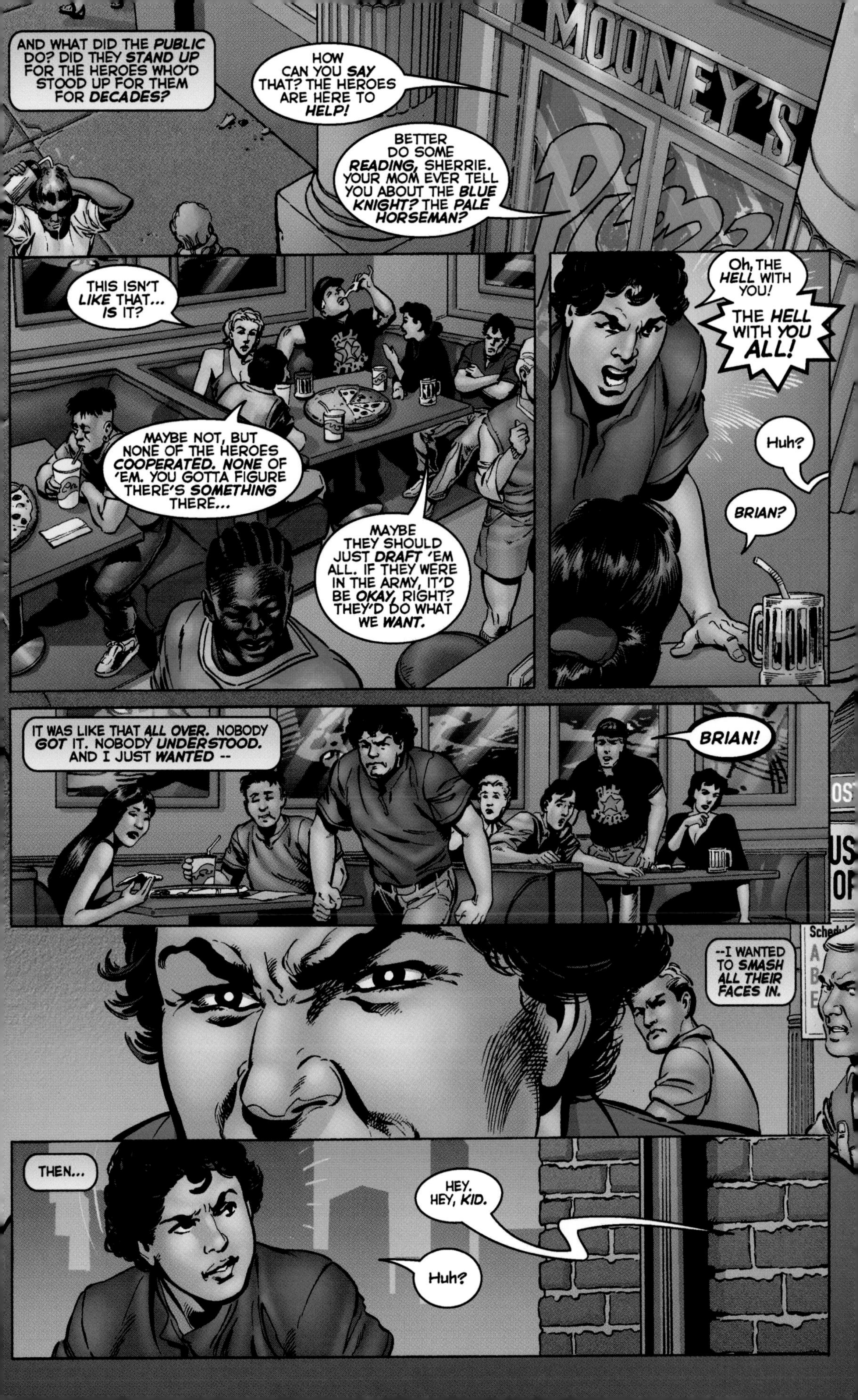
AND WHAT DID THE PUBLIC DO? DID THEY STAND UP FOR THE HEROES WHO'D STOOD UP FOR THEM FOR DECADES?
HOW CAN YOU SAY THAT? THE HEROES ARE HERE TO HELP!
BETTER DO SOME READING, SHERRIE. YOUR MOM EVER TELL YOU ABOUT THE BLUE KNIGHT? THE PALE HORSEMAN?
MOONEY'S
THIS ISN'T LIKE THAT... IS IT?
MAYBE NOT, BUT NONE OF THE HEROES COOPERATED. NONE OF 'EM. YOU GOTTA FIGURE THERE'S SOMETHING THERE...
MAYBE THEY SHOULD JUST DRAFT 'EM ALL. IF THEY WERE IN THE ARMY, IT'D BE OKAY, RIGHT? THEY'D DO WHAT WE WANT.
Oh, THE HELL WITH YOU!
THE HELL WITH YOU ALL!
Huh?
BRIAN?
IT WAS LIKE THAT ALL OVER. NOBODY GOT IT. NOBODY UNDERSTOOD. AND I JUST WANTED --
BRIAN!
--I WANTED TO SMASH ALL THEIR FACES IN.
THEN...
HEY. HEY, KID.
Huh?

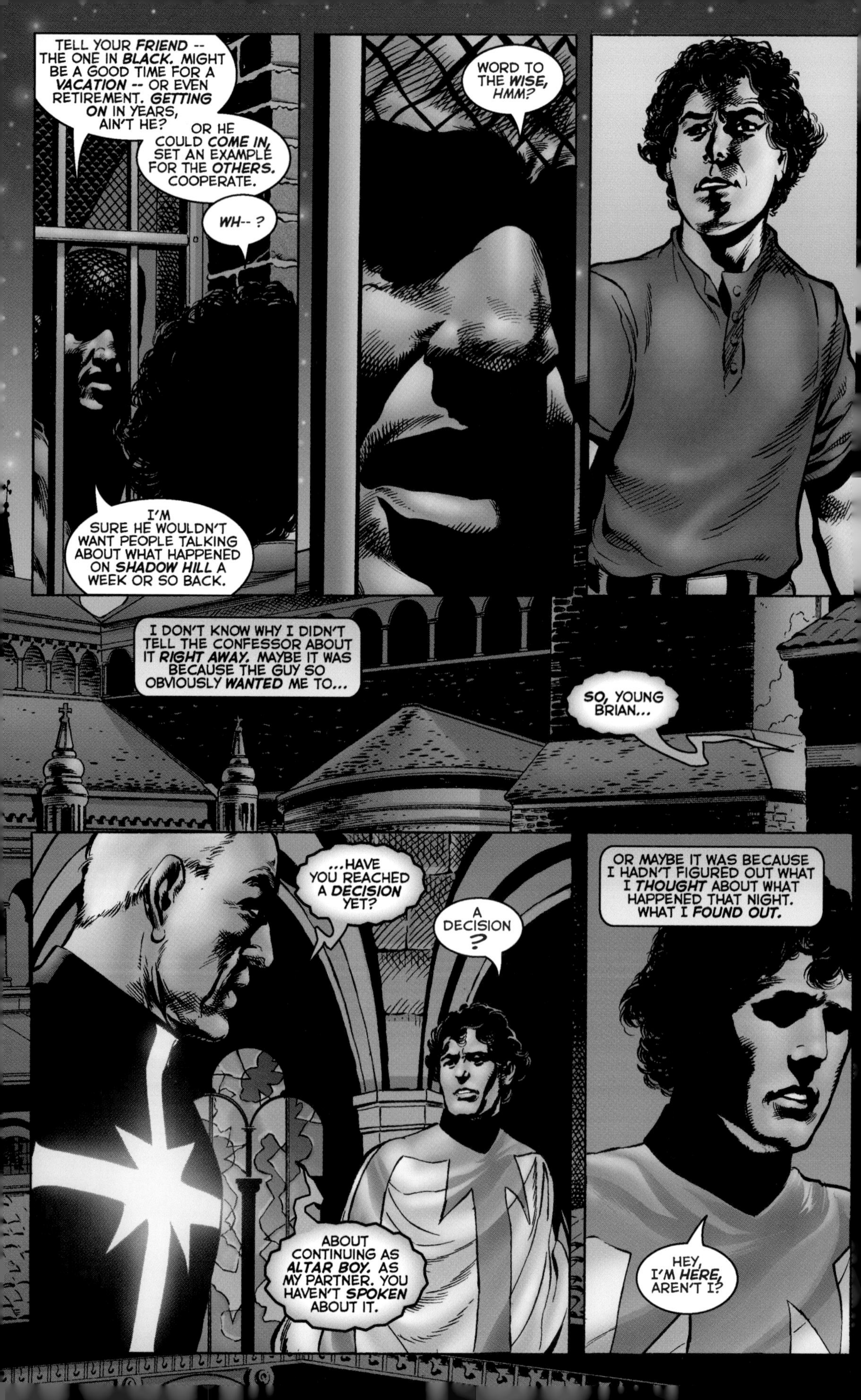
TELL YOUR FRIEND -- THE ONE IN BLACK. MIGHT BE A GOOD TIME FOR A VACATION -- OR EVEN RETIREMENT. GETTING ON IN YEARS, AIN'T HE?
OR HE COULD COME IN, SET AN EXAMPLE FOR THE OTHERS. COOPERATE.
WH-- ?
I'M SURE HE WOULDN'T WANT PEOPLE TALKING ABOUT WHAT HAPPENED ON SHADOW HILL A WEEK OR SO BACK.
WORD TO THE WISE, HMM?
I DON'T KNOW WHY I DIDN'T TELL THE CONFESSOR ABOUT IT RIGHT AWAY. MAYBE IT WAS BECAUSE THE GUY SO OBVIOUSLY WANTED ME TO...
SO, YOUNG BRIAN...
...HAVE YOU REACHED A DECISION YET?
A DECISION ?
ABOUT CONTINUING AS ALTAR BOY. AS MY PARTNER. YOU HAVEN'T SPOKEN ABOUT IT.
OR MAYBE IT WAS BECAUSE I HADN'T FIGURED OUT WHAT I THOUGHT ABOUT WHAT HAPPENED THAT NIGHT. WHAT I FOUND OUT.
HEY, I'M HERE, AREN'T I?

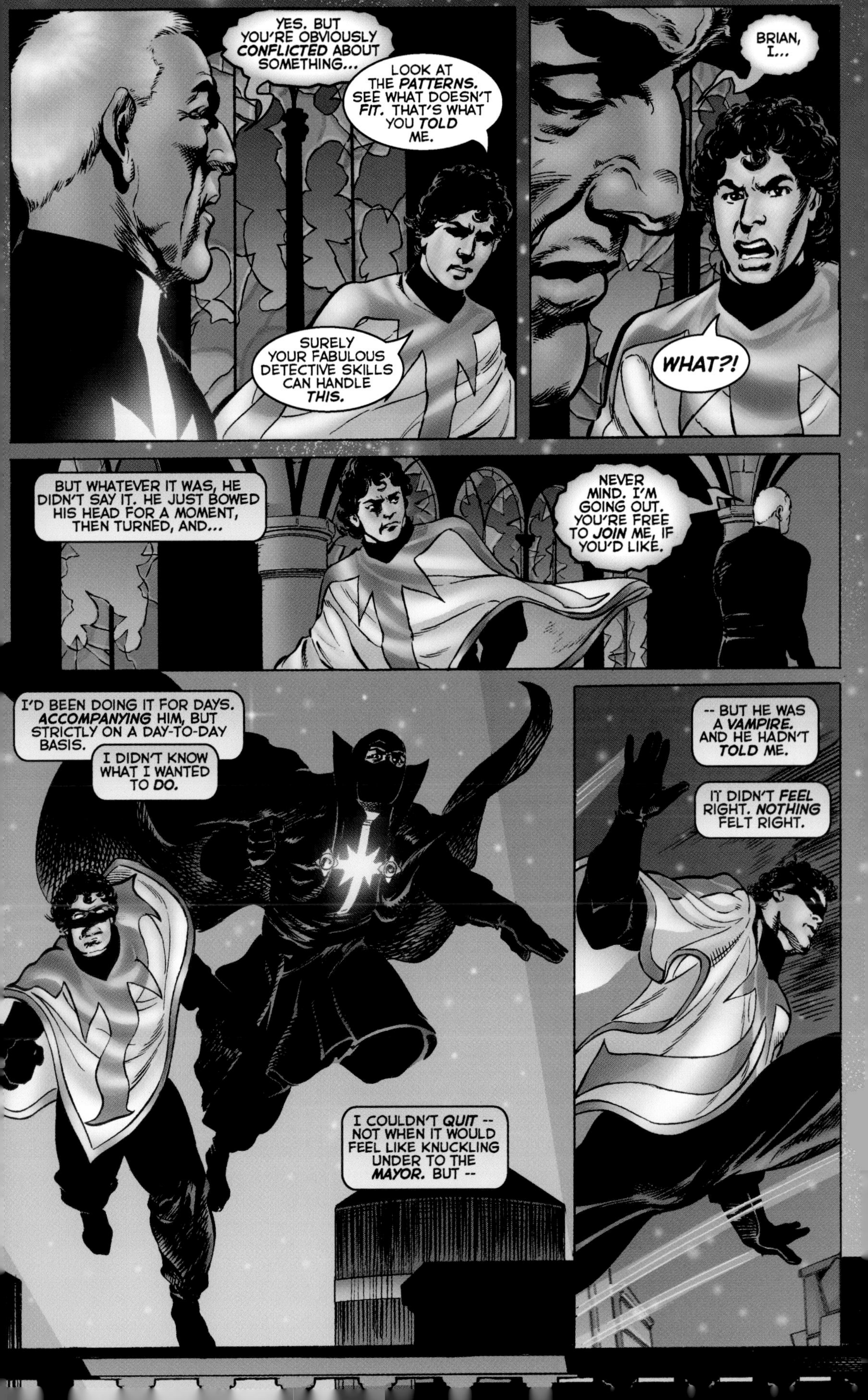
YES. BUT YOU'RE OBVIOUSLY CONFLICTED ABOUT SOMETHING...
LOOK AT THE PATTERNS. SEE WHAT DOESN'T FIT. THAT'S WHAT YOU TOLD ME.
SURELY YOUR FABULOUS DETECTIVE SKILLS CAN HANDLE THIS.
BRIAN, I...
WHAT?!
BUT WHATEVER IT WAS, HE DIDN'T SAY IT. HE JUST BOWED HIS HEAD FOR A MOMENT, THEN TURNED, AND...
NEVER MIND. I'M GOING OUT. YOU'RE FREE TO JOIN ME, IF YOU'D LIKE.
I'D BEEN DOING IT FOR DAYS. ACCOMPANYING HIM, BUT STRICTLY ON A DAY-TO-DAY BASIS.
I DIDN'T KNOW WHAT I WANTED TO DO.
I COULDN'T QUIT -- NOT WHEN IT WOULD FEEL LIKE KNUCKLING UNDER TO THE MAYOR. BUT --
-- BUT HE WAS A VAMPIRE. AND HE HADN'T TOLD ME.
IT DIDN'T FEEL RIGHT. NOTHING FELT RIGHT.

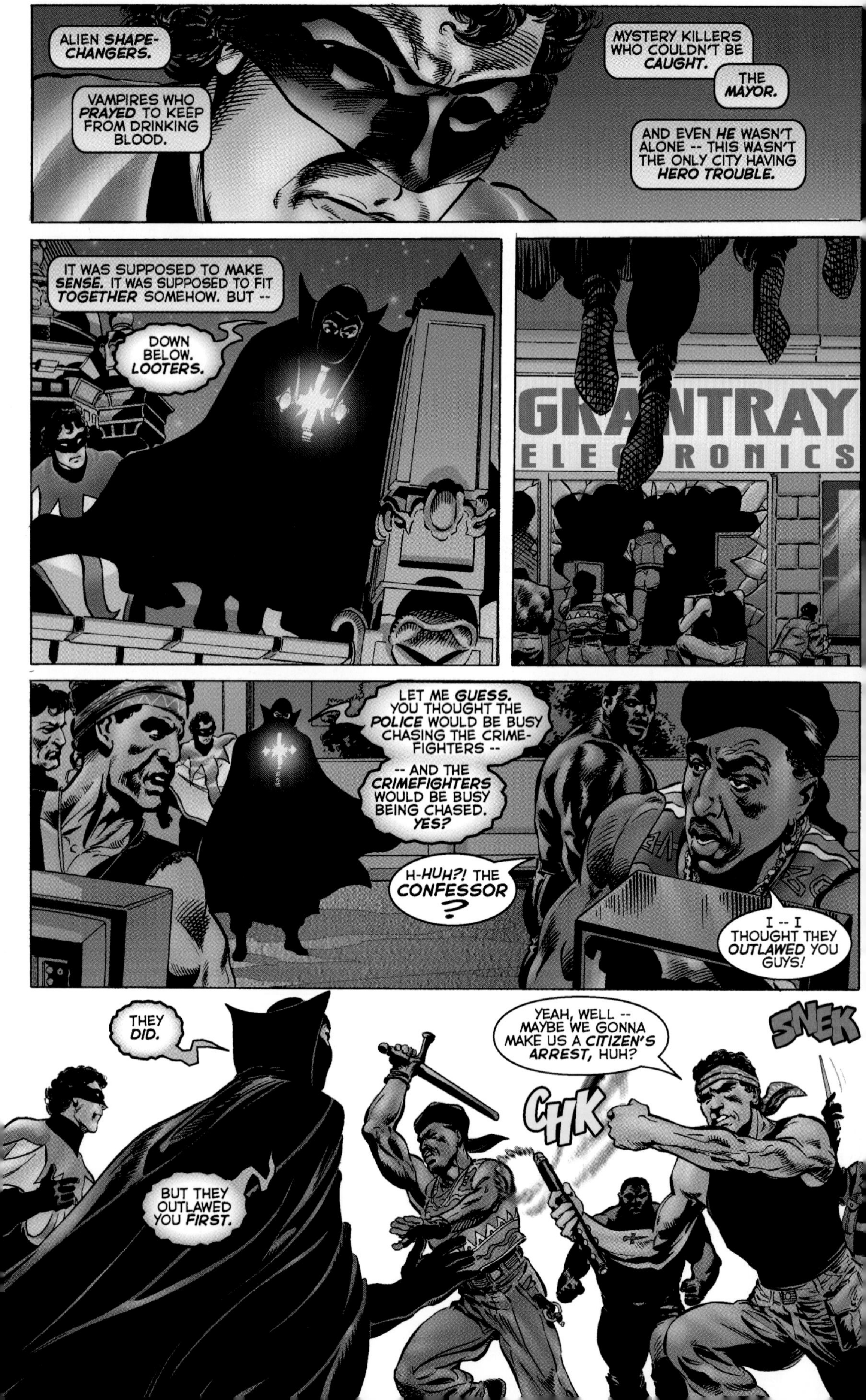

ALIEN SHAPE-CHANGERS.
VAMPIRES WHO PRAYED TO KEEP FROM DRINKING BLOOD.
MYSTERY KILLERS WHO COULDN'T BE CAUGHT.
THE MAYOR.
AND EVEN HE WASN'T ALONE -- THIS WASN'T THE ONLY CITY HAVING HERO TROUBLE.
IT WAS SUPPOSED TO MAKE SENSE. IT WAS SUPPOSED TO FIT TOGETHER SOMEHOW. BUT --
DOWN BELOW. LOOTERS.
GRANTRAY
ELECRONICS
LET ME GUESS. YOU THOUGHT THE POLICE WOULD BE BUSY CHASING THE CRIME-FIGHTERS --
-- AND THE CRIMEFIGHTERS WOULD BE BUSY BEING CHASED. YES?
H-HUH?! THE CONFESSOR?
I -- I THOUGHT THEY OUTLAWED YOU GUYS!
THEY DID.
BUT THEY OUTLAWED YOU FIRST.
YEAH, WELL -- MAYBE WE GONNA MAKE US A CITIZEN'S ARREST, HUH?
SNEK
CHK

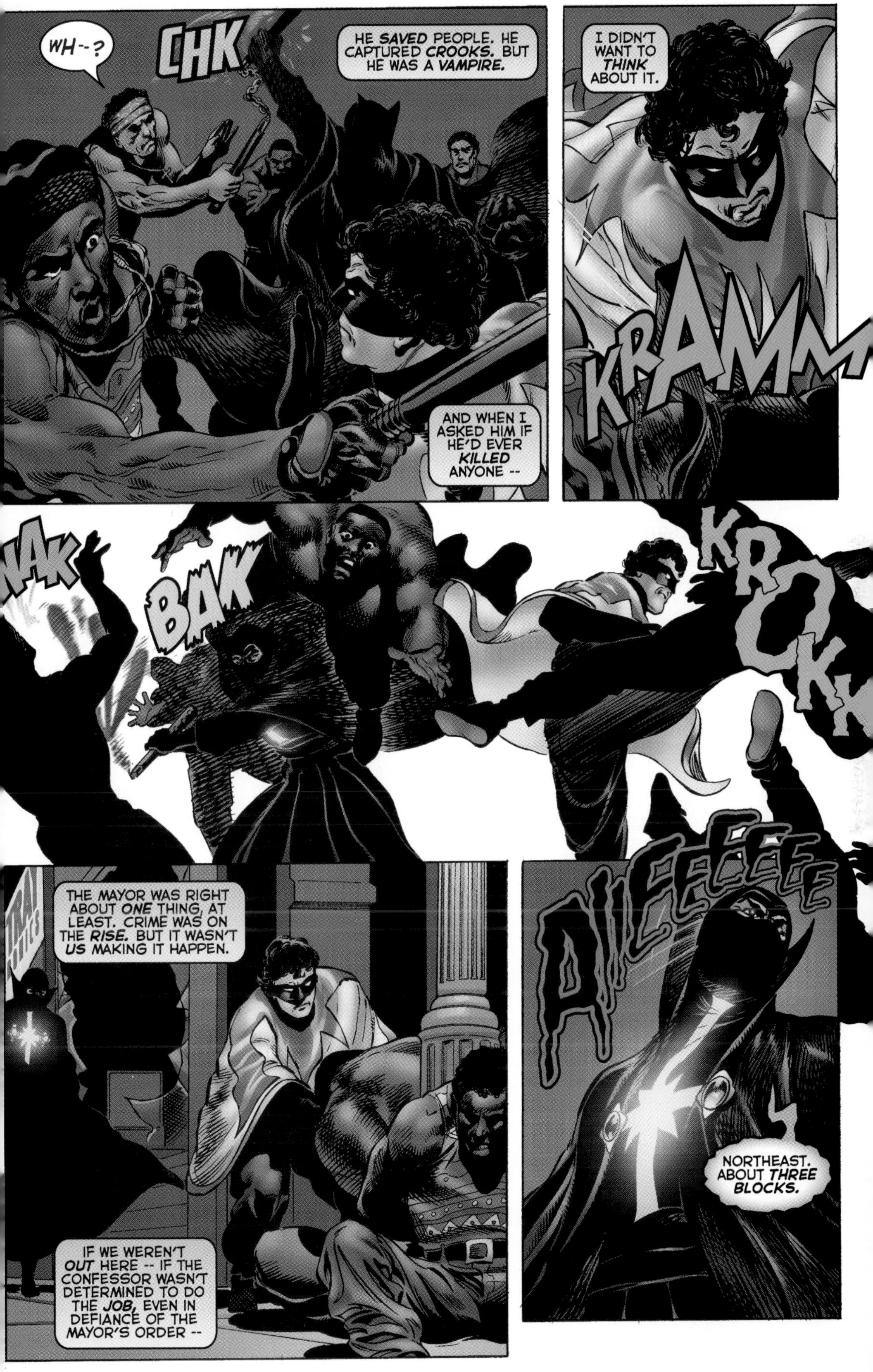
WH--?
CHK
HE SAVED PEOPLE. HE CAPTURED CROOKS. BUT HE WAS A VAMPIRE.
AND WHEN I ASKED HIM IF HE'D EVER KILLED ANYONE --
I DIDN'T WANT TO THINK ABOUT IT.
KRAMM
BAK
KROCKK
AIEEEEEE
THE MAYOR WAS RIGHT ABOUT ONE THING, AT LEAST. CRIME WAS ON THE RISE. BUT IT WASN'T US MAKING IT HAPPEN.
IF WE WEREN'T OUT HERE -- IF THE CONFESSOR WASN'T DETERMINED TO DO THE JOB, EVEN IN DEFIANCE OF THE MAYOR'S ORDER --
NORTHEAST. ABOUT THREE BLOCKS.

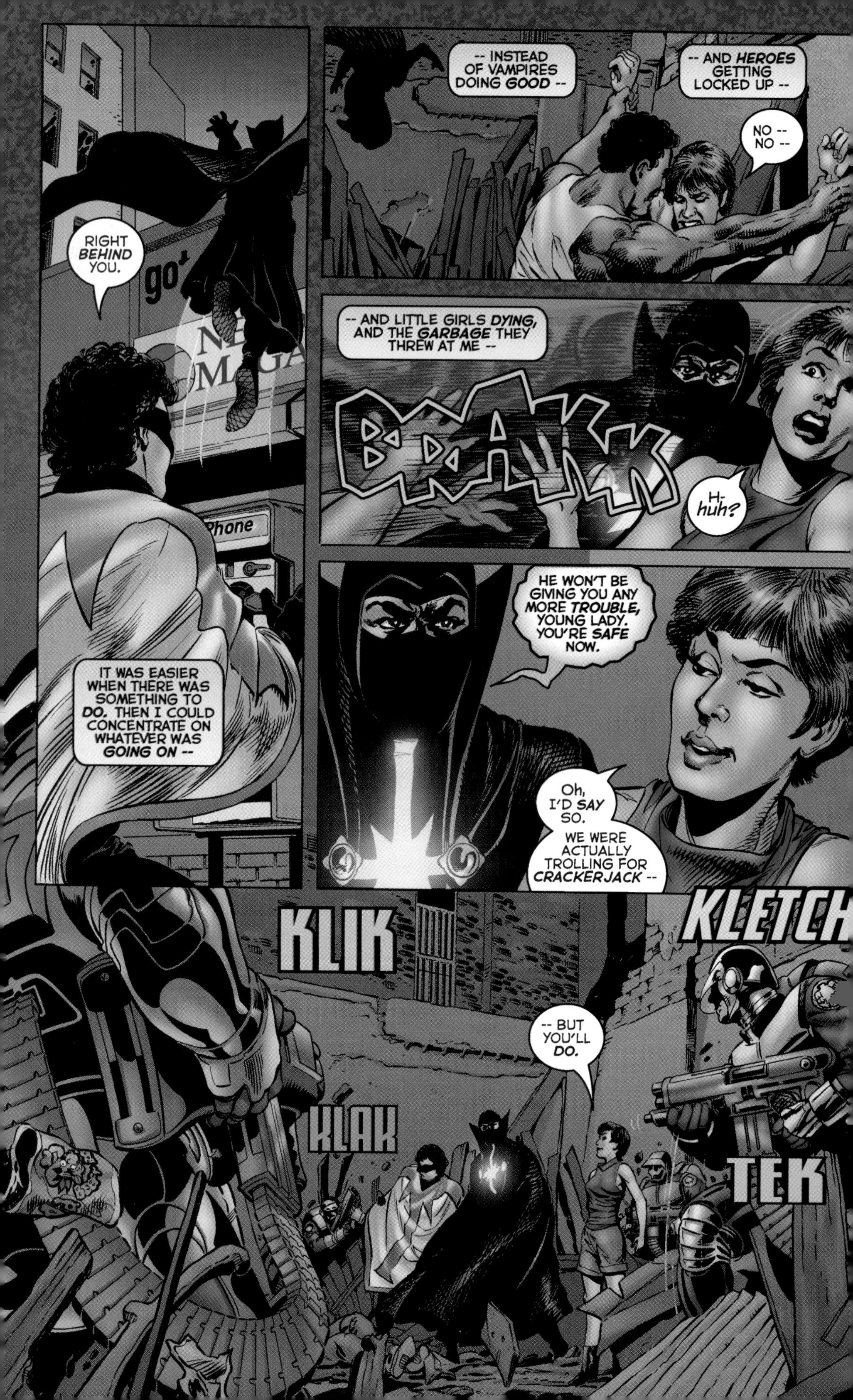
RIGHT BEHIND YOU.
go
Phone
IT WAS EASIER WHEN THERE WAS SOMETHING TO DO. THEN I COULD CONCENTRATE ON WHATEVER WAS GOING ON --
-- INSTEAD OF VAMPIRES DOING GOOD --
-- AND HEROES GETTING LOCKED UP --
NO -- NO --
-- AND LITTLE GIRLS DYING, AND THE GARBAGE THEY THREW AT ME --
BRAKK
H-huh?
HE WON'T BE GIVING YOU ANY MORE TROUBLE, YOUNG LADY. YOU'RE SAFE NOW.
Oh, I'D SAY SO.
WE WERE ACTUALLY TROLLING FOR CRACKERJACK --
KLIK
KLETCH
-- BUT YOU'LL DO.
KLAK
TEK

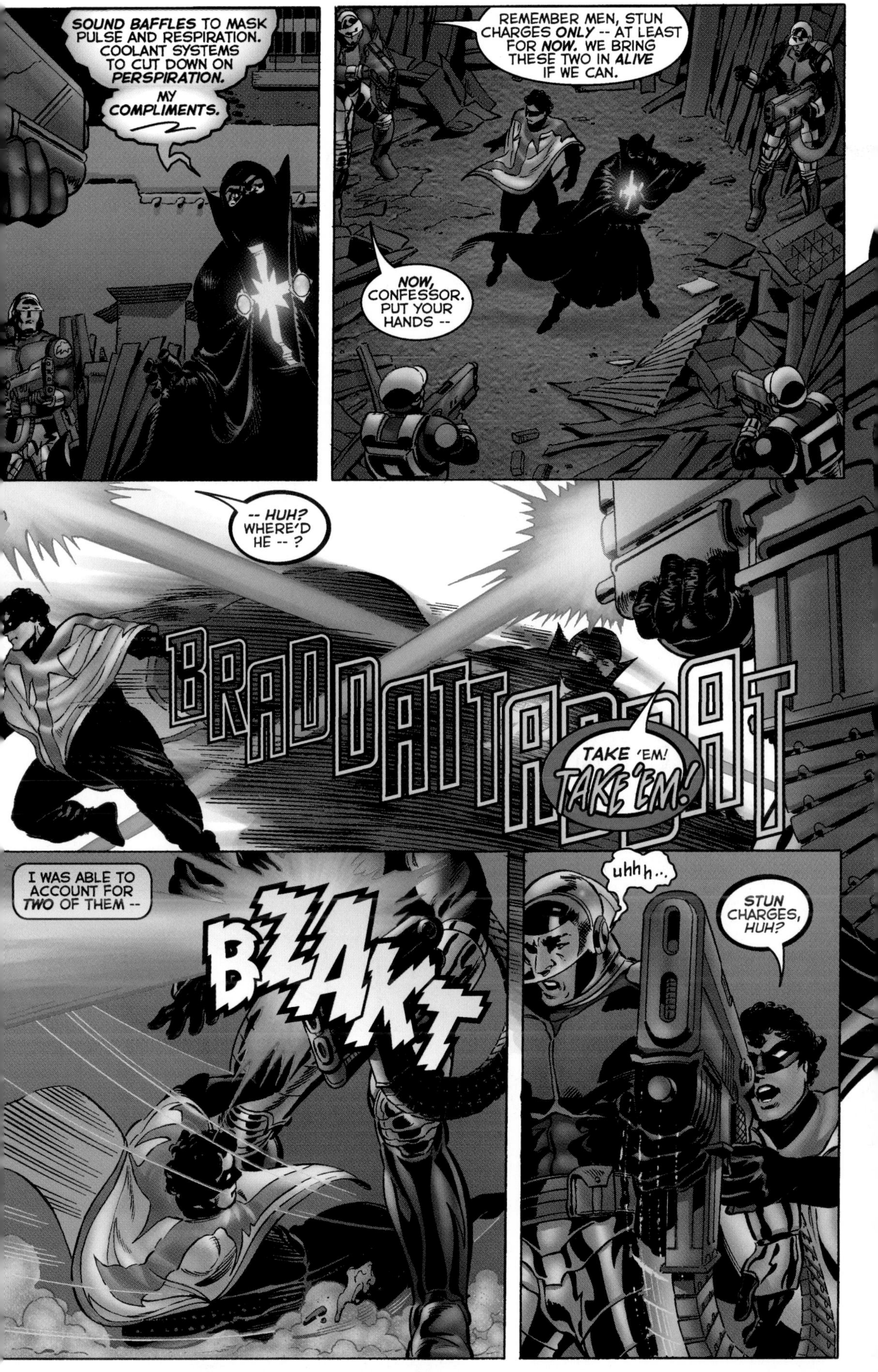

SOUND BAFFLES TO MASK PULSE AND RESPIRATION. COOLANT SYSTEMS TO CUT DOWN ON PERSPIRATION.
MY COMPLIMENTS.
REMEMBER MEN, STUN CHARGES ONLY -- AT LEAST FOR NOW. WE BRING THESE TWO IN ALIVE IF WE CAN.
NOW, CONFESSOR. PUT YOUR HANDS --
-- HUH? WHERE'D HE -- ?
BRADDATTADDAT
TAKE 'EM! TAKE 'EM!
I WAS ABLE TO ACCOUNT FOR TWO OF THEM --
BZAKT
uhhh...
STUN CHARGES, HUH?

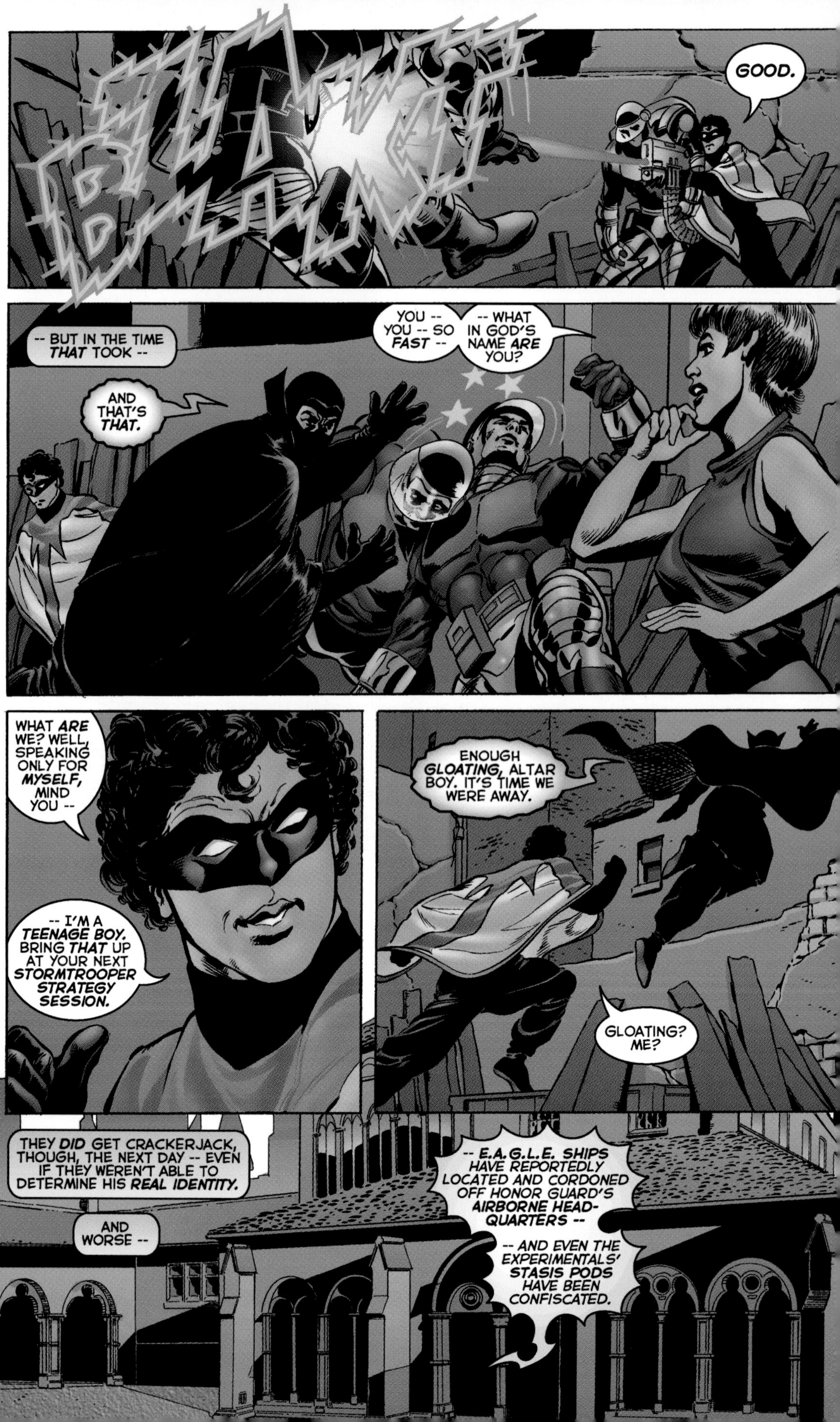
GOOD.
-- BUT IN THE TIME THAT TOOK --
AND THAT'S THAT.
YOU -- YOU -- SO FAST --
-- WHAT IN GOD'S NAME ARE YOU?
WHAT ARE WE? WELL, SPEAKING ONLY FOR MYSELF, MIND YOU --
-- I'M A TEENAGE BOY. BRING THAT UP AT YOUR NEXT STORMTROOPER STRATEGY SESSION.
ENOUGH GLOATING, ALTAR BOY. IT'S TIME WE WERE AWAY.
GLOATING? ME?
THEY DID GET CRACKERJACK, THOUGH, THE NEXT DAY -- EVEN IF THEY WEREN'T ABLE TO DETERMINE HIS REAL IDENTITY.
AND WORSE --
-- E.A.G.L.E. SHIPS HAVE REPORTEDLY LOCATED AND CORDONED OFF HONOR GUARD'S AIRBORNE HEAD-QUARTERS --
-- AND EVEN THE EXPERIMENTALS' STASIS PODS HAVE BEEN CONFISCATED.

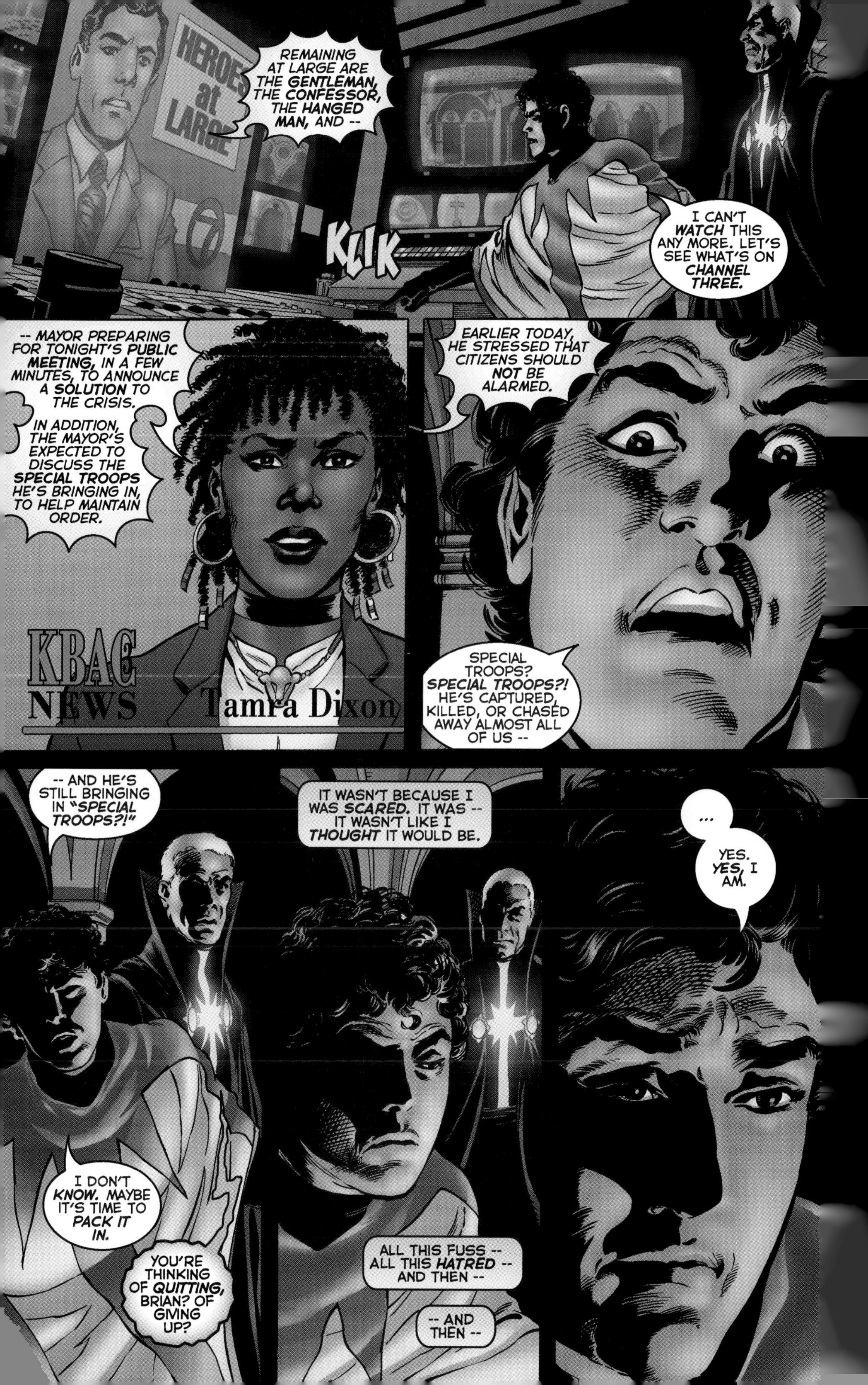
HEROES at LARGE
REMAINING AT LARGE ARE THE GENTLEMAN, THE CONFESSOR, THE HANGED MAN, AND --
KLIK
I CAN'T WATCH THIS ANY MORE. LET'S SEE WHAT'S ON CHANNEL THREE.
-- MAYOR PREPARING FOR TONIGHT'S PUBLIC MEETING, IN A FEW MINUTES, TO ANNOUNCE A SOLUTION TO THE CRISIS.
IN ADDITION, THE MAYOR'S EXPECTED TO DISCUSS THE SPECIAL TROOPS HE'S BRINGING IN, TO HELP MAINTAIN ORDER.
KBAC NEWS
Tamra Dixon
EARLIER TODAY, HE STRESSED THAT CITIZENS SHOULD NOT BE ALARMED.
SPECIAL TROOPS? SPECIAL TROOPS?! HE'S CAPTURED, KILLED, OR CHASED AWAY ALMOST ALL OF US --
-- AND HE'S STILL BRINGING IN "SPECIAL TROOPS?!"
I DON'T KNOW. MAYBE IT'S TIME TO PACK IT IN.
YOU'RE THINKING OF QUITTING, BRIAN? OF GIVING UP?
IT WASN'T BECAUSE I WAS SCARED. IT WAS -- IT WASN'T LIKE I THOUGHT IT WOULD BE.
ALL THIS FUSS -- ALL THIS HATRED -- AND THEN --
-- AND THEN --
...
YES. YES, I AM.

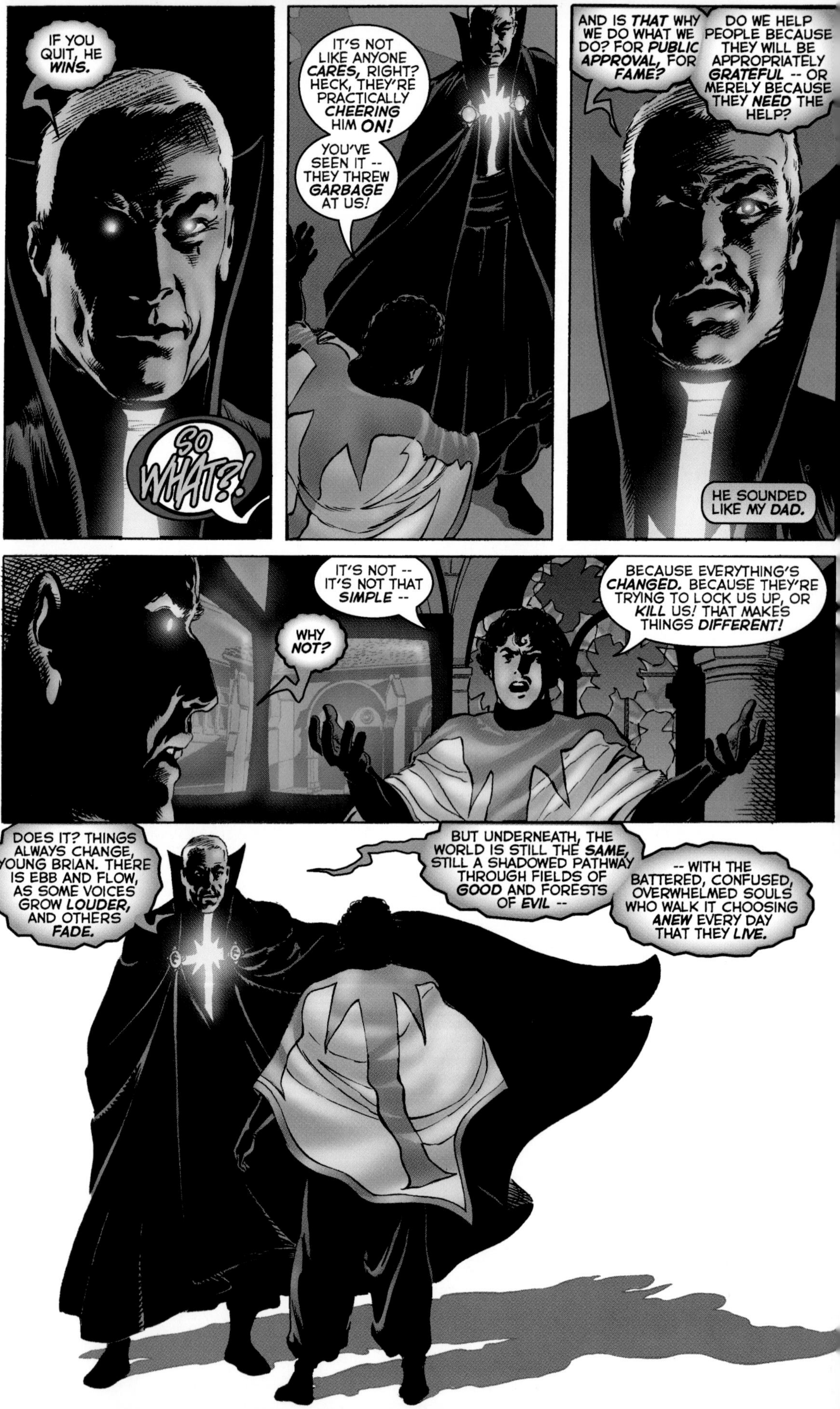
IF YOU QUIT, HE WINS.
SO WHAT?!
IT'S NOT LIKE ANYONE CARES, RIGHT? HECK, THEY'RE PRACTICALLY CHEERING HIM ON!
YOU'VE SEEN IT -- THEY THREW GARBAGE AT US!
AND IS THAT WHY WE DO WHAT WE DO? FOR PUBLIC APPROVAL, FOR FAME?
DO WE HELP PEOPLE BECAUSE THEY WILL BE APPROPRIATELY GRATEFUL -- OR MERELY BECAUSE THEY NEED THE HELP?
HE SOUNDED LIKE MY DAD.
WHY NOT?
IT'S NOT -- IT'S NOT THAT SIMPLE --
BECAUSE EVERYTHING'S CHANGED. BECAUSE THEY'RE TRYING TO LOCK US UP, OR KILL US! THAT MAKES THINGS DIFFERENT!
DOES IT? THINGS ALWAYS CHANGE, YOUNG BRIAN. THERE IS EBB AND FLOW, AS SOME VOICES GROW LOUDER, AND OTHERS FADE.
BUT UNDERNEATH, THE WORLD IS STILL THE SAME, STILL A SHADOWED PATHWAY THROUGH FIELDS OF GOOD AND FORESTS OF EVIL --
-- WITH THE BATTERED, CONFUSED, OVERWHELMED SOULS WHO WALK IT CHOOSING ANEW EVERY DAY THAT THEY LIVE.

AND IF THE FORCES OF ANGER AND UNREASON ARE *GROWING*, IF HUMANITY IS LOSING SIGHT OF THEIR *PATH* --

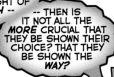

-- THEN IS IT NOT ALL THE *MORE* CRUCIAL THAT THEY BE SHOWN THEIR CHOICE? THAT THEY BE SHOWN THE *WAY*?

I TAKE IT *BACK.* YOU'RE *WORSE* THAN MY DAD.

YOUR FATHER SOUNDS LIKE A VERY *ADMIRABLE* MAN. I'D LIKE TO HAVE *MET* HIM.

MY FATHER WAS AN *IDIOT* -- WHO DIED *BROKE* AND *LAUGHED AT!* AND YOU, A *VAMPIRE,* TALKING ABOUT THIS KIND OF --

-- DO YOU THINK FOR A *MINUTE* THAT ANYONE WOULD LISTEN TO YOU IF -- IF --

THEY *KNOW,* CONFESSOR! THEY *KNOW!*

ONE OF THE MAYOR'S STOOGES TOLD ME YESTERDAY, YOU SHOULD *LEAVE TOWN,* OR *RETIRE* --

-- *OR* THEY'D *EXPOSE YOU!* THEY'D LET PEOPLE KNOW WHAT YOU REALLY *ARE!*

THINK ABOUT HOW THEY'D *REACT* -- AND THEN ASK YOURSELF IF YOU STILL *WANT* TO SAVE 'EM ALL!

THEY...

...THEY *KNOW?*

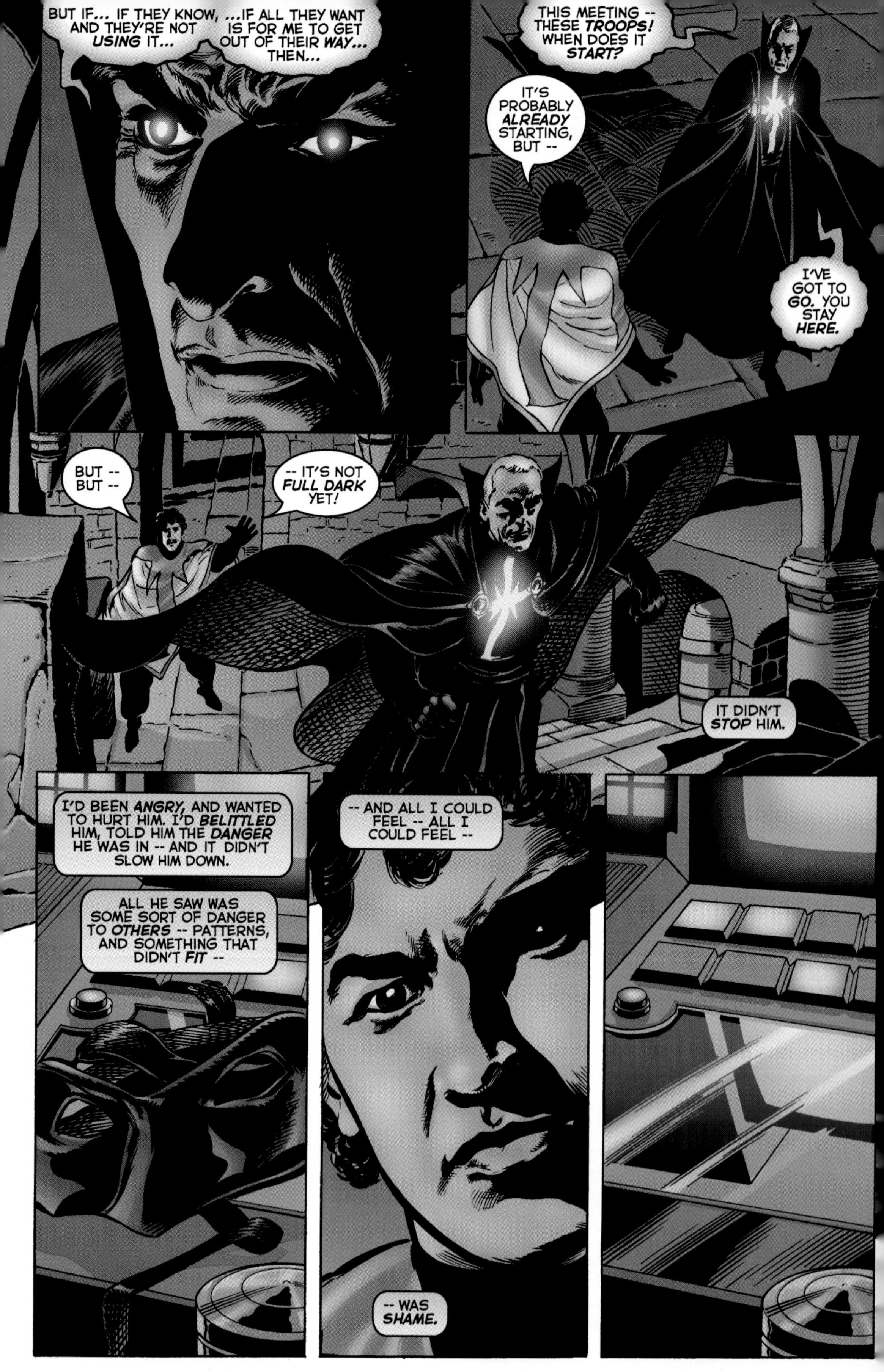

BUT IF... IF THEY KNOW, AND THEY'RE NOT USING IT...
...IF ALL THEY WANT IS FOR ME TO GET OUT OF THEIR WAY... THEN...
THIS MEETING -- THESE TROOPS! WHEN DOES IT START?
IT'S PROBABLY ALREADY STARTING, BUT --
I'VE GOT TO GO. YOU STAY HERE.
BUT -- BUT --
-- IT'S NOT FULL DARK YET!
IT DIDN'T STOP HIM.
I'D BEEN ANGRY, AND WANTED TO HURT HIM. I'D BELITTLED HIM, TOLD HIM THE DANGER HE WAS IN -- AND IT DIDN'T SLOW HIM DOWN.
ALL HE SAW WAS SOME SORT OF DANGER TO OTHERS -- PATTERNS, AND SOMETHING THAT DIDN'T FIT --
-- AND ALL I COULD FEEL -- ALL I COULD FEEL --
-- WAS SHAME.

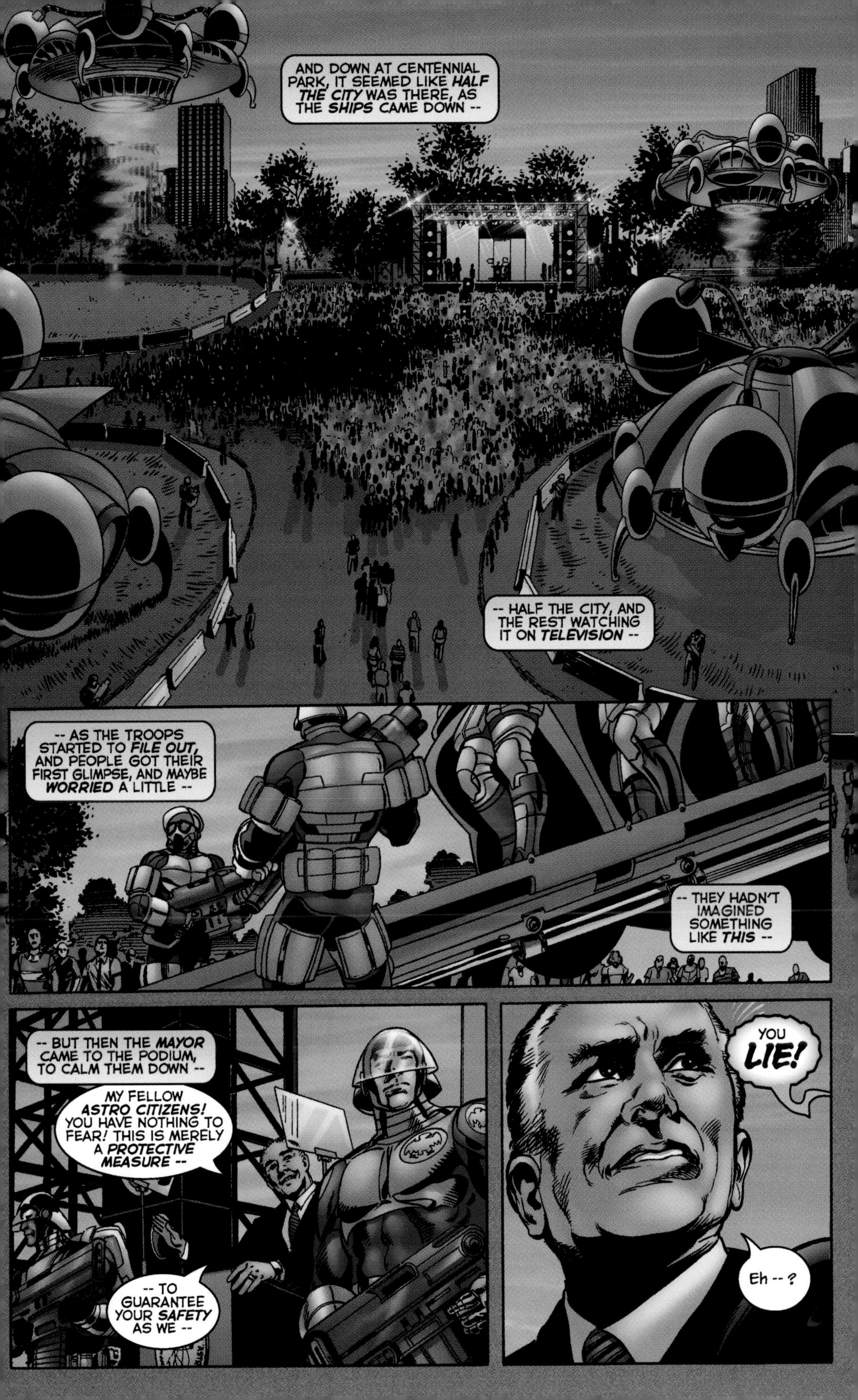
AND DOWN AT CENTENNIAL PARK, IT SEEMED LIKE HALF THE CITY WAS THERE, AS THE SHIPS CAME DOWN --
-- HALF THE CITY, AND THE REST WATCHING IT ON TELEVISION --
-- AS THE TROOPS STARTED TO FILE OUT, AND PEOPLE GOT THEIR FIRST GLIMPSE, AND MAYBE WORRIED A LITTLE --
-- THEY HADN'T IMAGINED SOMETHING LIKE THIS --
-- BUT THEN THE MAYOR CAME TO THE PODIUM, TO CALM THEM DOWN --
MY FELLOW ASTRO CITIZENS! YOU HAVE NOTHING TO FEAR! THIS IS MERELY A PROTECTIVE MEASURE --
-- TO GUARANTEE YOUR SAFETY AS WE --
YOU LIE!
Eh -- ?

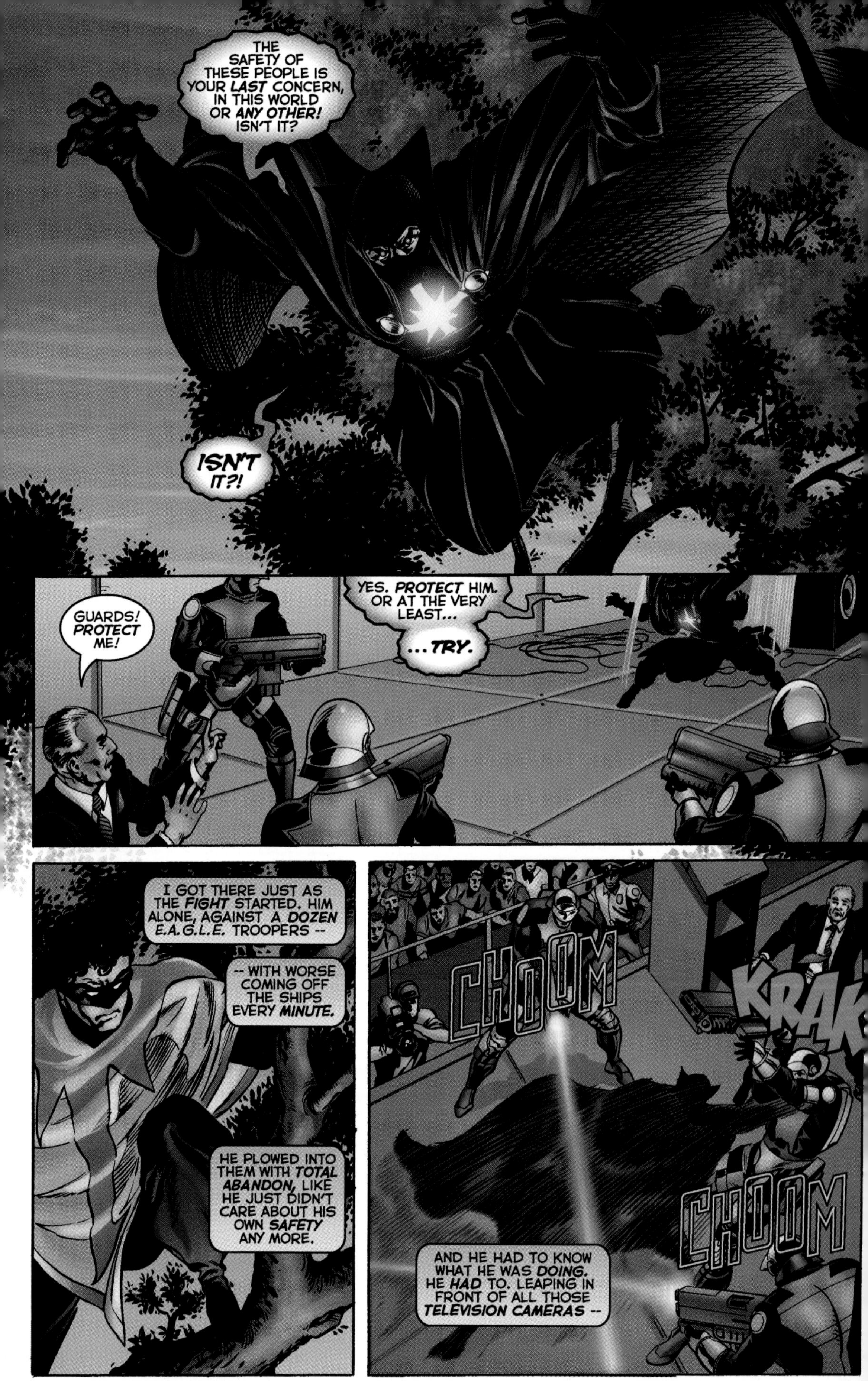
THE SAFETY OF THESE PEOPLE IS YOUR LAST CONCERN, IN THIS WORLD OR ANY OTHER! ISN'T IT?
ISN'T IT?!
GUARDS! PROTECT ME!
YES. PROTECT HIM. OR AT THE VERY LEAST...
...TRY.
I GOT THERE JUST AS THE FIGHT STARTED. HIM ALONE, AGAINST A DOZEN E.A.G.L.E. TROOPERS --
-- WITH WORSE COMING OFF THE SHIPS EVERY MINUTE.
HE PLOWED INTO THEM WITH TOTAL ABANDON, LIKE HE JUST DIDN'T CARE ABOUT HIS OWN SAFETY ANY MORE.
CHOOM
KRAK
CHOOM
AND HE HAD TO KNOW WHAT HE WAS DOING. HE HAD TO. LEAPING IN FRONT OF ALL THOSE TELEVISION CAMERAS --

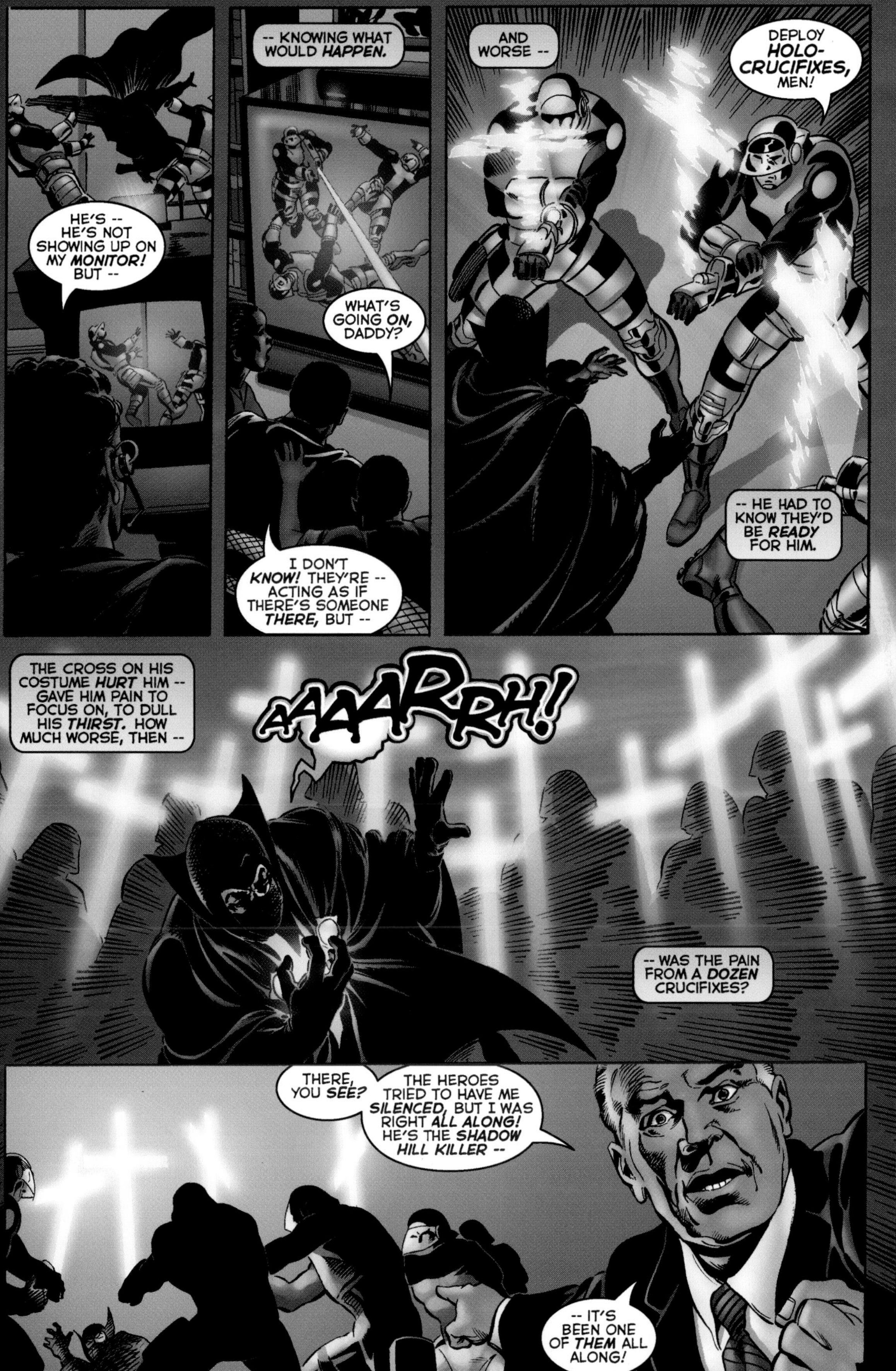
HE'S -- HE'S NOT SHOWING UP ON MY MONITOR! BUT --
-- KNOWING WHAT WOULD HAPPEN.
WHAT'S GOING ON, DADDY?
I DON'T KNOW! THEY'RE -- ACTING AS IF THERE'S SOMEONE THERE, BUT --
AND WORSE --
DEPLOY HOLO-CRUCIFIXES, MEN!
-- HE HAD TO KNOW THEY'D BE READY FOR HIM.
THE CROSS ON HIS COSTUME HURT HIM -- GAVE HIM PAIN TO FOCUS ON, TO DULL HIS THIRST. HOW MUCH WORSE, THEN --
AAAARRH!
-- WAS THE PAIN FROM A DOZEN CRUCIFIXES?
THERE, YOU SEE?
THE HEROES TRIED TO HAVE ME SILENCED, BUT I WAS RIGHT ALL ALONG! HE'S THE SHADOW HILL KILLER --
-- IT'S BEEN ONE OF THEM ALL ALONG!

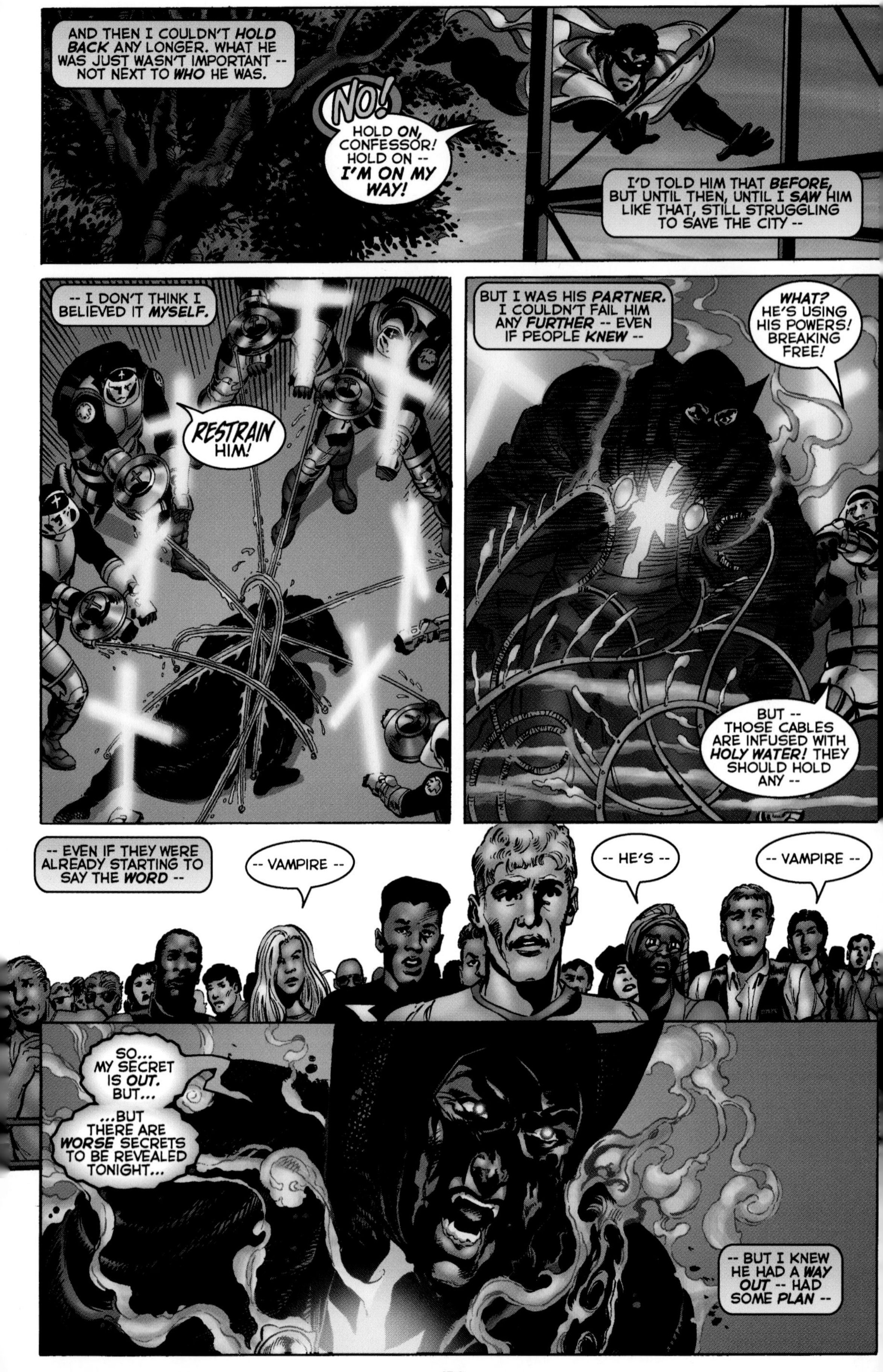
AND THEN I COULDN'T HOLD BACK ANY LONGER. WHAT HE WAS JUST WASN'T IMPORTANT -- NOT NEXT TO WHO HE WAS.
NO! HOLD ON, CONFESSOR! HOLD ON -- I'M ON MY WAY!
I'D TOLD HIM THAT BEFORE, BUT UNTIL THEN, UNTIL I SAW HIM LIKE THAT, STILL STRUGGLING TO SAVE THE CITY --
-- I DON'T THINK I BELIEVED IT MYSELF.
RESTRAIN HIM!
BUT I WAS HIS PARTNER. I COULDN'T FAIL HIM ANY FURTHER -- EVEN IF PEOPLE KNEW --
WHAT? HE'S USING HIS POWERS! BREAKING FREE!
BUT -- THOSE CABLES ARE INFUSED WITH HOLY WATER! THEY SHOULD HOLD ANY --
-- EVEN IF THEY WERE ALREADY STARTING TO SAY THE WORD --
-- VAMPIRE --
-- HE'S --
-- VAMPIRE --
SO... MY SECRET IS OUT. BUT...
...BUT THERE ARE WORSE SECRETS TO BE REVEALED TONIGHT...
-- BUT I KNEW HE HAD A WAY OUT -- HAD SOME PLAN --

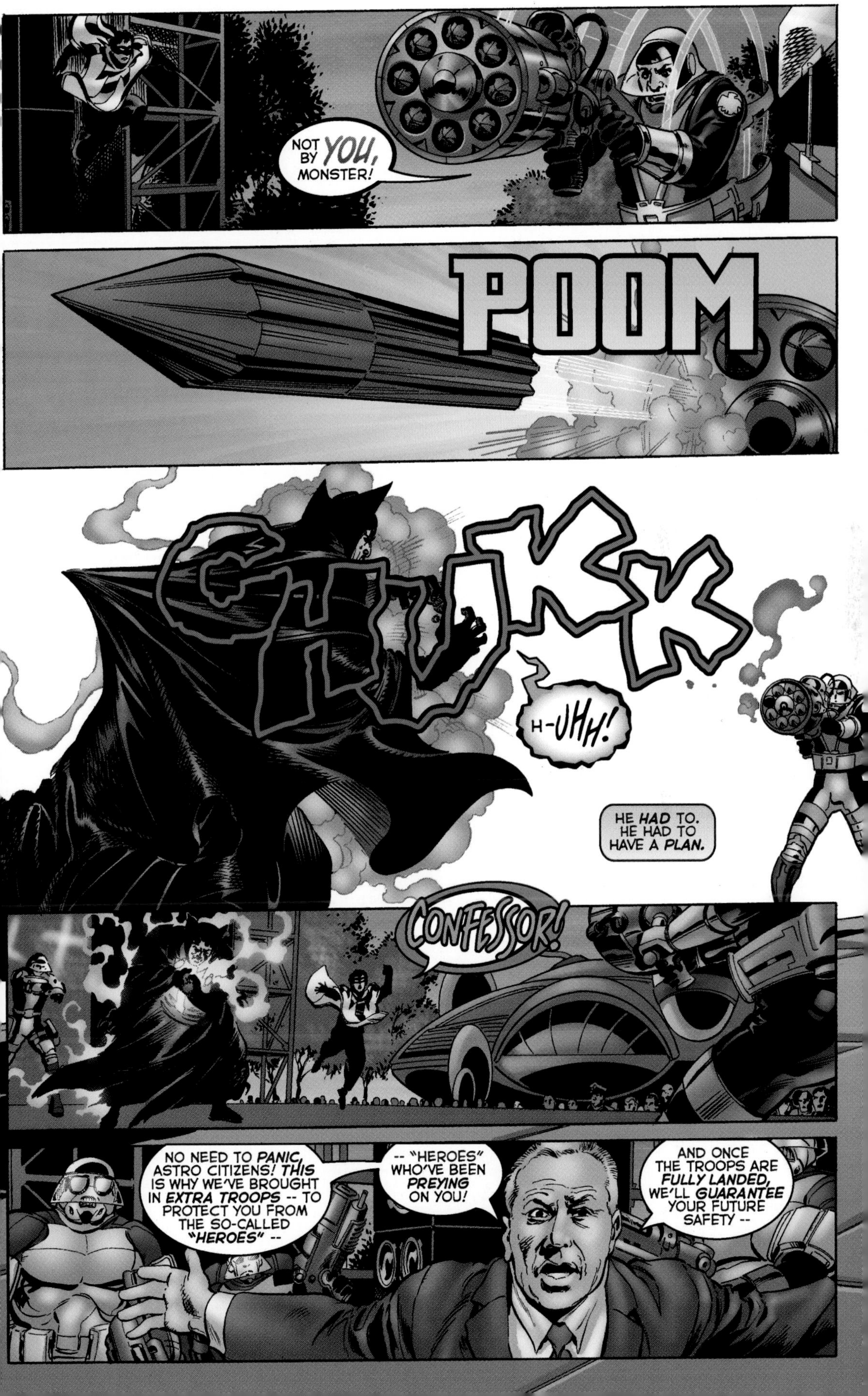
NOT BY YOU, MONSTER!
POOM
CHUKK
H-UHH!
HE HAD TO. HE HAD TO HAVE A PLAN.
CONFESSOR!
NO NEED TO PANIC, ASTRO CITIZENS! THIS IS WHY WE'VE BROUGHT IN EXTRA TROOPS -- TO PROTECT YOU FROM THE SO-CALLED "HEROES" --
-- "HEROES" WHO'VE BEEN PREYING ON YOU!
AND ONCE THE TROOPS ARE FULLY LANDED, WE'LL GUARANTEE YOUR FUTURE SAFETY --

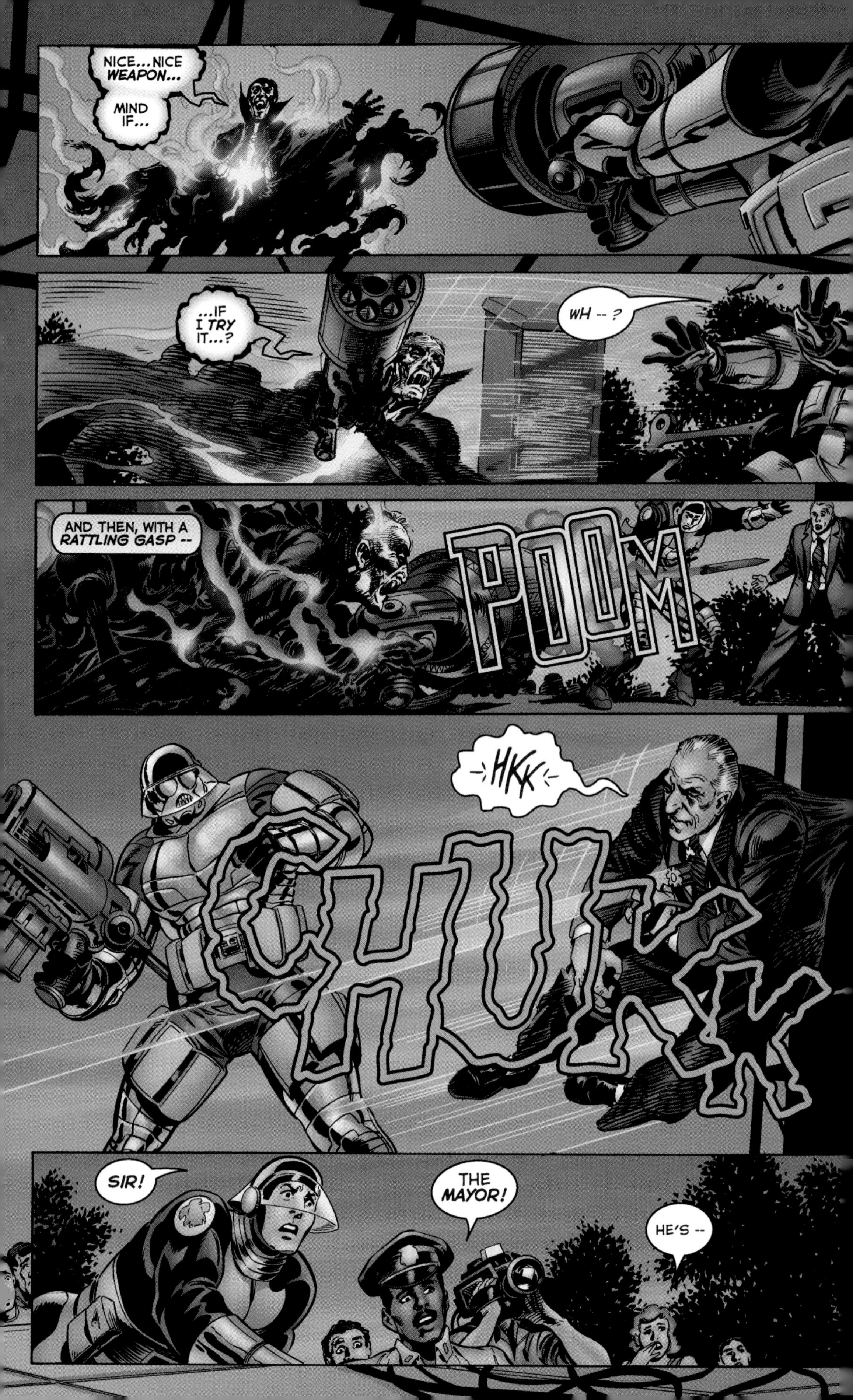
NICE...NICE WEAPON...
MIND IF...
...IF I TRY IT...?
WH -- ?
AND THEN, WITH A RATTLING GASP --
POOM
HKK
CHUKK
SIR!
THE MAYOR!
HE'S --

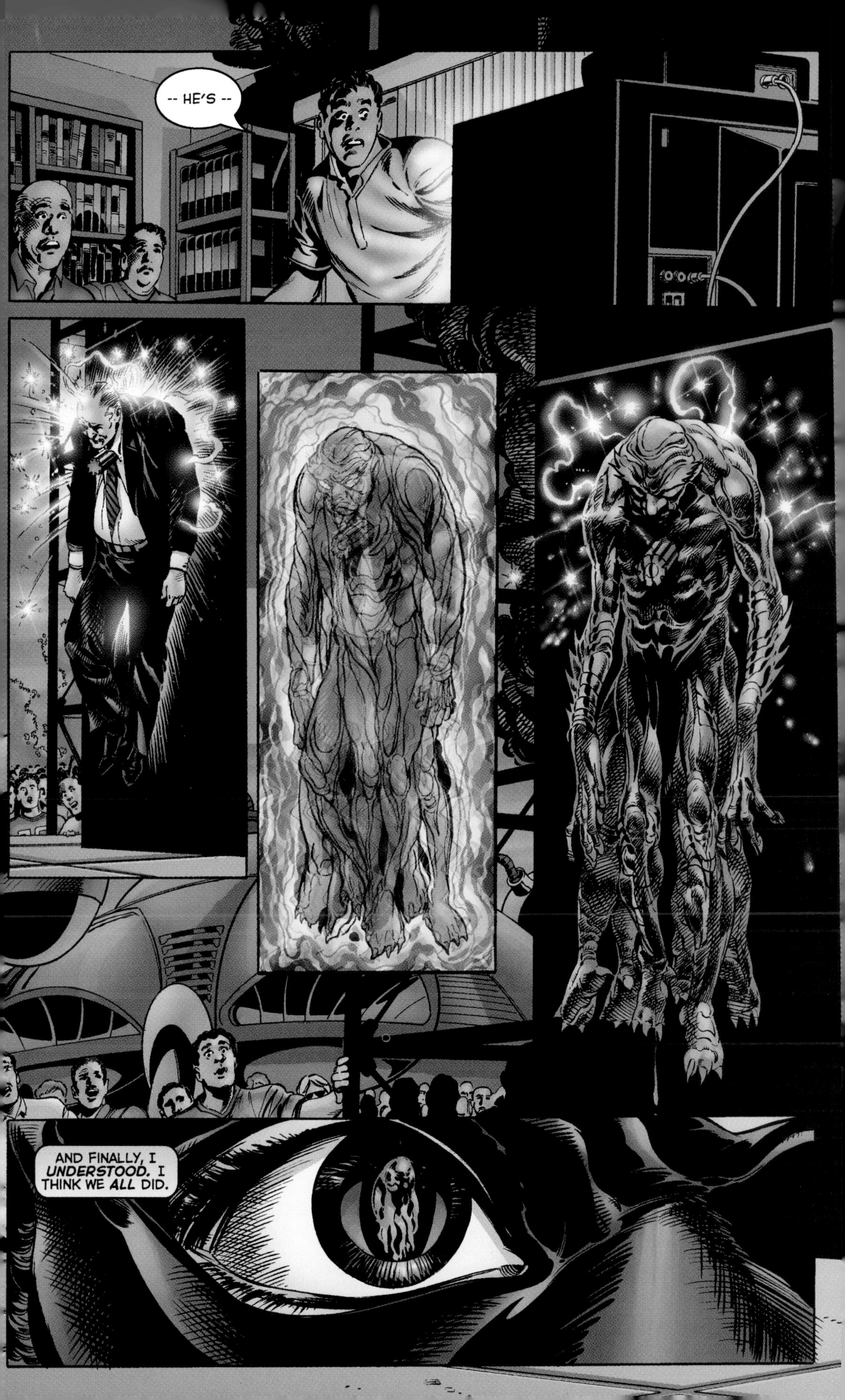
-- HE'S --
AND FINALLY, I UNDERSTOOD. I THINK WE ALL DID.

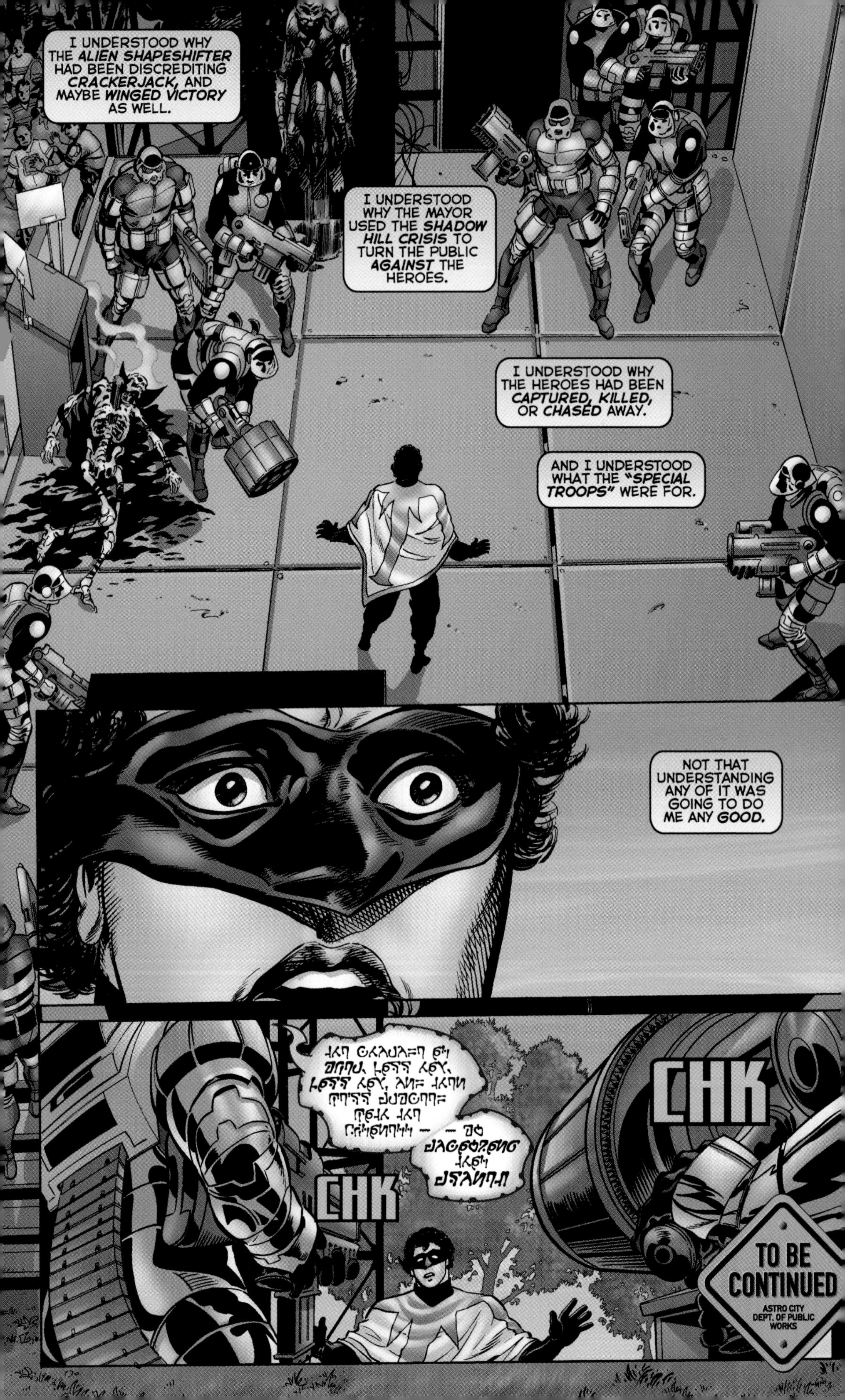
I UNDERSTOOD WHY THE ALIEN SHAPESHIFTER HAD BEEN DISCREDITING CRACKERJACK, AND MAYBE WINGED VICTORY AS WELL.
I UNDERSTOOD WHY THE MAYOR USED THE SHADOW HILL CRISIS TO TURN THE PUBLIC AGAINST THE HEROES.
I UNDERSTOOD WHY THE HEROES HAD BEEN CAPTURED, KILLED, OR CHASED AWAY.
AND I UNDERSTOOD WHAT THE "SPECIAL TROOPS" WERE FOR.
NOT THAT UNDERSTANDING ANY OF IT WAS GOING TO DO ME ANY GOOD.
CHK
CHK
TO BE CONTINUED
ASTRO CITY DEPT. OF PUBLIC WORKS

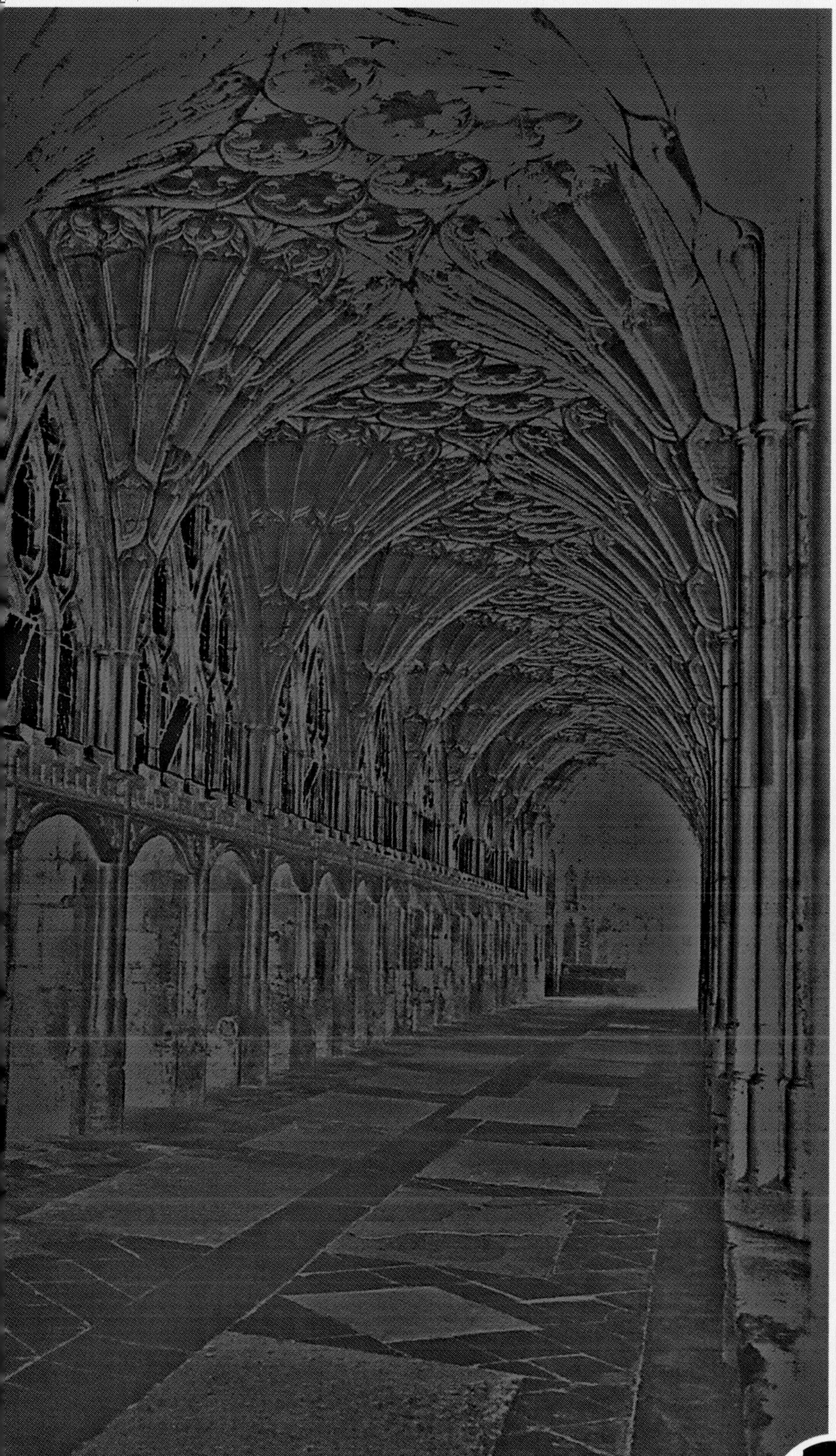

C H A P T E R

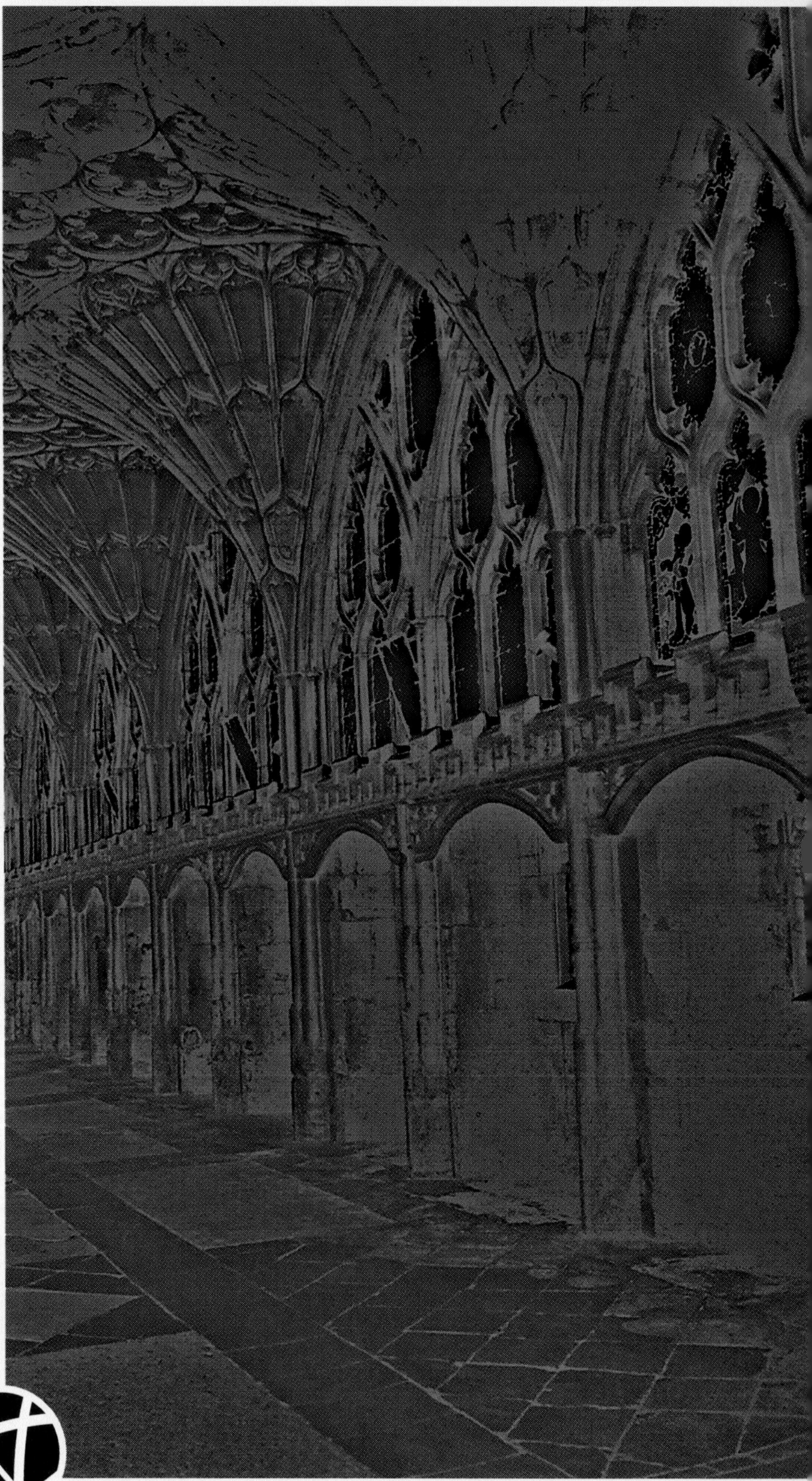

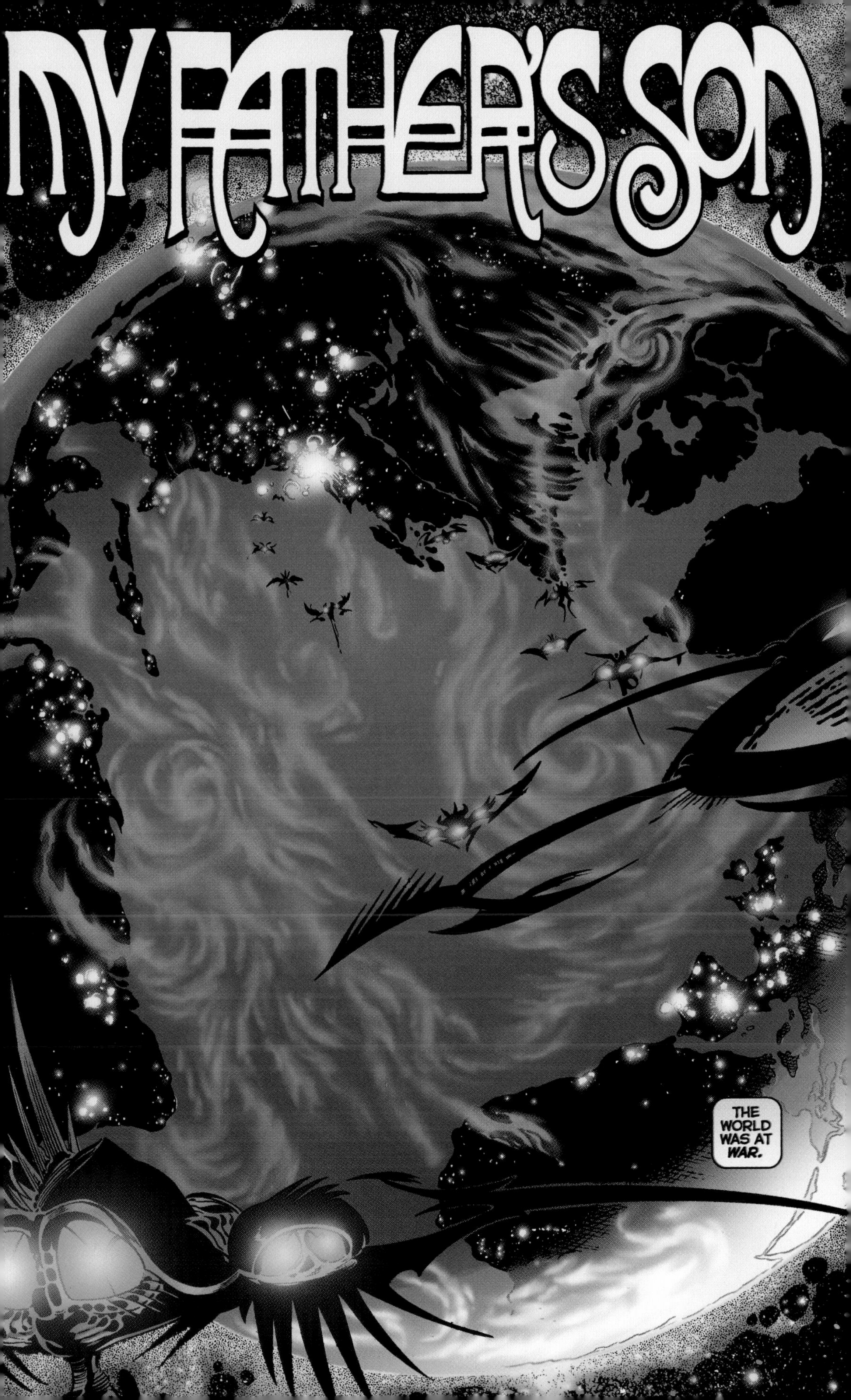
MY FATHER'S SON
THE WORLD WAS AT WAR.

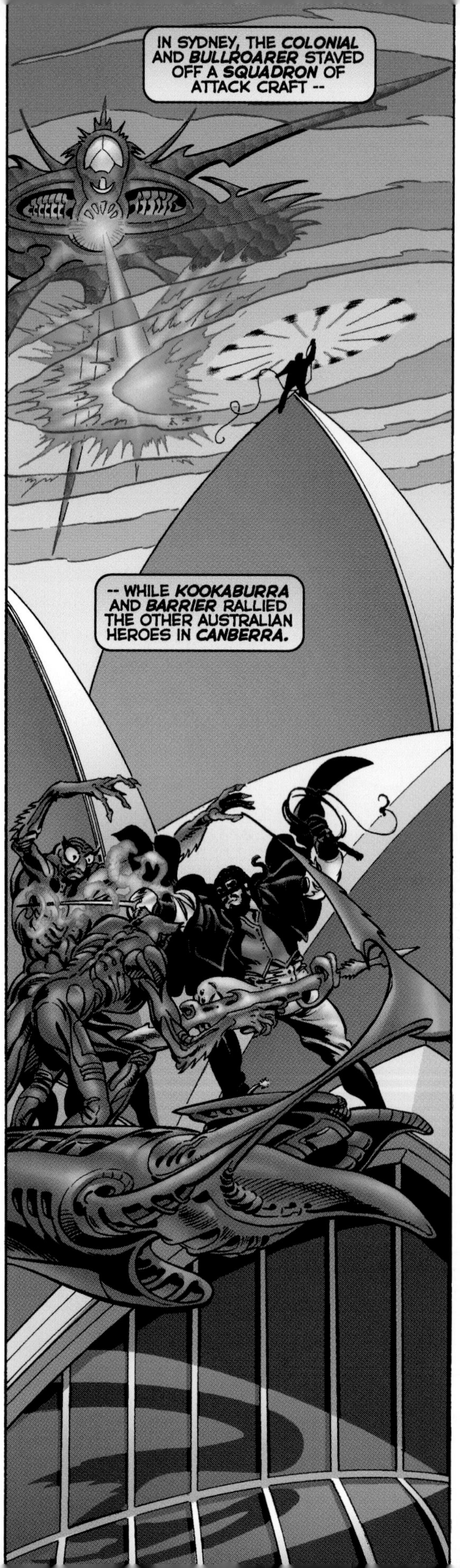
IN SYDNEY, THE COLONIAL AND BULLROARER STAVED OFF A SQUADRON OF ATTACK CRAFT --
-- WHILE KOOKABURRA AND BARRIER RALLIED THE OTHER AUSTRALIAN HEROES IN CANBERRA.
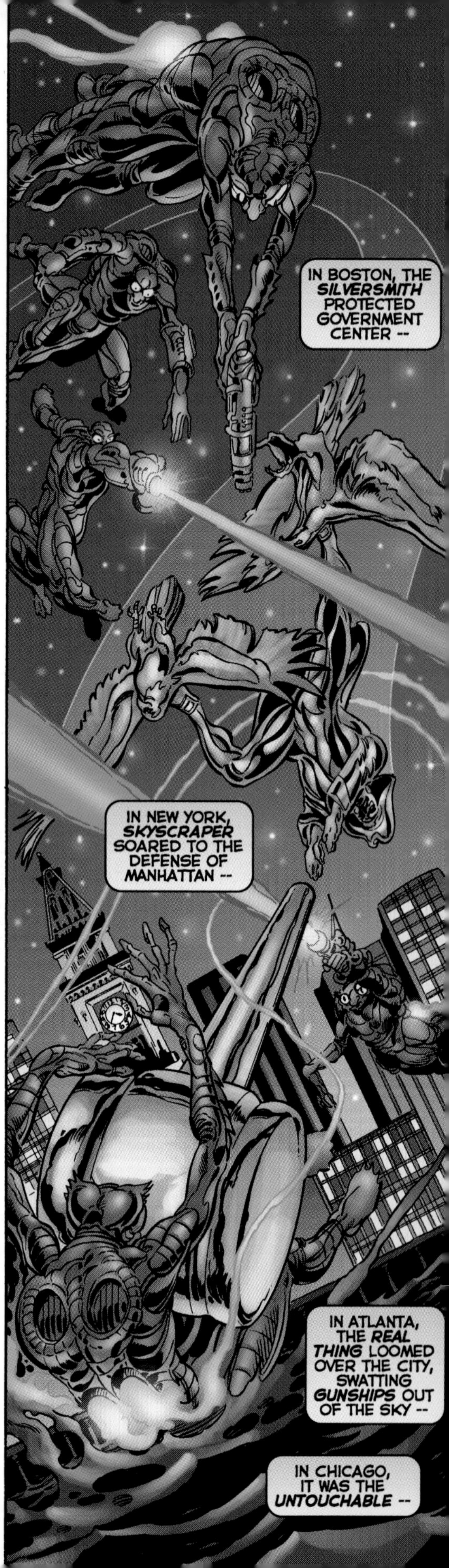
IN BOSTON, THE SILVERSMITH PROTECTED GOVERNMENT CENTER --
IN NEW YORK, SKYSCRAPER SOARED TO THE DEFENSE OF MANHATTAN --
IN ATLANTA, THE REAL THING LOOMED OVER THE CITY, SWATTING GUNSHIPS OUT OF THE SKY --
IN CHICAGO, IT WAS THE UNTOUCHABLE --

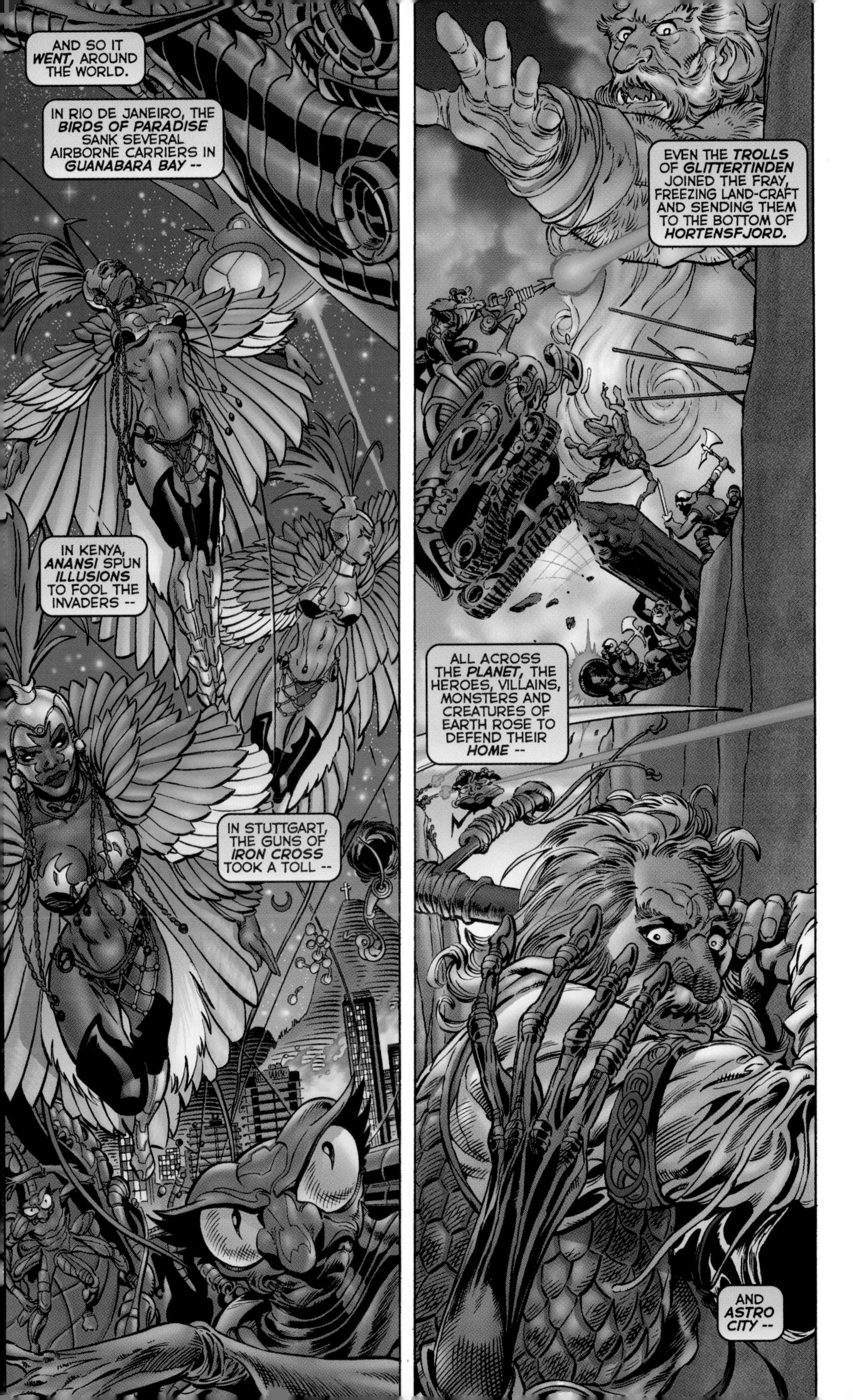
AND SO IT WENT, AROUND THE WORLD.
IN RIO DE JANEIRO, THE BIRDS OF PARADISE SANK SEVERAL AIRBORNE CARRIERS IN GUANABARA BAY --
IN KENYA, ANANSI SPUN ILLUSIONS TO FOOL THE INVADERS --
IN STUTTGART, THE GUNS OF IRON CROSS TOOK A TOLL --
EVEN THE TROLLS OF GLITTERTINDEN JOINED THE FRAY, FREEZING LAND-CRAFT AND SENDING THEM TO THE BOTTOM OF HORTENSFJORD.
ALL ACROSS THE PLANET, THE HEROES, VILLAINS, MONSTERS AND CREATURES OF EARTH ROSE TO DEFEND THEIR HOME --
AND ASTRO CITY --

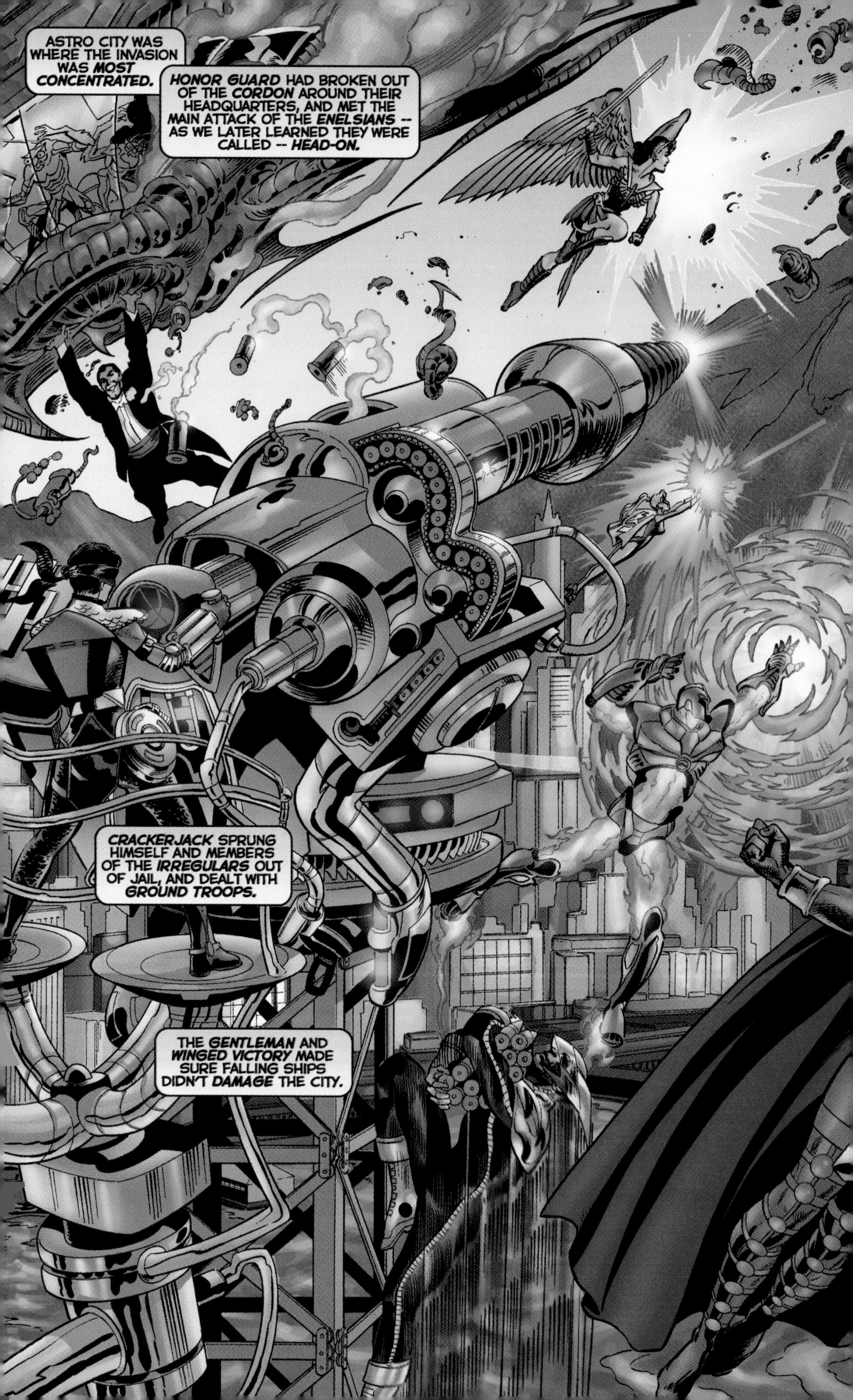
ASTRO CITY WAS WHERE THE INVASION WAS MOST CONCENTRATED.
HONOR GUARD HAD BROKEN OUT OF THE CORDON AROUND THEIR HEADQUARTERS, AND MET THE MAIN ATTACK OF THE ENELSIANS -- AS WE LATER LEARNED THEY WERE CALLED -- HEAD-ON.
CRACKERJACK SPRUNG HIMSELF AND MEMBERS OF THE IRREGULARS OUT OF JAIL, AND DEALT WITH GROUND TROOPS.
THE GENTLEMAN AND WINGED VICTORY MADE SURE FALLING SHIPS DIDN'T DAMAGE THE CITY.

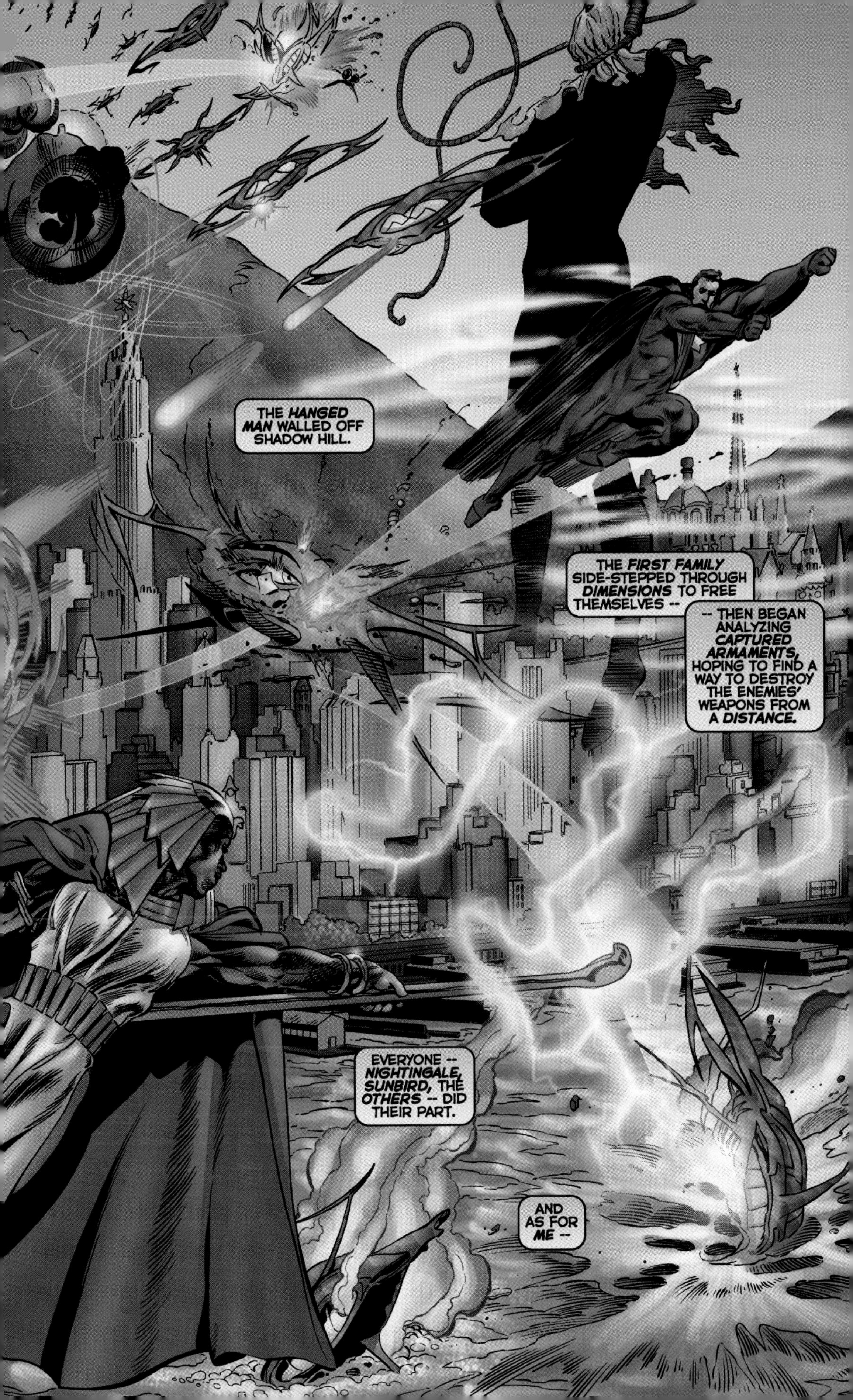
THE HANGED MAN WALLED OFF SHADOW HILL.
THE FIRST FAMILY SIDE-STEPPED THROUGH DIMENSIONS TO FREE THEMSELVES --
-- THEN BEGAN ANALYZING CAPTURED ARMAMENTS, HOPING TO FIND A WAY TO DESTROY THE ENEMIES' WEAPONS FROM A DISTANCE.
EVERYONE -- NIGHTINGALE, SUNBIRD, THE OTHERS -- DID THEIR PART.
AND AS FOR ME --

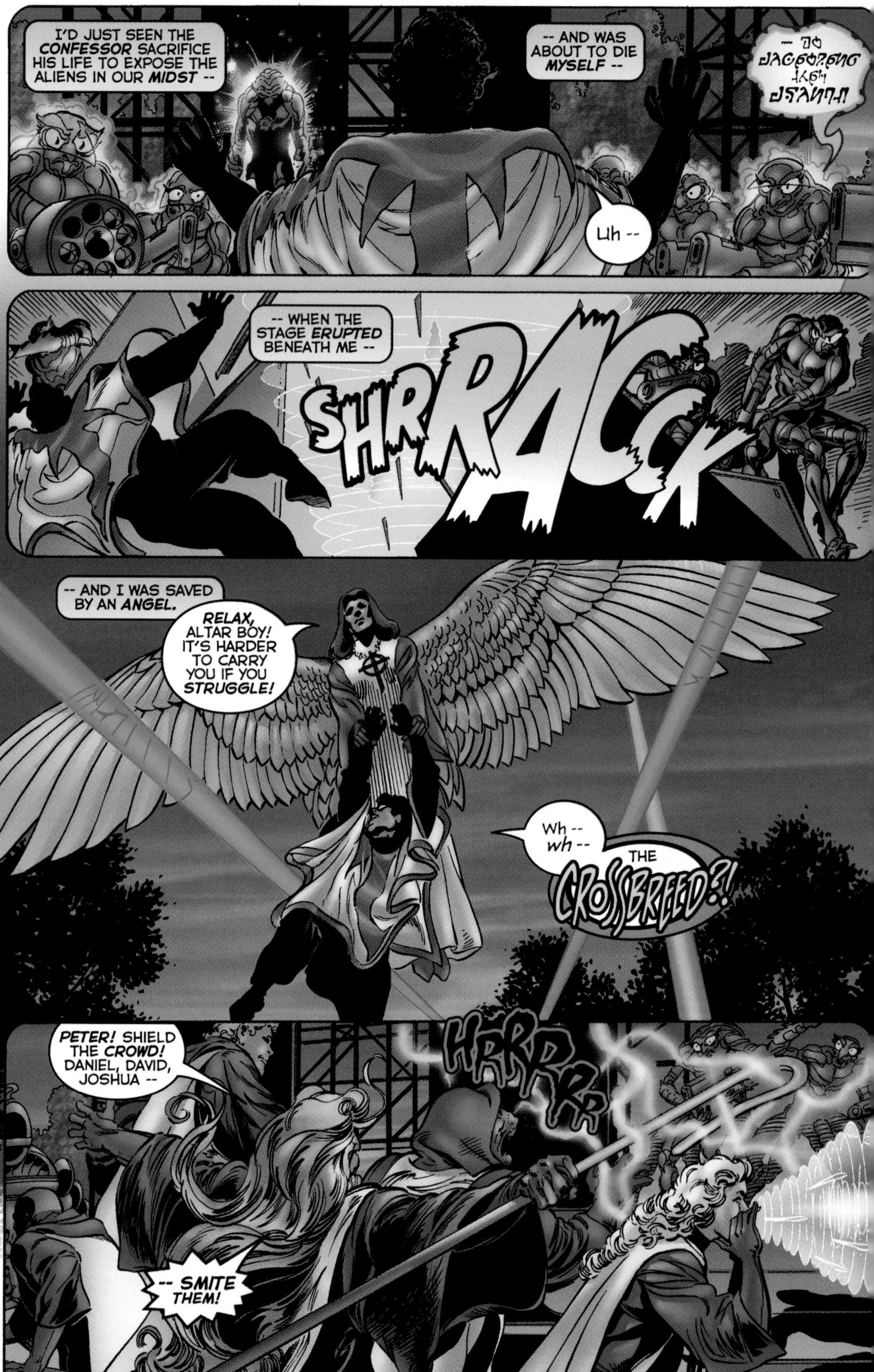
I'D JUST SEEN THE CONFESSOR SACRIFICE HIS LIFE TO EXPOSE THE ALIENS IN OUR MIDST --
-- AND WAS ABOUT TO DIE MYSELF --
Uh --
-- WHEN THE STAGE ERUPTED BENEATH ME --
SHRRACK
-- AND I WAS SAVED BY AN ANGEL.
RELAX, ALTAR BOY! IT'S HARDER TO CARRY YOU IF YOU STRUGGLE!
Wh -- wh --
THE CROSSBREED?!
PETER! SHIELD THE CROWD! DANIEL, DAVID, JOSHUA --
HRRRRRR
-- SMITE THEM!

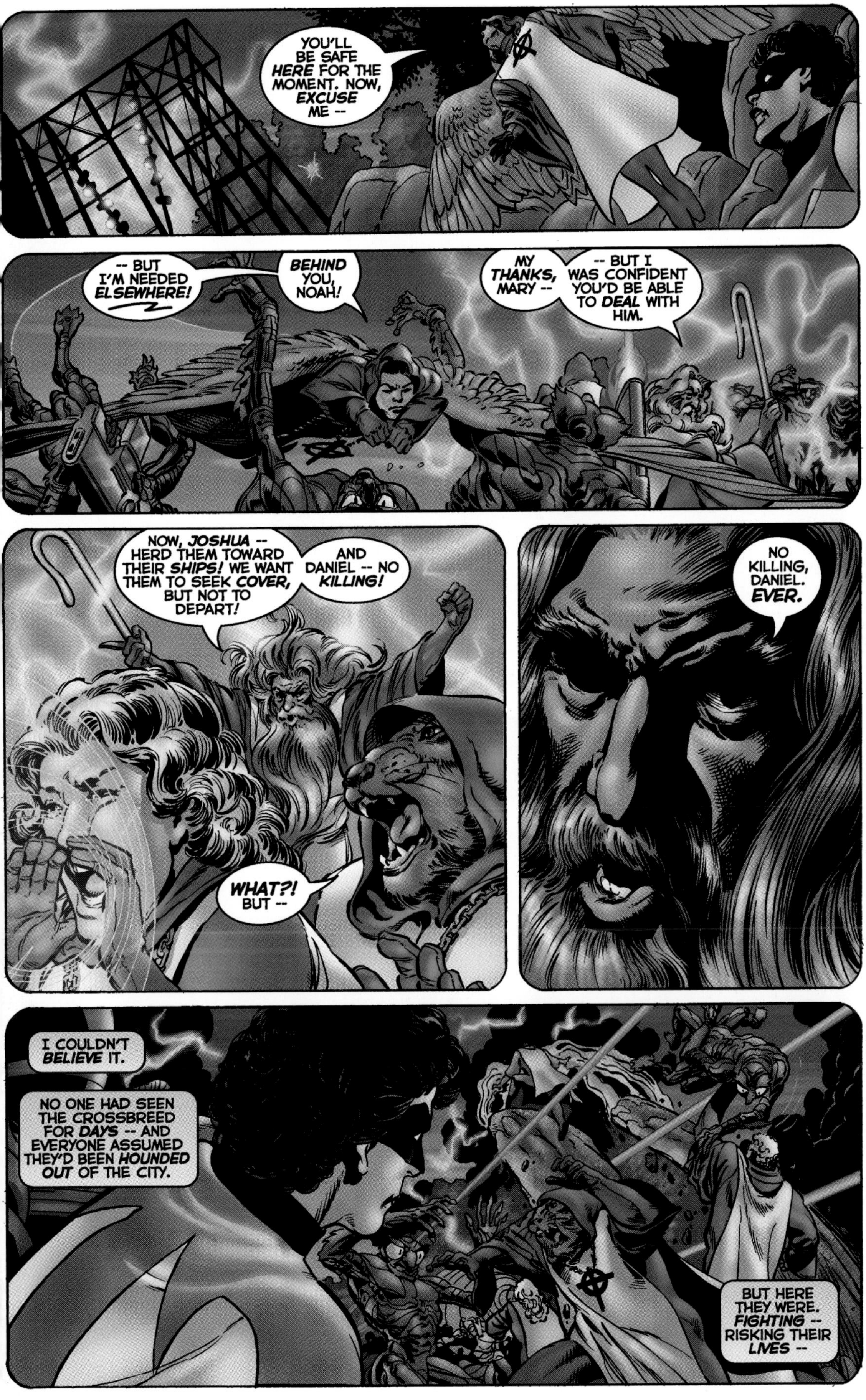
YOU'LL BE SAFE *HERE* FOR THE MOMENT. NOW, *EXCUSE* ME --
-- BUT I'M NEEDED *ELSEWHERE!*
BEHIND YOU, NOAH!
MY *THANKS,* MARY --
-- BUT I WAS CONFIDENT YOU'D BE ABLE TO *DEAL* WITH HIM.
NOW, *JOSHUA* -- HERD THEM TOWARD THEIR *SHIPS!* WE WANT THEM TO SEEK *COVER,* BUT NOT TO DEPART!
AND DANIEL -- NO *KILLING!*
WHAT?! BUT --
NO KILLING, DANIEL. *EVER.*
I COULDN'T *BELIEVE* IT.
NO ONE HAD SEEN THE CROSSBREED FOR *DAYS* -- AND EVERYONE ASSUMED THEY'D BEEN *HOUNDED OUT* OF THE CITY.
BUT HERE THEY WERE. *FIGHTING* -- RISKING THEIR *LIVES* --

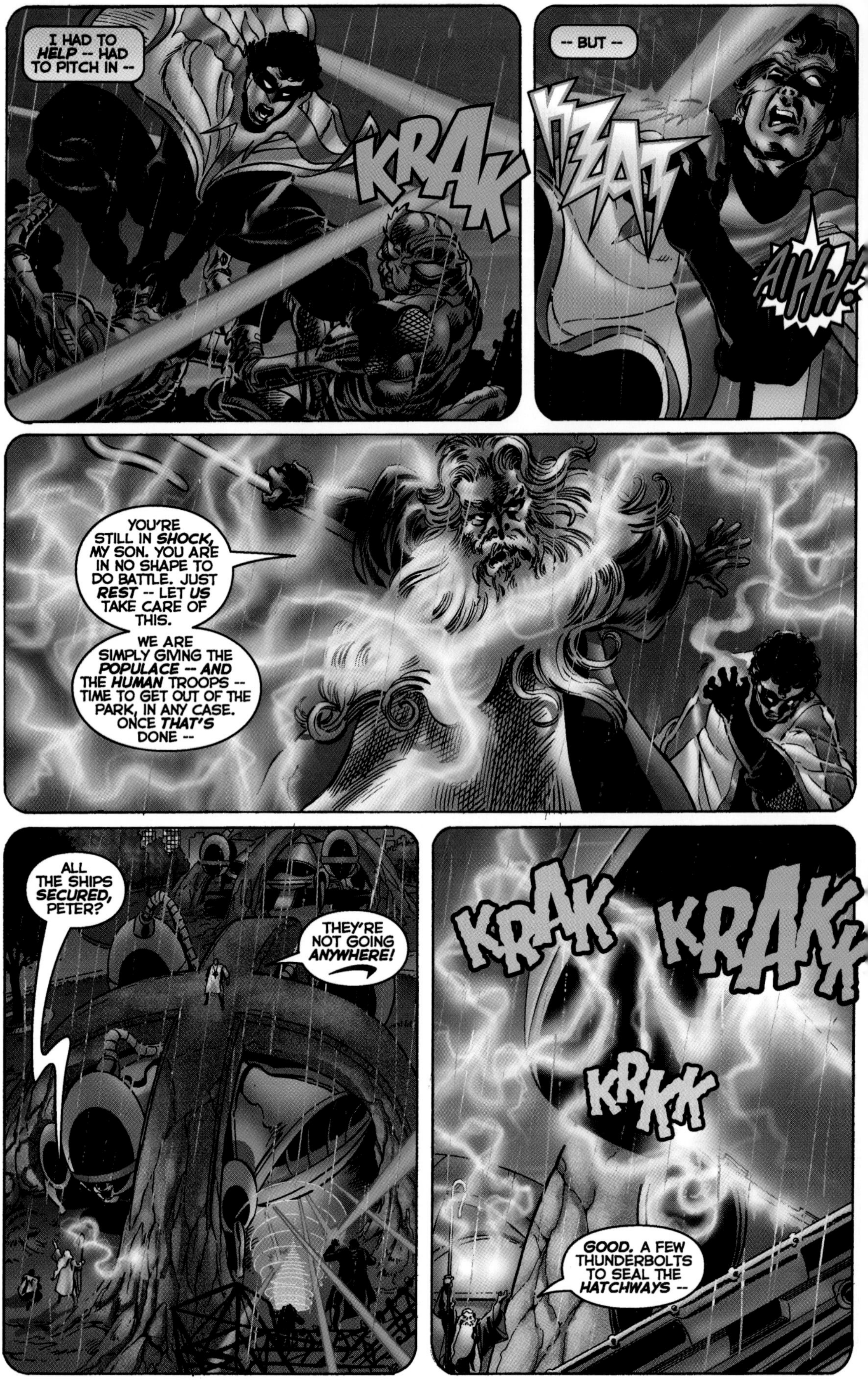
I HAD TO HELP -- HAD TO PITCH IN --
KRAK
-- BUT --
KZZAT
AHHH!
YOU'RE STILL IN SHOCK, MY SON. YOU ARE IN NO SHAPE TO DO BATTLE. JUST REST -- LET US TAKE CARE OF THIS.
WE ARE SIMPLY GIVING THE POPULACE -- AND THE HUMAN TROOPS -- TIME TO GET OUT OF THE PARK, IN ANY CASE. ONCE THAT'S DONE --
ALL THE SHIPS SECURED, PETER?
THEY'RE NOT GOING ANYWHERE!
KRAK
KRAKK
KRKK
GOOD. A FEW THUNDERBOLTS TO SEAL THE HATCHWAYS --

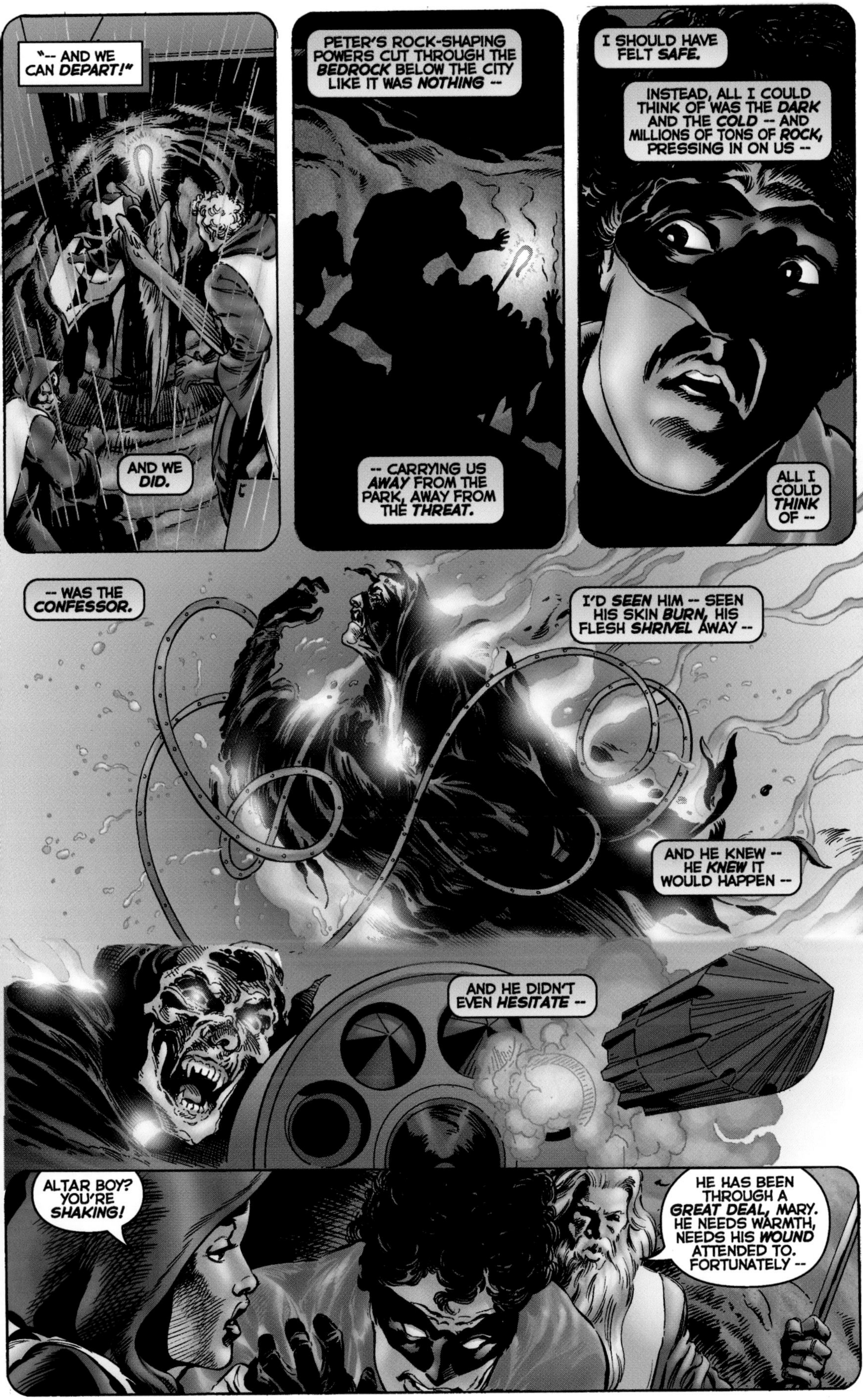
"-- AND WE CAN DEPART!"
AND WE DID.
PETER'S ROCK-SHAPING POWERS CUT THROUGH THE BEDROCK BELOW THE CITY LIKE IT WAS NOTHING --
-- CARRYING US AWAY FROM THE PARK, AWAY FROM THE THREAT.
I SHOULD HAVE FELT SAFE.
INSTEAD, ALL I COULD THINK OF WAS THE DARK AND THE COLD -- AND MILLIONS OF TONS OF ROCK, PRESSING IN ON US --
ALL I COULD THINK OF --
-- WAS THE CONFESSOR.
I'D SEEN HIM -- SEEN HIS SKIN BURN, HIS FLESH SHRIVEL AWAY --
AND HE KNEW -- HE KNEW IT WOULD HAPPEN --
AND HE DIDN'T EVEN HESITATE --
ALTAR BOY? YOU'RE SHAKING!
HE HAS BEEN THROUGH A GREAT DEAL, MARY. HE NEEDS WARMTH, NEEDS HIS WOUND ATTENDED TO. FORTUNATELY --

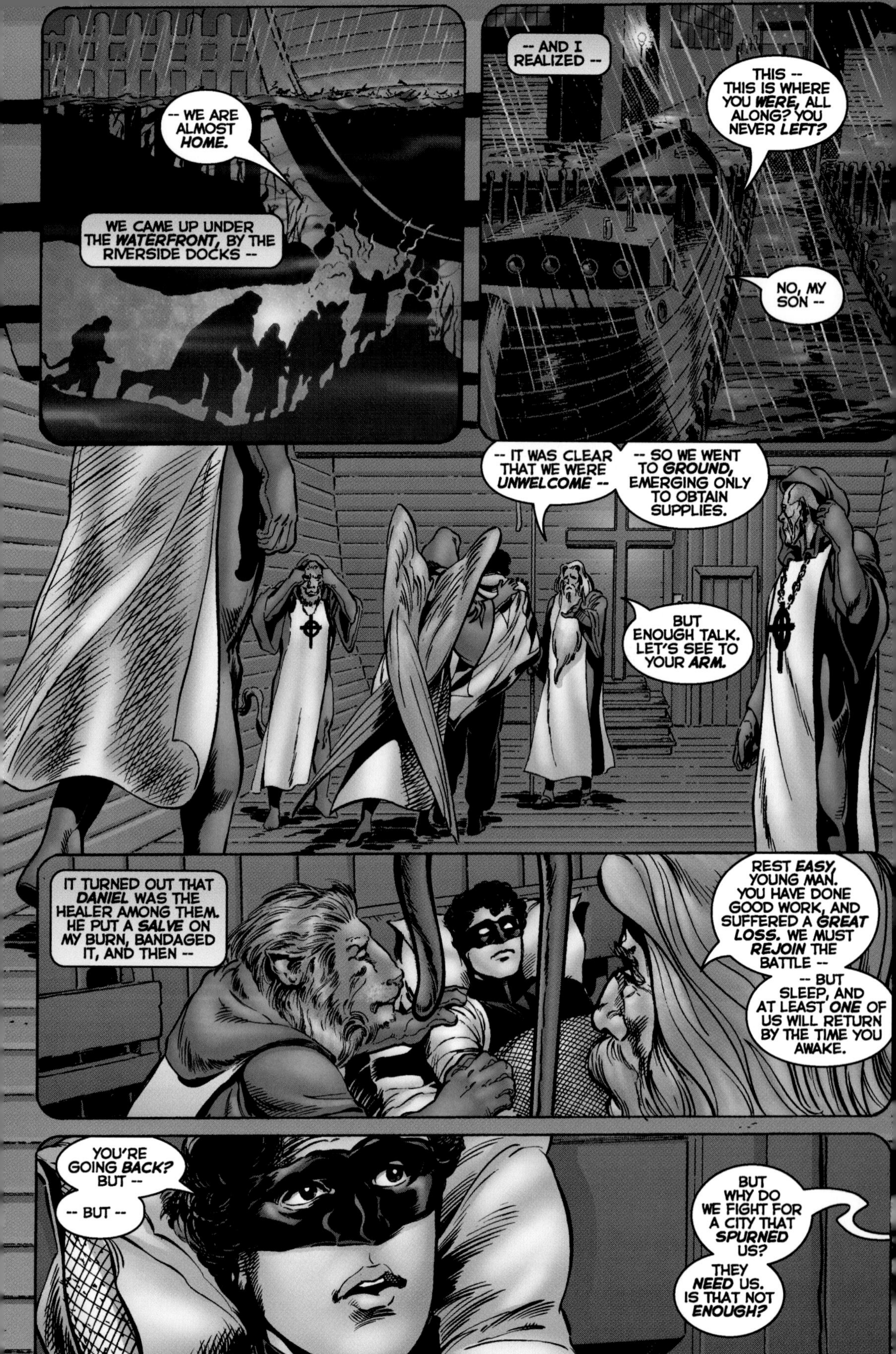
-- WE ARE ALMOST HOME.
WE CAME UP UNDER THE WATERFRONT, BY THE RIVERSIDE DOCKS --
-- AND I REALIZED --
THIS -- THIS IS WHERE YOU WERE, ALL ALONG? YOU NEVER LEFT?
NO, MY SON --
-- IT WAS CLEAR THAT WE WERE UNWELCOME --
-- SO WE WENT TO GROUND, EMERGING ONLY TO OBTAIN SUPPLIES.
BUT ENOUGH TALK. LET'S SEE TO YOUR ARM.
IT TURNED OUT THAT DANIEL WAS THE HEALER AMONG THEM. HE PUT A SALVE ON MY BURN, BANDAGED IT, AND THEN --
REST EASY, YOUNG MAN. YOU HAVE DONE GOOD WORK, AND SUFFERED A GREAT LOSS. WE MUST REJOIN THE BATTLE --
-- BUT SLEEP, AND AT LEAST ONE OF US WILL RETURN BY THE TIME YOU AWAKE.
YOU'RE GOING BACK? BUT --
-- BUT --
BUT WHY DO WE FIGHT FOR A CITY THAT SPURNED US?
THEY NEED US. IS THAT NOT ENOUGH?

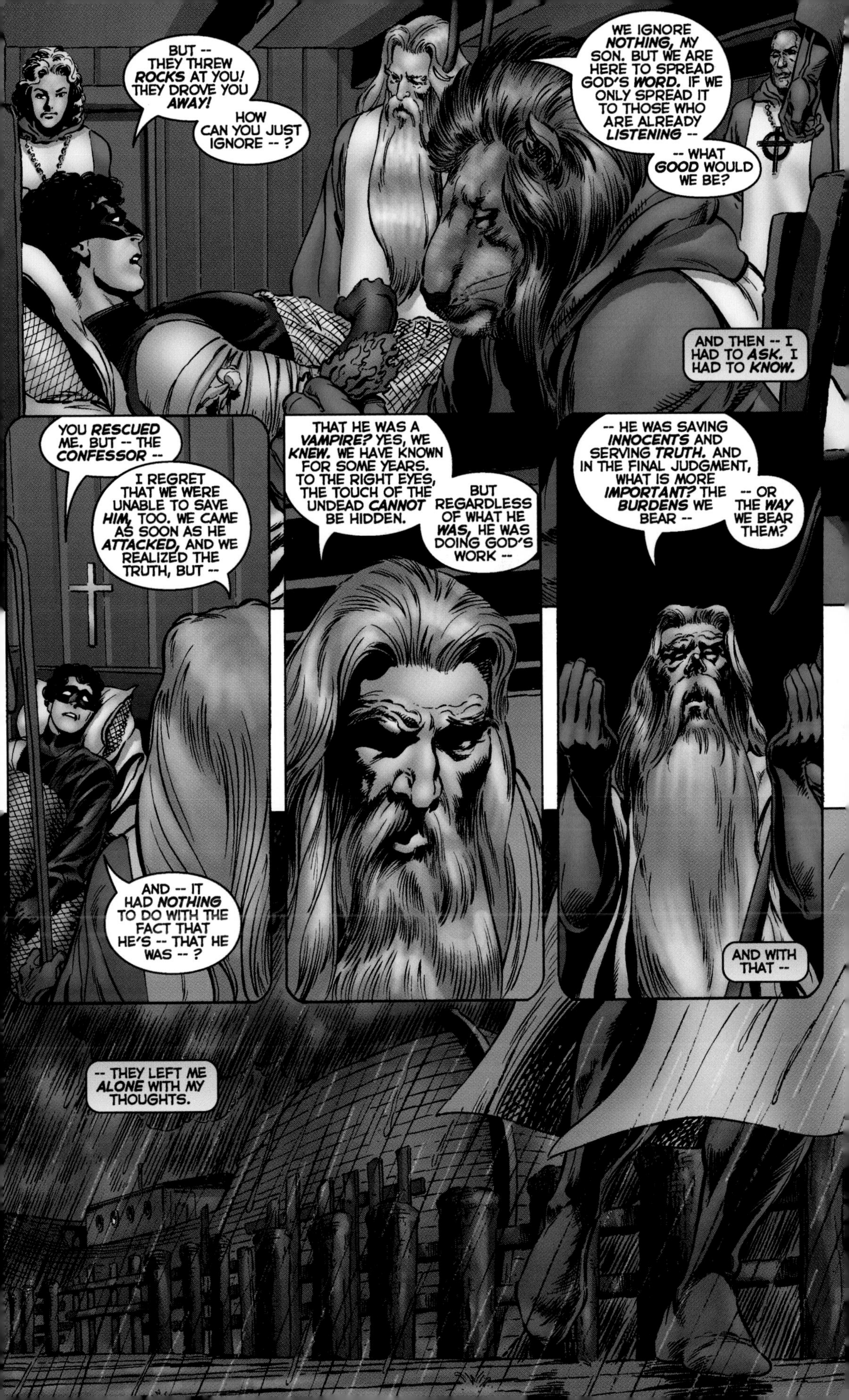
BUT -- THEY THREW ROCKS AT YOU! THEY DROVE YOU AWAY!
HOW CAN YOU JUST IGNORE -- ?
WE IGNORE NOTHING, MY SON. BUT WE ARE HERE TO SPREAD GOD'S WORD. IF WE ONLY SPREAD IT TO THOSE WHO ARE ALREADY LISTENING --
-- WHAT GOOD WOULD WE BE?
AND THEN -- I HAD TO ASK. I HAD TO KNOW.
YOU RESCUED ME. BUT -- THE CONFESSOR --
I REGRET THAT WE WERE UNABLE TO SAVE HIM, TOO. WE CAME AS SOON AS HE ATTACKED, AND WE REALIZED THE TRUTH, BUT --
AND -- IT HAD NOTHING TO DO WITH THE FACT THAT HE'S -- THAT HE WAS -- ?
THAT HE WAS A VAMPIRE? YES, WE KNEW. WE HAVE KNOWN FOR SOME YEARS. TO THE RIGHT EYES, THE TOUCH OF THE UNDEAD CANNOT BE HIDDEN.
BUT REGARDLESS OF WHAT HE WAS, HE WAS DOING GOD'S WORK --
-- HE WAS SAVING INNOCENTS AND SERVING TRUTH. AND IN THE FINAL JUDGMENT, WHAT IS MORE IMPORTANT? THE BURDENS WE BEAR --
-- OR THE WAY WE BEAR THEM?
AND WITH THAT --
-- THEY LEFT ME ALONE WITH MY THOUGHTS.

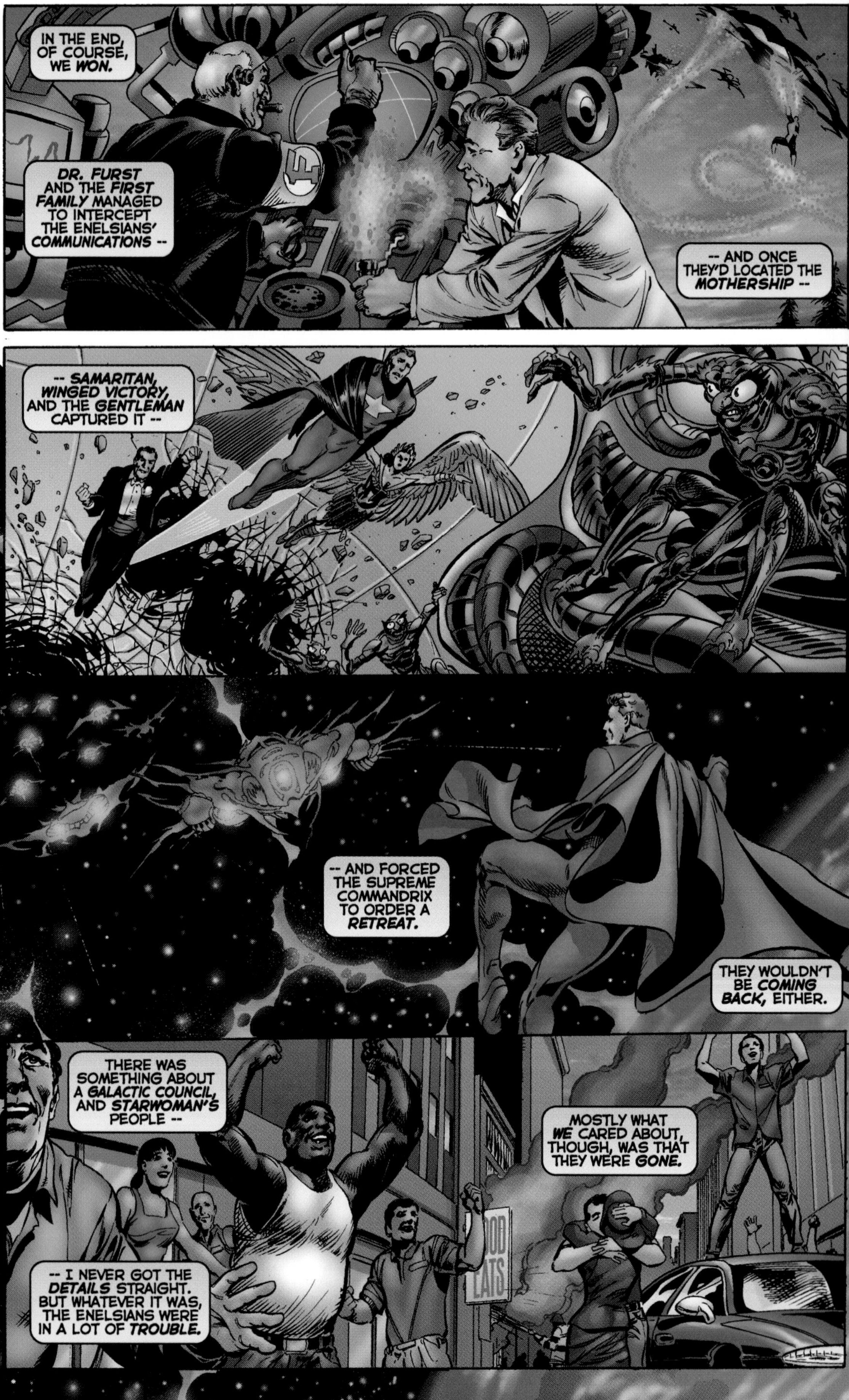
IN THE END, OF COURSE, WE WON.
DR. FURST AND THE FIRST FAMILY MANAGED TO INTERCEPT THE ENELSIANS' COMMUNICATIONS --
-- AND ONCE THEY'D LOCATED THE MOTHERSHIP --
-- SAMARITAN, WINGED VICTORY, AND THE GENTLEMAN CAPTURED IT --
-- AND FORCED THE SUPREME COMMANDRIX TO ORDER A RETREAT.
THEY WOULDN'T BE COMING BACK, EITHER.
THERE WAS SOMETHING ABOUT A GALACTIC COUNCIL, AND STARWOMAN'S PEOPLE --
-- I NEVER GOT THE DETAILS STRAIGHT. BUT WHATEVER IT WAS, THE ENELSIANS WERE IN A LOT OF TROUBLE.
MOSTLY WHAT WE CARED ABOUT, THOUGH, WAS THAT THEY WERE GONE.
GOOD EATS

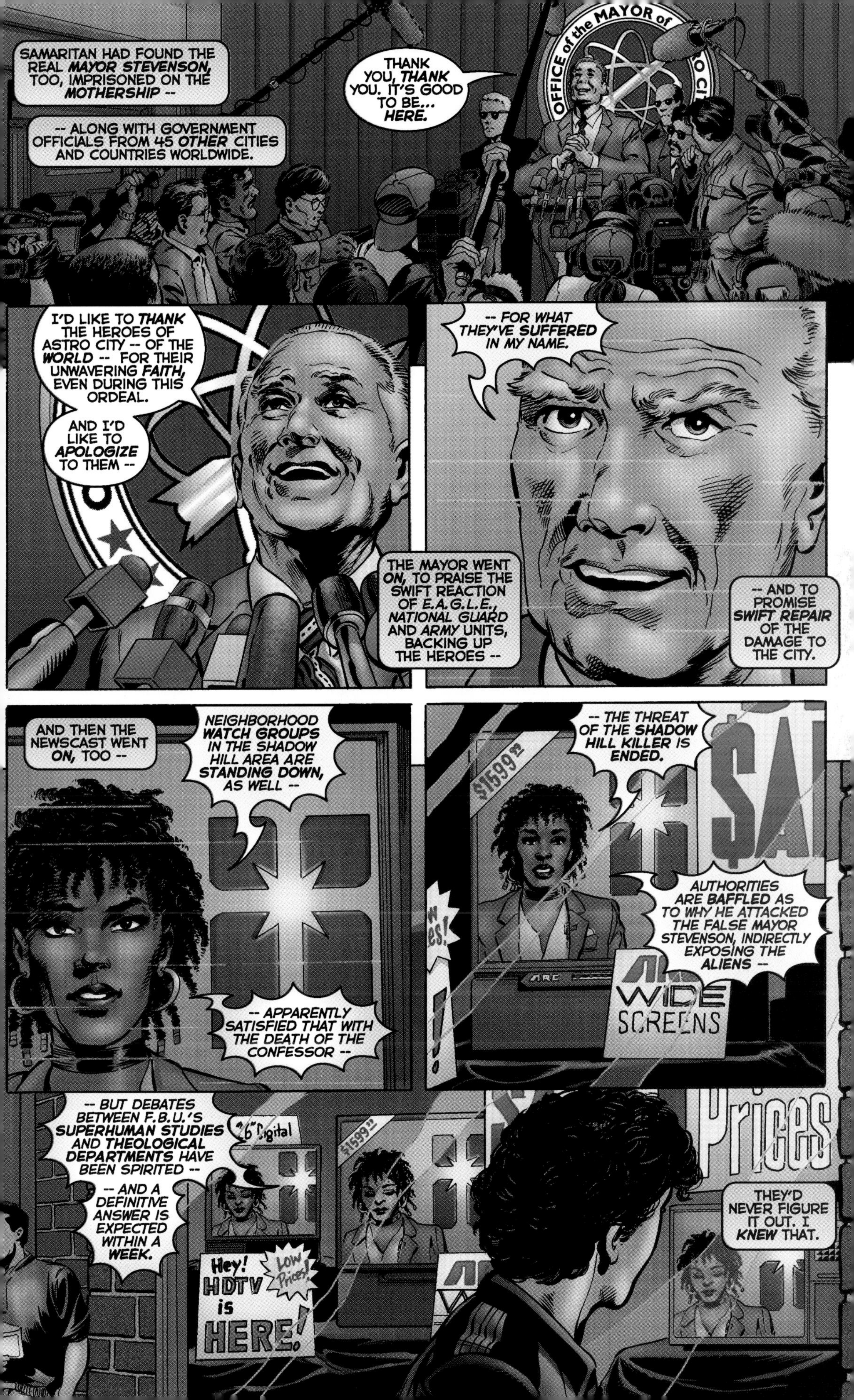
OFFICE of the MAYOR of
SAMARITAN HAD FOUND THE REAL MAYOR STEVENSON, TOO, IMPRISONED ON THE MOTHERSHIP --
-- ALONG WITH GOVERNMENT OFFICIALS FROM 45 OTHER CITIES AND COUNTRIES WORLDWIDE.
THANK YOU, THANK YOU. IT'S GOOD TO BE... HERE.
I'D LIKE TO THANK THE HEROES OF ASTRO CITY -- OF THE WORLD -- FOR THEIR UNWAVERING FAITH, EVEN DURING THIS ORDEAL.
AND I'D LIKE TO APOLOGIZE TO THEM --
-- FOR WHAT THEY'VE SUFFERED IN MY NAME.
THE MAYOR WENT ON, TO PRAISE THE SWIFT REACTION OF E.A.G.L.E., NATIONAL GUARD AND ARMY UNITS, BACKING UP THE HEROES --
-- AND TO PROMISE SWIFT REPAIR OF THE DAMAGE TO THE CITY.
AND THEN THE NEWSCAST WENT ON, TOO --
NEIGHBORHOOD WATCH GROUPS IN THE SHADOW HILL AREA ARE STANDING DOWN, AS WELL --
-- APPARENTLY SATISFIED THAT WITH THE DEATH OF THE CONFESSOR --
$1599.99
-- THE THREAT OF THE SHADOW HILL KILLER IS ENDED.
AUTHORITIES ARE BAFFLED AS TO WHY HE ATTACKED THE FALSE MAYOR STEVENSON, INDIRECTLY EXPOSING THE ALIENS --
WIDE SCREENS
-- BUT DEBATES BETWEEN F.B.U.'S SUPERHUMAN STUDIES AND THEOLOGICAL DEPARTMENTS HAVE BEEN SPIRITED --
-- AND A DEFINITIVE ANSWER IS EXPECTED WITHIN A WEEK.
26" Digital
$1599.99
Hey! HDTV is HERE!
Low Prices!
Prices
THEY'D NEVER FIGURE IT OUT. I KNEW THAT.

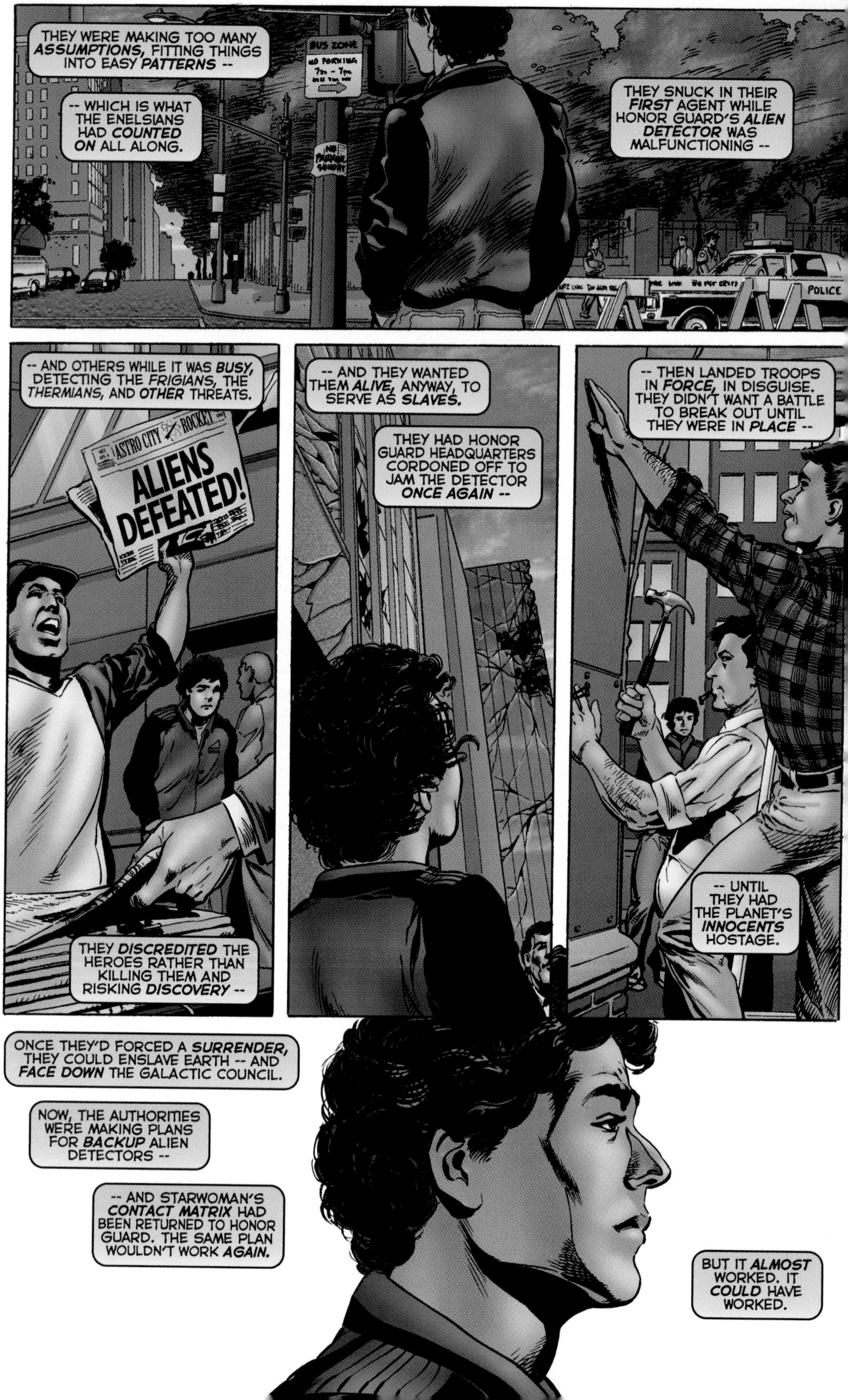

THEY WERE MAKING TOO MANY ASSUMPTIONS, FITTING THINGS INTO EASY PATTERNS --
-- WHICH IS WHAT THE ENELSIANS HAD COUNTED ON ALL ALONG.
BUS ZONE
THEY SNUCK IN THEIR FIRST AGENT WHILE HONOR GUARD'S ALIEN DETECTOR WAS MALFUNCTIONING --
POLICE
-- AND OTHERS WHILE IT WAS BUSY, DETECTING THE FRIGIANS, THE THERMIANS, AND OTHER THREATS.
ASTRO CITY ROCKET
ALIENS DEFEATED!
THEY DISCREDITED THE HEROES RATHER THAN KILLING THEM AND RISKING DISCOVERY --
-- AND THEY WANTED THEM ALIVE, ANYWAY, TO SERVE AS SLAVES.
THEY HAD HONOR GUARD HEADQUARTERS CORDONED OFF TO JAM THE DETECTOR ONCE AGAIN --
-- THEN LANDED TROOPS IN FORCE, IN DISGUISE. THEY DIDN'T WANT A BATTLE TO BREAK OUT UNTIL THEY WERE IN PLACE --
-- UNTIL THEY HAD THE PLANET'S INNOCENTS HOSTAGE.
ONCE THEY'D FORCED A SURRENDER, THEY COULD ENSLAVE EARTH -- AND FACE DOWN THE GALACTIC COUNCIL.
NOW, THE AUTHORITIES WERE MAKING PLANS FOR BACKUP ALIEN DETECTORS --
-- AND STARWOMAN'S CONTACT MATRIX HAD BEEN RETURNED TO HONOR GUARD. THE SAME PLAN WOULDN'T WORK AGAIN.
BUT IT ALMOST WORKED. IT COULD HAVE WORKED.

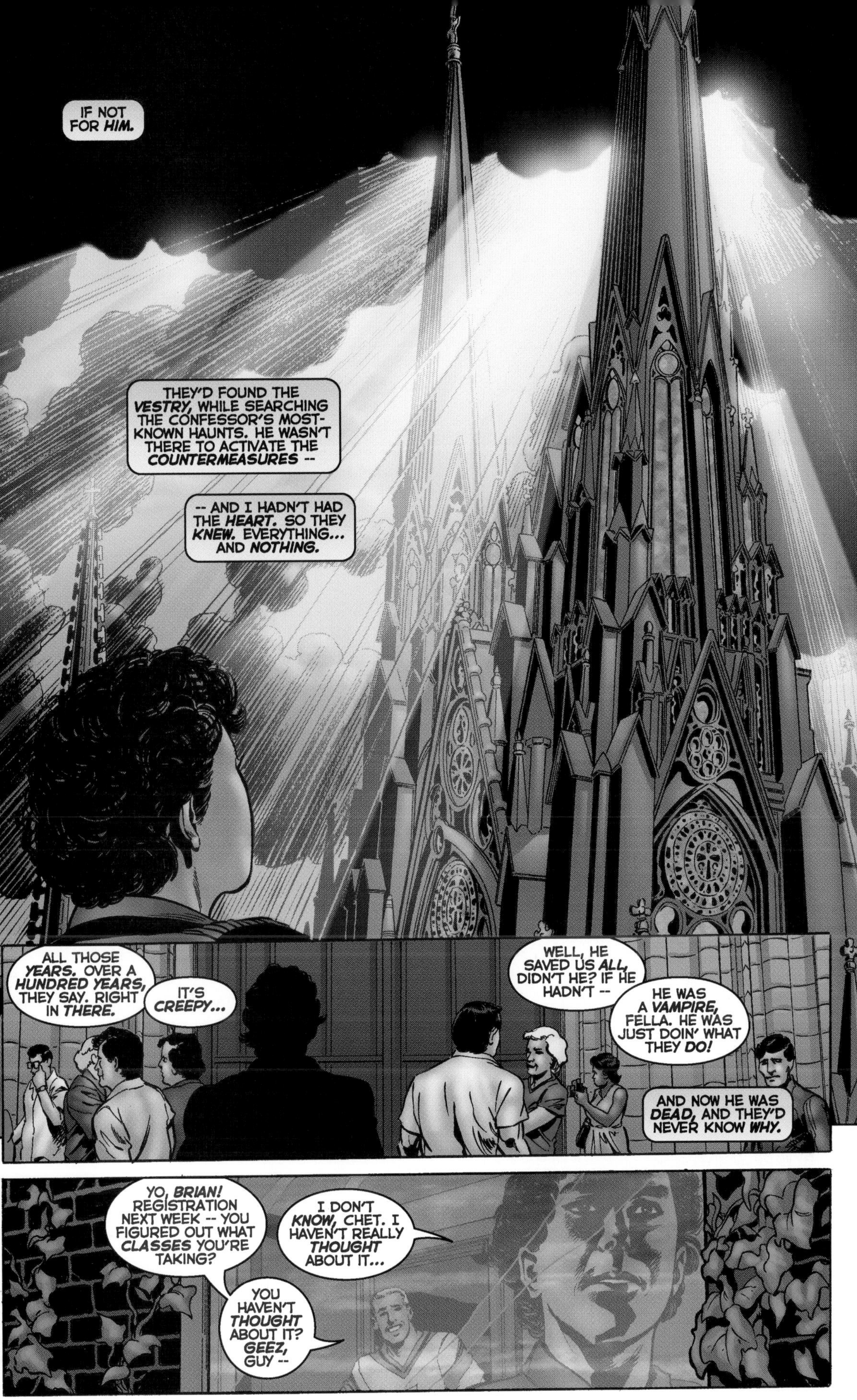
IF NOT FOR HIM.
THEY'D FOUND THE VESTRY, WHILE SEARCHING THE CONFESSOR'S MOST-KNOWN HAUNTS. HE WASN'T THERE TO ACTIVATE THE COUNTERMEASURES --
-- AND I HADN'T HAD THE HEART. SO THEY KNEW. EVERYTHING... AND NOTHING.
ALL THOSE YEARS. OVER A HUNDRED YEARS, THEY SAY. RIGHT IN THERE.
IT'S CREEPY...
WELL, HE SAVED US ALL, DIDN'T HE? IF HE HADN'T --
HE WAS A VAMPIRE, FELLA. HE WAS JUST DOIN' WHAT THEY DO!
AND NOW HE WAS DEAD, AND THEY'D NEVER KNOW WHY.
YO, BRIAN! REGISTRATION NEXT WEEK -- YOU FIGURED OUT WHAT CLASSES YOU'RE TAKING?
I DON'T KNOW, CHET. I HAVEN'T REALLY THOUGHT ABOUT IT...
YOU HAVEN'T THOUGHT ABOUT IT? GEEZ, GUY --

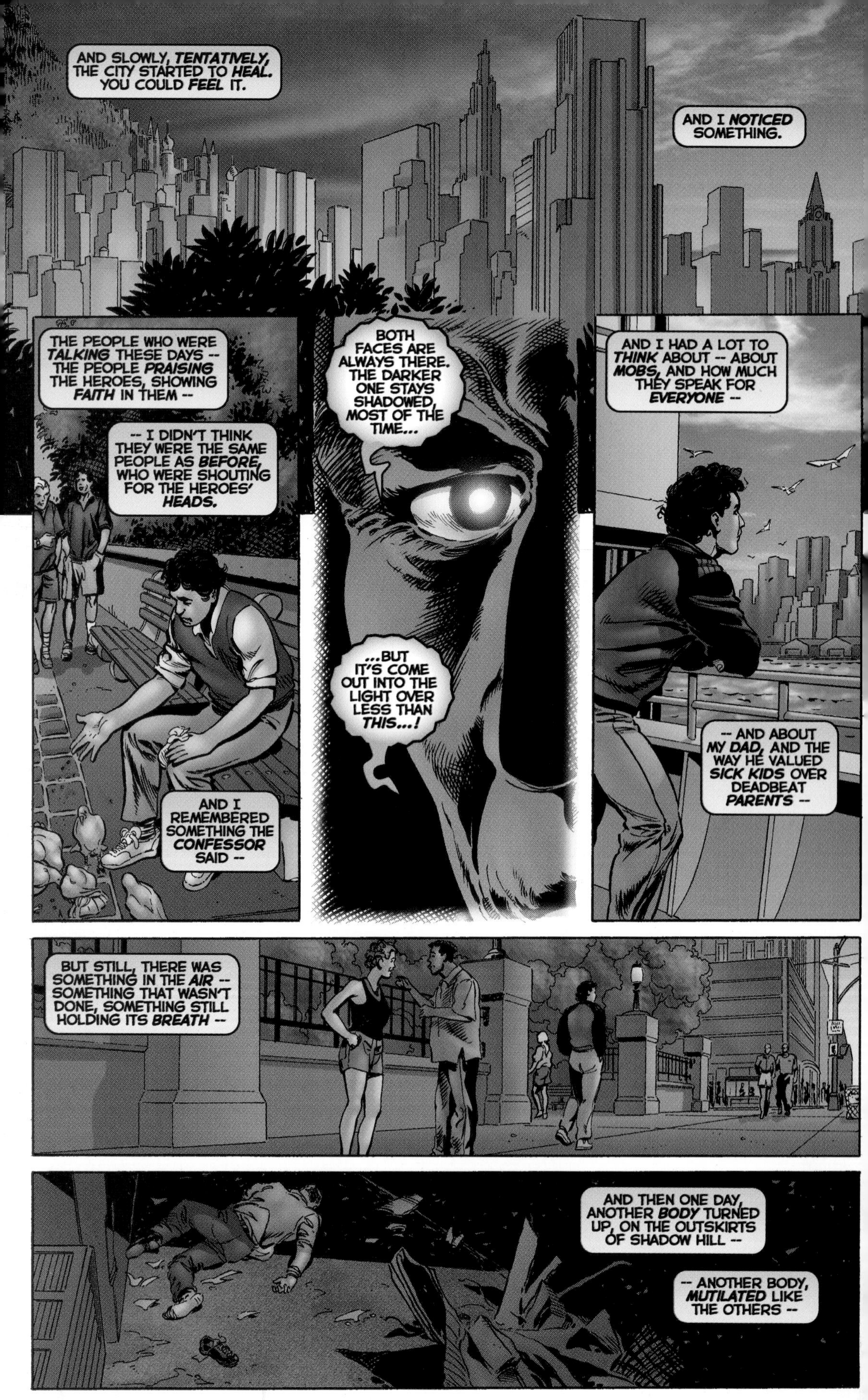
AND SLOWLY, TENTATIVELY, THE CITY STARTED TO HEAL. YOU COULD FEEL IT.
AND I NOTICED SOMETHING.
THE PEOPLE WHO WERE TALKING THESE DAYS -- THE PEOPLE PRAISING THE HEROES, SHOWING FAITH IN THEM --
-- I DIDN'T THINK THEY WERE THE SAME PEOPLE AS BEFORE, WHO WERE SHOUTING FOR THE HEROES' HEADS.
AND I REMEMBERED SOMETHING THE CONFESSOR SAID --
BOTH FACES ARE ALWAYS THERE. THE DARKER ONE STAYS SHADOWED, MOST OF THE TIME...
...BUT IT'S COME OUT INTO THE LIGHT OVER LESS THAN THIS...!
AND I HAD A LOT TO THINK ABOUT -- ABOUT MOBS, AND HOW MUCH THEY SPEAK FOR EVERYONE --
-- AND ABOUT MY DAD, AND THE WAY HE VALUED SICK KIDS OVER DEADBEAT PARENTS --
BUT STILL, THERE WAS SOMETHING IN THE AIR -- SOMETHING THAT WASN'T DONE, SOMETHING STILL HOLDING ITS BREATH --
AND THEN ONE DAY, ANOTHER BODY TURNED UP, ON THE OUTSKIRTS OF SHADOW HILL --
-- ANOTHER BODY, MUTILATED LIKE THE OTHERS --

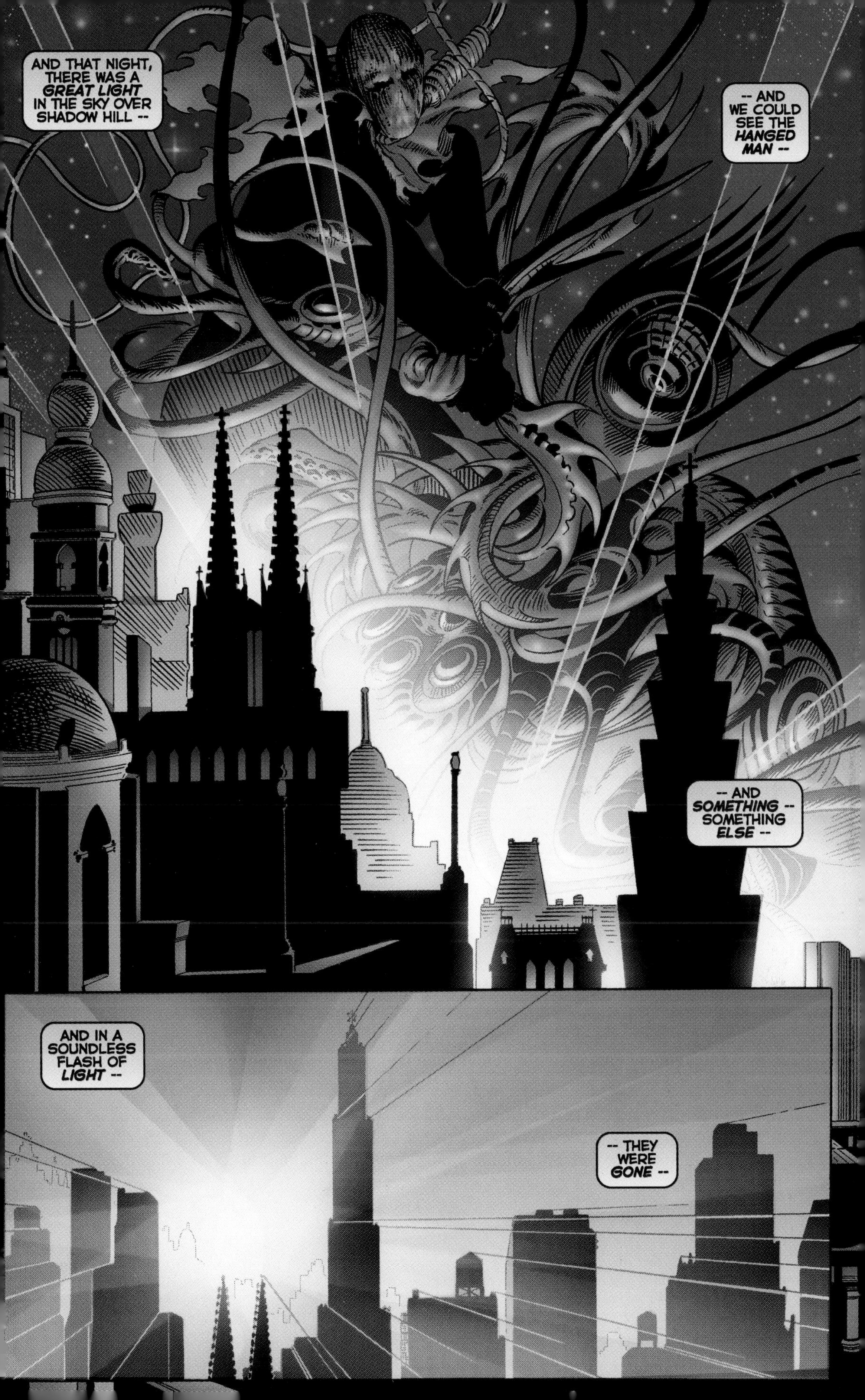
AND THAT NIGHT, THERE WAS A GREAT LIGHT IN THE SKY OVER SHADOW HILL --
-- AND WE COULD SEE THE HANGED MAN --
-- AND SOMETHING -- SOMETHING ELSE --
AND IN A SOUNDLESS FLASH OF LIGHT --
-- THEY WERE GONE --

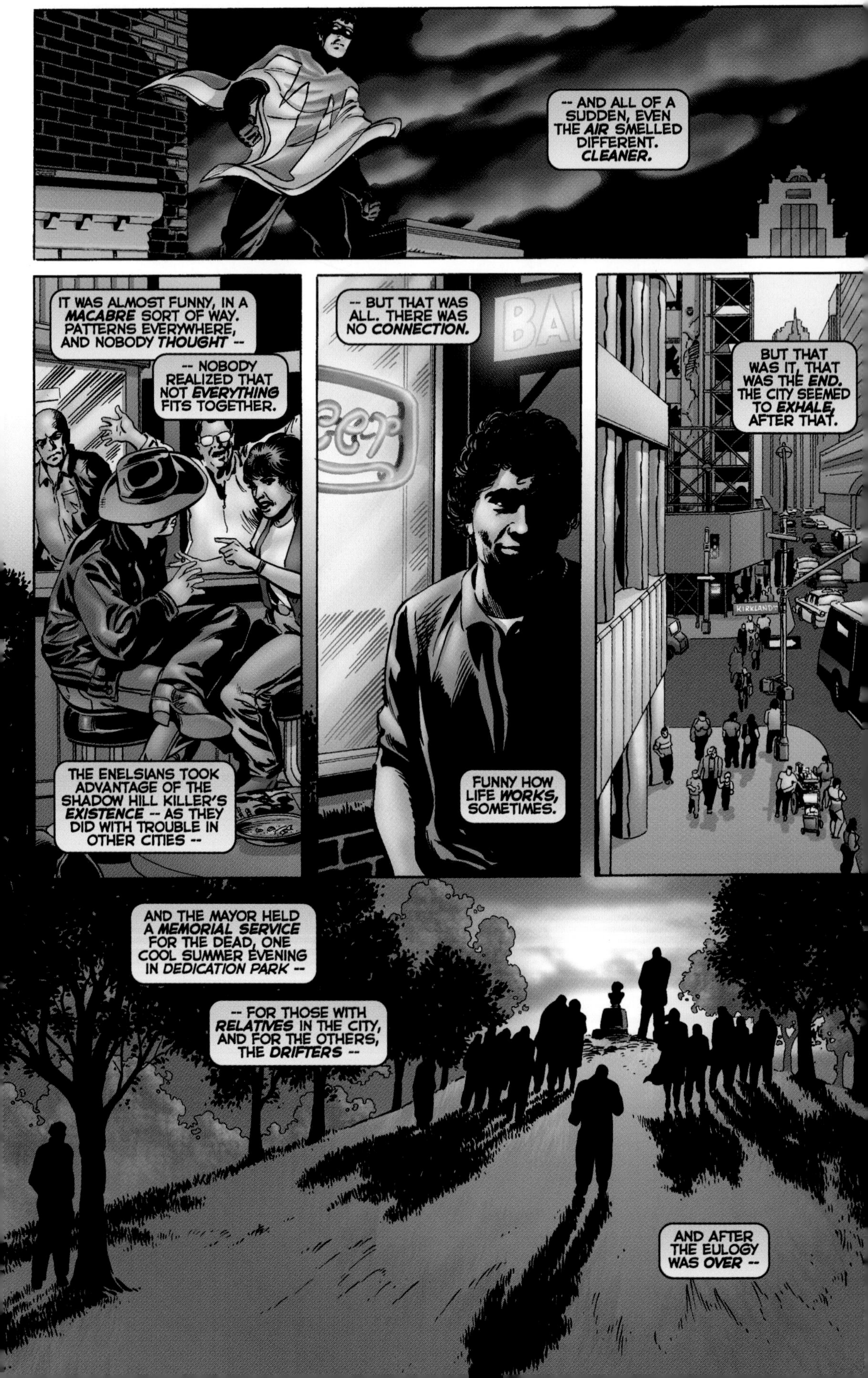
-- AND ALL OF A SUDDEN, EVEN THE *AIR* SMELLED DIFFERENT. *CLEANER.*
IT WAS ALMOST FUNNY, IN A *MACABRE* SORT OF WAY. PATTERNS EVERYWHERE, AND NOBODY *THOUGHT* --
-- NOBODY REALIZED THAT NOT *EVERYTHING* FITS TOGETHER.
THE ENELSIANS TOOK ADVANTAGE OF THE SHADOW HILL KILLER'S *EXISTENCE* -- AS THEY DID WITH TROUBLE IN OTHER CITIES --
-- BUT THAT WAS ALL. THERE WAS NO *CONNECTION.*
FUNNY HOW LIFE *WORKS,* SOMETIMES.
BUT THAT WAS IT, THAT WAS THE *END.* THE CITY SEEMED TO *EXHALE,* AFTER THAT.
AND THE MAYOR HELD A *MEMORIAL SERVICE* FOR THE DEAD, ONE COOL SUMMER EVENING IN *DEDICATION PARK* --
-- FOR THOSE WITH *RELATIVES* IN THE CITY, AND FOR THE OTHERS, THE *DRIFTERS* --
AND AFTER THE EULOGY WAS *OVER* --

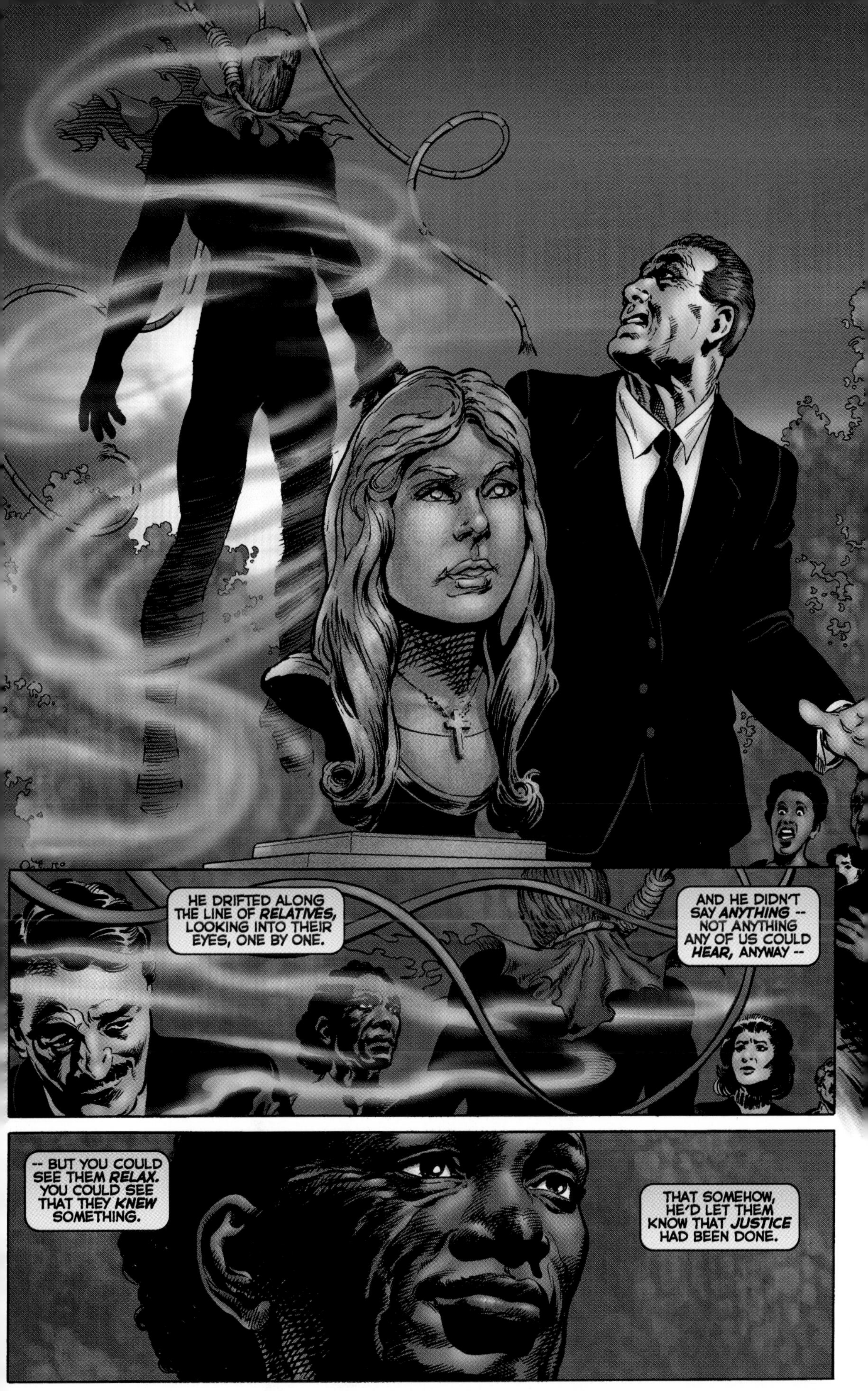
HE DRIFTED ALONG THE LINE OF RELATIVES, LOOKING INTO THEIR EYES, ONE BY ONE.
AND HE DIDN'T SAY ANYTHING -- NOT ANYTHING ANY OF US COULD HEAR, ANYWAY --
-- BUT YOU COULD SEE THEM RELAX. YOU COULD SEE THAT THEY KNEW SOMETHING.
THAT SOMEHOW, HE'D LET THEM KNOW THAT JUSTICE HAD BEEN DONE.

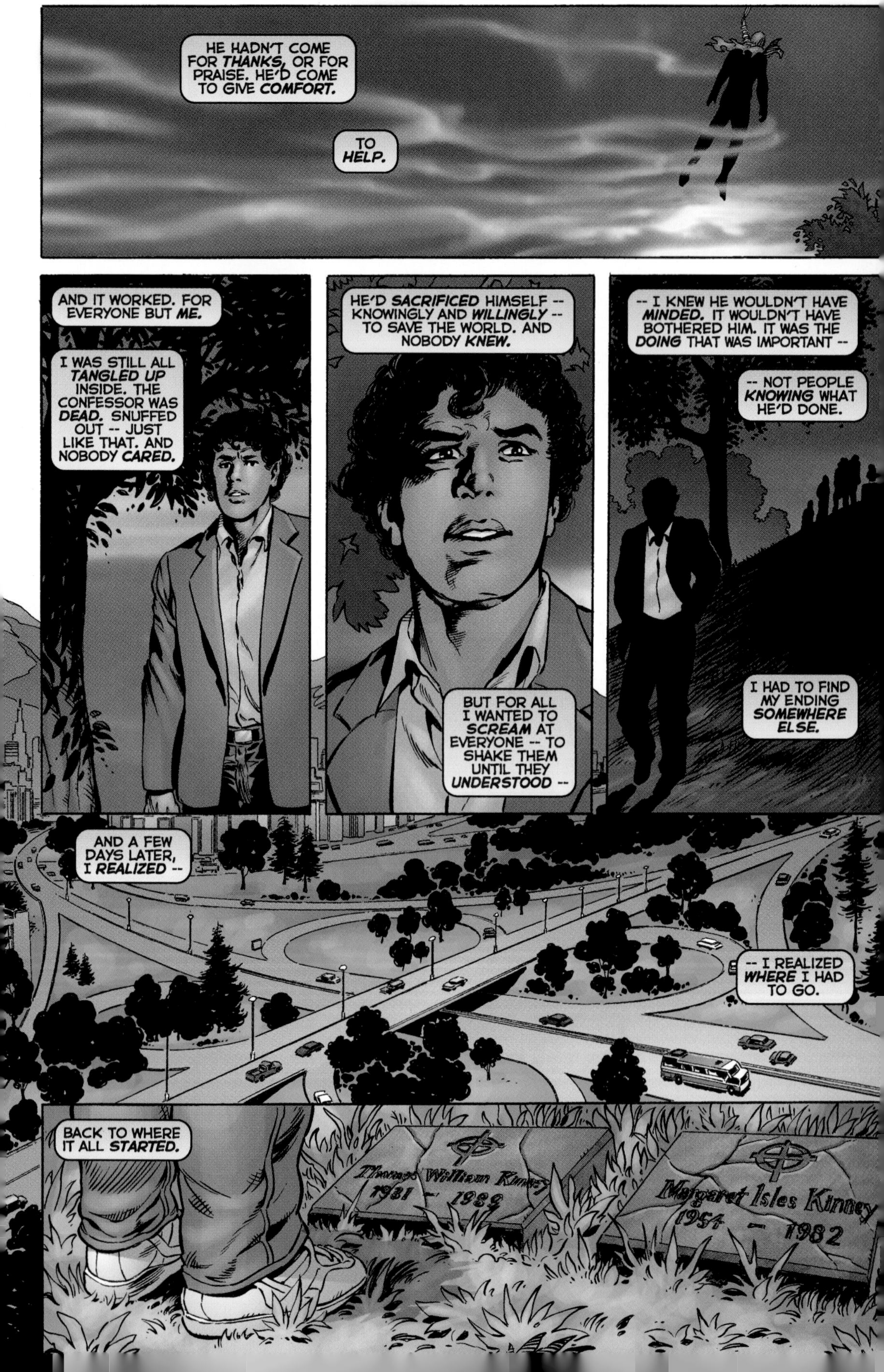
HE HADN'T COME FOR THANKS, OR FOR PRAISE. HE'D COME TO GIVE COMFORT.
TO HELP.
AND IT WORKED. FOR EVERYONE BUT ME.
I WAS STILL ALL TANGLED UP INSIDE. THE CONFESSOR WAS DEAD. SNUFFED OUT -- JUST LIKE THAT. AND NOBODY CARED.
HE'D SACRIFICED HIMSELF -- KNOWINGLY AND WILLINGLY -- TO SAVE THE WORLD. AND NOBODY KNEW.
BUT FOR ALL I WANTED TO SCREAM AT EVERYONE -- TO SHAKE THEM UNTIL THEY UNDERSTOOD --
-- I KNEW HE WOULDN'T HAVE MINDED. IT WOULDN'T HAVE BOTHERED HIM. IT WAS THE DOING THAT WAS IMPORTANT --
-- NOT PEOPLE KNOWING WHAT HE'D DONE.
I HAD TO FIND MY ENDING SOMEWHERE ELSE.
AND A FEW DAYS LATER, I REALIZED --
-- I REALIZED WHERE I HAD TO GO.
BACK TO WHERE IT ALL STARTED.
Thomas William Kinney
1931 - 1989
Margaret Isles Kinney
1954 - 1982

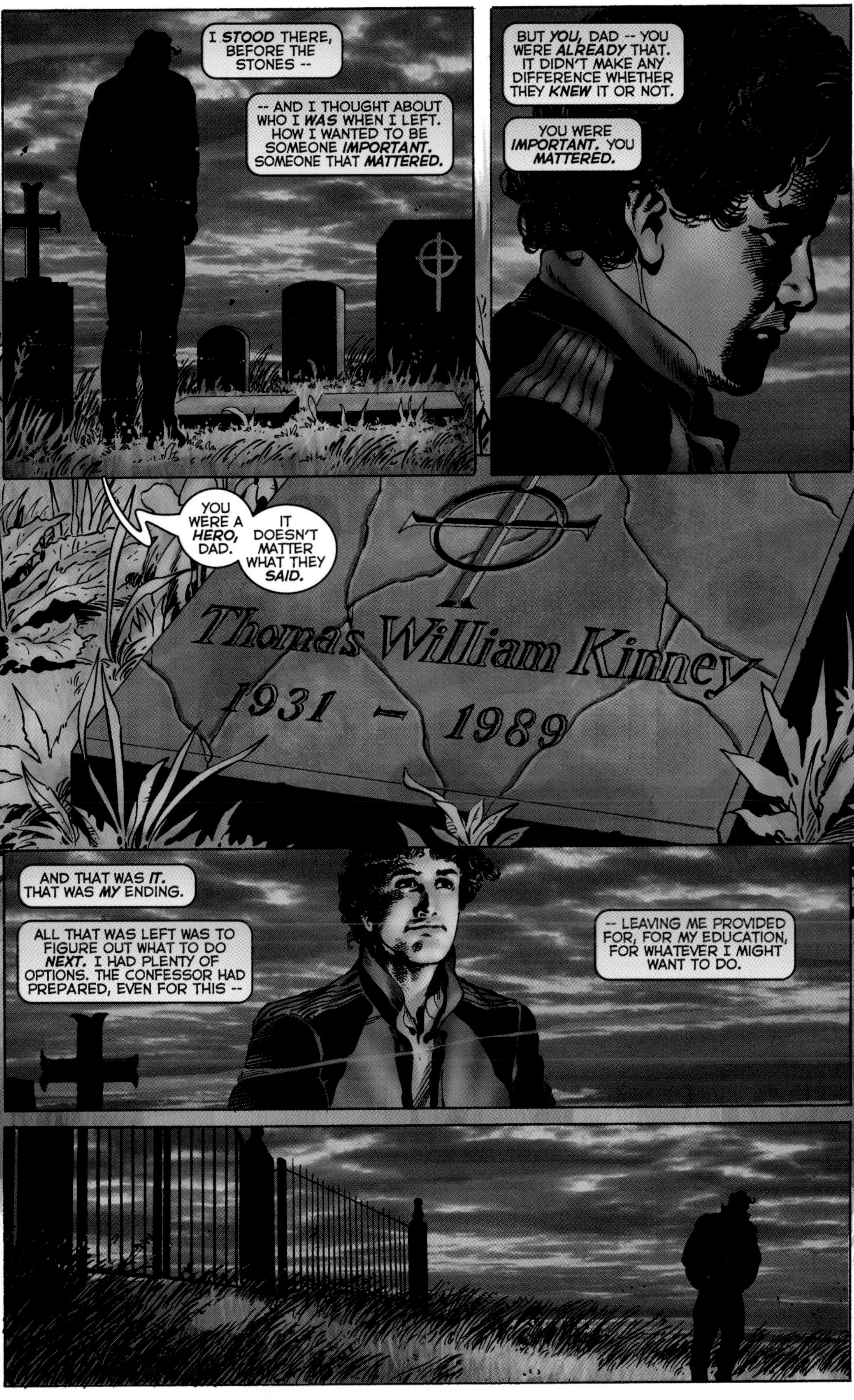
I STOOD THERE, BEFORE THE STONES --
-- AND I THOUGHT ABOUT WHO I WAS WHEN I LEFT. HOW I WANTED TO BE SOMEONE IMPORTANT. SOMEONE THAT MATTERED.
BUT YOU, DAD -- YOU WERE ALREADY THAT. IT DIDN'T MAKE ANY DIFFERENCE WHETHER THEY KNEW IT OR NOT.
YOU WERE IMPORTANT. YOU MATTERED.
YOU WERE A HERO, DAD.
IT DOESN'T MATTER WHAT THEY SAID.
Thomas William Kinney
1931 – 1989
AND THAT WAS IT. THAT WAS MY ENDING.
ALL THAT WAS LEFT WAS TO FIGURE OUT WHAT TO DO NEXT. I HAD PLENTY OF OPTIONS. THE CONFESSOR HAD PREPARED, EVEN FOR THIS --
-- LEAVING ME PROVIDED FOR, FOR MY EDUCATION, FOR WHATEVER I MIGHT WANT TO DO.

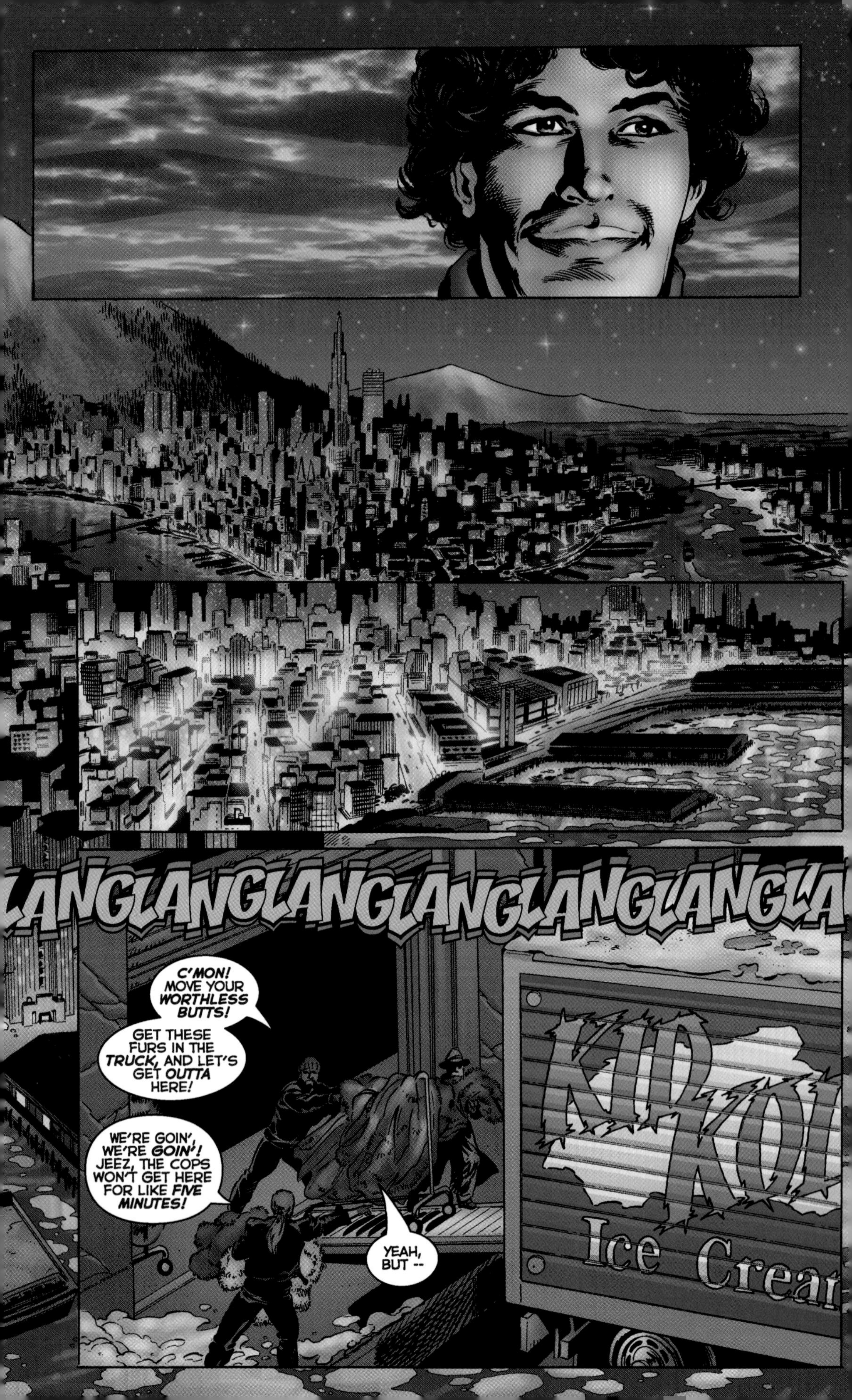
LANGLANGLANGLANGLANGLANGLANGLANGLA
C'MON! MOVE YOUR WORTHLESS BUTTS!
GET THESE FURS IN THE TRUCK, AND LET'S GET OUTTA HERE!
WE'RE GOIN', WE'RE GOIN'! JEEZ, THE COPS WON'T GET HERE FOR LIKE FIVE MINUTES!
YEAH, BUT --
Ice Crea

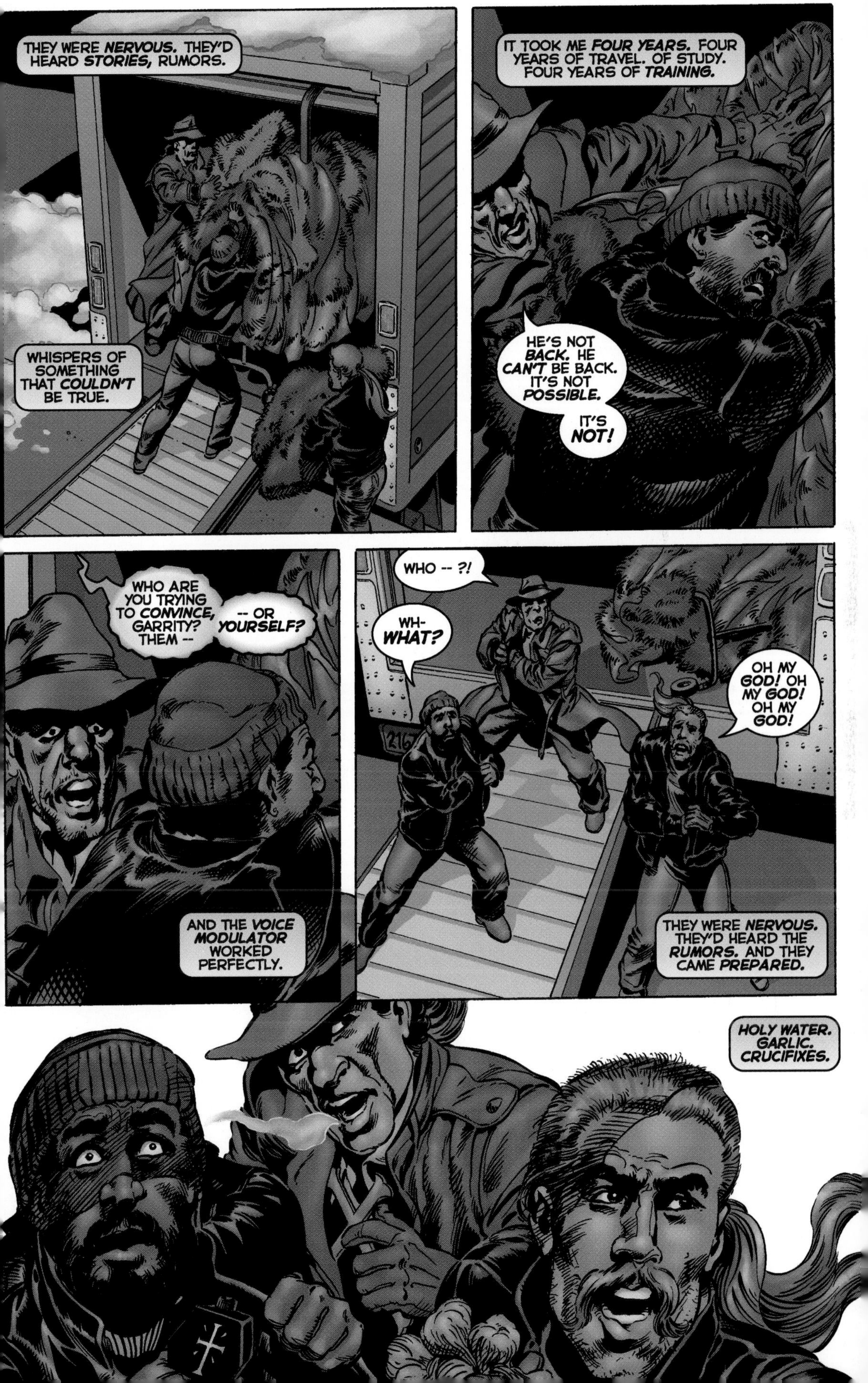
THEY WERE NERVOUS. THEY'D HEARD STORIES, RUMORS.
WHISPERS OF SOMETHING THAT COULDN'T BE TRUE.
IT TOOK ME FOUR YEARS. FOUR YEARS OF TRAVEL. OF STUDY. FOUR YEARS OF TRAINING.
HE'S NOT BACK. HE CAN'T BE BACK. IT'S NOT POSSIBLE.
IT'S NOT!
WHO ARE YOU TRYING TO CONVINCE, GARRITY? THEM --
-- OR YOURSELF?
AND THE VOICE MODULATOR WORKED PERFECTLY.
WHO -- ?!
WH- WHAT?
OH MY GOD! OH MY GOD! OH MY GOD!
THEY WERE NERVOUS. THEY'D HEARD THE RUMORS. AND THEY CAME PREPARED.
HOLY WATER. GARLIC. CRUCIFIXES.

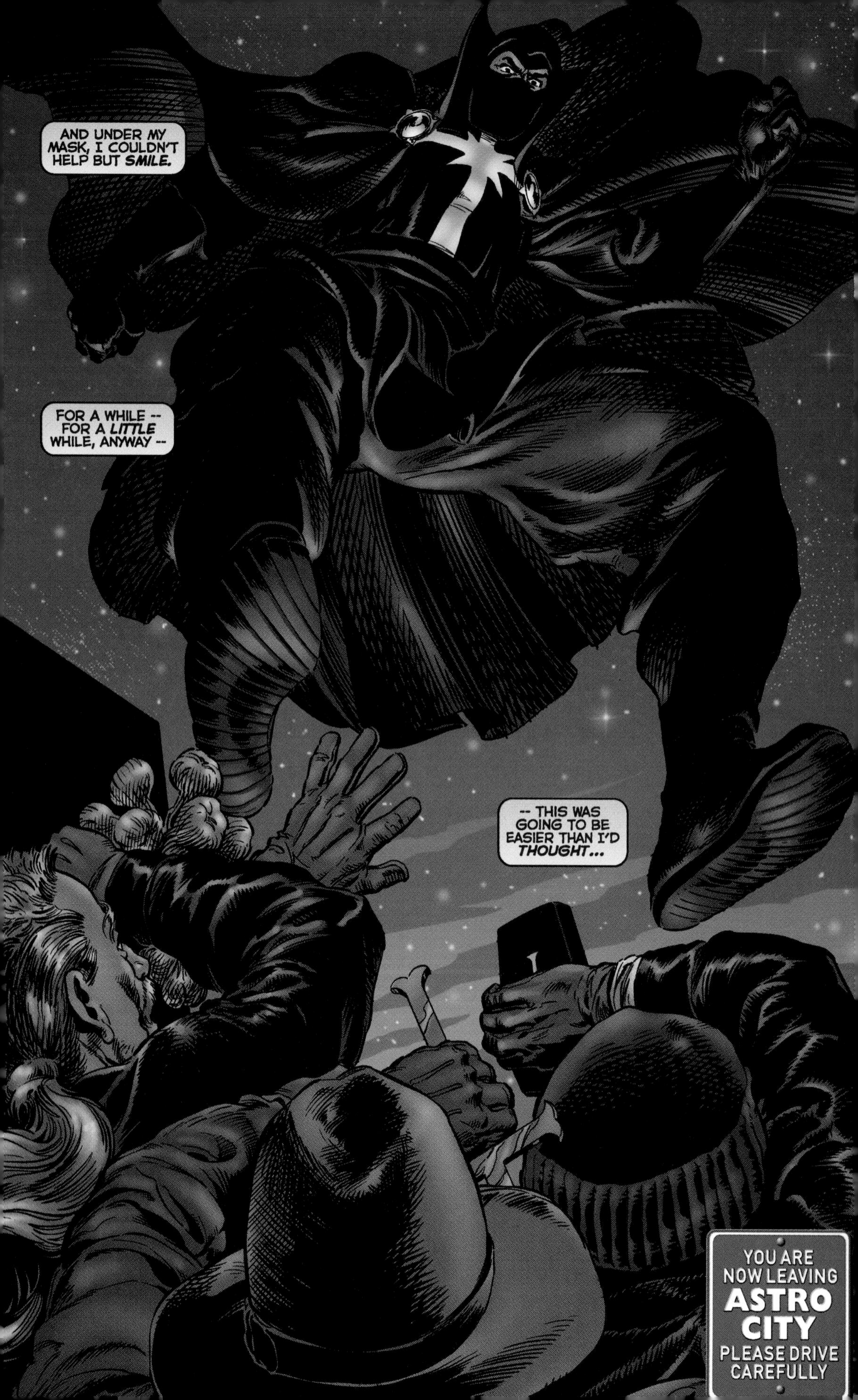
AND UNDER MY MASK, I COULDN'T HELP BUT SMILE.
FOR A WHILE -- FOR A LITTLE WHILE, ANYWAY --
-- THIS WAS GOING TO BE EASIER THAN I'D THOUGHT...
YOU ARE NOW LEAVING ASTRO CITY PLEASE DRIVE CAREFULLY

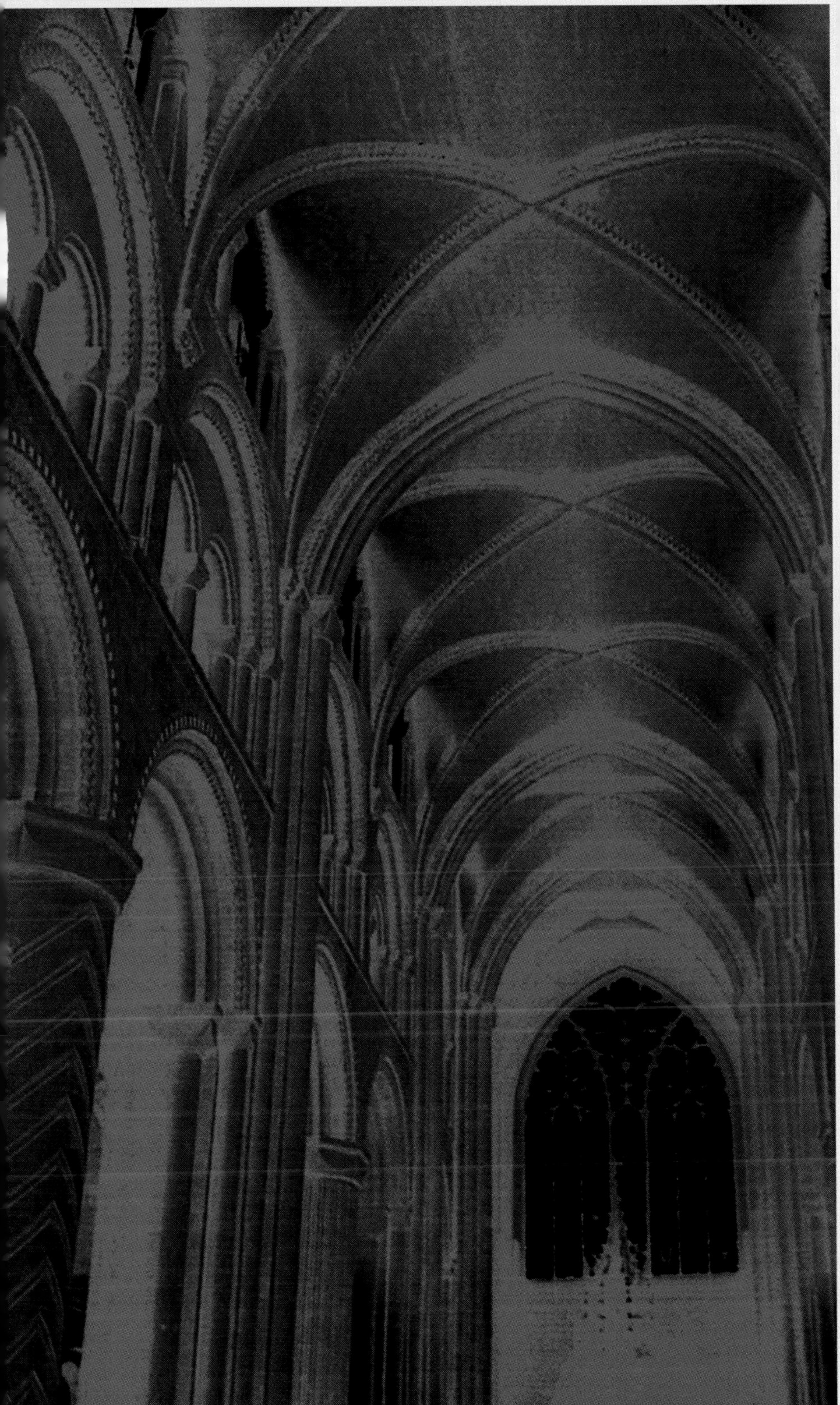

THE NEARNESS OF

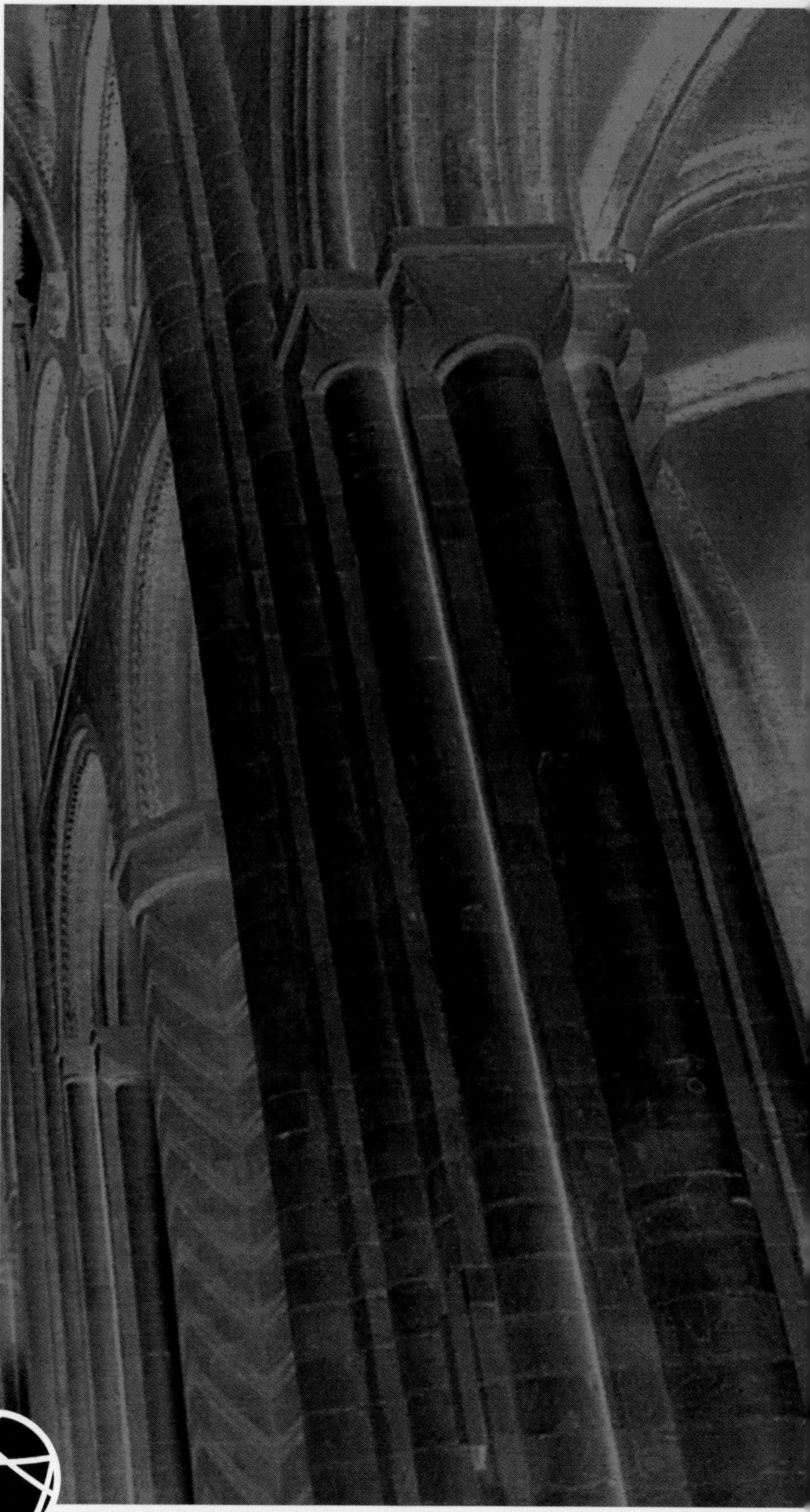

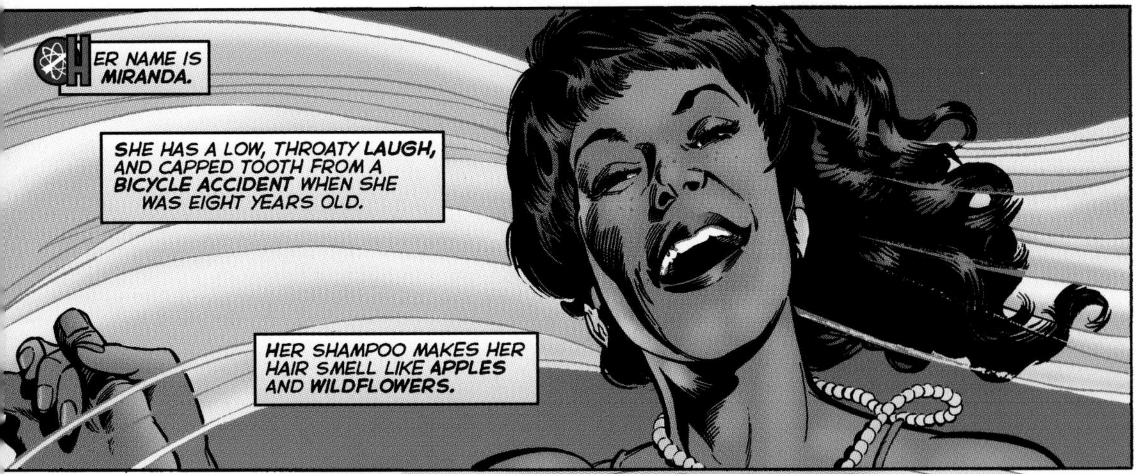
HER NAME IS MIRANDA.
SHE HAS A LOW, THROATY LAUGH, AND CAPPED TOOTH FROM A BICYCLE ACCIDENT WHEN SHE WAS EIGHT YEARS OLD.
HER SHAMPOO MAKES HER HAIR SMELL LIKE APPLES AND WILDFLOWERS.

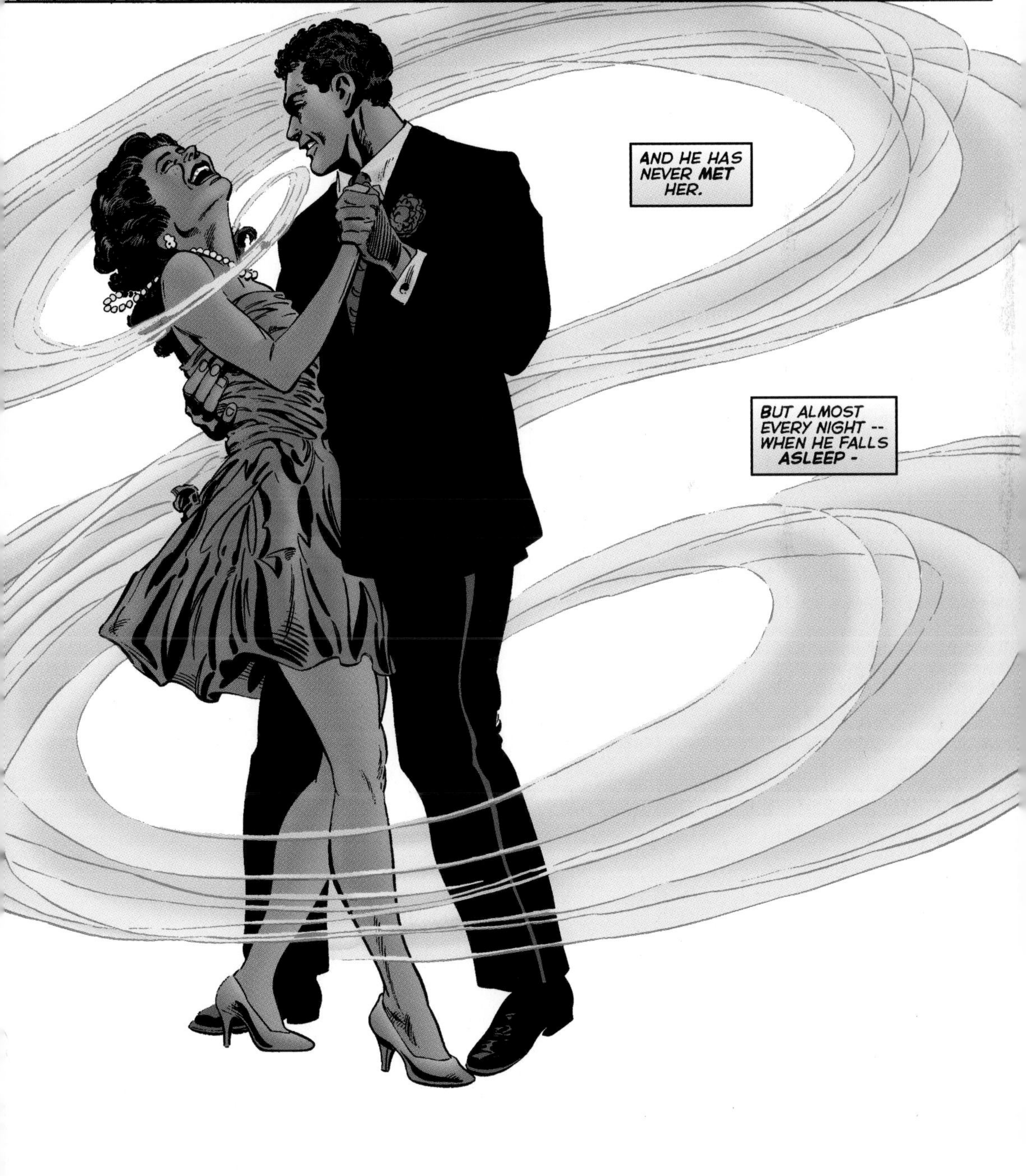
AND HE HAS NEVER MET HER.
BUT ALMOST EVERY NIGHT -- WHEN HE FALLS ASLEEP -

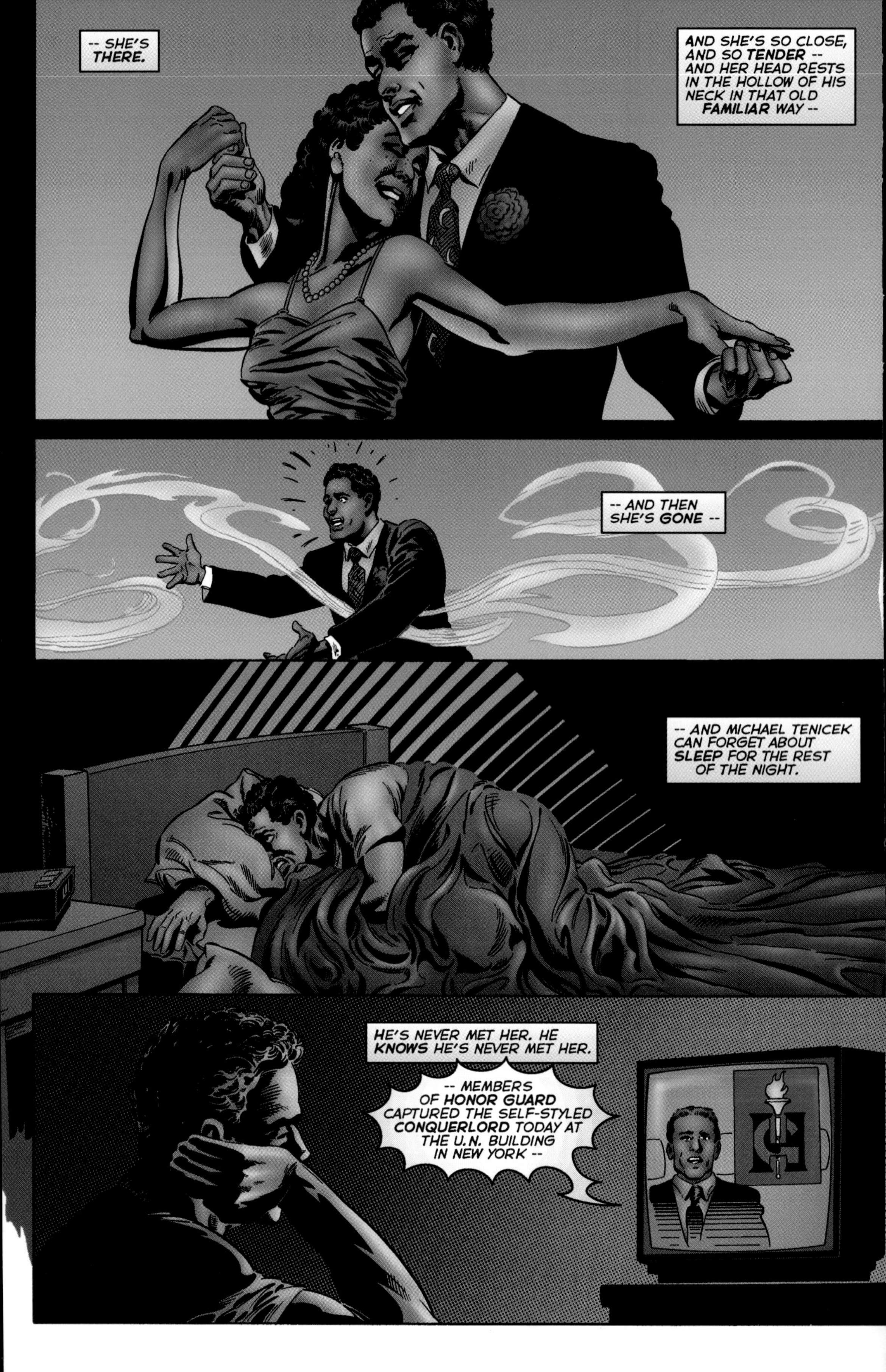

-- SHE'S THERE.
AND SHE'S SO CLOSE, AND SO TENDER -- AND HER HEAD RESTS IN THE HOLLOW OF HIS NECK IN THAT OLD FAMILIAR WAY --
-- AND THEN SHE'S GONE --
-- AND MICHAEL TENICEK CAN FORGET ABOUT SLEEP FOR THE REST OF THE NIGHT.
HE'S NEVER MET HER. HE KNOWS HE'S NEVER MET HER.
-- MEMBERS OF HONOR GUARD CAPTURED THE SELF-STYLED CONQUERLORD TODAY AT THE U.N. BUILDING IN NEW YORK --

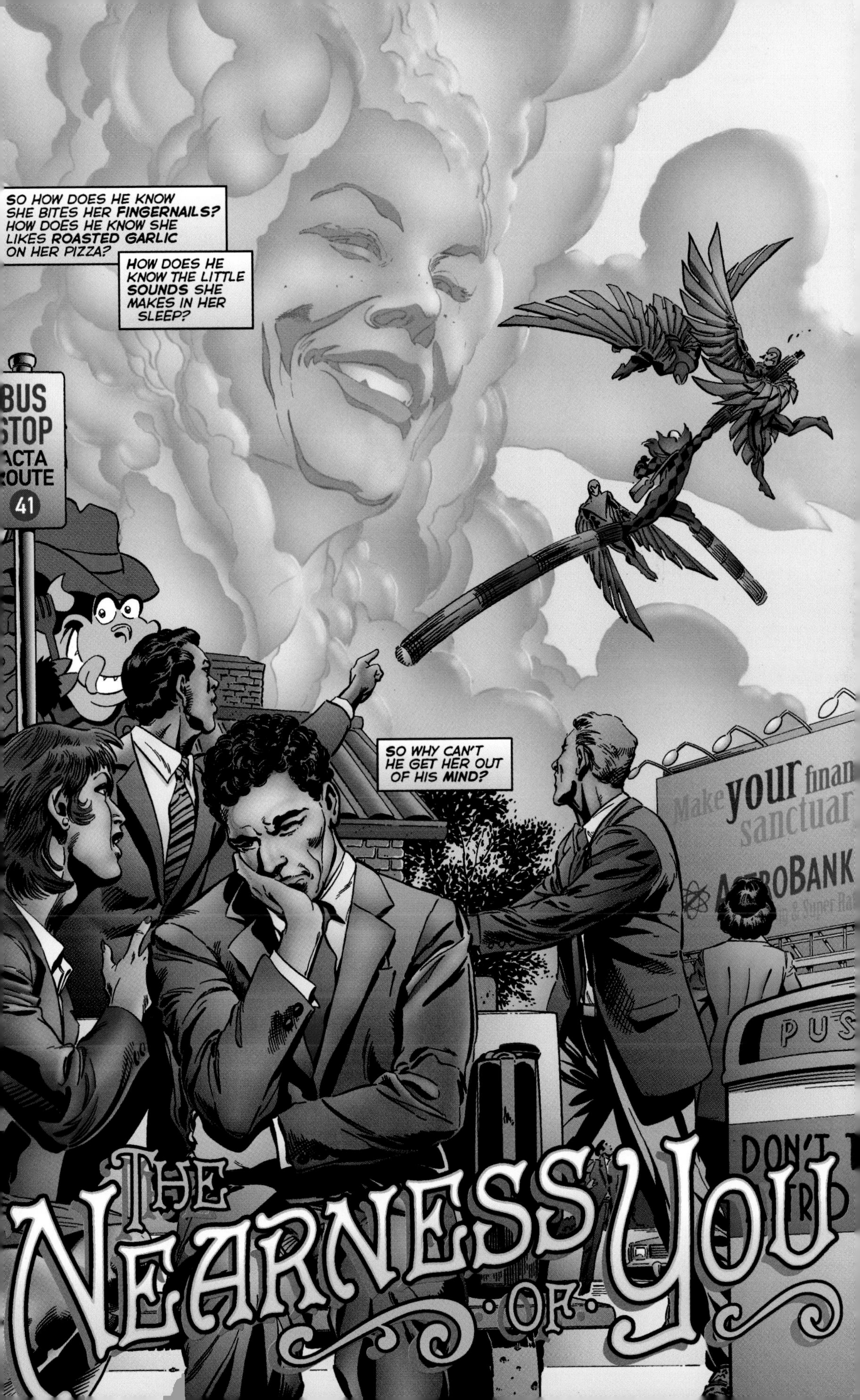
SO HOW DOES HE KNOW SHE BITES HER FINGERNAILS? HOW DOES HE KNOW SHE LIKES ROASTED GARLIC ON HER PIZZA?
HOW DOES HE KNOW THE LITTLE SOUNDS SHE MAKES IN HER SLEEP?
BUS STOP ACTA ROUTE 41
SO WHY CAN'T HE GET HER OUT OF HIS MIND?
Make your finan sanctuar
ASTROBANK
THE NEARNESS OF YOU

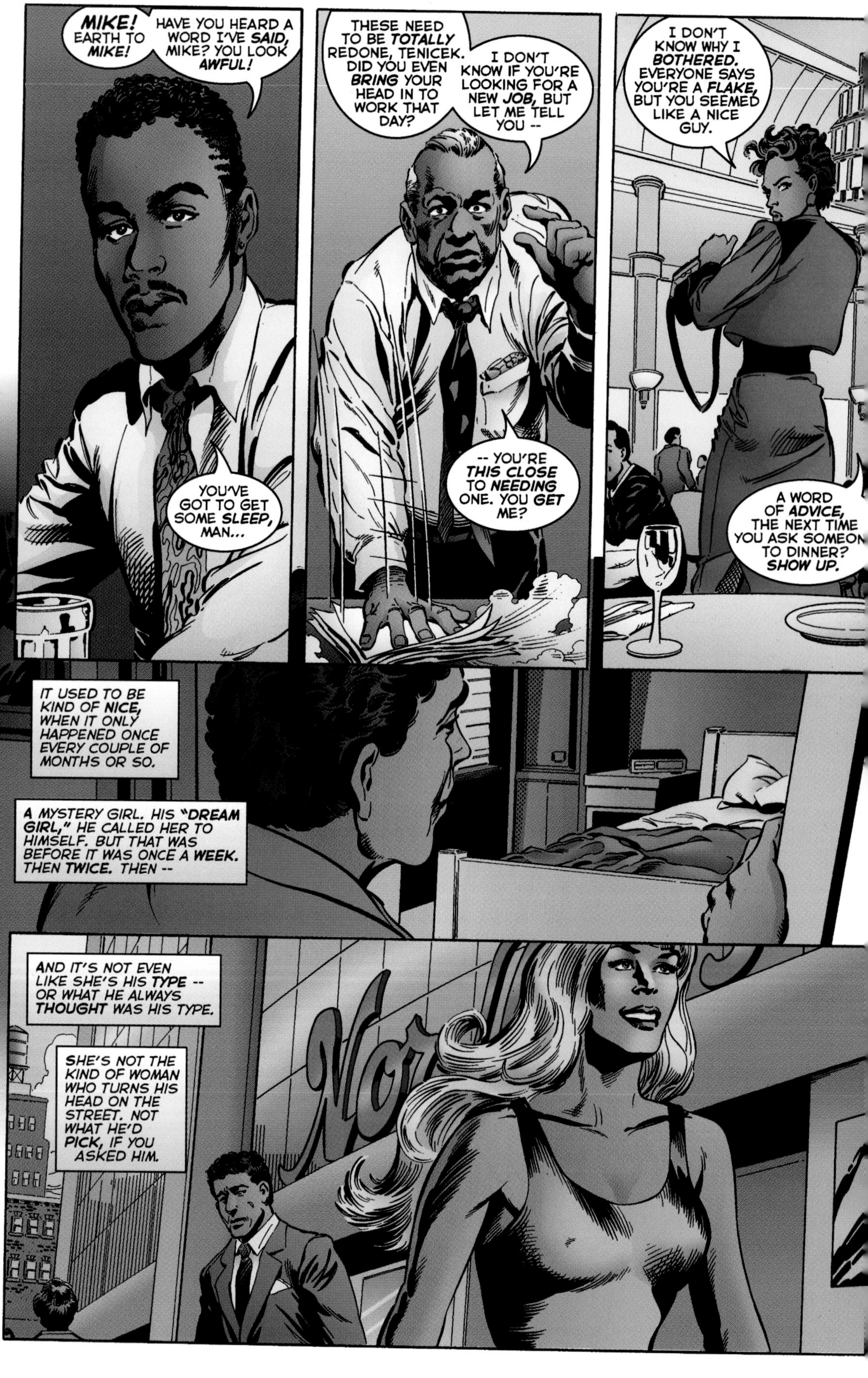

MIKE! EARTH TO MIKE!
HAVE YOU HEARD A WORD I'VE SAID, MIKE? YOU LOOK AWFUL!
YOU'VE GOT TO GET SOME SLEEP, MAN...
THESE NEED TO BE TOTALLY REDONE, TENICEK. DID YOU EVEN BRING YOUR HEAD IN TO WORK THAT DAY?
I DON'T KNOW IF YOU'RE LOOKING FOR A NEW JOB, BUT LET ME TELL YOU --
-- YOU'RE THIS CLOSE TO NEEDING ONE. YOU GET ME?
I DON'T KNOW WHY I BOTHERED. EVERYONE SAYS YOU'RE A FLAKE, BUT YOU SEEMED LIKE A NICE GUY.
A WORD OF ADVICE, THE NEXT TIME YOU ASK SOMEON TO DINNER? SHOW UP.
IT USED TO BE KIND OF NICE, WHEN IT ONLY HAPPENED ONCE EVERY COUPLE OF MONTHS OR SO.
A MYSTERY GIRL. HIS "DREAM GIRL," HE CALLED HER TO HIMSELF. BUT THAT WAS BEFORE IT WAS ONCE A WEEK. THEN TWICE. THEN --
AND IT'S NOT EVEN LIKE SHE'S HIS TYPE -- OR WHAT HE ALWAYS THOUGHT WAS HIS TYPE.
SHE'S NOT THE KIND OF WOMAN WHO TURNS HIS HEAD ON THE STREET. NOT WHAT HE'D PICK, IF YOU ASKED HIM.

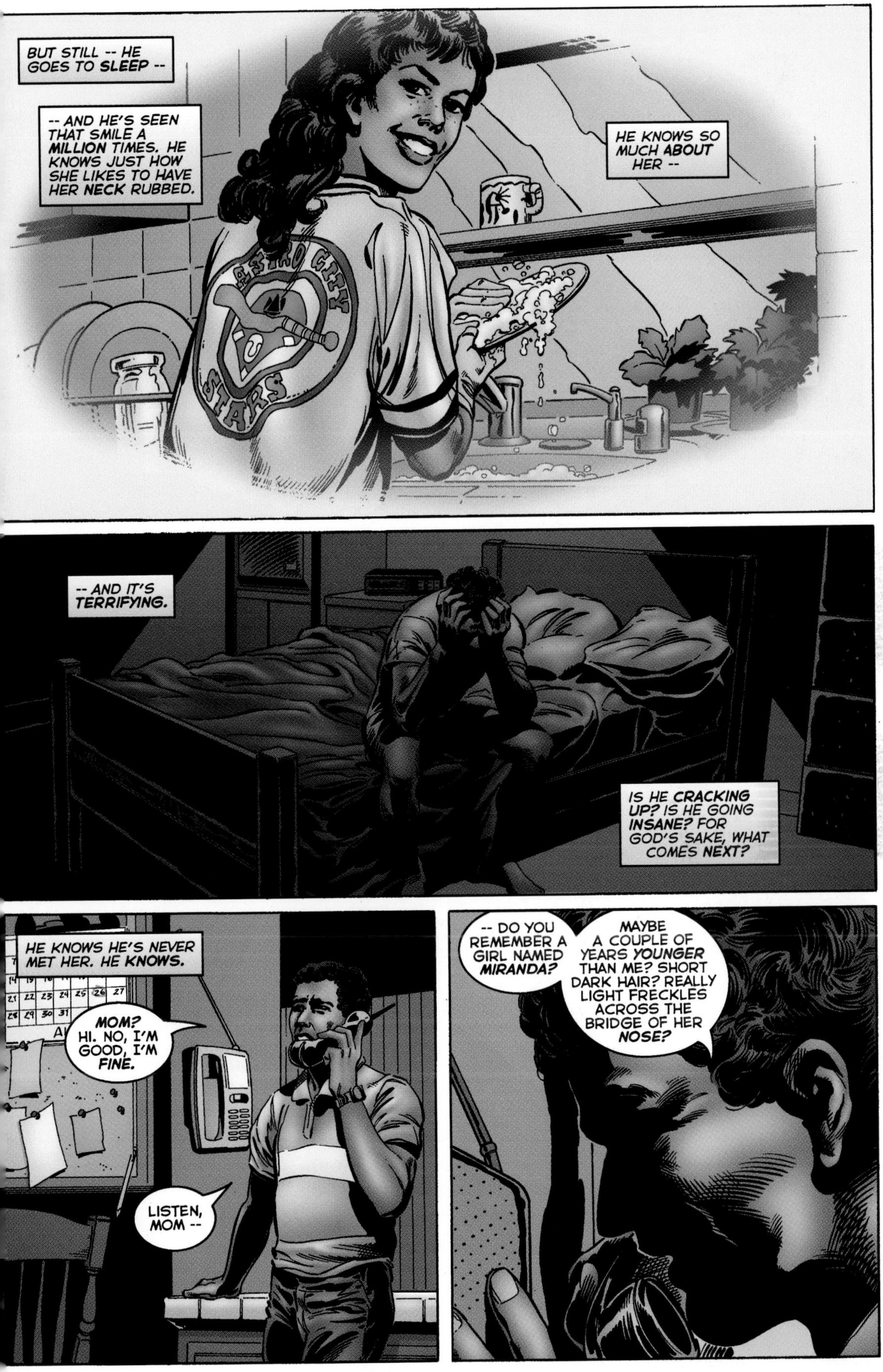
BUT STILL -- HE GOES TO SLEEP --
-- AND HE'S SEEN THAT SMILE A MILLION TIMES. HE KNOWS JUST HOW SHE LIKES TO HAVE HER NECK RUBBED.
HE KNOWS SO MUCH ABOUT HER --
-- AND IT'S TERRIFYING.
IS HE CRACKING UP? IS HE GOING INSANE? FOR GOD'S SAKE, WHAT COMES NEXT?
HE KNOWS HE'S NEVER MET HER. HE KNOWS.
MOM? HI. NO, I'M GOOD, I'M FINE.
LISTEN, MOM --
-- DO YOU REMEMBER A GIRL NAMED MIRANDA?
MAYBE A COUPLE OF YEARS YOUNGER THAN ME? SHORT DARK HAIR? REALLY LIGHT FRECKLES ACROSS THE BRIDGE OF HER NOSE?

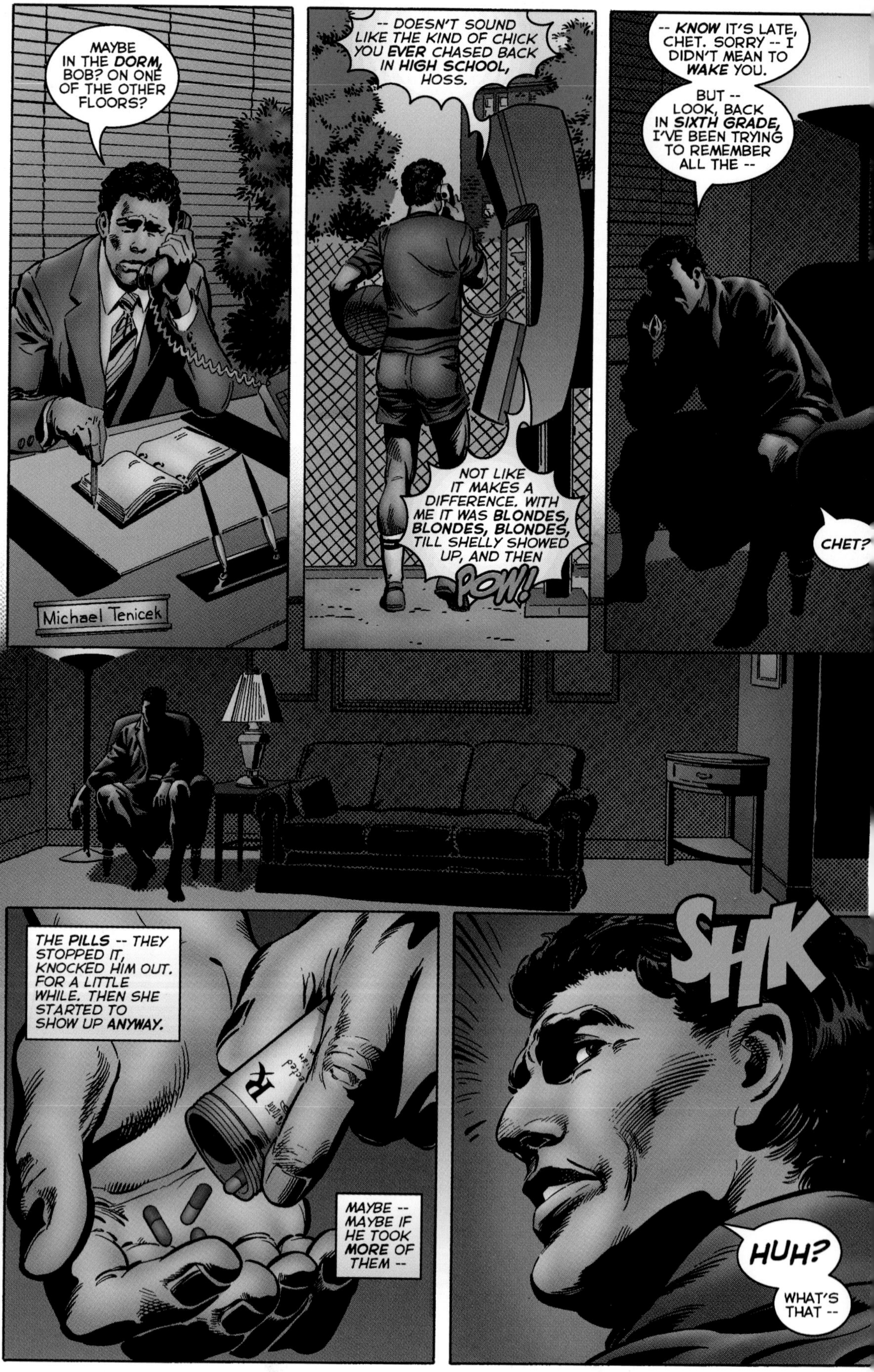
MAYBE IN THE DORM, BOB? ON ONE OF THE OTHER FLOORS?
Michael Tenicek
-- DOESN'T SOUND LIKE THE KIND OF CHICK YOU EVER CHASED BACK IN HIGH SCHOOL, HOSS.
NOT LIKE IT MAKES A DIFFERENCE. WITH ME IT WAS BLONDES, BLONDES, BLONDES, TILL SHELLY SHOWED UP, AND THEN
POW!
-- KNOW IT'S LATE, CHET. SORRY -- I DIDN'T MEAN TO WAKE YOU.
BUT -- LOOK, BACK IN SIXTH GRADE, I'VE BEEN TRYING TO REMEMBER ALL THE --
CHET?
THE PILLS -- THEY STOPPED IT, KNOCKED HIM OUT. FOR A LITTLE WHILE. THEN SHE STARTED TO SHOW UP ANYWAY.
MAYBE -- MAYBE IF HE TOOK MORE OF THEM --
SHK
HUH?
WHAT'S THAT --

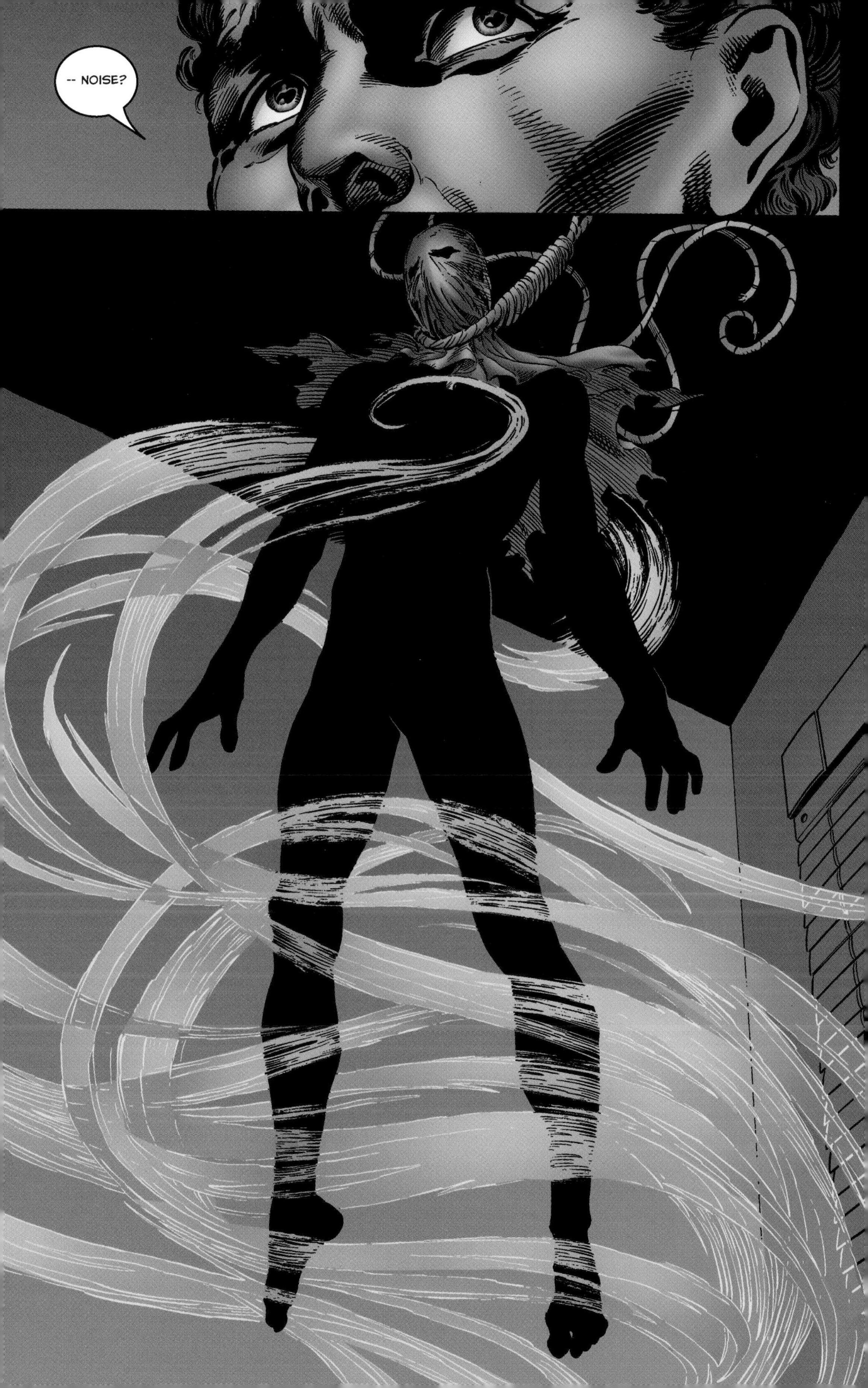
-- NOISE?

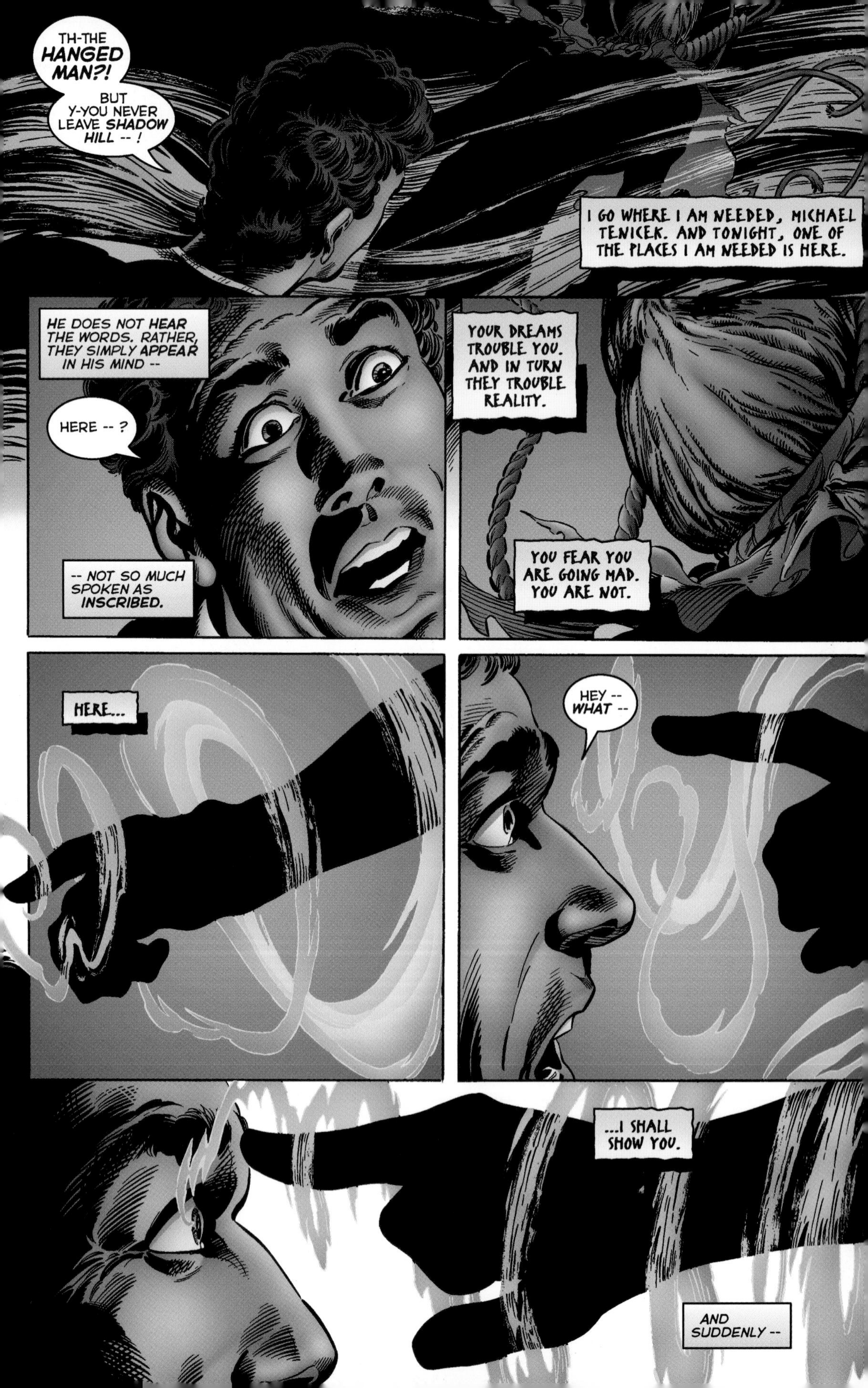
TH-THE HANGED MAN?!
BUT Y-YOU NEVER LEAVE SHADOW HILL -- !
I GO WHERE I AM NEEDED, MICHAEL TENICEK. AND TONIGHT, ONE OF THE PLACES I AM NEEDED IS HERE.
HE DOES NOT HEAR THE WORDS. RATHER, THEY SIMPLY APPEAR IN HIS MIND --
HERE -- ?
-- NOT SO MUCH SPOKEN AS INSCRIBED.
YOUR DREAMS TROUBLE YOU. AND IN TURN THEY TROUBLE REALITY.
YOU FEAR YOU ARE GOING MAD. YOU ARE NOT.
HERE...
HEY -- WHAT --
...I SHALL SHOW YOU.
AND SUDDENLY --

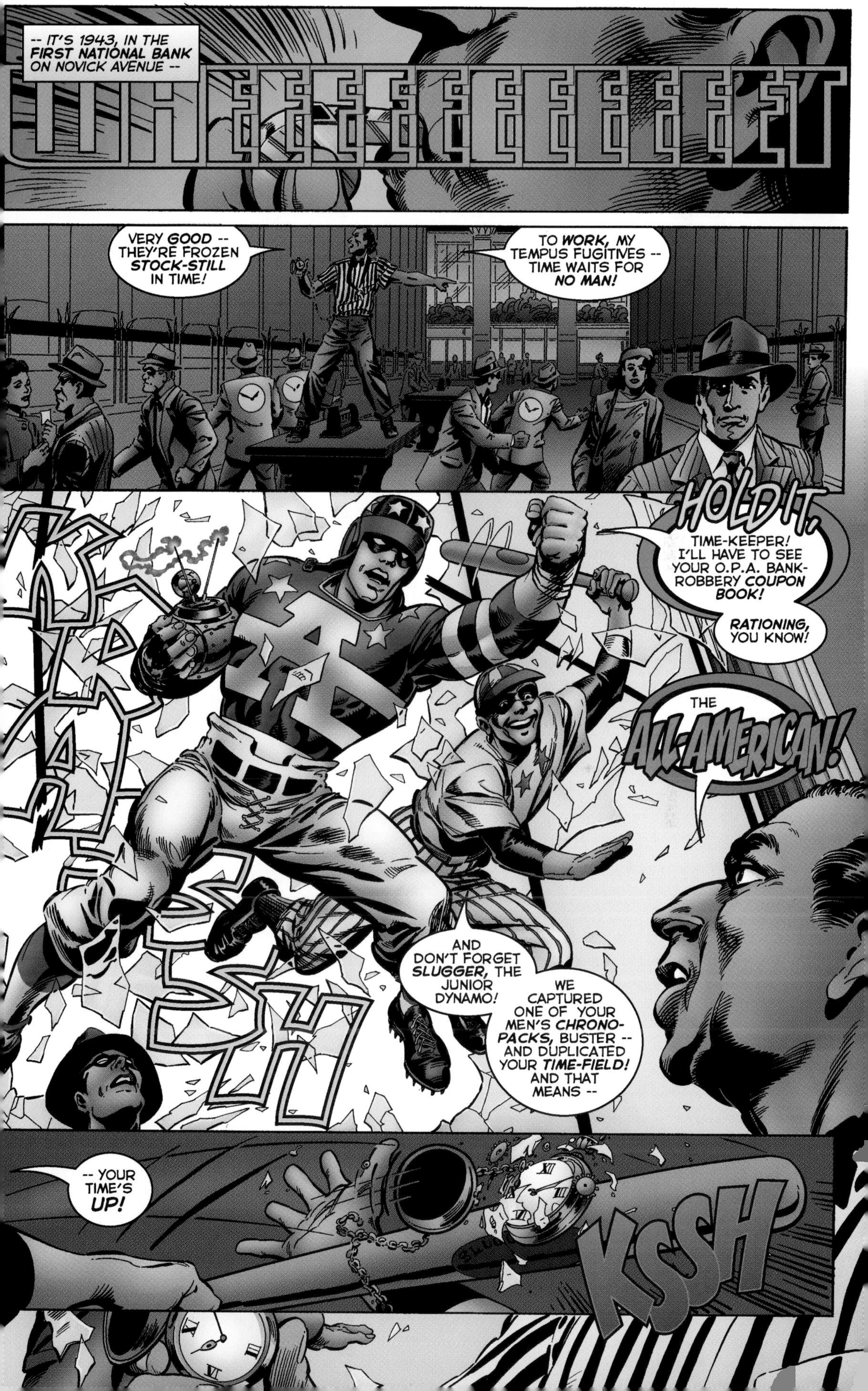
-- IT'S 1943, IN THE FIRST NATIONAL BANK ON NOVICK AVENUE --
VERY GOOD -- THEY'RE FROZEN STOCK-STILL IN TIME!
TO WORK, MY TEMPUS FUGITIVES -- TIME WAITS FOR NO MAN!
HOLD IT,
TIME-KEEPER! I'LL HAVE TO SEE YOUR O.P.A. BANK-ROBBERY COUPON BOOK!
RATIONING, YOU KNOW!
THE ALL-AMERICAN!
AND DON'T FORGET SLUGGER, THE JUNIOR DYNAMO!
WE CAPTURED ONE OF YOUR MEN'S CHRONO-PACKS, BUSTER -- AND DUPLICATED YOUR TIME-FIELD! AND THAT MEANS --
-- YOUR TIME'S UP!
KSSH

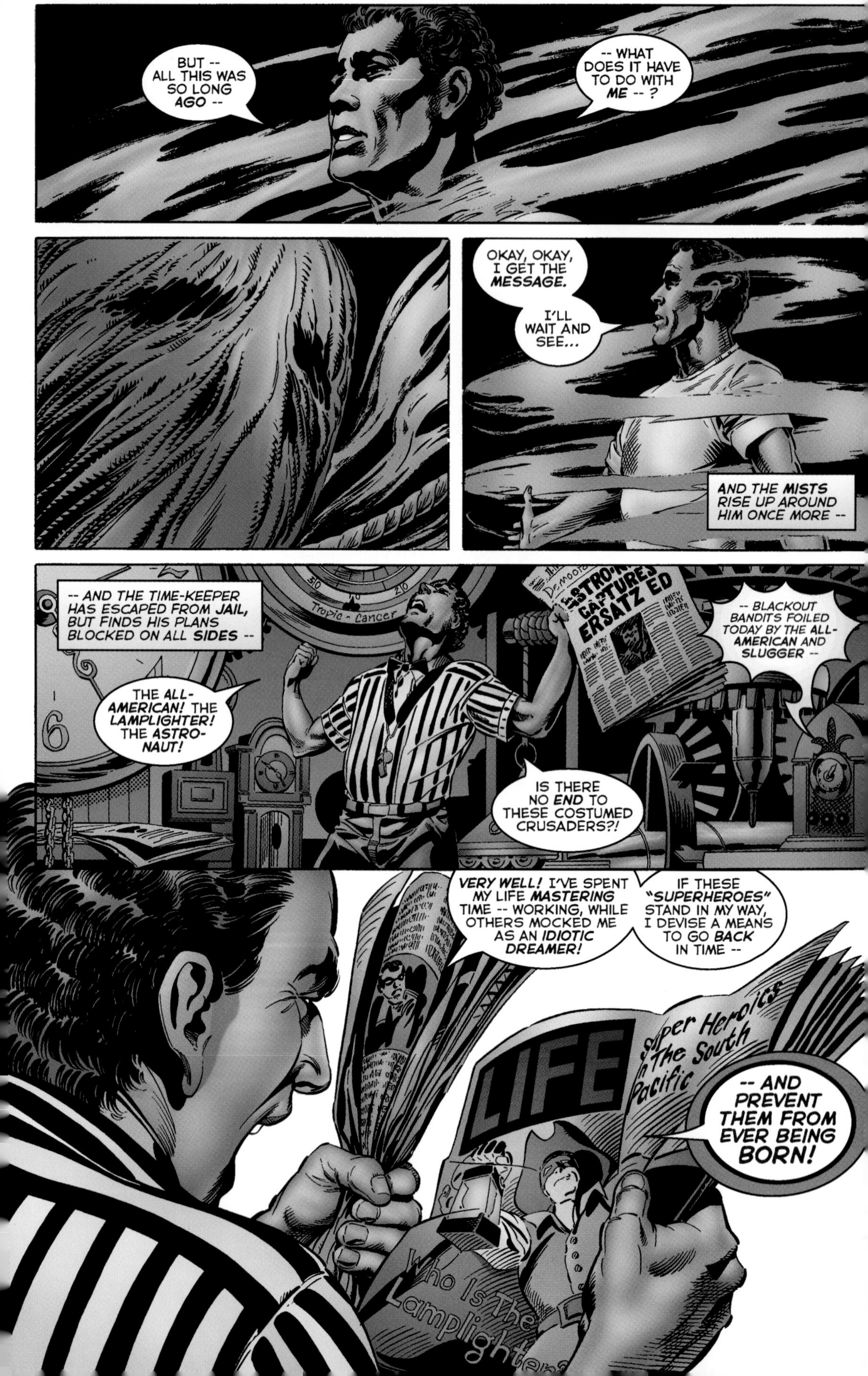
BUT -- ALL THIS WAS SO LONG AGO --
-- WHAT DOES IT HAVE TO DO WITH ME -- ?
OKAY, OKAY, I GET THE MESSAGE.
I'LL WAIT AND SEE...
AND THE MISTS RISE UP AROUND HIM ONCE MORE --
-- AND THE TIME-KEEPER HAS ESCAPED FROM JAIL, BUT FINDS HIS PLANS BLOCKED ON ALL SIDES --
ERSATZ ED
-- BLACKOUT BANDITS FOILED TODAY BY THE ALL-AMERICAN AND SLUGGER --
THE ALL-AMERICAN! THE LAMPLIGHTER! THE ASTRONAUT!
IS THERE NO END TO THESE COSTUMED CRUSADERS?!
VERY WELL! I'VE SPENT MY LIFE MASTERING TIME -- WORKING, WHILE OTHERS MOCKED ME AS AN IDIOTIC DREAMER!
IF THESE "SUPERHEROES" STAND IN MY WAY, I DEVISE A MEANS TO GO BACK IN TIME --
LIFE
Super Heroics in The South Pacific
-- AND PREVENT THEM FROM EVER BEING BORN!
Who Is The Lamplighter?

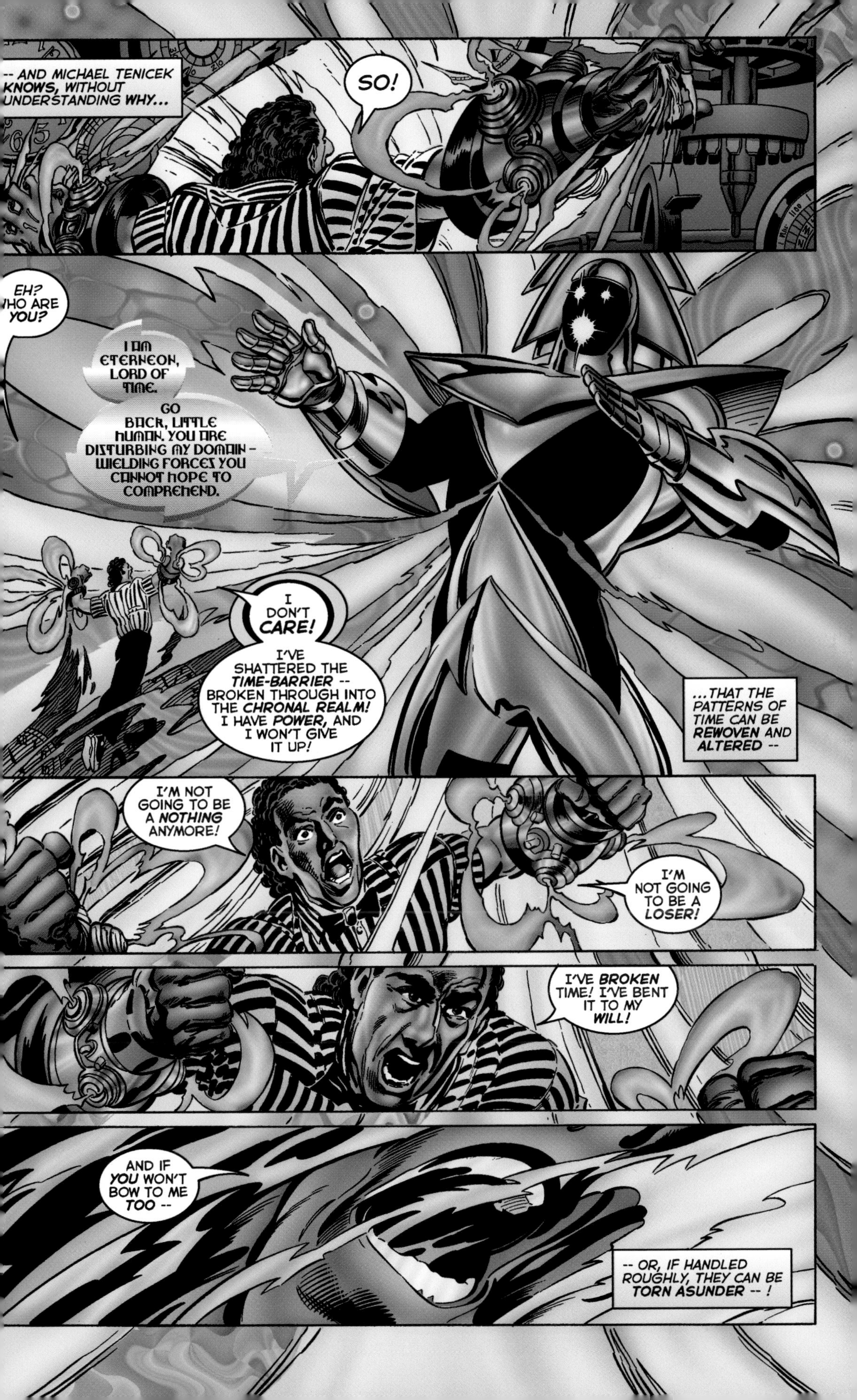
-- AND MICHAEL TENICEK KNOWS, WITHOUT UNDERSTANDING WHY...
SO!
EH? WHO ARE YOU?
I AM ETERNEON, LORD OF TIME.
GO BACK, LITTLE HUMAN. YOU ARE DISTURBING MY DOMAIN -- WIELDING FORCES YOU CANNOT HOPE TO COMPREHEND.
I DON'T CARE!
I'VE SHATTERED THE TIME-BARRIER -- BROKEN THROUGH INTO THE CHRONAL REALM! I HAVE POWER, AND I WON'T GIVE IT UP!
...THAT THE PATTERNS OF TIME CAN BE REWOVEN AND ALTERED --
I'M NOT GOING TO BE A NOTHING ANYMORE!
I'M NOT GOING TO BE A LOSER!
I'VE BROKEN TIME! I'VE BENT IT TO MY WILL!
AND IF YOU WON'T BOW TO ME TOO --
-- OR, IF HANDLED ROUGHLY, THEY CAN BE TORN ASUNDER -- !

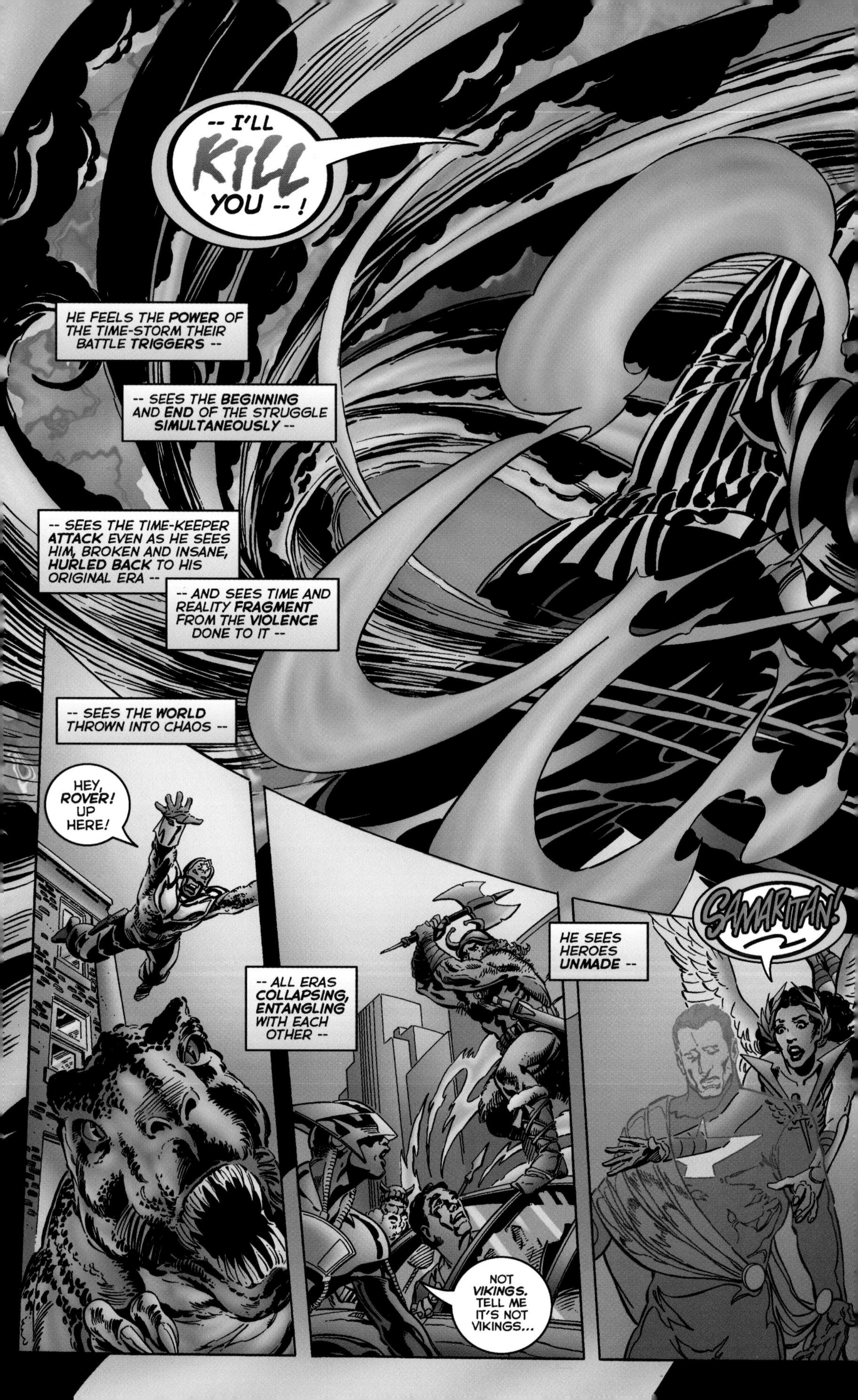

-- I'LL KILL YOU -- !
HE FEELS THE POWER OF THE TIME-STORM THEIR BATTLE TRIGGERS --
-- SEES THE BEGINNING AND END OF THE STRUGGLE SIMULTANEOUSLY --
-- SEES THE TIME-KEEPER ATTACK EVEN AS HE SEES HIM, BROKEN AND INSANE, HURLED BACK TO HIS ORIGINAL ERA --
-- AND SEES TIME AND REALITY FRAGMENT FROM THE VIOLENCE DONE TO IT --
-- SEES THE WORLD THROWN INTO CHAOS --
HEY, ROVER! UP HERE!
-- ALL ERAS COLLAPSING, ENTANGLING WITH EACH OTHER --
NOT VIKINGS. TELL ME IT'S NOT VIKINGS...
HE SEES HEROES UNMADE --
SAMARITAN!

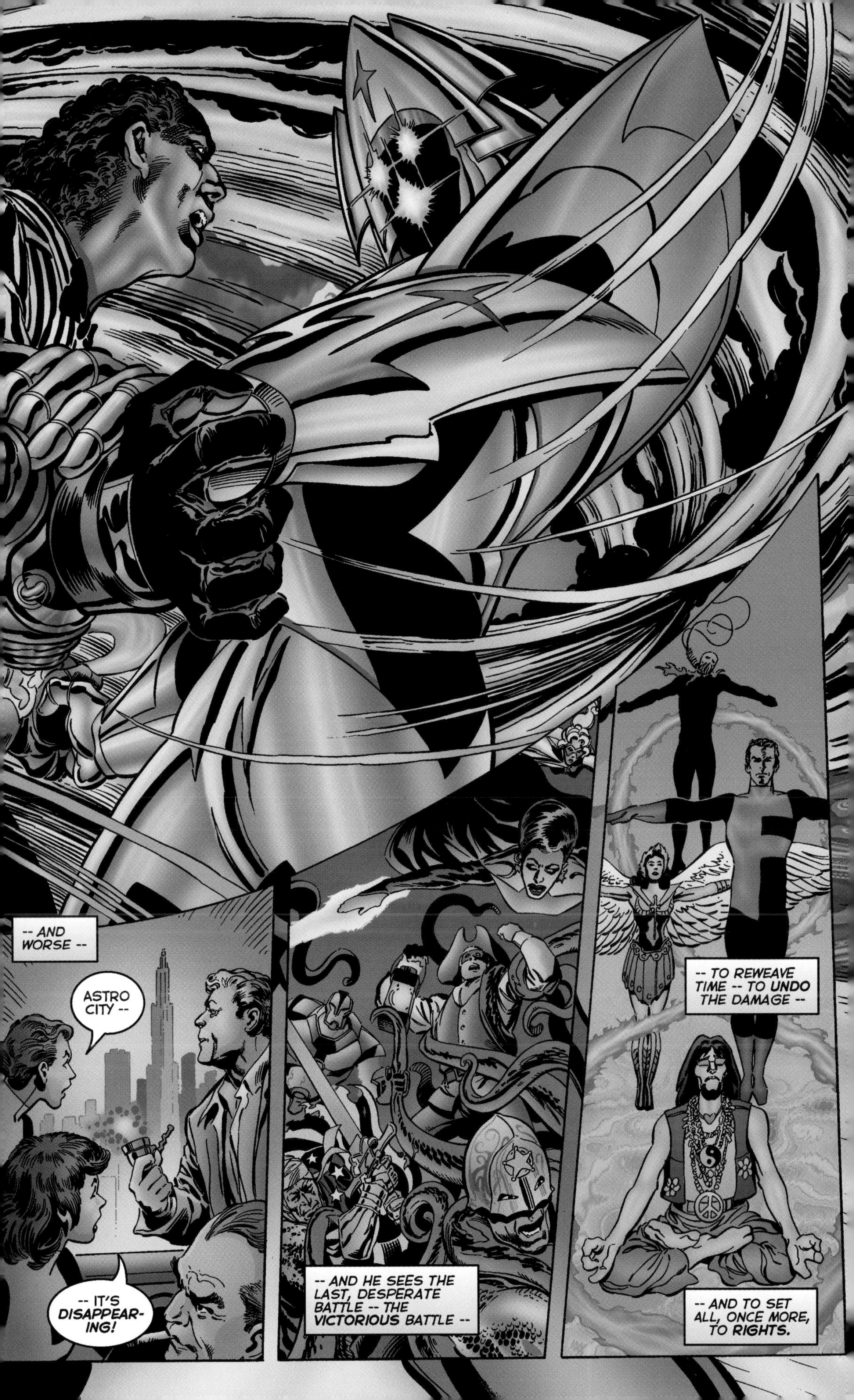
-- AND WORSE --
ASTRO CITY --
-- IT'S DISAPPEAR-ING!
-- AND HE SEES THE LAST, DESPERATE BATTLE -- THE VICTORIOUS BATTLE --
-- TO REWEAVE TIME -- TO UNDO THE DAMAGE --
-- AND TO SET ALL, ONCE MORE, TO RIGHTS.

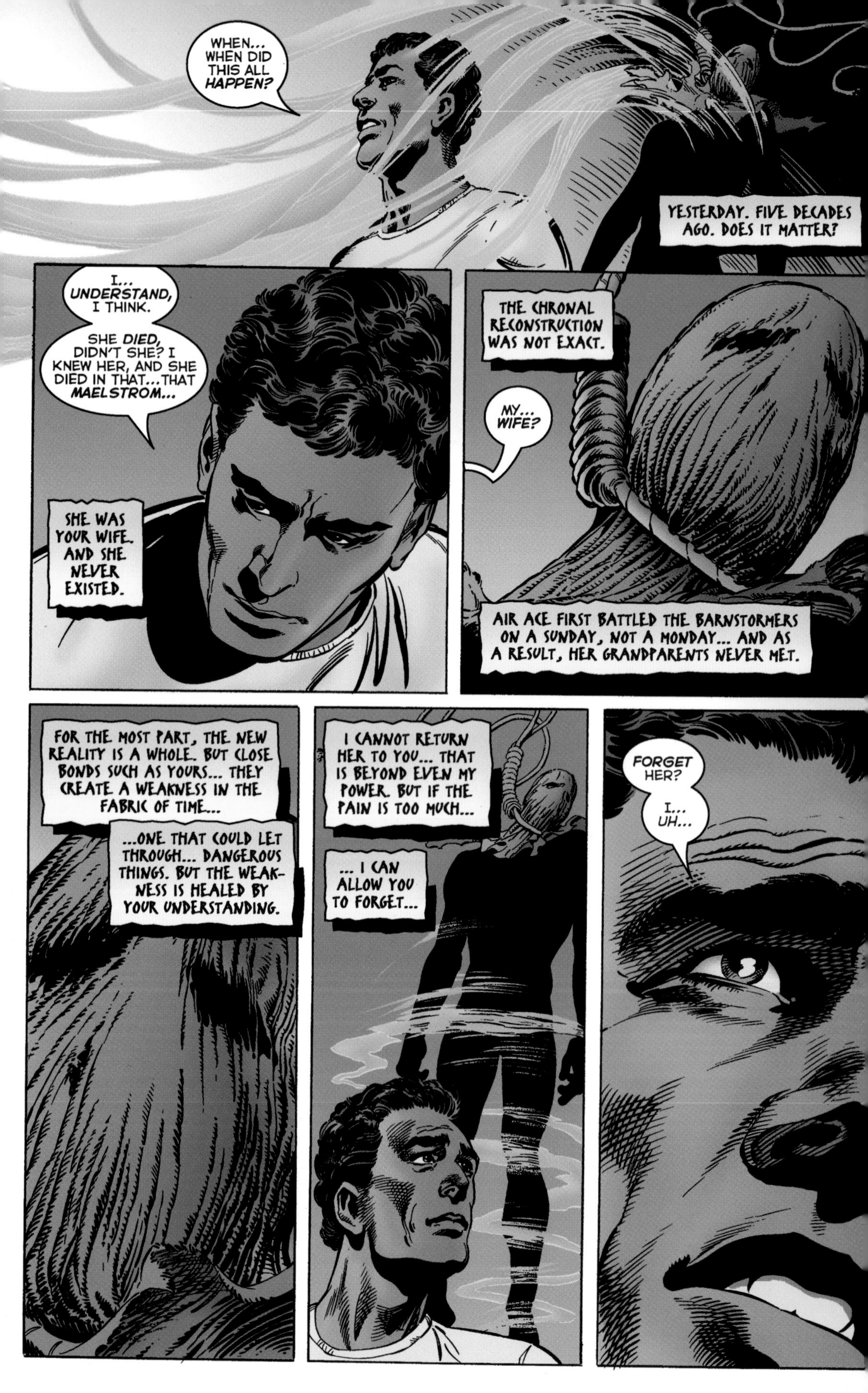
WHEN... WHEN DID THIS ALL *HAPPEN?*
YESTERDAY. FIVE DECADES AGO. DOES IT MATTER?
I... *UNDERSTAND,* I THINK.
SHE *DIED,* DIDN'T SHE? I KNEW HER, AND SHE DIED IN THAT... THAT *MAELSTROM...*
SHE WAS YOUR WIFE. AND SHE NEVER EXISTED.
THE CHRONAL RECONSTRUCTION WAS NOT EXACT.
MY... *WIFE?*
AIR ACE FIRST BATTLED THE BARNSTORMERS ON A SUNDAY, NOT A MONDAY... AND AS A RESULT, HER GRANDPARENTS NEVER MET.
FOR THE MOST PART, THE NEW REALITY IS A WHOLE. BUT CLOSE BONDS SUCH AS YOURS... THEY CREATE A WEAKNESS IN THE FABRIC OF TIME...
...ONE THAT COULD LET THROUGH... DANGEROUS THINGS. BUT THE WEAK-NESS IS HEALED BY YOUR UNDERSTANDING.
I CANNOT RETURN HER TO YOU... THAT IS BEYOND EVEN MY POWER. BUT IF THE PAIN IS TOO MUCH...
... I CAN ALLOW YOU TO FORGET...
FORGET HER?
I... UH...

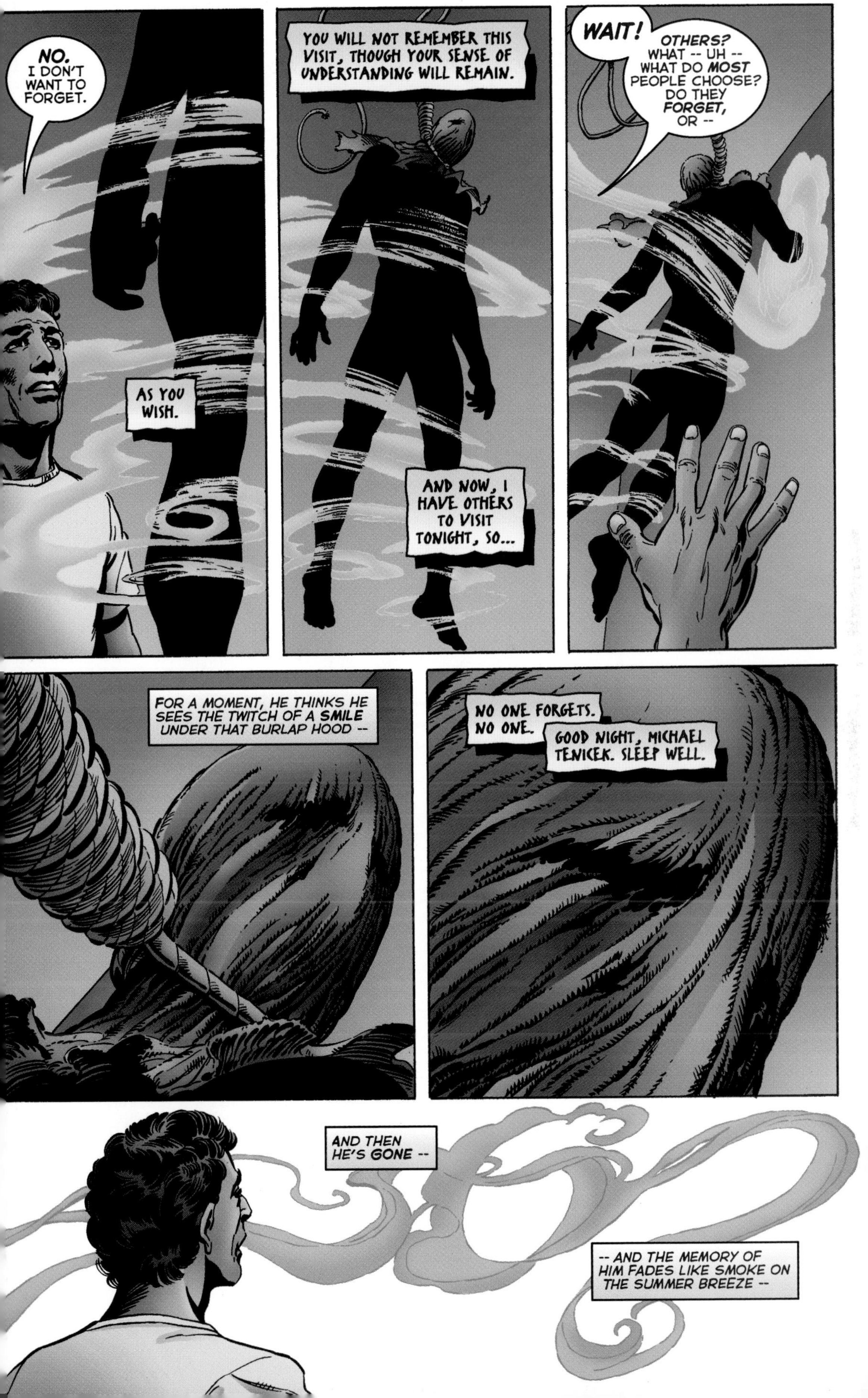
NO. I DON'T WANT TO FORGET.
AS YOU WISH.
YOU WILL NOT REMEMBER THIS VISIT, THOUGH YOUR SENSE OF UNDERSTANDING WILL REMAIN.
AND NOW, I HAVE OTHERS TO VISIT TONIGHT, SO...
WAIT!
OTHERS? WHAT -- UH -- WHAT DO MOST PEOPLE CHOOSE? DO THEY FORGET, OR --
FOR A MOMENT, HE THINKS HE SEES THE TWITCH OF A SMILE UNDER THAT BURLAP HOOD --
NO ONE FORGETS. NO ONE.
GOOD NIGHT, MICHAEL TENICEK. SLEEP WELL.
AND THEN HE'S GONE --
-- AND THE MEMORY OF HIM FADES LIKE SMOKE ON THE SUMMER BREEZE --

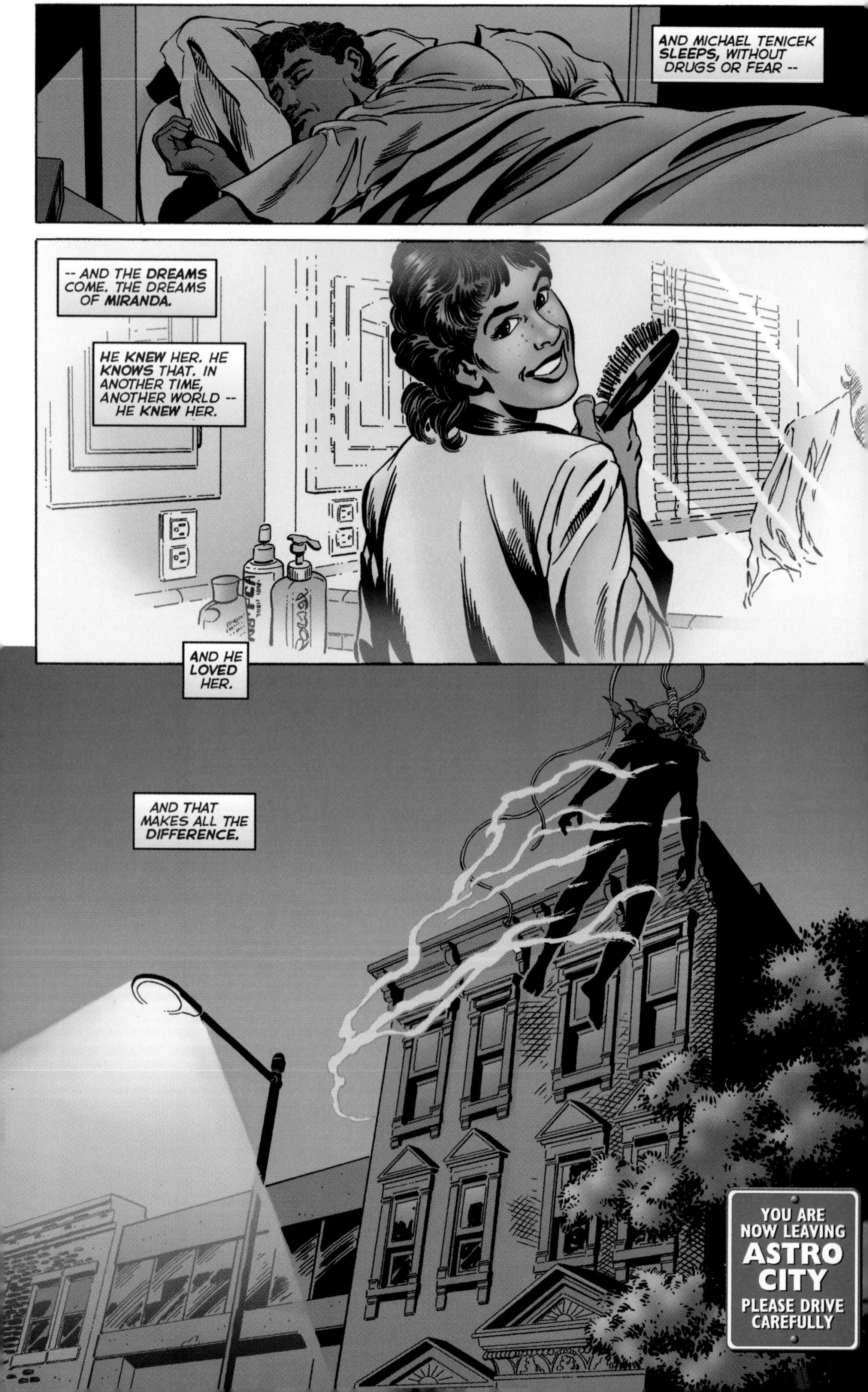
AND MICHAEL TENICEK SLEEPS, WITHOUT DRUGS OR FEAR --
-- AND THE DREAMS COME. THE DREAMS OF MIRANDA.
HE KNEW HER. HE KNOWS THAT. IN ANOTHER TIME, ANOTHER WORLD -- HE KNEW HER.
AND HE LOVED HER.
AND THAT MAKES ALL THE DIFFERENCE.
YOU ARE NOW LEAVING ASTRO CITY PLEASE DRIVE CAREFULLY

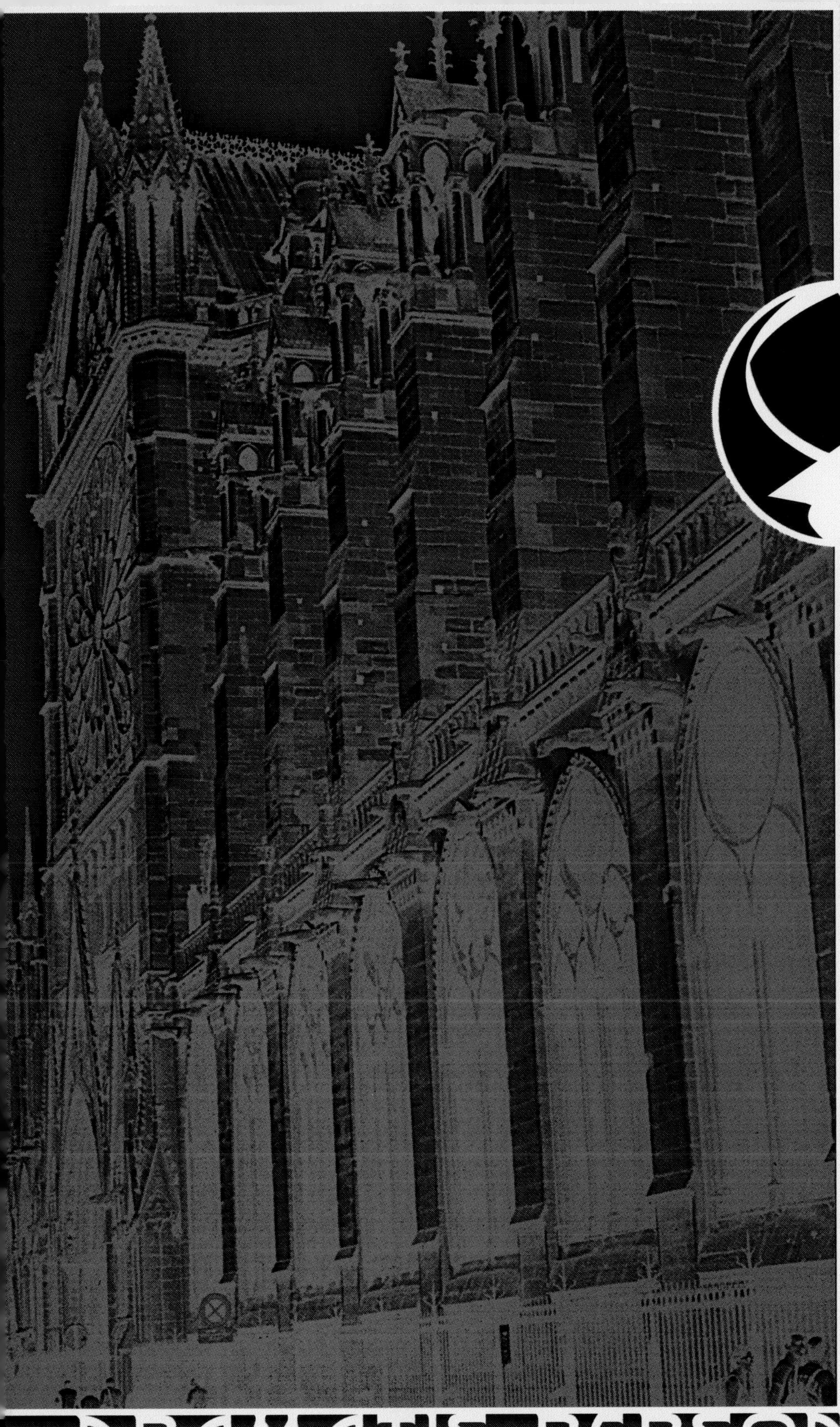

DRAMATIS PERSON

STAR BRAND

MUNK HOOD

CLERICAL LOOK

EVENING STAR SYMBOL

PENTACLE

TO CLOSE TO STAR BRAND & ECLIPSE SYMBOL

A BALD HEAD?

WHITE HEADDRESS?

DARK PURPLE & WHITE TRIM

MAYBE EYES JUST TURN WHITE WHEN HE'S IN COSTUME

GLOWING EYES

The most compelling personality, set of superpowers, mission — none of it will matter if the character doesn't look right, if the idea at the character's core doesn't come through. And that can take a lot of work.

The Confessor was originally called "Vesper," which combined nighttime and a religious touch, but an independent comic called *Vespers* was announced, so we renamed him "Confessor" for the way it straddled the line between religious and criminal confessions. For a visual, we wanted something that said both "priest" and "superhero," and eventually found it by combining a ninja mask with some outré priest's robes — but not before Alex tried dozens of masks, from influences as varied as opera, medieval armor and Dick Sprang.

Altar Boy came faster, once we combined a choirboy's robe with a Musketeer's surplice. And, of course, Alex worked out distinctive, involving faces for both of them.

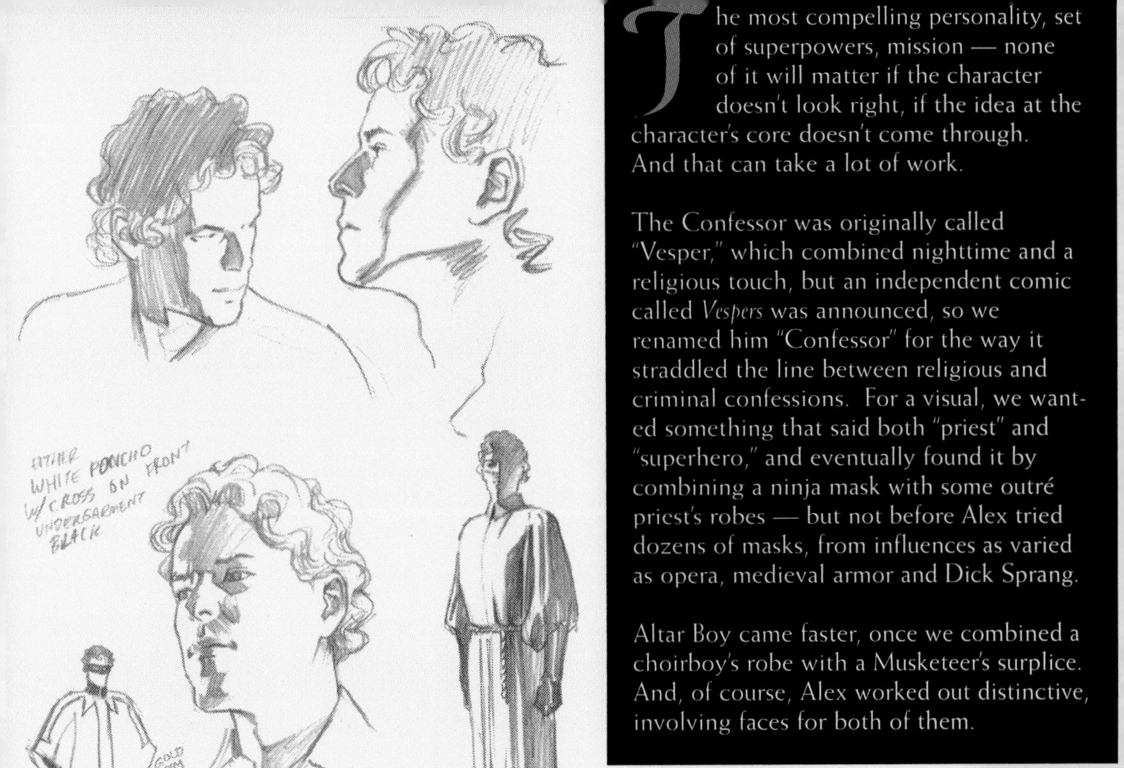

EITHER WHITE PONCHO W/ CROSS ON FRONT
UNDERGARMENT BLACK

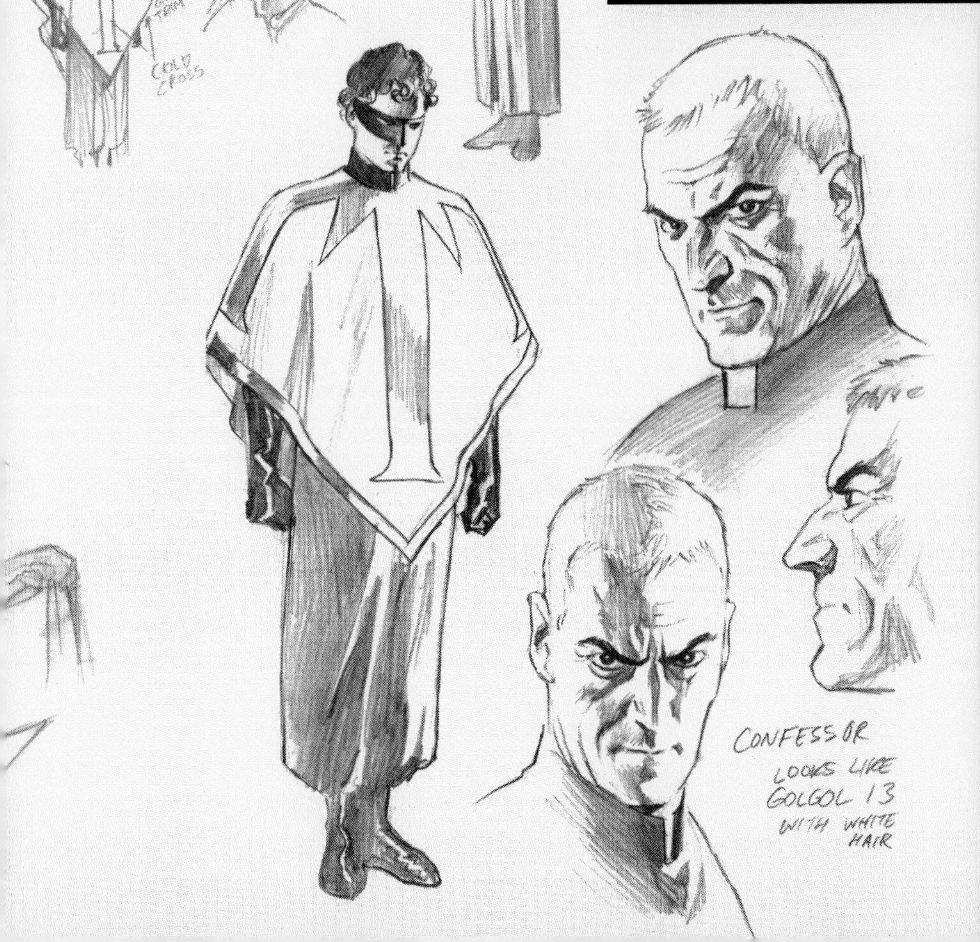

GOLD TRIM
GOLD CROSS
CONFESSOR LOOKS LIKE GOLGOL 13 WITH WHITE HAIR

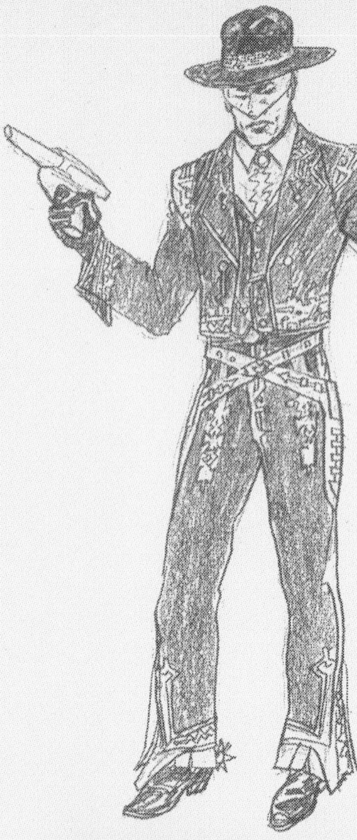

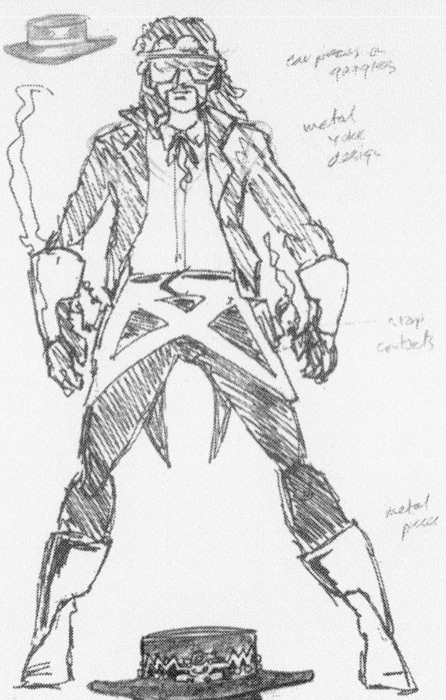
metal yoke design
metal piece

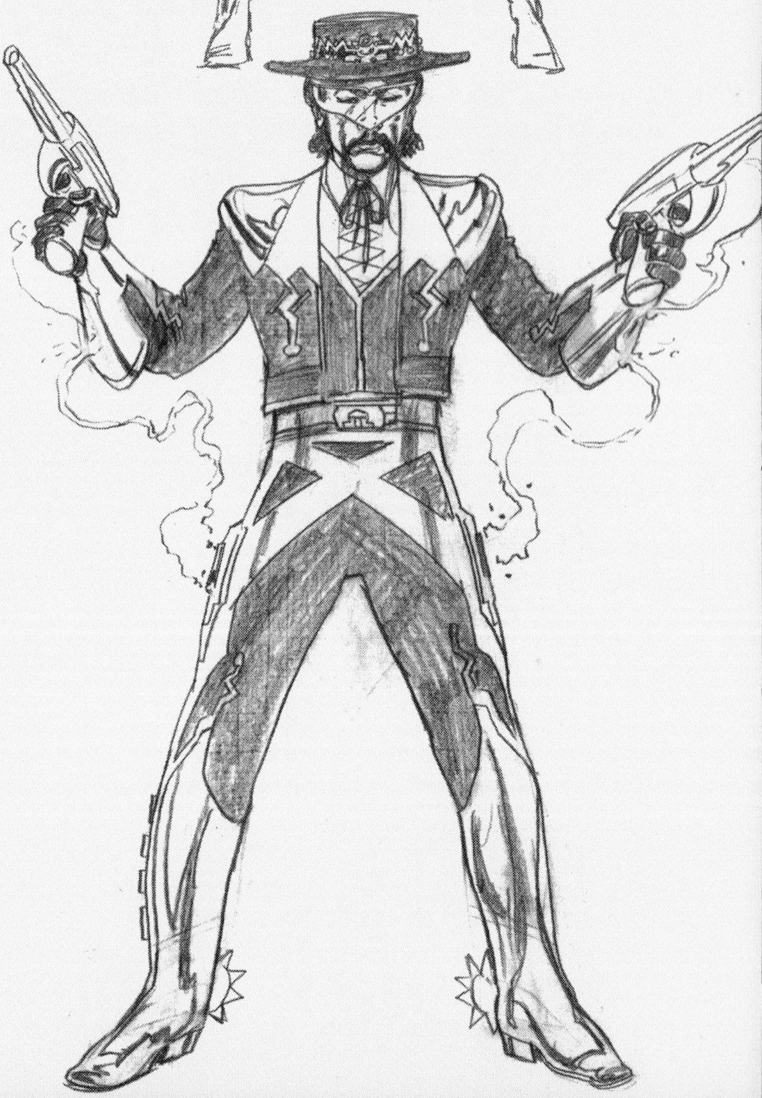

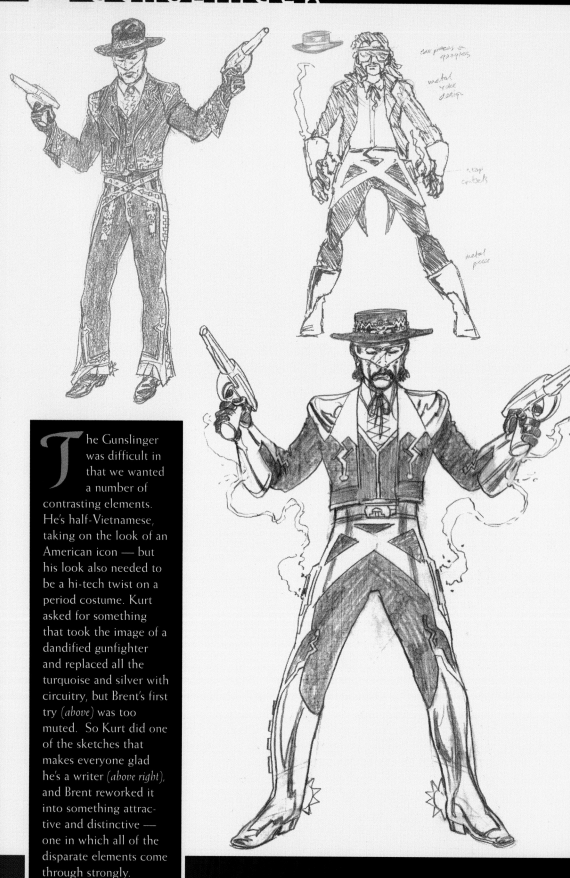

The Gunslinger was difficult in that we wanted a number of contrasting elements. He's half-Vietnamese, taking on the look of an American icon — but his look also needed to be a hi-tech twist on a period costume. Kurt asked for something that took the image of a dandified gunfighter and replaced all the turquoise and silver with circuitry, but Brent's first try *(above)* was too muted. So Kurt did one of the sketches that makes everyone glad he's a writer *(above right)*, and Brent reworked it into something attractive and distinctive — one in which all of the disparate elements come through strongly.

Ironhorse was created, at least at first, to give Rex someone to arm-wrestle with, and in looking for a visual idea to contrast with Rex's saurian look, we hit on a mechanical hero. Kurt came up with the name "Ironhorse, the Human Locomotive," which in turn suggested a 19th century hero, and everything coalesced around that. Visually, he was somewhat tricky — steam engine elements were easy enough to find, but reworking them into a human form that looked both impressive and old-fashioned took some delicate design work.

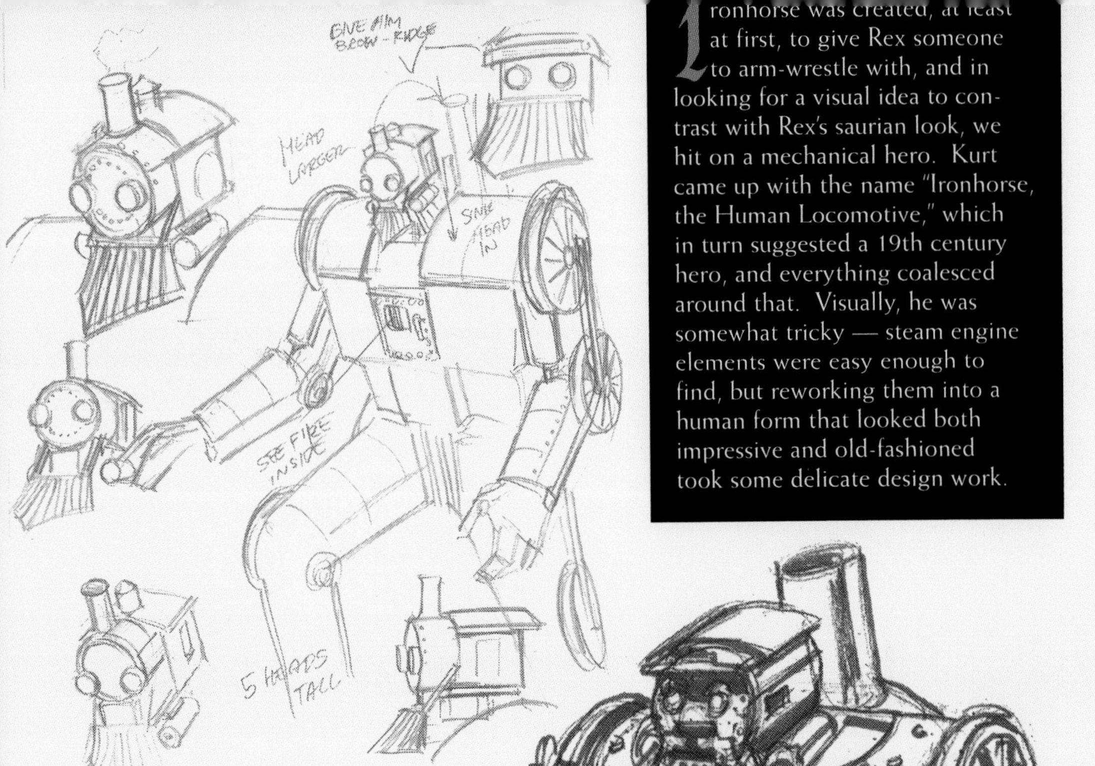
GIVE HIM BROW-RIDGE
HEAD LARGER
SINK HEAD IN
SEE FIRE INSIDE
5 HEADS TALL

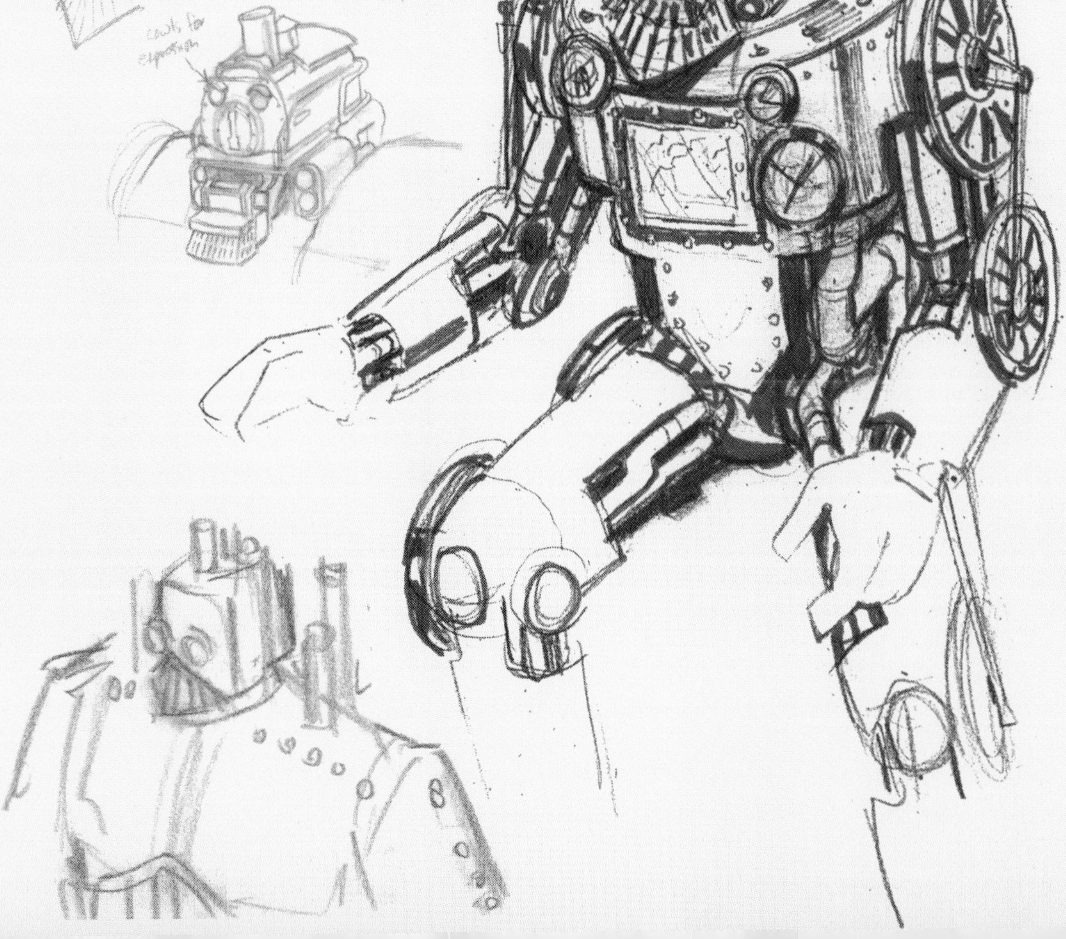

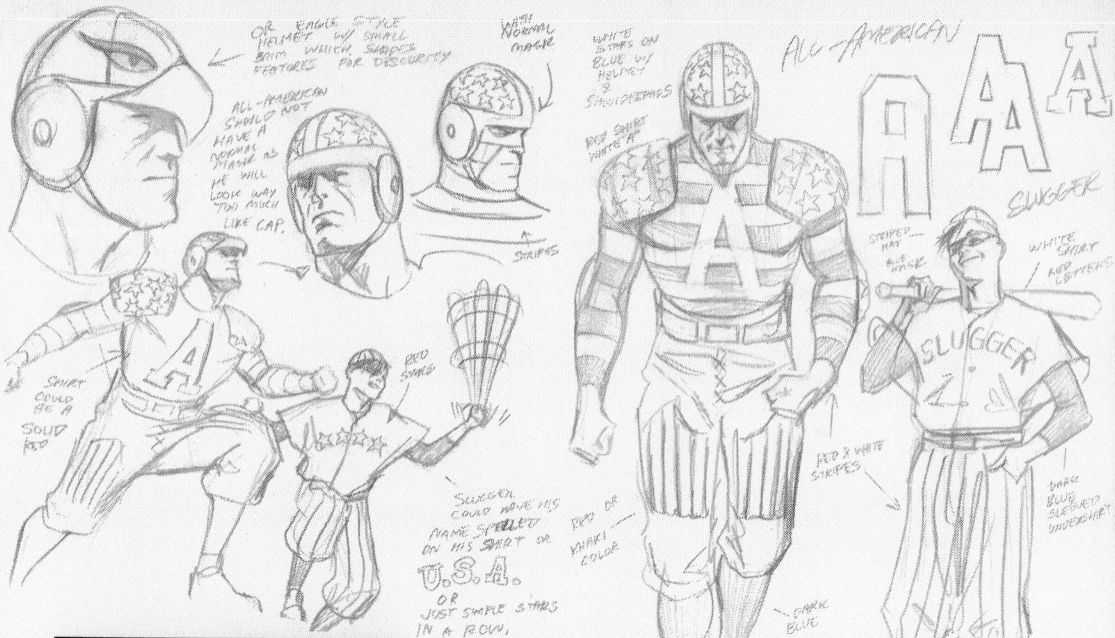
OR EAGLE STYLE HELMET W/ SMALL BRIM WHICH SHADES FEATURES FOR OBSCURITY
WITH NORMAL MASK
ALL-AMERICAN SHOULD NOT HAVE A NORMAL MASK AS HE WILL LOOK WAY TOO MUCH LIKE CAP.
STRIPES
WHITE STARS ON BLUE W/ HELMET & SHOULDERPADS
RED SHIRT WHITE 'A'
ALL-AMERICAN
SLUGGER
STRIPED HAT
BLUE MASK
WHITE SHIRT RED LETTERS
SLUGGER
SHIRT COULD BE A SOLID RED
RED STARS
SLUGGER COULD HAVE HIS NAME SPELLED ON HIS SHIRT OR
U.S.A.
OR JUST SIMPLE STARS IN A ROW.
RED OR KHAKI COLOR
RED & WHITE STRIPES
DARK BLUE SLEEVED UNDERSHIRT
DARK BLUE

The All-American was another balancing act — we knew from the start that he was a patriotic hero built around the visual icon of a football player, but we needed him to look like an early-Forties football player, without the bulkier padding and helmet of the modern day. Ultimately, we gave him a build that gave him enough bulk to make any question of pads pointless, and a noble-athlete look inspired in part by a J.C. Leyendecker *Saturday Evening Post* cover. After that, it was just a matter of figuring out how to anchor that 'A' on his chest without emphasizing his stomach over his pectorals. And after all that work, he's only appeared in one panel to date.

Slugger, comparatively, was a snap. The only part that even slowed Alex down was the question of what to put on the front

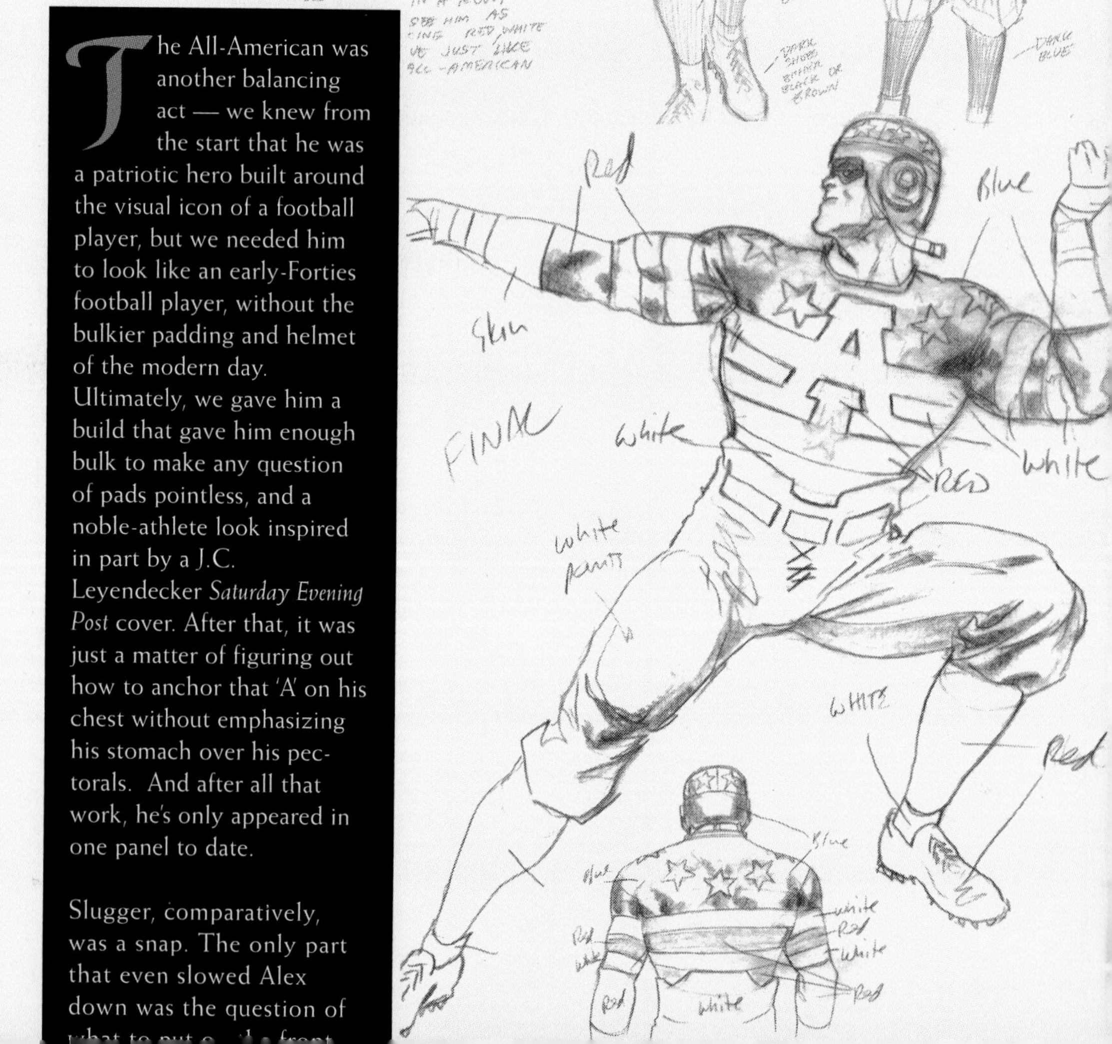
DARK BLUE
Red
Blue
Skin
FINAL
White
White
RED
White Knit
WHITE
Red
Blue
White
Red
White
Red
White

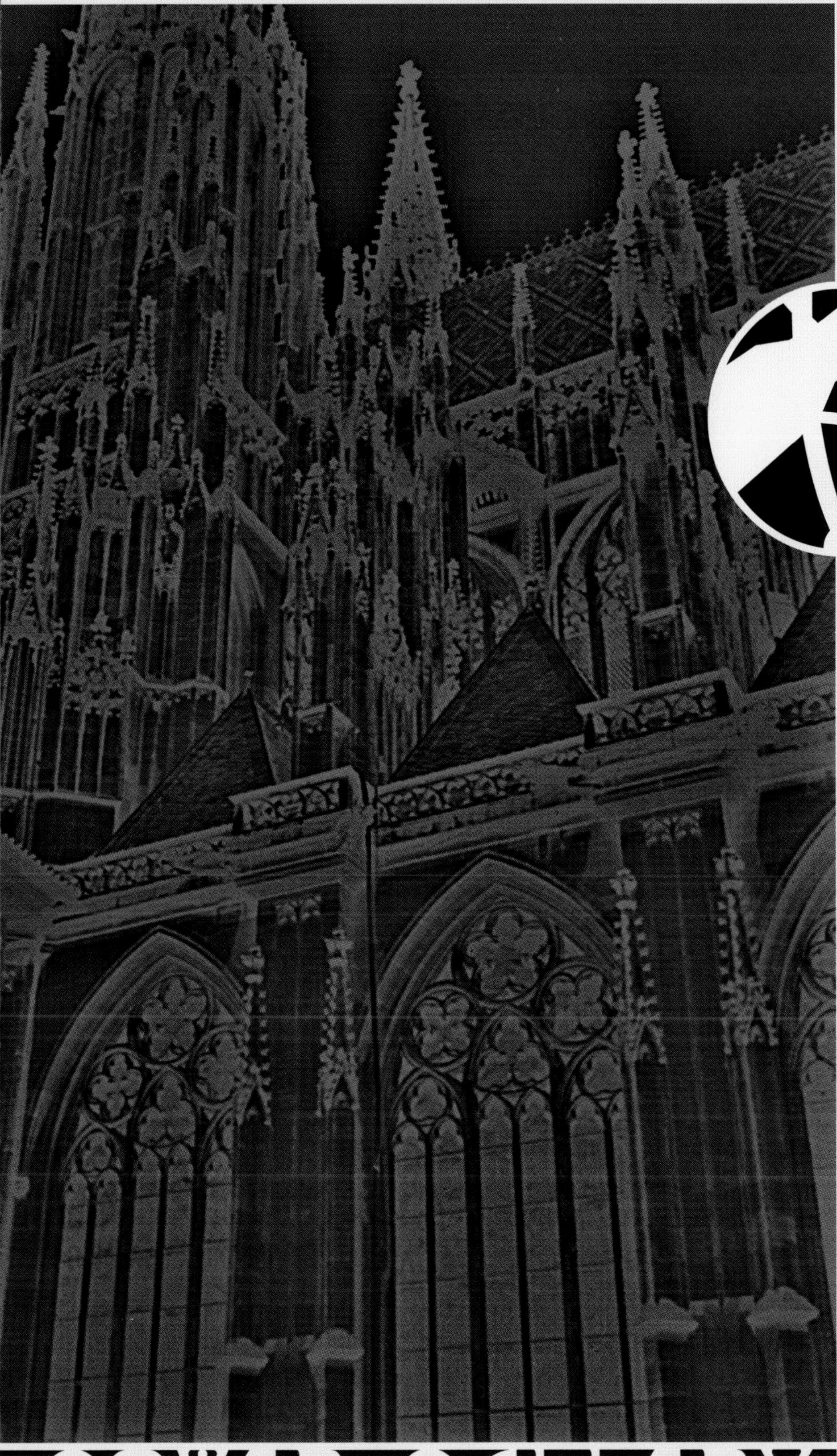

COVER GALLERY

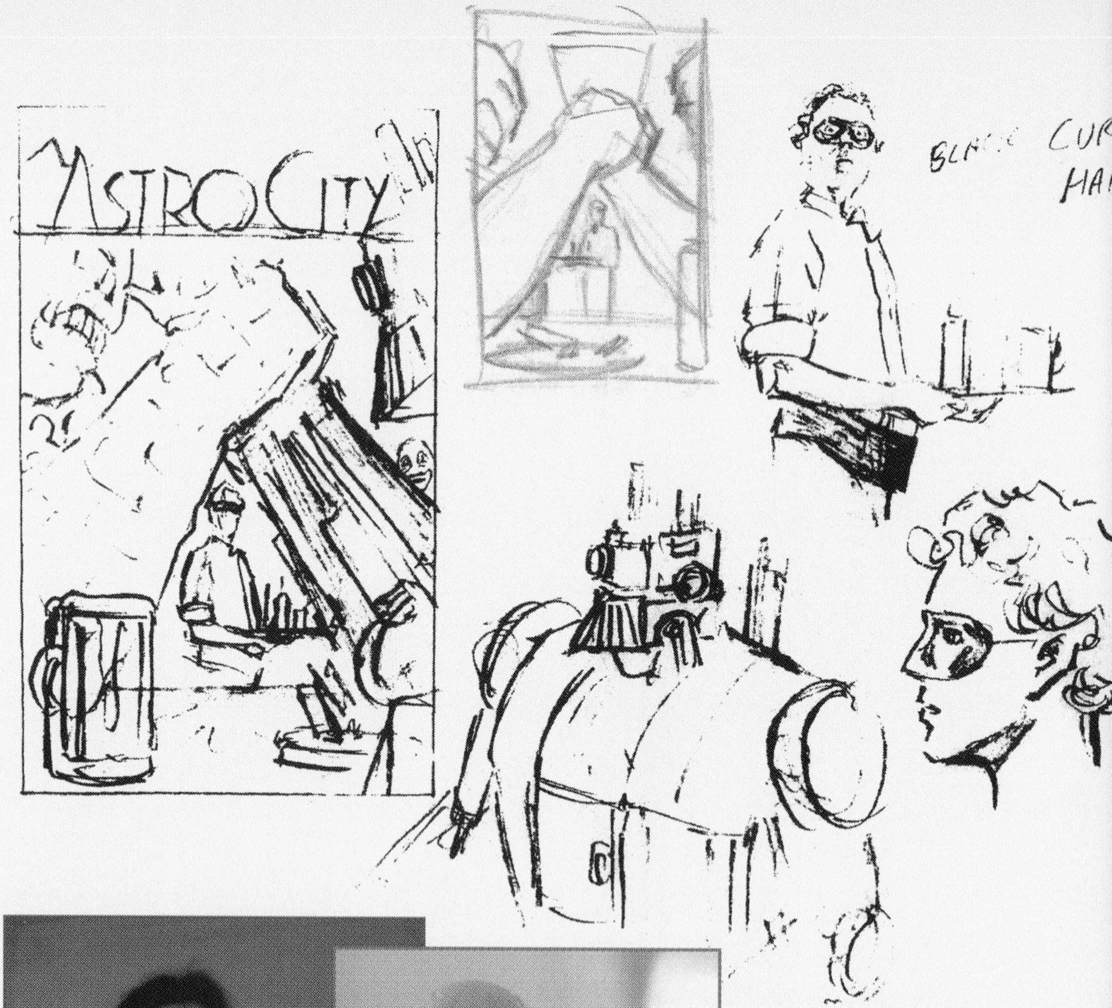
ASTRO CITY

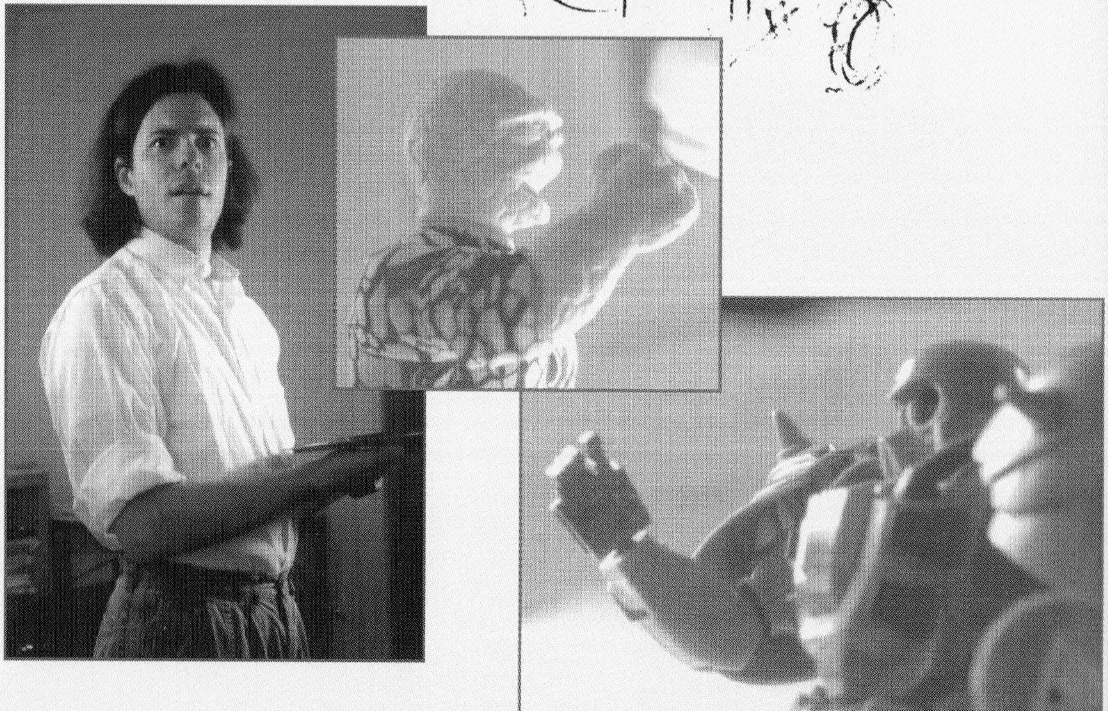

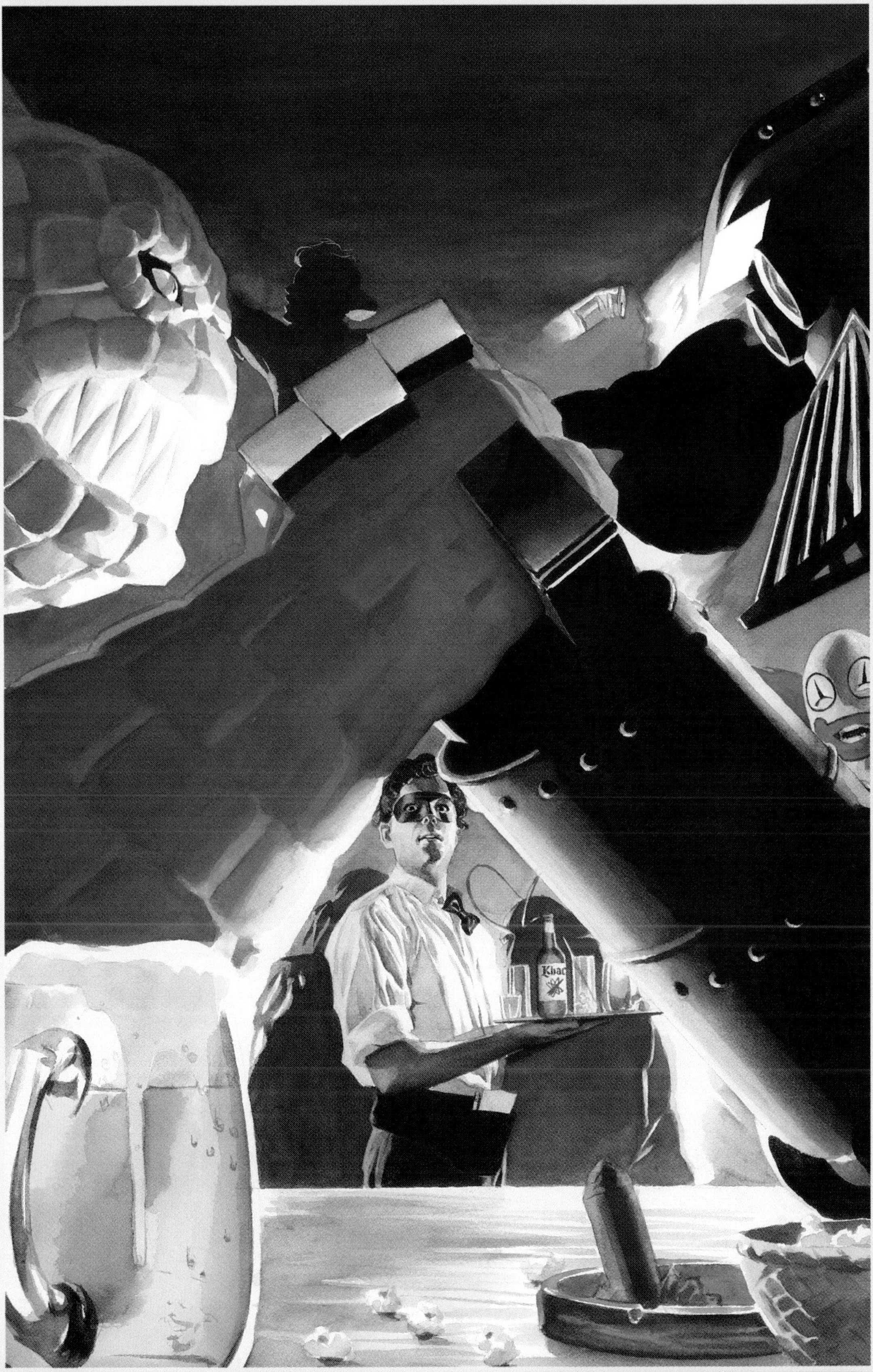

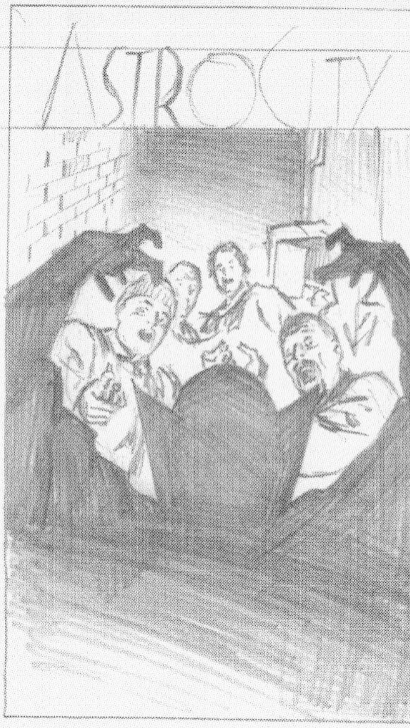
ASTRO CITY

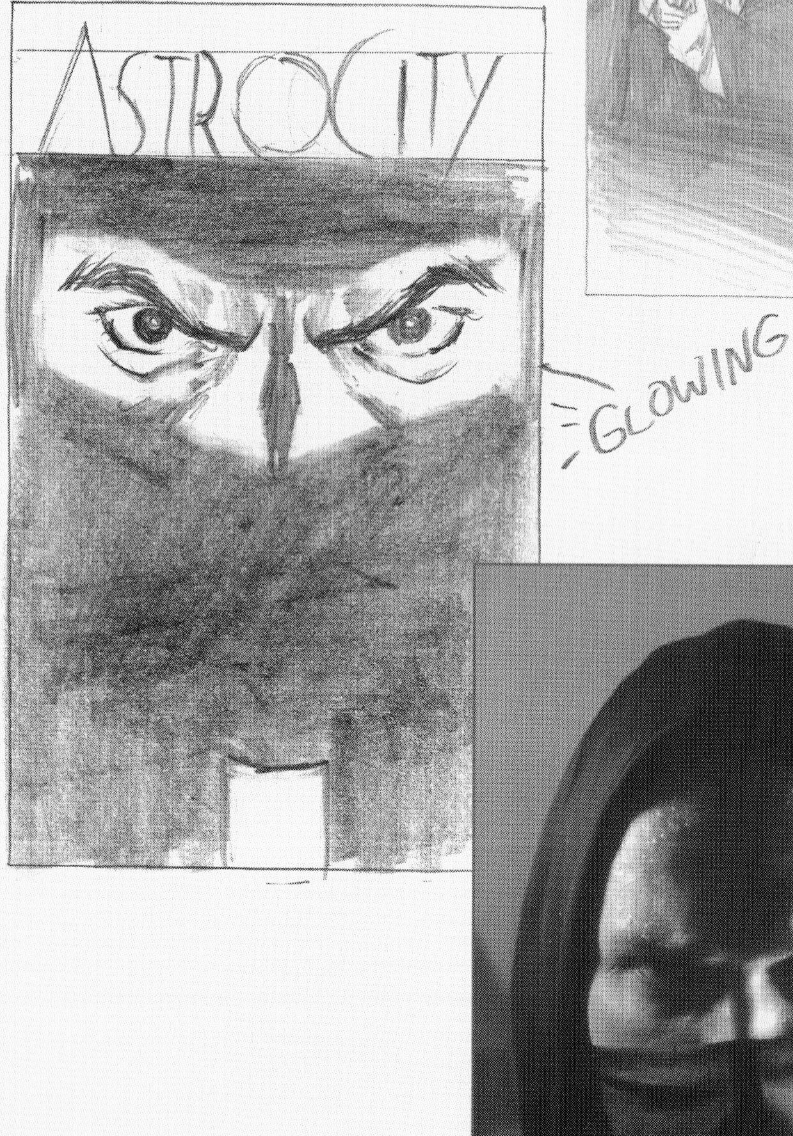
ASTRO CITY
GLOWING

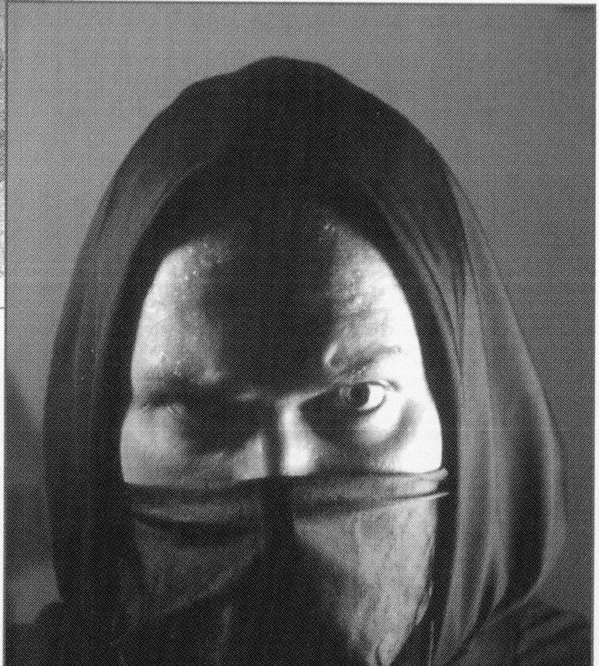

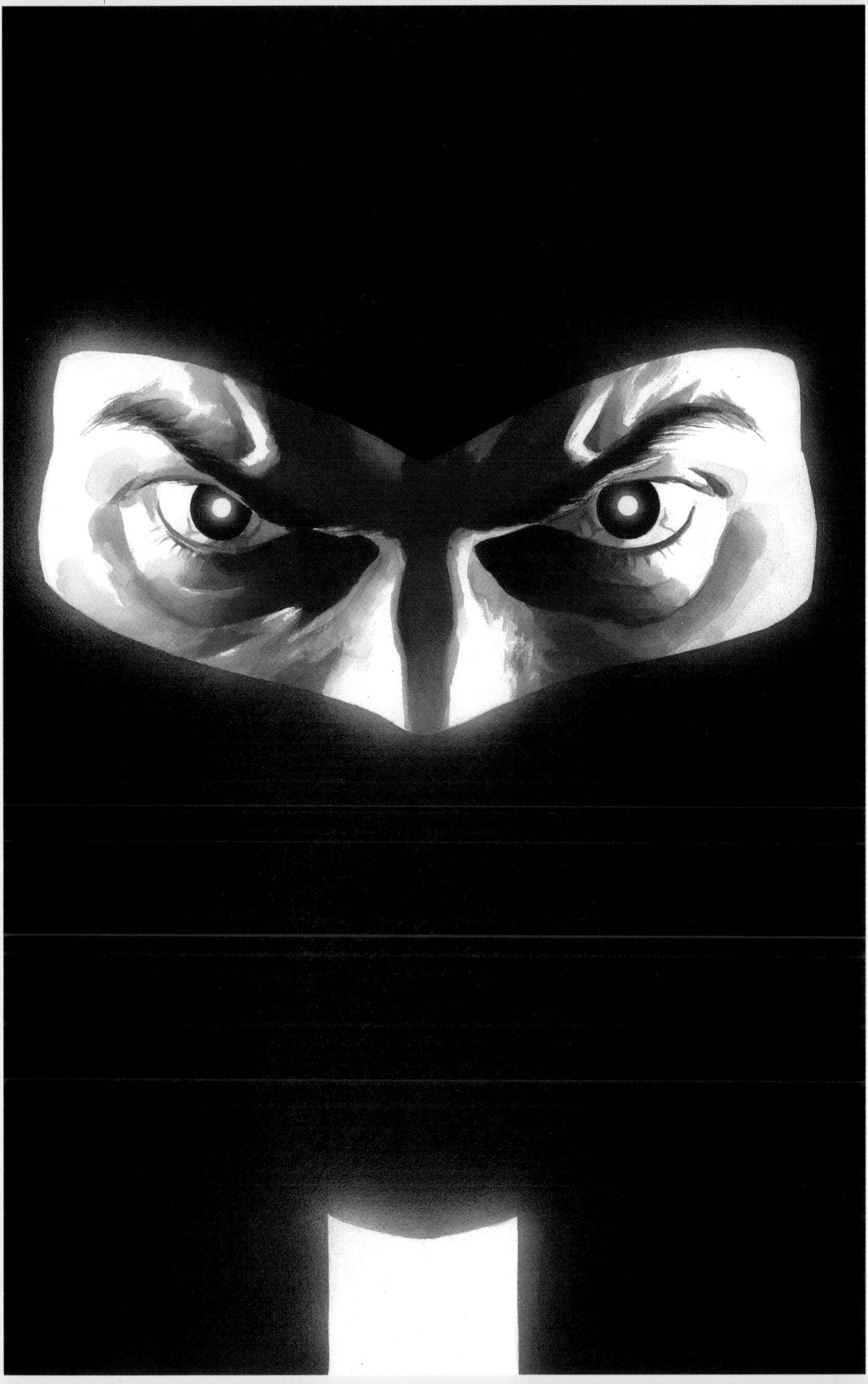

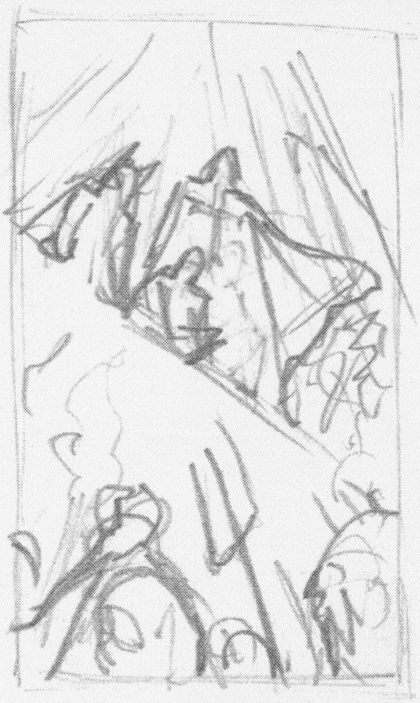

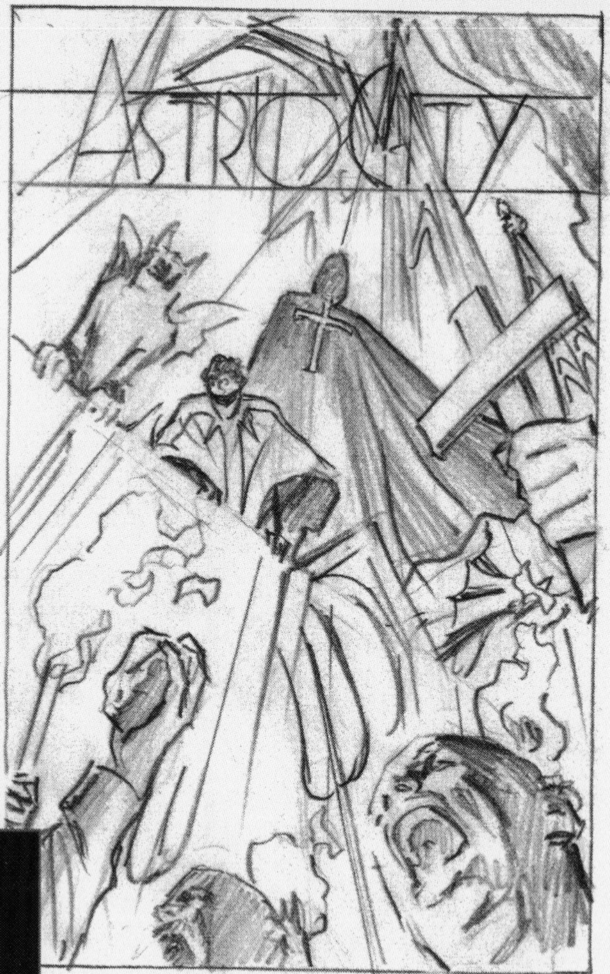
ASTRO CITY

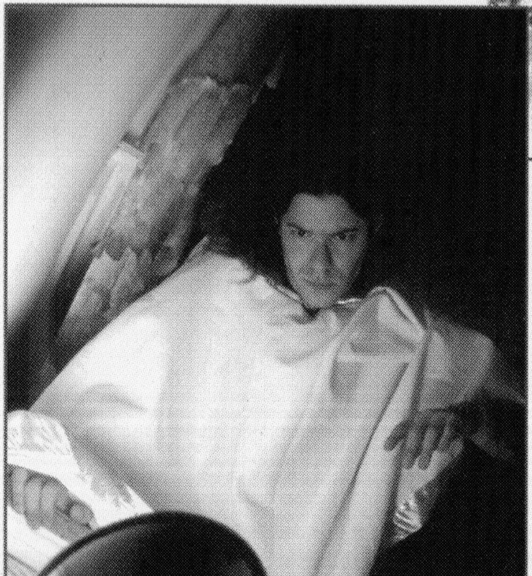

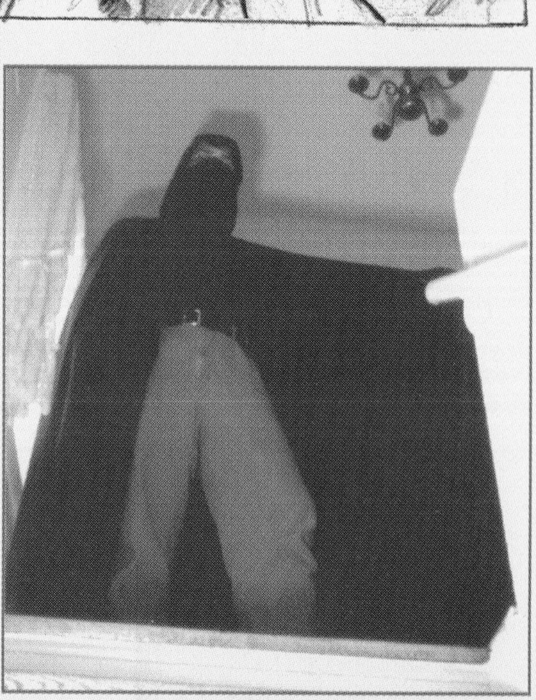

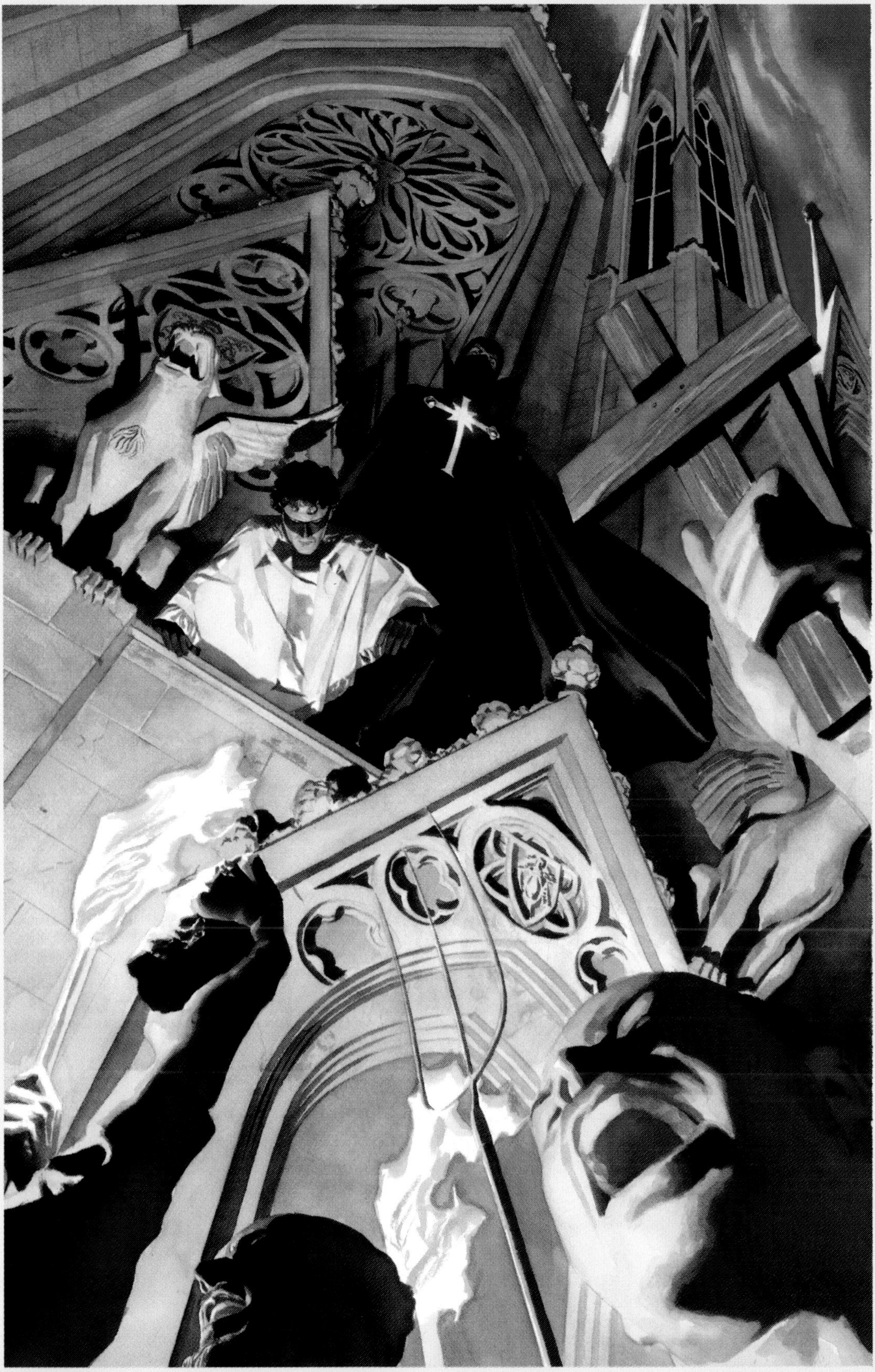

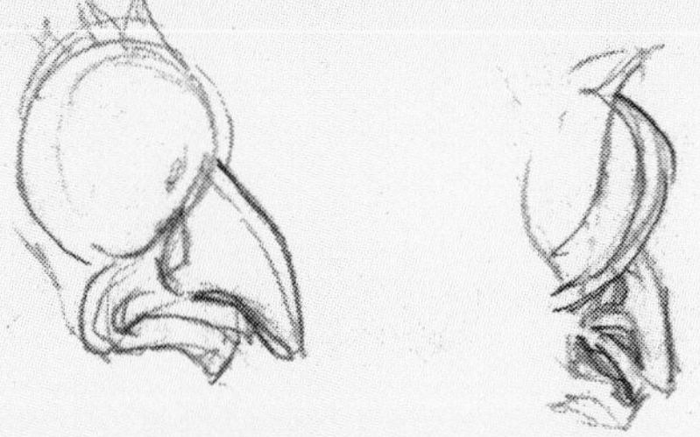

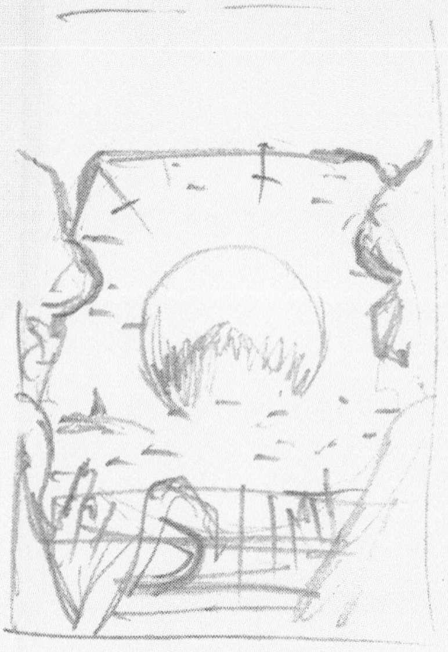

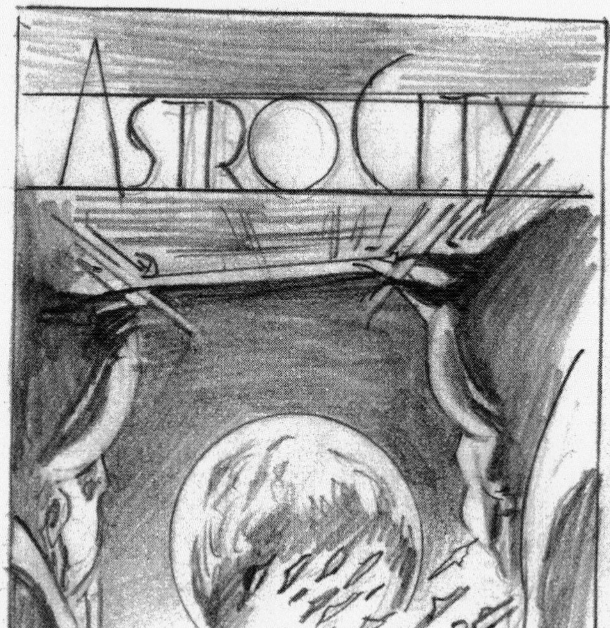
ASTRO CITY

MAKE FLEET
COMING IN
FROM TOP
INSTEAD OF
BOTTOM

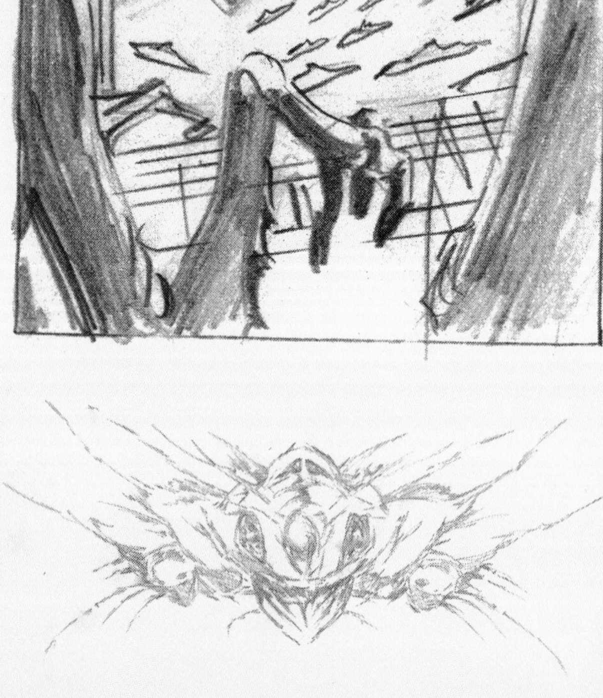

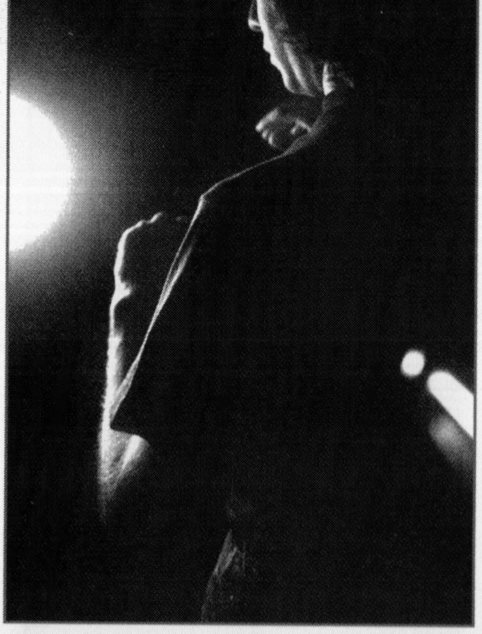

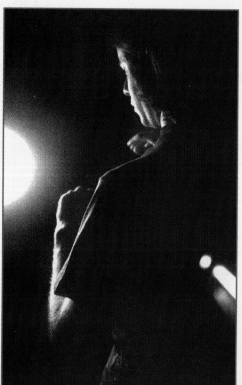

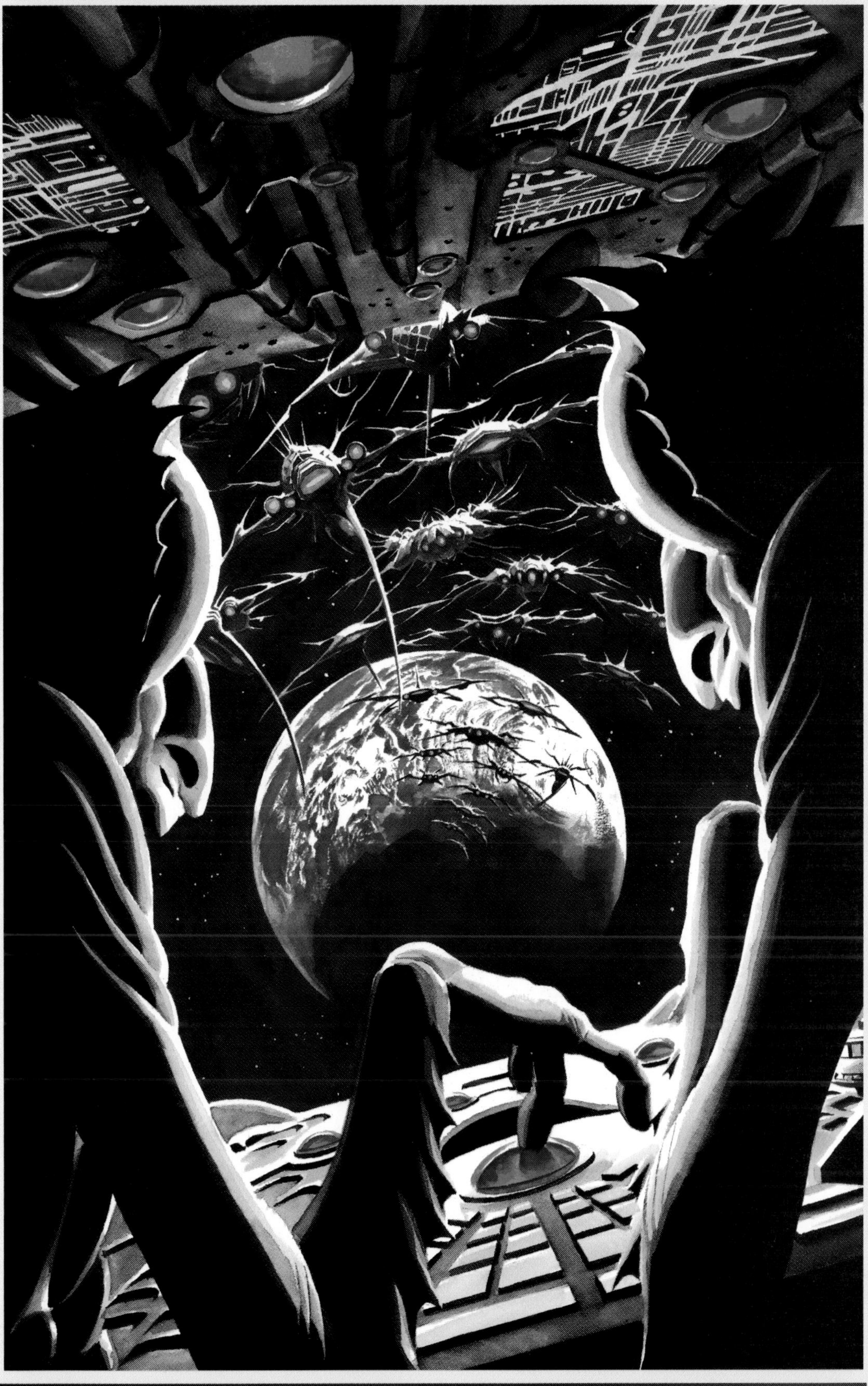

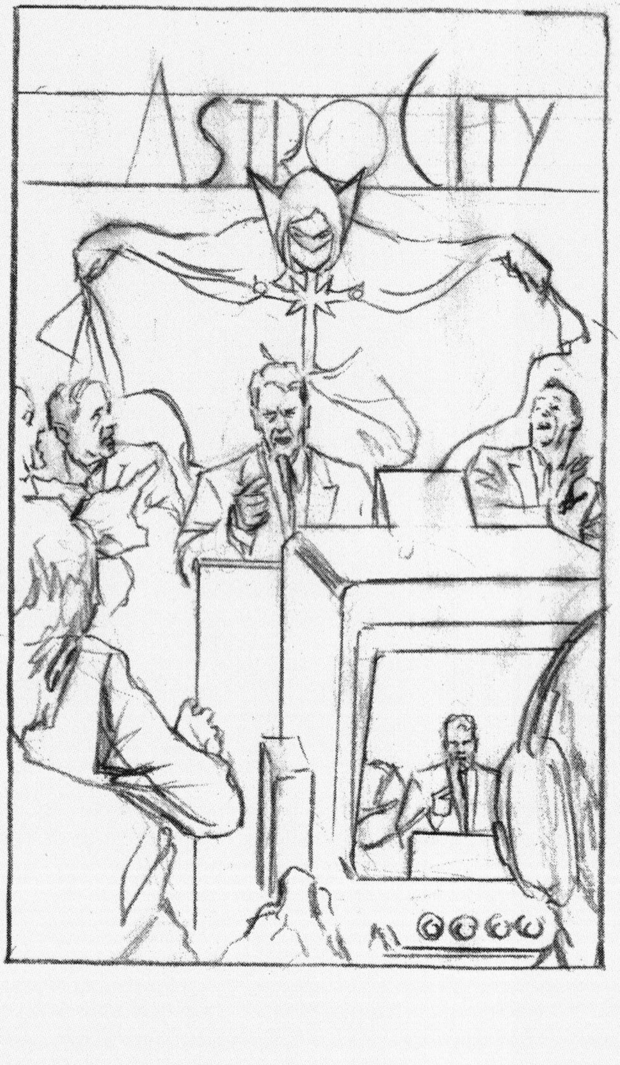
ASTRO CITY

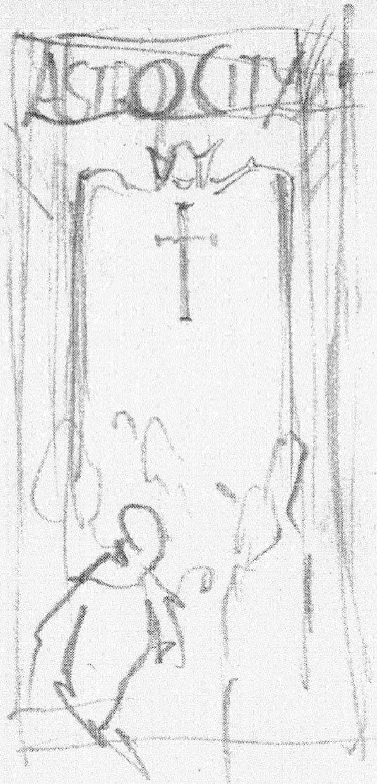
ASTRO CITY

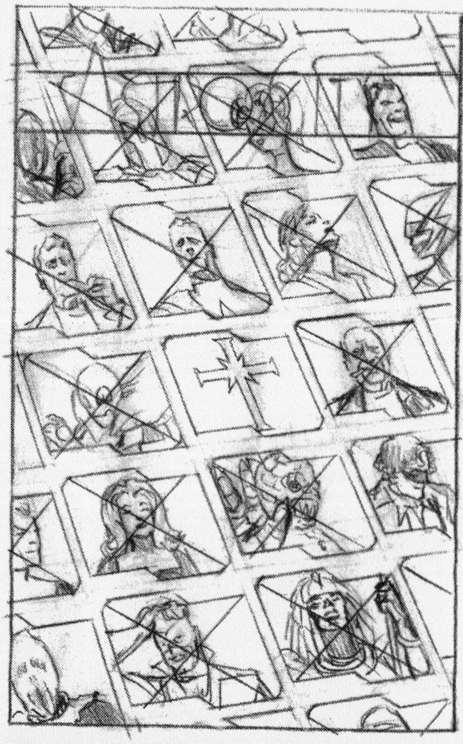

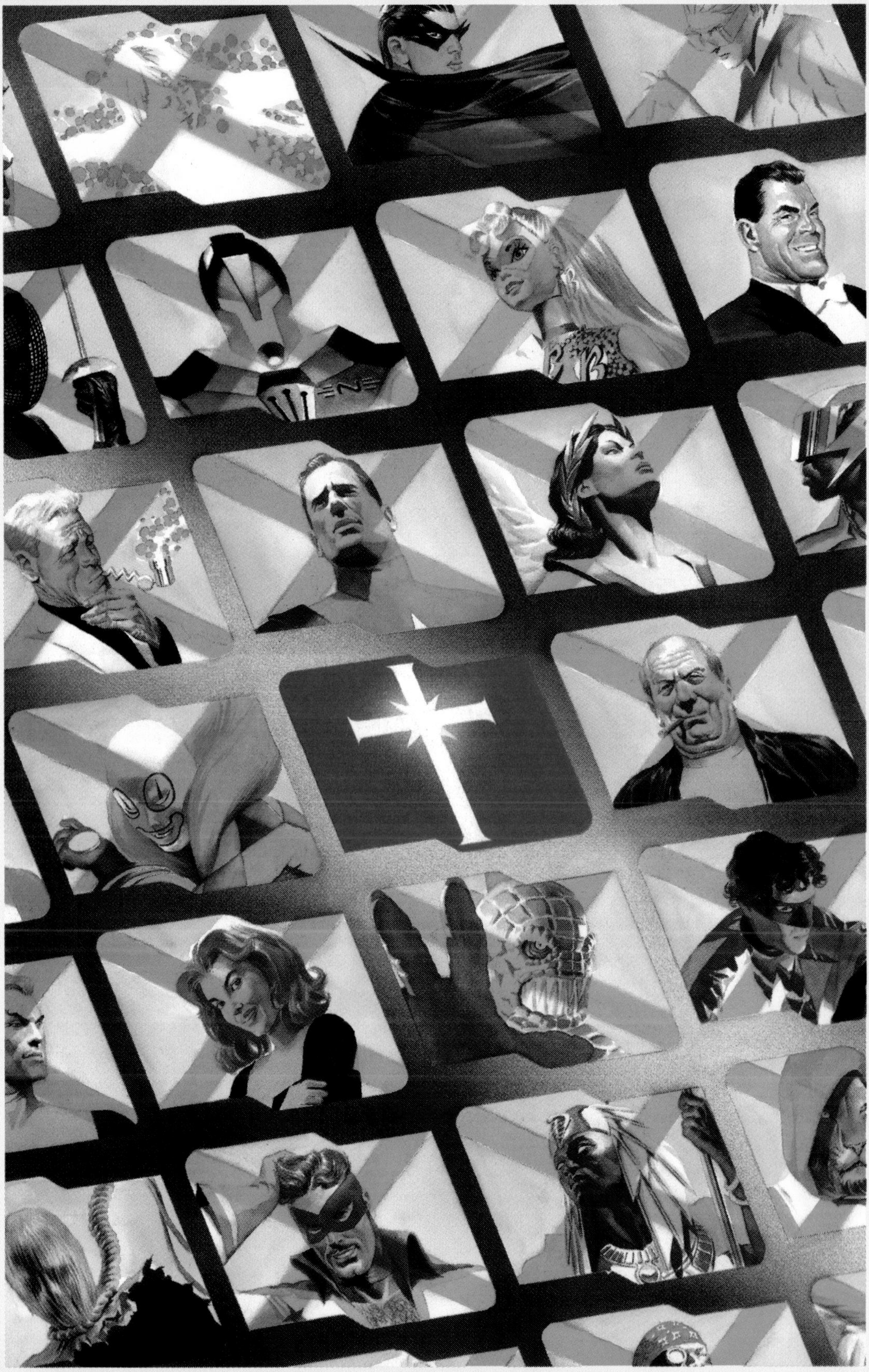

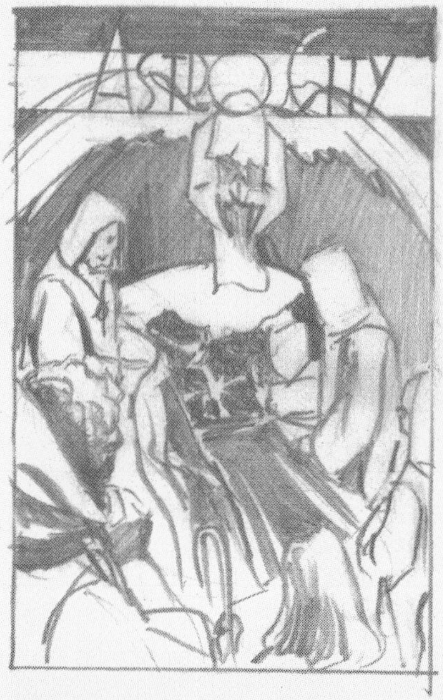
ASTRO CITY

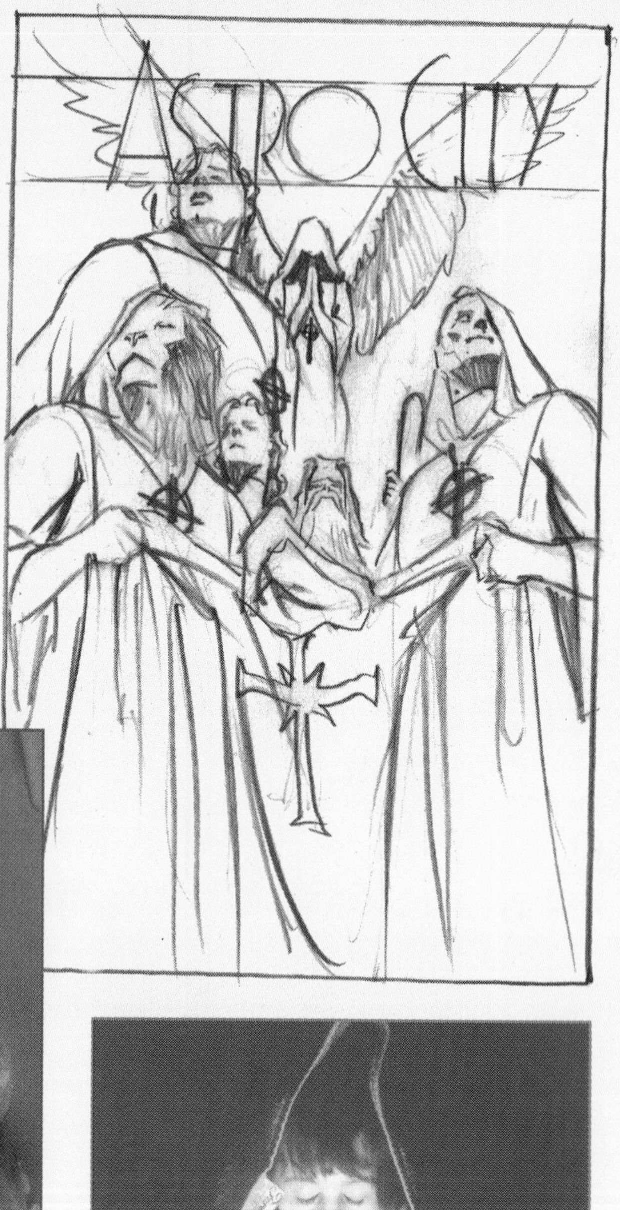
ASTRO CITY

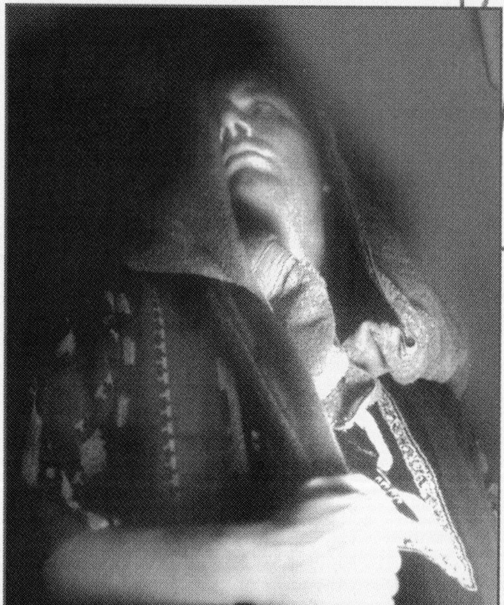

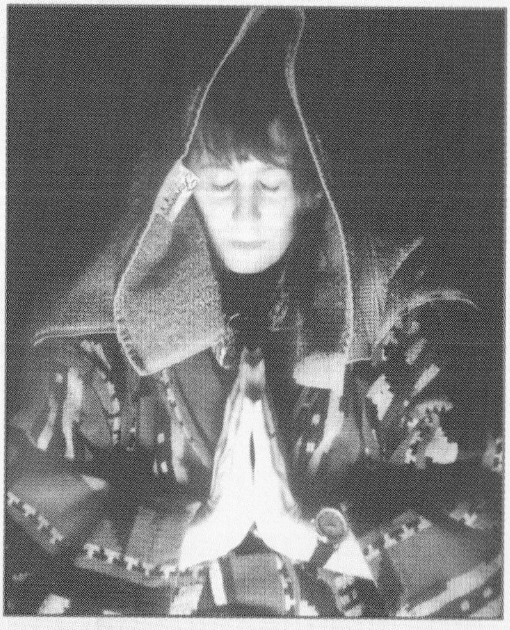

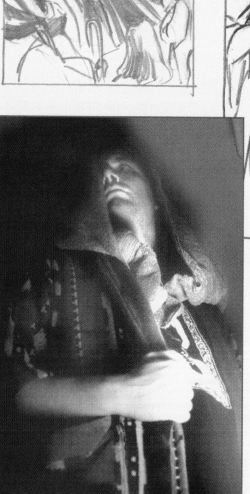

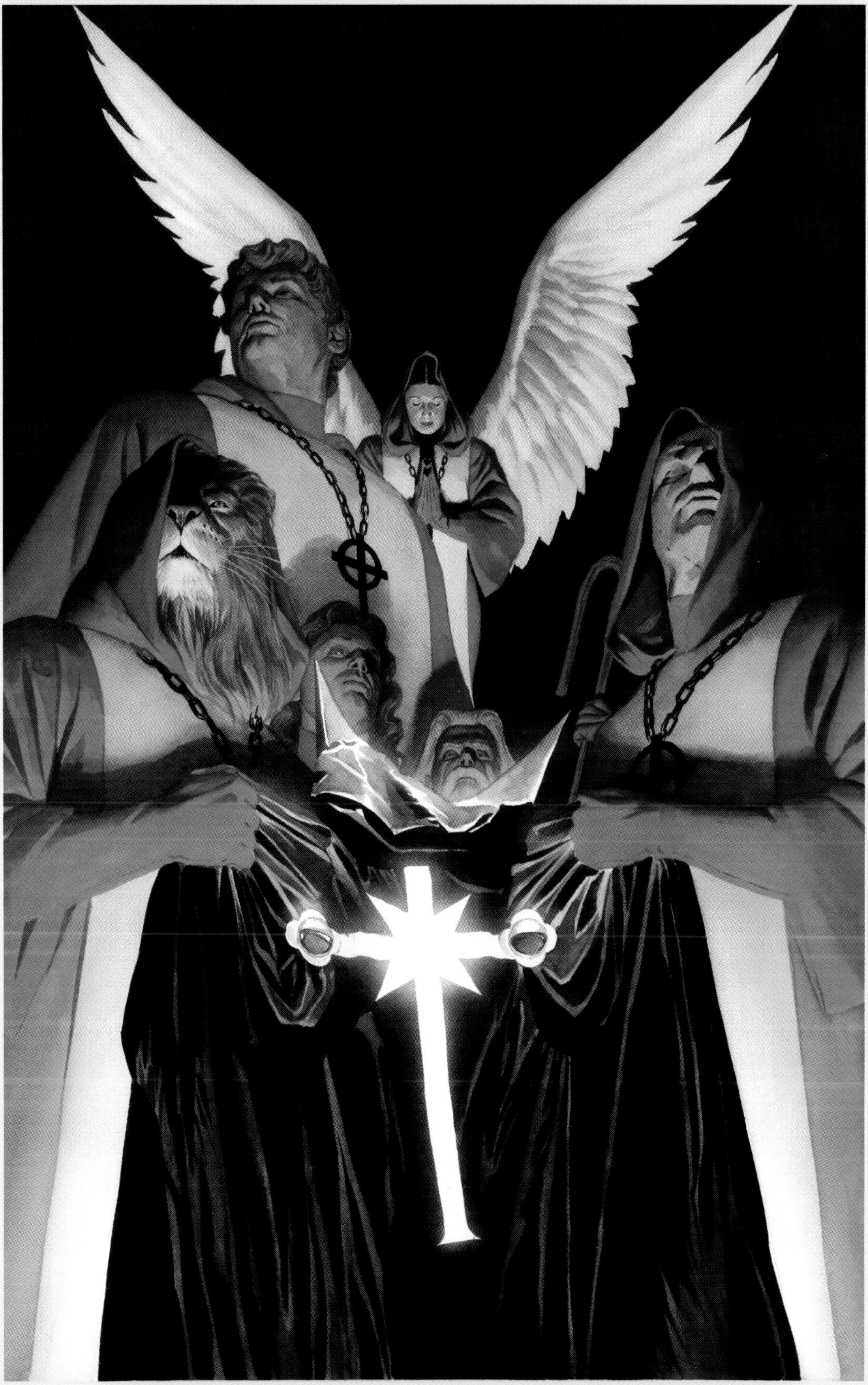

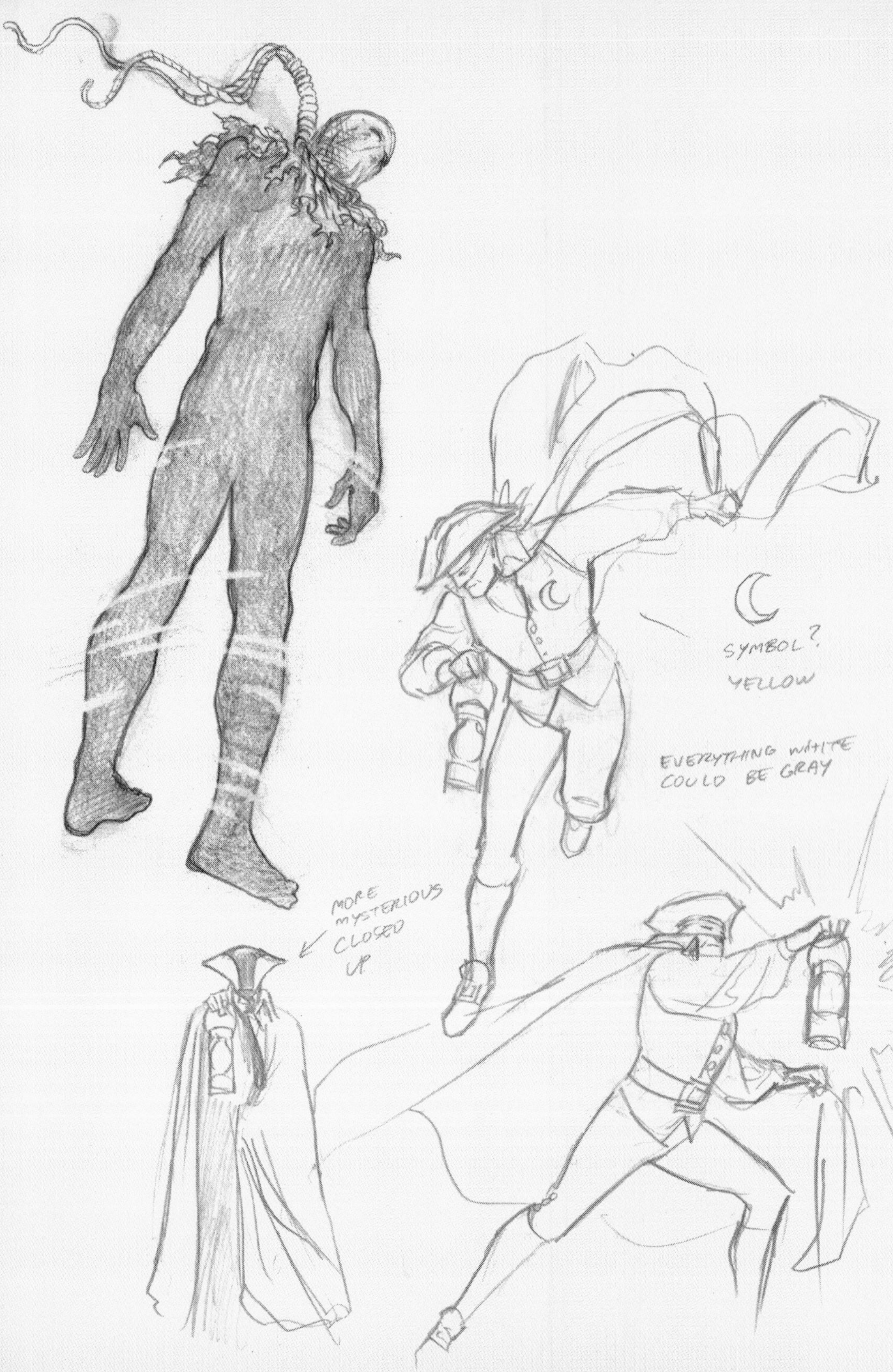
SYMBOL?
YELLOW
EVERYTHING WHITE
COULD BE GRAY
MORE
MYSTERIOUS
CLOSED
UP

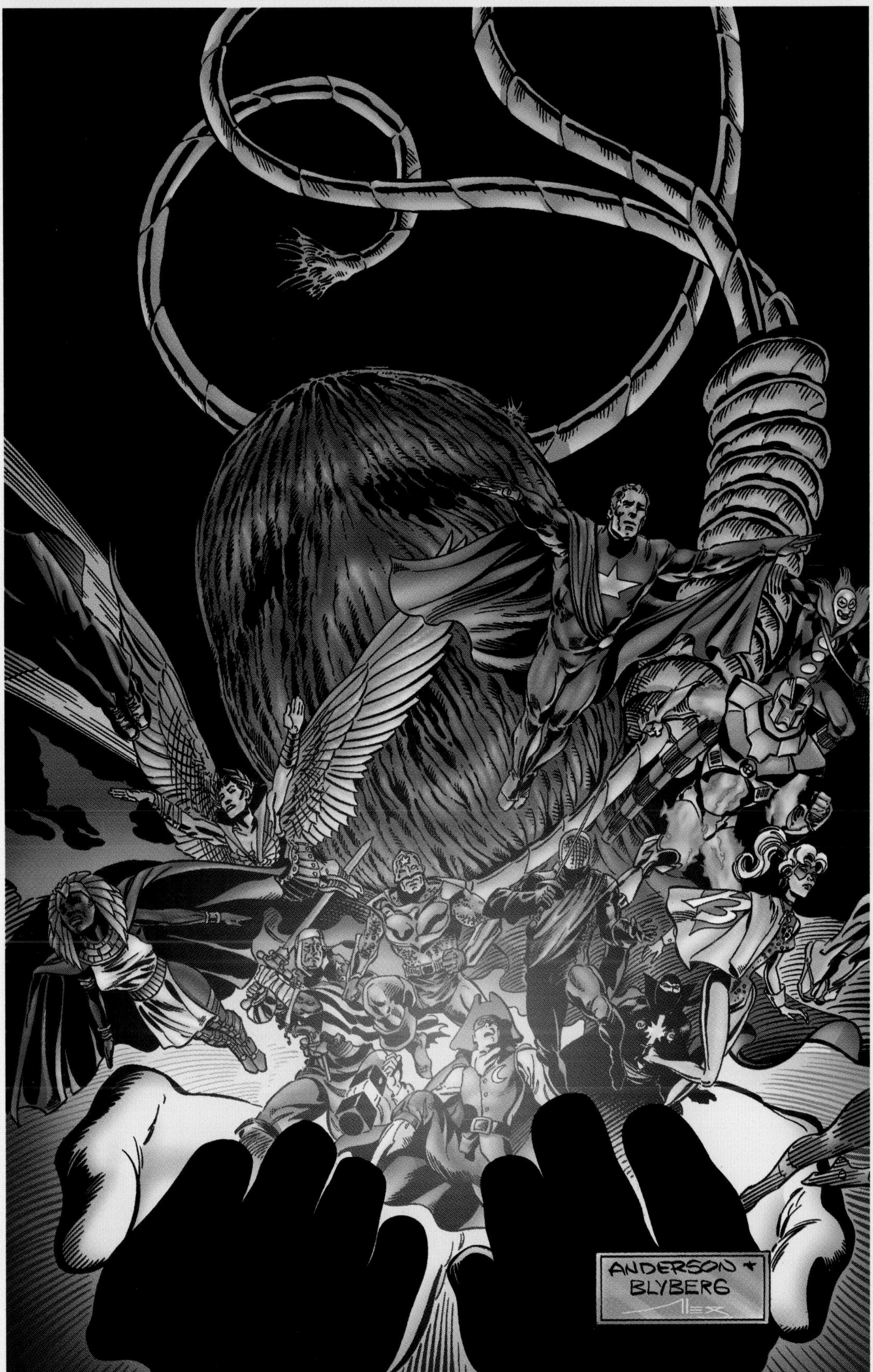
ANDERSON + BLYBERG

ACKNOWLEDGMENTS

Aside from everyone I thanked in the last volume, I've got to thank Lawrence Watt-Evans and my mother, for fielding questions about the priesthood and cathedrals that they had no reason to know the answers to, Michael Grabois for stuff that went into the last volume (and my apologies for leaving you off the list then, Mike), and everyone who got increasingly strung-out phone calls from me as the story wore on, especially Karl Kesel, Richard Howell, James Fry, Roger Stern and Mark Waid. Thanks to the folks at *Wizard*, for giving me the opportunity to tell a story I otherwise wouldn't have been able to get to for I-don't-know-how-long, with the #1/2 issue. Thanks to Jim Lee and the Homage gang for their patience, and to everyone who supported the series, even when it took us nine months to get six issues out. And thanks, as always, to Ann.

— *Kurt Busiek*

First, to correct an oversight, a special thanks to my fellow Spellbinder, Marge Windus, who with all the other Spellbinders obliged my work in progress a look in lieu of a reading; to my friend Scott Burdman for his help and support at John Muir Junior High, and to his father Hy for encouraging me to draw better than Chester Gould; to Frank, Gary, Ron, Ken and Chuck, my HO!B.O.B. lodge brothers, for many meaningful father hours; to my friend Harold R. Johnston for being Harold; to Mike Lovins for his unyielding friendship and support; to Hal and Mary Ella Johnston for producing their daughter Shirley; to Kurt and Ann Busiek for the fertility of their friendship; to Caroline and Alfred Cirocco and Anne and Irv Winnick for helping personify the abstract fidelities of parenthood; and finally to my mother Carol for standing in as father when necessary.

— *Brent Eric Anderson*

Principally, I'd like to thank Mark Kolodny, who modeled for Brian and helped out with a lot of the reference photography. Also, I thank Steve Darnall and Meg Guttmann for their assistance with the Crossbreed cover, and Sal Abbinanti for the design of the alien ships.

— *Alex Ross*

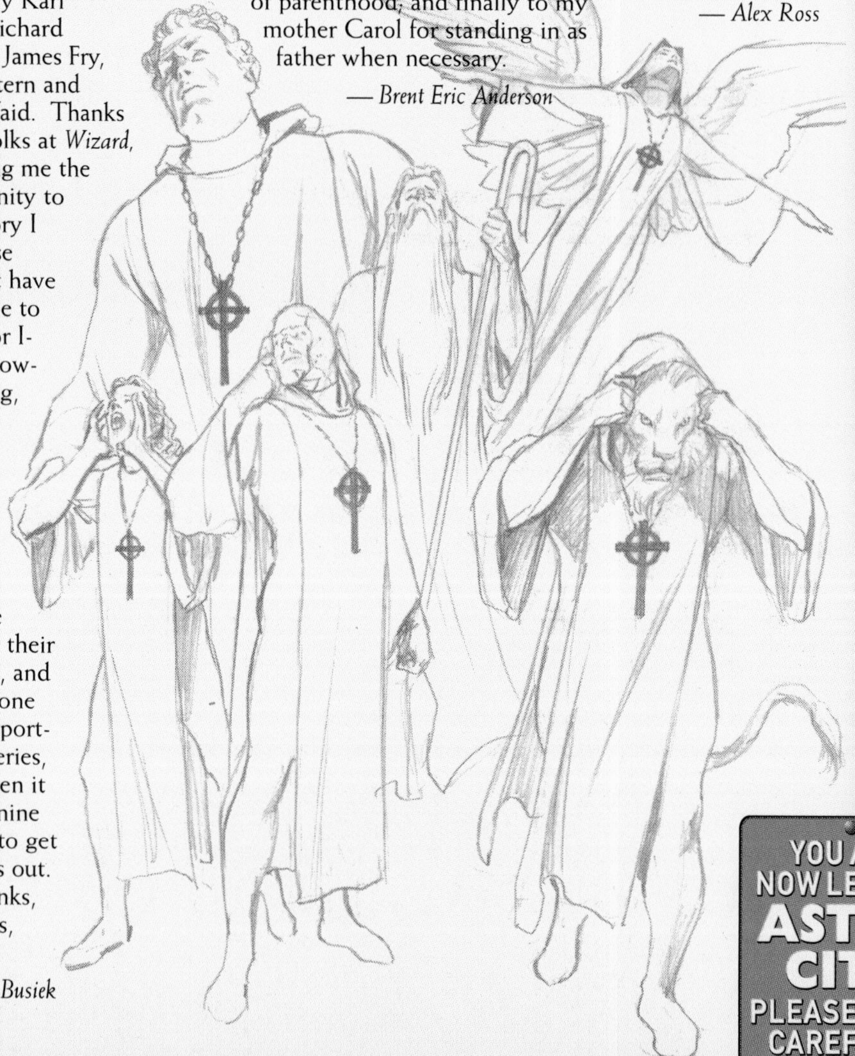

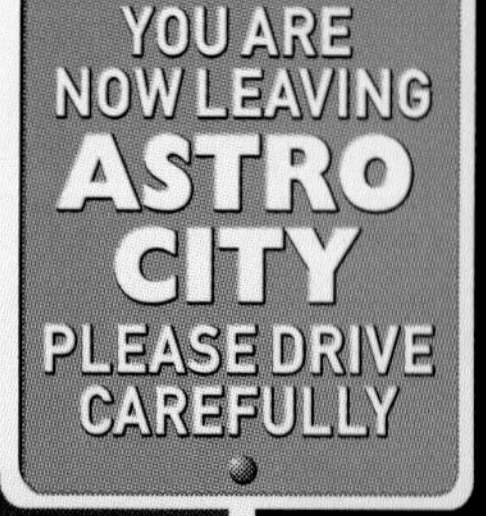
YOU ARE
NOW LEAVING
ASTRO
CITY
PLEASE DRIVE
CAREFULLY